THE CITIES OF PAMPHYLIA

Other Books by John D. Grainger:

Ancient History:
The Ancient Sea (forthcoming, Hambledon Continuum)
Alexander the Great Failure (Hambledon Continuum, 2008)
The Cities of Seleukid Syria (Oxford 1990)
A Seleukid Prosopography and Gazetteer (Brill, 1997)
Seleukos Nikator (Routledge, 1991)
Hellenistic Phoenicia (Oxford 1991)
The League of the Aitolians (Brill, 2000)
The Roman War of Antiochos the Great (Brill, 2002)
Nerva and the Imperial Succession Crisis, AD 96–99 (Routledge, 2002, paperback 2004)

Modern History:
Cromewll Against the Scots (Tuckwell, 1997)
The Battle of Yorktown 1781: a Reassessment (Boydell, 2005)
The Amiens Truce, Britain and Bonaparte 1801–1803 (Boydell, 2004)
The Royal Navy in the River Plate (Navy Records Society, 1996)
The First Pacific War, Britain and Russia 1854–1856 (Boydell, 2008)
The Maritime Blocade of Germany in the Great War (Navy Records Society, 2004)
The Battle for Palestine, 1917 (Boydell)

THE CITIES
OF PAMPHYLIA

by

JOHN D. GRAINGER

OXBOW BOOKS
Oxford and Oakville

Published by
Oxbow Books, Oxford, UK

© Oxbow Books and the individual author, 2009

ISBN 978-1-84217-334-3

This book is available direct from:

Oxbow Books, Oxford, UK
(Phone: 01865-241249; Fax: 01865-794449)

and

The David Brown Book Company
PO Box 511, Oakville, CT 06779, USA
(Phone: 860-945-9329; Fax: 860-945-9468)

or from our website

www.oxbowbooks.com

Library of Congress Cataloging-in-Publication Data

Grainger, John D., 1939-
  The cities of Pamphylia / by John D. Grainger.
     p. cm.
  Includes bibliographical references and index.
  ISBN 978-1-84217-334-3
  1. Pamphylia (Turkey)--History. 2. Pamphylia (Turkey)--History, Local. 3. Cities
and towns, Ancient--Turkey--Pamphylia. 4. City and town life--Turkey--Pamphylia-
-History. 5. Political culture--Turkey--Pamphylia--History. 6. Pamphylia (Turkey)-
-Social conditions. 7. Pamphylia (Turkey)--Politics and government. 8. Greeks--
Turkey--Pamphylia--History. I. Title.
  DS156.P27G73 2009
  939'.29--dc22
                                        2009024735

Printed and bound by Hobbs the Printers Ltd,
Totton, Hampshire

Contents

List of Figures

Abbreviations

ABSA	*Annual of the British School at Athens*
AE	*Année Épigraphique*
AJA	*American Journal of Archaeology*
AMS	*Asia Minor Studien*
Anat. St.	*Anatolian Studies*
ANRW	*Aufstieg under Niedergang des Römische Welt*
ANSMN	*American Numismatic Society Museum Notes*
AST	*Arastirma Sonuclari Toplantısı*
BAR	British Achaeological Reports
BCH	*Bulletin de Correspondence Hellenique*
BE	*Bulletin Épigraphique*
Bean	G. E. Bean, 'Inscriptions in the Antalya Museum', *Belleten* 22, 1958, 21–70
Bean, *TSS*	G. E. Bean, *Turkey's Southern Shore*, 2nd ed., London 1979
BJ	*Bonner Jahrbucher*
Blumenthal, *Siedlungscolonisation*	
	E. Blumenthal, *Die altgriechische Siedlungscolonisation in Mittelmeerraum unter besondere Berichigung der Südkuste Kleinasiens*, Tübingen 1963
BMC	British Museum Catalogue
Bosch/Atlan	E. Bosch and S. Atlan, 'Epigraphica: Antalya Kitabaleri', *Belleten* 11, 1946
Brixhe, *Dialecte grec.*	C. Brixhe, *Le Dialecte grec de Pamphylie*, Paris 1976
DOP	*Dumbarton Oaks Papers*
Ep. Anat.	*Epigraphica Anatolica*
FGrH	*Fragmente Greichische Historiker*
Foss, 'Cities'	C. Foss, 'The Cities of Pamphylia', in *Cities, Fortresses and Villages of Byzantine Asia Minor,* Aldershot 1996
GGM	*Geographi Graeci Minores*
Haensch, *Capita*	R. Haensch, *Capita Provinciarum, Statthaltersitze und Provinzialverwaltung in der römischen Kaizerzeit*, Mainz 1997

Head, *HN*	B. V. Head, *Historia Numorum*, London 1911
Hiepp-Tamer, *Phaselis*	C. Hiepp-Tamer, *Die Münzpragung de Lykischen Stadt Phaselis in Greichischen Zeit*, Saarbrucken 1993
IG	*Inscriptiones Graecae*
IGCH	*Inventory of Greek Coin Hoards*
IGRRP	*Inscriptiones Graecae ad Res Pertinentes*, ed. A. Degrassi
I. Perge	*Inschriften von Perge*, ed. J. Merkelbach
I. Side	*Inschriften von Side*, ed. J. Nolle
Ist. Mitt.	*Istanbuler Mitteilungen*
JHS	*Journal of Hellenic Studies*
JNG	*Jahreschrift für Numismatik und Geldgeschichte*
JRS	*Journal of Roman Studies*
Kazı	*Kazi Sonuclari Toplantısı*
Merkelbach and Sahin	R. Merkelbach and S. Sahin, 'Die Publizierten Inschriften von Perge', *Ep. Anat.* 11, 1988, 97–169
Num. Chron.	*Numismatic Chronicle*
OGIS	*Orientis Graeci Inscriptiones Selectae*
RE	*Real Encyclopadie der classischen Altertumsissenschaft*
REA	*Revue des Etudes Anciennes*
Rev. Num.	*Revue Numismatique*
Robert, *Docs*	L. Robert, *Documents d'Asie Mineure méridionale*, Paris 1966
Schafer, *Phaselis*	J. Schafer (ed.), *Phaselis*, Tubingen, 1981
SEG	*Supplementum Epigraphicarum Graecorum*
SNG	*Sylloge Numorum Graecorum*
TAM	*Tituli Asia Minoris*
TAPA	*Transactions of the American Philosophical Association*
TIB	*Tabula Imperii Bizantini* 8, ed. H. Hellenkamper and F. Hild, Vienna 2004
YCS	*Yale Classical Studies*
ZPE	*Zeitschrift für Papyrologie und Epigrafik*

Introduction

Pamphylia is that part of modern Turkey which faces south into the Mediterranean and is hemmed in by mountains in all other directions; its main centre is now Antalya, the former Attaleia. To the west are the Lykian Mountains; to its east are the hills of Rough Kilikia, and these two highland areas are joined to the long high range of the Taurus Mountains on the north. The sea, the Bay of Antalya, or Pamphylian Sea, is to the south. On the map, especially a contour map, the region looks well defined, and this is also the case on the ground, where the mountains rise abruptly from the plain; its eastern and western boundaries along the coast are not so clear; ancient writers never agreed on where they were.[1]

These boundaries were dictated not so much by the actual definition of Pamphylia as by the contexts of the writers. Hekataios in the sixth century BC, as reported by Strabo in the time of the Emperor Augustus, included the whole coast from Cape Gelidonya to Syedra,[2] but the author now referred to as 'Pseudo-Skylax', who composed a *periplus* (a set of sailing directions) in about 360 BC referred to the western coast, which trends almost due south-north, as Lykian, and the coast from its turn to the east (just west of modern Antalya) as Pamphylia – for sailors who were sailing north along the coast the point at which it turned was the important item of information.[3]

The geographical bounds were not in fact crucial for defining the land, for it was the cities and their territories which constituted Pamphylia, and the allocation of cities to it varied with political events. So at times Phaselis was counted as Pamphylian, but at other times it was reckoned to be Lykian; at the other end of the Bay, Syedra could be thought of as Pamphylian at times, but was normally Kilikian; Korakesion (modern Alanya) is only just part of Pamphylia.

Within this area, which is about two hundred kilometres from west to east, and at most fifty kilometres inland from the coast to the hills, there were seven

---

[1] A map, showing the varying definitions, is in *RE* XVIII.3.355–356, 'Pamphylia'.
[2] Strabo 14.41–2.
[3] Ps.-Skylax, *GGM*, 100.

substantial cities in the ancient world; it is these which are my central subject (Map 1). From east to west the cities were: Korakesion (modern Alanya), on a high, steep hill, where the coastal plain is virtually non-existent; Side, also on the coast, at the mouth of the Melas River, close to the hills of Rough Kilikia; Aspendos, Sillyon, and Perge in the Pamphylian plain, all on flat, steep-sided hills a few kilometres inland from the coast, and spread roughly equidistantly along the plain where it is at its widest; south of Perge, directly on the coast, and with a small harbour, was Attaleia, founded much later, now the large city of Antalya; on either side of Attaleia were two smaller settlements, Olbia to the west and Magydos to the east, both near or on the coast; Phaselis is to the south, directly on the coast where it trends almost due south, blocked in by the Lykian Mountains. There were also several other small settlements, most of which are barely known, Idyros, Syedra, Hamaxia, Kibyra – called Kibyra Minor – Seleukeia, Ptolemais, and some others.

   Four main rivers flow through the plain from the Taurus mountains: the Katarrhaktes (the modern Duden), the Kestros (Aksu-chai), the Eurymedon (Kopru-chai), and the Melas (Manavgat-chai), respectively reaching the sea in the neighbourhoods of Attaleia and Magydos, Perge, Aspendos, and Side; other rivers, or rather mountain streams, flow out of the Kilikian and Lykian hills. The valleys of the Kestros and the Melas rivers provide important routes out of Pamphylia towards the north and the north-east, but they were, and are, by no

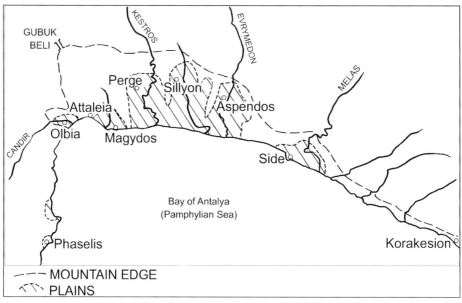

Map 1. The Cities of Pamphylia

means easy to travel along. The main route was north along the Kestros valley and then by the steep, ten-kilometre climb through the pass called Gubuk Beli towards the Turkish Lake District to the north; the route along the Melas valley led from Side east and north-east into central Anatolia and Lykaonia. A third route led westwards along the Yenice bogaz in front of and below the Pisidian city of Termessos, towards Isinda and Kibyra Major, and the cities of Ionia and Karia; again the route climbs through an awkward pass, Golcuk Beli. Despite these several passes, by land Pamphylia was not easy to reach. Within Pamphylia there was just one main road, running parallel to the coast, as it still does, linking the cities, and reaching eastwards towards Lykia and westwards along the Kilikian coast. Pamphylia was well isolated.

It might be thought that the sea would provide a more congenial method of communications out of Pamphylia and between the cities, but it is not quite so useful as might appear from a glance at the map. Several of the Pamphylian cities were actually situated inland, and only those to the east (Side, Korakesion) and west (Attaleia, Magydos, Olbia, Phaselis) were directly on or close to the coast. Their harbours are generally small and exposed to storms out of the sea from the south, and the coast is made even less approachable by an uncomfortable westward-flowing current. The sea was of less importance in Pamphylia than for many other areas of the ancient Mediterranean.

In the western half of the country the land rises from the coast in shelves of limestone,[4] over which the Katarrhaktes falls twice, and the Kestros once. At the Taurus Mountains the land rises steeply and abruptly and the mountains are forested where not too steep (Plates 1, 13). To the east fingers of hilly limestone extend southwards across and through the lower plain, separating the alluvial plains of the rivers into varying-sized sections (e.g., Plates 17, 18); at Antalya a limestone shelf reaches the sea as cliffs, and the Katarrhaktes falls directly into the sea between that city and Magydos. The sea level has fluctuated somewhat in the last 10,000 years, and the sea has receded for some distance along the middle part of Pamphylia; on the other hand, at Phaselis some of the quays of the ancient city are now under water.

The land is well watered (by Mediterranean standards) by the streams and rivers from the Taurus, so much so that it has a tendency to waterlogging in winter and spring, and without drainage some parts degenerate into marsh. It is generally fertile, but there are areas of poor soil, notably of sand along the coast, and low jagged limestone hills stick up out of the plain here and there, especially in the eastern half; the eastern coast is sandy, with an area of dunes penetrating some

---

[4] Bean, *TSS*, 21: 'steps'.

way inland. The natural vegetation ever since the climate stabilized after the Ice Age is Mediterranean scrub and conifers, with some deciduous and more pine forests in the hills; the generally flat terrain also encourages marshy vegetation. All of this has been much modified by man's activities, of course.[5]

Pamphylia is therefore a relatively well-defined geographical region which in the ancient world contained a group of cities regarded as distinctive largely because of their geographical situation. The cities and the regions were not, however, central to Greek history at any time. The region was isolated by the sea and the hills, and those dominating hills were also inhabited by non-Greek peoples – Lykians, Pisidians, Kilikians – who accepted Greek civilization and Roman authority, but who were never seen as Greek. Pamphylia was thus an island of Greek cities on the frontier of Greek society, a close neighbour to non-Greek lands, and was also somewhat isolated from the Greek and Roman mainstream.

One result of the area's political isolation is that it has been relatively little studied. There is, for example, only one (very short) book discussing the history of the area,[6] though there are accounts of some of its cities. In any general account of Asia Minor Pamphylia necessarily suffers by comparison with the better sources available for other regions, and by their greater centrality in wider affairs. It was one of the targets for western travellers in the eighteenth and nineteenth centuries, such as Captain Beaufort, Charles Robert Cockerell, Lieutenant Spratt, and others in the early nineteenth, and the diligent Count Lanckoronski at the end of that century, and Freya Stark in the mid-twentieth. That Freya Stark could, in the 1950s, embark on an 'exploration' of the area is a telling indication of its isolation even then. The brevity of past investigations means that the account of the elaborate archaeological explorations of Count Lanckoronski in the 1880s is still useful,[7] though more recent excavations have now rendered it rather less so than it was.

This region is therefore both well defined and neglected, yet it was the scene of a continuing society of cities and their citizens for two thousand years. Being small and compact it provides a field of study where it is possible to follow through its history for the whole of that lengthy period, from the origins of the cities to their final extinction; in other areas the overwhelming number of sources tends to force a concentration on much shorter periods. So this is what

[5] For a detailed description of the geography of the region, cf. X. de Planhol, *De la plaine pamphylienne aux lacs pisidiens*, Paris 1958, ch. 1.

[6] C. E. Bosch, *Studien zur geschichte Pamphyliens*, Ankara 1957.

[7] F. Beaufort, *Karamania*, London 1817; C. R. Cockerell, *Travels in Europe and the Levant, 1810–1817*, London 1903; T. A. B. Spratt and E. Forbes, *Travels in Lycia*, London 1947; Count K. Lanckoronski, *Städte Pamphyliens und Pisidiens*, Vienna 1890; F. Stark, *The Lycian Shore*, London 1956, and *Alexander's Path*, London 1958.

I am attempting here: to reconstruct the history of this small area, which indeed happens to have some quite remarkable ancient remains, but which was never important in affairs at any time. The aim is, besides teasing out the regional history, to consider the effects of outside forces on the society of the cities: it seems to me that these are crucial elements in the region's history. It follows that a more or less strict chronological approach is needed, but the effects of the local geography will be constantly borne in mind.

There is no ancient account of the region apart from Strabo's brief description. The written sources available for the study of the region are largely accounts of occasional outside interventions, for example by Alexander. The result is like a series of intermittent lights being shone on the region, separated by rather longer periods of darkness and silence. These sources can be supplemented by the collections of ancient inscriptions gathered by explorers, notably in the early twentieth century, of which some are now being re-edited into more conventional publications.[8] Archaeologists have also been busy, particularly at Perge and Side, but it cannot be said that any of the other cities have been properly investigated, and this goes double for the countryside. Numismatists have collected the coins of the cities, but the study of them, as with the written sources, is intermittent and partial. The study of the area thus requires repeated switches between these various sources.

The physical remains of the ancient cities are the main reasons for visiting the region. Aspendos and its theatre, Perge and its street and gate and theatre and stadium, Side and its walls, Phaselis and its street and harbour and theatre, are all places worth travelling great distances to see and examine. These are all sites where a good deal of excavation and investigation work has been and is being done as the value of such places for attracting tourists is realized. The excavation results are variously well reported, but mainly in fairly obscure journals, some of which have had only a brief life, while others are only occasional, and not all of them are easy, or even at times possible, to locate. The words of G. E. Bean in 1968 are still relevant: 'there is hardly anything for the English reader outside the learned journals'.[9] Further, the investigators' attention has been largely concentrated on those cities, and little has been done to investigate the countryside, while the remains in the cities, largely of Roman date, prevent much investigation of earlier periods of occupation. Pamphylia is still, that is to say, off the beaten track, a judgment which applies to its archaeology as well as to its history and geography.

---

[8] E.g., *I. Perge, I. Side*.
[9] Bean, *TSS*, vii.

1

The Arrival of the Greeks

The name 'Pamphylia' signified, in Greek, 'many tribes', or even 'all tribes', or perhaps 'all languages',[1] and implies a land inhabited by a much-divided, mixed population, composed of Greeks and other peoples. The settlement of Greeks in Pamphylia is traditionally dated to the post-Bronze Age migrations,[2] but they arrived in a land that was already settled by non-Greeks, and they were only ever part of the population.

Evidence for the sort of settlement and population which existed before the Greeks' arrival is very scarce. Such excavations as have taken place – usually at the sites of the Greek cities – have found little archaeological evidence for occupation before the Iron Age. The cave at Karain, in the mountains on the western side of Pamphylia, looking over the plain (Plate 1), has revealed a long sequence of intermittent occupations dating back deep into the Holocene, and the skull of a Neanderthal child has been found there;[3] the grave of a child of the Chalcolithic period and some flint arrowheads have been found on the acropolis of Perge, which has also produced graves and pottery of the Early Iron Age; there is a single Early Bronze Age sherd from Sillyon.[4] These are the only archaeological evidences of early occupation, but the region certainly had a human population throughout prehistory. Linguistic evidence indicates that

---

[1] Liddell and Scott, *Greek-English Lexicon*, 'Pamphylia'; C. Brixhe, *Le Dialecte Grec de Pamphylie*, Paris 1976, 145.

[2] Summarised by Bean TSS, 3–6; Blumenthal, *Siedlungscolonisation*, takes this early dating seriously, even placing it as Mycenaean; it is generally not actually discussed, merely referred to briefly.

[3] E. Y. Bostanci, 'Researches on the Mediterranean coast of Anatolia: a new Palaeolithic Site at Belbina near Antalya', *Anatolia*, 11, 1967, 203–217; G. Albrecht *et al.*, 'Late Pleistocene and Early Holocene Finds from Okuzini, a Contribution to the Settlement History of the Bay of Antalya, Turkey', *Paleorient* 18, 1992, 123–141; reports by I. Yalçinkaya, 'Karain Kazılari 1994', XVII *Kazı* I, 1995, and 'Yili Karain Kazı', XXI *Kazı* II, 1999, 15–36; a summary of other palaeolithic investigations in the area is in I. Kayan, A. Minzoni-Deroche and I. Yalçinkaya, 'Prospection préhistorique dans la région d'Antalya, notice préliminaire', in B. Rémy (ed.), *Anatolia Antiqua/Eski Anadolu*, Istanbul and Paris 1988, 9–12.

[4] W. Martini, 'Die Akropolis von Perge, Survey und Sondagen, 1994–1996', *AMS* 34, 1999, 155–161; M. Küpper, 'Sillyon, Research Work, 1995', XIV *AST*, II, 1996, 451–462.

peoples speaking a Luwian language – the ancestor of the later Pidisian and Lykian – gave names to several places, including Perge and the major rivers, and from this it may be inferred that people speaking that language were already present when the Greeks arrived.[5]

The evidence of earlier occupation is therefore discontinuous, and yet the area was surely attractive to settlers. It is flat, well-watered, and agriculturally rich, especially by contrast with the surrounding mountains and the dry Anatolian interior. Farmers had occupied all the lands around from at least the seventh millennium BC, perhaps even earlier – the age-old sites of Catal Hüyük and Hacilar are just north of the mountains. Presumably people moved into the lower Pamphylian lands as they became available with the increase in the temperature as the Ice Age released its grip, and as farming techniques improved, but little has yet been found. Perhaps it is merely the result of a lack of research, on the assumption that archaeologists tend to find what they are looking for, and so it is widely assumed that there is little to find. But it may be more than that, for, if early occupation had been really extensive, then the evidence would be obvious, in the form of tells, pottery scatters, and occasional finds, which would become known. Possibly there was too much water for ease of agriculture. Strabo, as late as the first century AD, notes a lake near Aspendos, Lake Capria,[6] and parts of the land are marshy even now, especially in the winter and spring. The techniques of farming on the dry plateau may not have suited the wetter lowland.

Historical rather than geographical reasons may also have limited occupation, but some written evidence for it does exist. In the second millennium BC the Anatolian plateau was organized as a series of kingdoms, of which the Hittite state became the most powerful. For a long time researchers ignored Pamphylia, leaving it as a blank on maps of the region.[7] More recently, the discovery of more Hittite records has led to the theory that Pamphylia was for a time part of a sub-kingdom of the Hittite empire called Tarhuntassa.[8] This was both a territory and a city, set apart for governing by a younger son of the Hittite Great King in the thirteenth century BC – the word is in the genitive, and so

---

[5] See note 11.

[6] Strabo 14.4.2.

[7] For example, A. J. Toynbee, *A Study of History*, XI, *Historical Atlas and Gazetteer*, London 1959, map 15, pp. 106–107, where it is marked as part of an '(?) Enclave of Khatti Territory', (see the appendix, 203–216); J. Garstang and O. R. Gurney, *A Geography of the Hittite Empire*, London 1959, or T. Bryce, *The Kingdom of the Hittites*, Oxford 1998, map 5, p. xvi, where the area is left blank, though the scale is very small. The situation is no different for J. Yakar, *The Later Prehistory of Anatolia, the Late Chalcolithic and Early Bronze Ages*, BAR S268, Oxford 1985.

[8] The crucial document, an inscribed bronze plaque, was published by H. Otten, *Die Bronzetafel aus*

would translate as 'Tarhunta's land', that is, it was named from the man placed in command or perhaps from a god's name, though the two are not mutually exclusive; this suggests that it was not a recognized geographical area with a name of its own until then.

One of these Hittite sources describes the boundaries of the sub-kingdom. These have been located so as to encompass not only almost all Pamphylia and part of the Taurus mountain area to the north, and including much of the future Pisidia, Isauria to the north-east, and part of Rough Kilikia to the east.[9] The western boundary ran along the Kastaraya river, plausibly interpreted as the later Kestros (the present Aksu-chai); a place called Parha is mentioned and is interpreted as the old name for Perge – it is thus left outside Tarhuntassa, being west of the river. (Its naming in the description implies that a settlement existed there; the archaeologists have not yet found it; this is not the only puzzle about Perge.) Several other places are named – notably 'Sallusa, Sanhata, and Surimma' – but their exact positions are unknown; they may have been small places on the coast to the east of the later Side, perhaps in Rough Kilikia – one, possibly Sanhata, may be the later Syedra.

There is therefore a gap in the recorded settlements between Parha in the west and the eastern coast, covering the region where the later cities of the plain were. The line of the coast of Pamphylia between Side and Attaleia has changed over the millennia, but the actual shore has never been worth settling. It is now sandy and marshy, and probably was always that way; only holiday hotels, to whom the beaches are of use, reach the shore nowadays; working villages and towns are invariably set back from the coast amid their fields, and away from the agriculturally unusable coastal strip. This was the case in the Greco-Roman period, and there is no reason to suppose that the situation was different in the Bronze Age, though the coastline was then some distance north of its present position. So the gap may well represent reality: there was probably little settlement between the Kestros and the Melas Rivers.

The purpose of the establishment of the sub-kingdom of Tarhuntassa was for

---

Boghasköy: ein Staatsvertrag Tuthalijas IV, Wiesbaden 1988; discussions since then include, particularly, O. R. Gurney, 'The Annals of Hattusilis III', *Anat. St.* 47, 1997, 127–139, and A. M. and B. Dincol, J. Yakar, and A. Taffia, 'The Borders of the Appanage Kingdom of Tarhuntassa – A Geographical and Archaeological Assessment', *Anatolica* 26, 2000, 1–19; see also A. M. Jasink, 'Kizzuwatna and Tarhuntassa, their historical evolution and interactions with Hatti', in *La Cilicie, Espaces et Pouvoirs Locales*, Istanbul 2001, 47–56, who tends to locate the kingdom in Rough Cilicia, and H. Abbasoğlu, 'The Founding of Perge and its Development in the Hellenistic and Roman Periods', in D. Parrish (ed.), *Urbanism in Western Asia Minor*, *Journal of Roman Archaeology*, Supplement 45, Portsmouth, RI, 2001, 173–188.

[9] By Dincol *et al.* (previous note).

it to act as a buffer between the Hittite realm proper, which reached south to the Taurus and into Kilikia and northern Syria, and the 'Lukka Lands', whose location would seem to be mainly in Lykia.[10] Parha/Perge therefore was left in the Lukka Lands, and this would fit with the influence of the Luwian language, which has been detected in the later Greek inscriptions.[11] The Tarhuntassa boundary along the Kestros looks very like the work of a group of negotiators who chose the river as a clear and unambiguous boundary line after a war – which we know had happened – in which neither side could claim an overwhelming victory. Behind the boundary (that is, to the east), the Pamphylian parts of Tarhuntassa may well have been largely empty space, an area which, in combination with the formidable mountains, was deliberately kept clear as a buffer separating the main Hittite polity from the awkward and hostile Lukka Lands.

The location of the city of Tarhuntassa – 'Tarhunta's city' – from which the principality was ruled, is not known; all too often it is placed vaguely somewhere in the mountains, usually marked by a large dot on a small-scale map. The most serious attempt to locate it has suggested a site somewhat to the south of Konya, close to the mountains' northern side. This would place it close to the route along the Melas River, which connects the inland plateau, the heartland of the Hittite state, and Pamphylia.[12] This location, while by no means certain, fits in very well with the concept of Tarhuntassa as a buffer state between the Hittite kingdom and its enemies in Lykia. An invasion force from the Lukka Lands would have a long hard march through country with few supplies – the mountains will have had few, even if Pamphylia was productive – before it reached any vital Hittite interests. The sub-king in the city of Tarhuntassa – a prince called Tarhunta, presumably, at least at the beginning – would thus have plenty of time to prepare to meet the invaders with his full force, perhaps by an ambush in the mountains.

All this leads to the necessary conclusion that Pamphylia was surely inhabited in the Late Bronze Age as well as earlier, that it was a land with which the Hittite empire had relations, and that its people were in contact with the people of the hills to the north, their landward neighbours, and with the Lykians to the west.

---

[10] Assumed from the similarity of names, of course.

[11] Brixhe, *Dialecte grec*; also P. H. J. Houwink ten Cate, *The Luwian Population Groups of Lycia and Cilicia Aspera during the Hellenistic Period*, Leiden 1965; J. Yakar, *Ethnoarchaeology of Anatolia: Rural Socio-Economy in the Bronze and Iron Ages*, Tel Aviv 2000, suggests that Perge was a 'centre' in the Late Bronze Age.

[12] Dincol *et al.*, and Jasink (note 8). Three kings of Tarhuntassa are known by name; two were sons of Hittite Great Kings; it looks as though they attempted to seize the Great Kingship itself, thus contributing to the instability which led to the kingdom's collapse.

They were also in contact by sea with other lands, for Bronze Age shipwrecks have been discovered off Cape Gelidonya, their cargoes implying a voyage from east to west.[13] And this is so even if the precise archaeological evidence from within Pamphylia is not yet available. It also suggests that it was only a thinly peopled land, partly because it was obviously a fought-over buffer between the Lukka Lands and the Hittite kingdom, but also because it does not appear to figure, by name, in any of the sources except as Tarhuntassa. Thus there are reasonably convincing historical explanations for the absence of evidence, as well as geographical and political reasons. It may also be that the land was difficult to cultivate with Bronze Age methods and tools; the soil is heavy and at times the land is waterlogged; other areas are sandy; neither would be easy to farm with the light Bronze Age agricultural implements.

The fact that there is little or no evidence for habitation in Pamphylia in the Bronze Age is, however, also due to the fact that such settlement has not been seriously looked for. Excavations have been largely confined to the cave sites and the Greek cities. The cave sites by definition tend to be located in land not easily cultivable – Karain is 150 metres above the plain, a stiff climb (Plate 1). Many of the cities are on rocky hills which would not be the first choice of farmers as places to inhabit (Plates 4, 8, 11, 19); their Greek and Roman remains are both substantial and impossible to remove, for good aesthetic and tourist industry reasons, and so it is difficult to excavate deeply into them. Other investigations have been generally superficial surveys, which have concluded that there is nothing to find.[14] That conclusion has discouraged further investigations, which makes the surveys' conclusions more of a self-fulfilling prophecy than the result of scientific investigations. Recently some extra-civic surveys have been made, as in the neighbourhood of Sillyon, but they have done little more than detect Roman-period farmsteads.[15] It is not reasonable to believe that the land has been empty at any time since the arrival of farmers in the region. The evidence is surely there; it has just not been found yet. We must conclude that Pamphylia was probably occupied throughout the Bronze Age, and for several millennia before that, but that the occupation was only ever thin and rural – even the superficial surveys are unlikely to have missed a Bronze Age city.

The post-Hittite population was thus already in place when the Greek settlers

[13] G. F. Bass, 'Cape Gelidonya: a Bronze Age shipwreck', *TAPA*, 57/58, 1967.
[14] For example, by J. Mellaart, 'Preclassical Remains in Southern Turkey', *Anat. St.* 5, 1955, 176–178; see also the discussion by A. Erzen 'Das Besiedlungsproblem Pamphyliens im Altertum', *Archäologischer Anzeiger*, 1973, 388–401.
[15] Küpper's work (note 4). Also the later periods, after AD 400, are ably covered by *TIB*, which also regularly refers to earlier periods.

arrived. They were the descendants of people who had inhabited the land in the centuries following the disappearance of the Hittite Empire; that is, they were the descendants of the Bronze Age population, the subjects of the brief kingdom of Tarhuntassa. The Hittite state was destroyed by the invasions of its myriad enemies at some time after 1200 BC (the last Great King that we know of seems to have succeeded some six or seven years earlier than that, but how long he lasted, or if he had a successor, we don't know).[16] The capital Hattusas was burned, and is later seen to be occupied by the Kaskas, old Hittite enemies from the northern hills. The centre of Anatolia was subsequently divided among several local kingdoms, and in the south the Kilikians formed the separate kingdom of Que.[17] The situation in Pamphylia is once more quite unknown, but there is no reference to any kingdom in the area at any time after the disappearance of Tarhuntassa. This is not to say that one did not exist, but one would certainly have expected a reference to it somewhere. It is, however, reasonably safe to assume that the inhabitants were speakers of a Luwian language or dialect.

The basis for this conclusion is a set of studies of the names of people who are recorded much later, in Greek and usually in inscriptions, plus the general conclusions to be drawn from the history of the area. The studies show a spread of non-Greek personal names throughout Pamphylia and the surrounding lands, and all these areas show the same selection of names.[18] In other words, these names are those inherited by and used by the populations of all three areas from before Greek naming conventions arrived. The name given to this language, and so to the people who used it, is Luwian, from the name of the whole southern coastal region given in Hittite records. With this as a clue it can also be seen that the gods worshipped in the area in the later period were in fact the gods and goddesses of the area in pre-Greek times. They are usually portrayed in Greek guise, or are assimilated to the standard Greek gods: Zeus Solymos at Termessos is probably the Luwian god Tarhunt;[19] *Wanassa Preiia*, the 'Lady of Perge' is

---

[16] 'The early years of the twelfth century (BC)' is the dating suggested by Bryce, *Kingdom*, ch. 13; the Egyptian pharaoh Rameses III, who took the throne about 1185, included 'Hatti' in the list of the kingdoms destroyed in his day.

[17] Bryce, *Kingdom*, 387–388.

[18] Houwink ten Cate, *Luwian Population Groups*, lists names from inscriptions from southern Asia Minor in his appendix, 216–235; S. Colvin, 'Names in Hellenistic and Roman Lycia', in S. Colvin (ed.), *The Greco-Roman East*, YCS 31, Cambridge 2004, 44–84, provides another list in his appendix; T. Bryce, *The Lycians*, vol. 1, Copenhagen 1986, provides lists of place names and personal names, 229–252.

[19] Colvin (previous note) 45; the most common male personal name in the area was Trokondas, a hellenised version of Tarhunta.

assimilated as Artemis and was portrayed on Pergean coins as a barely human shape, so she was not originally a Greek goddess.[20] Many of the place names show signs of being pre-Greek as well – the names of several of the cities, for example, and at least one of the rivers, the previously noted Kestros/Kastaraya. That is, these studies show that the Greeks of Pamphylia arrived to settle in a land already populated by a sedentary Luwian-speaking population which had its own set of personal names and its own names for the rivers and hills of the country. The Luwian names, and therefore the Luwian-speaking population, survived and even predominated after the arrival of the Greeks.

This, of course, has so far begged the question of the time at which the Greeks actually arrived. Tarhuntassa was a thirteenth century BC kingdom, and it vanished in the post-imperial chaos of the early twelfth century. The earliest record of Greeks living in Pamphylia is archaeological material of the Geometric period, which has been found at Sillyon.[21] This is pottery first made in Greece in the early ninth century BC; it will have reached Sillyon some time later, say, in the latter part of the ninth century. This is assuming that it was actually used by Greeks, of course, and not simply bought by native Luwians from traders, but at all events it puts Sillyon in touch with Greece at that time. So we may say that Greeks arrived in Pamphylia some time after the end of the Hittite kingdom and by the time of the Geometric period, between perhaps 1190 BC and about 800 BC. It remains to be seen if something less vague can be achieved.

The Greeks are traditionally said to have arrived to settle amongst the older inhabitants of Pamphylia in the aftermath of the Trojan War, though actually the migration took place as part of the much wider movement of peoples which marked the end of the Bronze Age, a rather looser and longer period of time. This would put their arrival in Pamphylia well into the migration period, but also well after the Trojan War (which is to be dated late in the thirteenth or very early in the twelfth century); that is, Greeks reached Pamphylia in the twelfth century BC, according to this theory. Stories link the Greeks of Pamphylia with supposed individuals who participated in the Trojan War: Amphilochos, Kalchas, Mopsos (all of them seers, curiously), and others.[22] The occurrence of the name of Mopsos in that of the city of Mopsuhestia in Kilikia, and a reference in a local eighth century inscription in Phoenician to 'Bt Mps' (taken

---

[20] T.S. McKay, 'The Major Sanctuaries of Pamphylia and Cilicia', *ANRW* II, 8.3, 2045–2130, at 2072–2075; see also various coins of Perge of the Roman period, as in *SNG*, Paris 3.

[21] Küpper, 'Sillyon', XIV *AST* II, 1996.

[22] Strabo 14.4.3; Herodotos 7.91.

to mean 'House of Mopsu'),[23] are claimed to validate these myths. Mopsos is also identified with a king of 'Lydia' who is supposed to have reigned at the time of the Trojan War.[24]

These details, in fact, do not provide any validation at all for the Mopsos theory. It is not an acceptable procedure to link such fragmentary and disparate items together into a coherent story; the gaps, both geographical and chronological, are far too wide. What is required to make a real connection is the discovery in Pamphylia of some clear and unambiguous archaeological evidence, firmly dated to the twelfth century BC, and connected with Mycenaean Greece. Even then this would be no more than an indication of a connection between these lands (like the Geometric pottery at Sillyon), and by no means a proof of the existence and historicity of Mopsos and his supposed activities.

No such evidence exists. What the mythmakers did was to select likely heroes out of the old stories and appropriate them to their communities, so providing themselves with recognizable Greek lineages. This was invariably done after, and usually long after, the time the stories supposedly refer to. Modern theorists, using a great deal of wishful thinking, have at times fallen for this all too readily. The process continued for centuries; at Phaselis, for instance, which we know was founded by Rhodians in about 690 BC, Mopsos is also mentioned much later as a founder.[25] His presumed date is at least four centuries earlier than Phaselis' founding, if he ever existed. At the city of Perge in the second century AD a whole gallery of founders was on display at the South Gate, including Mopsos, a variety of other men, some of them notably obscure, and two Roman citizens, who were contemporary with the gate itself.[26] At Sillyon a gravestone inscribed with the name Mopsos has been taken as some sort of proof of his existence, and of his activity in the area;[27] actually it is only 'proof' of the use of the name by a man who had died at the time of the inscription. Aspendos is claimed to have been ruled by Mopsos,[28] and the local name for the city, Estwediiys, is linked to the local king of Kilikia named on the Karatepe inscription, Asitawadas, and claimed to be identical.[29] Since Asitawadas refers

---

[23] The whole inscription has now been published by H. Cambel and J.D. Hawkins, *Corpus of Hieroglyphic Luwian Inscriptions*, vol 2, 'Karatepe–Aslantas', 2000; in vol. 1 Hawkins discusses the text on pp. 45–68.

[24] Cf. Houwink ten Cate, *Luwian Population Groups*, 44–46.

[25] Pomponius Mela, 79.

[26] *I. Perge*, 24–28 (Mopsos is 27).

[27] D. Hereward, 'Inscriptions from Pamphylia and Isauria', *JHS* 78, 1958, 1.

[28] Eustathius, *Commentary on Dionysios Periegetes* 1.852, *GGM* II 366.

[29] The idea was floated by R. D. Barnett, 'Mopsos', *JHS* 73, 1953, 140–143, and 'A Phoenician Inscription from Eastern Cilicia', *Iraq* 10, 1948.

to a king of 'Bt Mps', the 'House of Mopsos', the connection is thus held to be verified. None of this is acceptable.

Aspendos developed an alternative origin-myth to the Mopsos story. In about 300 BC the city used this myth, that it was originally a colony of Argos, to forge an alliance of sorts with that Greek city. This was persistent and convenient enough to be repeated by Pomponius Mela in the first century AD. Of course, these two myths – Mopsos/Asitawadas and Argos – are mutually contradictory. They are also both inventions of later ages.[30]

It has to be said that a good deal of credulity of a strangely naive sort is displayed in the discussions on Mopsos and company. More than one historian simply piles up references from all periods of antiquity, and appears to regard the total mountain of comments as proof of the myth's validity,[31] whereas all that has happened is that successive authors have repeated one another. The alleged proofs in Kilikia – the city name Mopsuhestia, and the occurrence of 'Bt Mps' in the Karatepe inscription[32] – are not proof either, since neither is datable to the period immediately following the Trojan war, which must be within a decade or two of 1200 BC at the latest (unless the war was even earlier).[33] It is no good claiming that the use of the name 'Mopsos' must mean something. What is required is evidence susceptible to detailed proof, with careful attention to sources and chronology, and this the Mopsos material does not provide. It is sometimes ignored that the 'dark-age' period in Pamphylia – that is, when there are no available written sources, and precious little in the way of archaeological material – was at least six centuries long (c.1200 to c.600 BC), and this is far too long a time to allow 'tribal memories' or whatever to be reckoned accurate or reliable, particularly when they are recounted by poets and others from outside who were uninterested in accuracy.

The use of the term 'founder' – *ktistes* – in such displays as that at Perge's South Gate, or in claims such as that for Phaselis, cannot be taken as historical evidence. Either the 'founder' is an invention, as it certainly is in the case of Mopsos at Phaselis, or it is an honour awarded to men who were particularly

---

[30] R.S. Stroud, 'An Argive Decree from Nemea concerning Aspendos', *Hesperia* 53, 1984, 193–216.

[31] A particularly blatant example is Houwink ten Cate, *Luwian Population Groups*, 44–50; see also Erzen, 'Besiedlungsproblem Pamphyliens' (note 4).

[32] It is *'Bt Mps'* in the Phoenician section and *'Mukshash'* in the Hittite, and the inscription is of the eighth century BC; cf. G. Salmoni, 'Hellenism on the periphery: the case of Cilicia and an etymology of Soloikismos', in Colvin (ed.), *The Greco-Roman East*, YCS 2004, 181–206.

[33] If the war ended about 1260 BC, as the archaeology of Troy suggests (assuming there was a war at all, of course), the problem is redoubled, and the migrants were invading the Hittite empire when it was vigilant and powerful; for such an invasion there is no evidence for another two generations.

generous towards the city, as with the Romans at Perge – or indeed both of these. It is quite clear that the myths of the early so-called 'founders' such as Mopsos are wholly unreliable as foundation histories. They are not worthless, of course, but they were valuable for other reasons than providing accurate history, which indeed was not their purpose. They were a way of validating their society and community, in the same way that Sparta's kings and Rome's kings claimed long and highly improbable genealogies, or that Athens claimed a relationship with Theseus, or the Macedonian kings claimed to have originated from an Argive family. These stories were not intended to convey historical truth, and should not be interpreted in that way. Nor can they be used to date any activity at all, and certainly not the foundation of the Pamphylian cities, or even the arrival of Greeks in Pamphylia.

These myths and appropriations thus provide no evidence for the original migration, but are only evidence for later generations' desire to link themselves and their communities to that seminal Greek event, the Trojan War, and its aftermath. Yet the failure of the myths to be evidence in this matter does not disprove the migrations themselves. The destruction of the Hittite Empire (and of Troy), the violent extinction of the Mycenaean kingdoms, the settlement of Philistines in southern Palestine, and the actions of the groups of invaders whom the Egyptians fought in the twelfth century BC, now referred to as the 'Sea Peoples', all demonstrate that the movements of peoples throughout the Near East in the twelfth and eleventh centuries BC did take place.[34] It would thus be perverse to insist that the elimination of the myths as evidence for the movement into Pamphylia meant that such a movement did not occur. But removing the myth does allow a clearer vision, and compels a concentration on the real evidence. Such as it is.

The absence of hard evidence, written, archaeological, or any other, for the Greek settlement in Pamphylia is not a decisive bar to understanding what happened there, though it does mean that the problem has to be approached from a different direction. It is worth considering a neighbouring land, where the evidence does exist. Across the narrow sea to the south-east, the island of Cyprus quite certainly received Greek-speaking peoples during the migration period, and excavations have located settlements of people equipped with late Mycenaean gold and pottery in places such as Marion, Soloi, Paphos, and Lapithos.[35] The settlers

[34] M. K. Sanders, *The Sea Peoples, Warriors of the Ancient Mediteranean 1250–1150 BC*, rev. ed., London 1985, is as good an account as can be found; on the Mopsos myth cf. J. Vanschoonwinkel, 'Mopsos: legende et réalité', *Hethitica* 10, 1990, 185–211.

[35] J. N. Coldstream, 'Status symbols in Cyprus in the eleventh century BC', in E. Peltenburg (ed.), *Early Society in Cyprus*, Edinburgh 1989, 325–335.

were only small groups of people, perhaps no more than extended families and their dependents, possibly a few tens of people in each case, but they were strong enough, or violent enough, or persuasive enough, or rich enough, to impose their authority on a series of small territories, mainly along the coasts, and to defend these areas against any attack. Their success in imposing themselves in Cyprus also argues for a considerable disruption of Bronze Age Cypriot society at the time, and maybe their settlements took place in areas which were the less useful or attractive, which the native Cypriots were uninterested in occupying. Their settlements eventually developed into a series of city kingdoms, whose dynasties sometimes traced themselves back to the original settlers.[36]

This is just the sort of migration and settlement best envisaged for Pamphylia, though on an even smaller scale. Cyprus was a known quantity at the time, a Bronze Age kingdom with a substantial mineral wealth: it was, for groups leaving Greece for a new home, a sensible and likely target. Pamphylia, on the other hand, was not known, it was not rich, and it had no metals; what it perhaps did have was land and space.

Pamphylia would not be the first choice of the refugees who headed eastwards, therefore, and so it would not receive many of the migrants, and few of those who did arrive had any wealth or power. Those who arrived found a native population already there, but, if my theory of Tarhuntassa as a thinly inhabited buffer state is correct, there may not have been many people in occupation. This provides a satisfactory explanation for the later linguistic evidence, which shows that the Greek arrivals, speaking the Arkadian dialect,[37] came in the migration period, and that the local Luwian-speakers survived to pass on their own names for rivers, for example, to the newcomers, so that the two languages, and thus the two peoples, lived on side by side.

The Arkadian dialect was similar to that of the settlers in Cyprus, and we may therefore suppose that the migrants in both places arrived at much the same time. But the Pamphylian Greeks did not form any kingdoms; it may be assumed that Mycenaean chiefs were not involved, as they clearly were in Cyprus. The time of their arrival in the island was, very roughly, the eleventh century BC and later. Given the difference in the attractiveness of the two lands, Cyprus was probably the first target for the migrants, so that Pamphylia would be likely to be settled later than the island, by people unable to settle in Cyprus because the best places were already occupied by groups and kingdoms unwilling to accept more refugees.

---

[36] As at Paphos: F. G. Maier, 'Priest Kings in Cyprus', in Peltenburg (ed.) (previous note), 376–391.
[37] Brixhe, *Dialecte grec*, 147–149.

The migration was not a movement of large numbers of people, whatever may have been the scale of the initial upheaval in their homelands, and it took place over a lengthy period of time, perhaps a century or more. It cannot thus be described as an invasion, still less as a conquest – 'migration' is still the best term for it. In Pamphylia the linguistic evidence implies the addition, or perhaps even the inclusion, of speakers of the Dorian Greek dialect among the migrants as well as that of Arkadia, though this may be the result of later Rhodian influence from the foundation of Phaselis, and of Rhodian commercial activity.[38]

The problem with all this is that it is quite impossible to prove any of it on present evidence – at least with regard to Pamphylia. (I thus lay myself open to the same criticism I have levelled at those who accept Mopsos' activity – but I would claim that my theory is closer to such evidence as does exist, and that it is inherently more likely all round.) What is required is clear and datable archaeological evidence such as has emerged in Cyprus; for example, tombs of people whose possessions link them to Greece in the eleventh and tenth centuries, or a settlement site with post-Mycenaean or Protogeometric Greek pottery. In the absence of such evidence, but in the knowledge that Greeks certainly did arrive in Pamphylia and settled there – for they are discovered there later and were not there earlier – the modified speculation of the sort expressed in the last two paragraphs must be indulged.

The linguistic evidence may also perhaps be pressed a little further. In the third and second centuries BC the city of Perge began to issue coins with representations of the local goddess Artemis on them.[39] She was sometimes described as Artemis of Perge in Greek (or 'Diana Perg' in Latin later) and sometimes in a different dialect or language as *Wanassas Preiias*. (The title *Wanassa* is clearly a descendant of the Mycenaean title *Wanax* – 'king', so the title was one awarded by Greek-speakers.) The name Perge, of course, is not itself Greek, and would seem to have become Preia in the local dialect by the time of the coins; this is close to the name Parha which the place apparently bore in the Hittite texts. The name was thus, it would seem, Luwian. Similarly, the city of Aspendos had the alternative, or original, name of Estwediiys, which is interpreted as being basically an Anatolian – that is, Luwian – word. Sillyon was known originally as Selyviios; Side seems to have had the local name Sibdabiis. The speakers of Luwian were thus numerous enough to maintain their own names for such places and to impose them on the Greek arrivals. Indeed, Side has never been thought to be other than a Luwian city (or its equivalent); but

[38] *Ibid.*
[39] *BMC Pamphylia*, lxxvii–lxxix; Head *HN* 702.

since the three cities of the plain also had their Luwian names, which were used on their coins until the Hellenistic period, we must assume that Luwian was also spoken there for centuries after their foundation.[40]

So what may be envisaged in Pamphylia in the 'migration period' of the eleventh century BC and after is the slow infiltration of a variety of small Greek groups, mainly speaking the Arkadian dialect, into a fairly thinly populated land, where Luwian-speaking inhabitants were already much divided into separate tribal groups, hence the 'Pamphylian' name. The arrival of these Greek groups will have significantly increased the number of those clans or tribes. The Greek immigrants were not able to overwhelm the native peoples, though their language and culture did so successfully in the end, in a process which took centuries. The immigrants did not form themselves into local kingdoms; the name 'Pamphylia' implies that the whole country had a clan organization rather than anything more elaborate or concentrated.[41]

In that period of migration and after, which for Pamphylia may be considered to run from about 1100 BC to after 700 BC, a good deal happened, besides the arrival of the Greek immigrants. There is no indication of hostility between Greeks and Luwians; if there had been a long period of inter-communal hostility, this would be a condition both remembered and endemic. This does not 'prove' a lack of hostility, still less an absence of fighting and conflict, but it does suggest that any such hostility which did develop was never strong enough or nasty enough to colour the attitudes of later generations. More cynically, one might put it down to the inability of any one group to prevail over the rest.

If this interpretation is reasonable we may therefore assume that the Greeks and the Luwians mingled more or less amicably, and that their societies were, politically speaking, organized at the tribal or clan level. In this the Greeks would have resembled their fellows in central and north-west Greece in later centuries. Between 1100 BC and, say, 800 BC, the whole of Greece was effectively organized as a set of 'tribal' states, if such a designation as a preliminary to urbanization may be permitted. Urbanization developed only slowly, depending as it did on a pre-existing social organization of some complexity, on a minimal but rising level of individual and communal wealth, and hence commerce, and on the need for communal defence. Perhaps the earliest of these *poleis* were those which developed along the western coast of Anatolia in the ninth century, or in Euboia at about the same time, but there is no need to assume that the Pamphylians were as 'advanced' in this respect as Ionia. Of the three social requirements for

[40] These names are all found on the coins: *BMC Pamphylia* lxxi–lxxxvi; Head *HN* 705.
[41] See appendix 1.

the development of towns, the Pamphylians were not wealthy and had little trade, though the presence of some small amounts of Geometric Greek pottery would suggest that some trade did exist by the end of the ninth century; they were organized, as their name insists, in tribes, and for a long time they will have apprehended no external threat, being protected by the mountains all around, and by their generally inhospitable coast. For the period of the 'dark age', they had no incentive to urbanize.

To summarize, therefore. For some time during the centuries after the collapse of the Hittite empire, groups of Greek-speaking people arrived in Pamphylia. They were neither numerous nor aggressive enough to displace or absorb the existing Luwian-speaking population, but neither were the Luwians able to absorb the Greeks. The two peoples, politically and socially organized in clans and tribes and living in rural settlements, continued to live next to one another for several centuries. It was only after this period of (presumed) relatively amicable co-existence that outside events were to impinge sufficiently to force changes to their situation in the country – which is the subject of the next chapter. But during that time the two peoples – or rather the many tribes, Luwian, Greek, perhaps others – had found it possible to live together in relative peace and amity. This mutual tolerance was the foundation for the future phases of Pamphylian history.

2

The New Cities

The presence of Greeks living in Pamphylia in the eleventh or tenth centuries BC did not mean that they lived in cities; nor does it mean that the cities which later developed in Pamphylia were necessarily Greek. Investigation is necessary to determine, not just where the cities were, but how they developed, and when and by whom they were founded. It will emerge that urbanization did not begin with the Greeks, and that the Pamphylian cities were developed by both Greeks and non-Greeks.

The number of cities in Pamphylia increased over time. The initial set, which developed in the Archaic period (before c.700 BC), numbered seven (Side, Aspendos, Sillyon, Perge, Magydos, Olbia and Phaselis); two more were added during the Hellenistic period (Attaleia and Korakesion); some other places became counted as cities, if minor ones, in the Roman period. The original seven are the ones to be considered in this chapter; the later cities will be considered at the appropriate chronological place.

The first cities fall into two groups, four coastal and three inland. For two of the coastal cities, Phaselis and Side, we have some written information attesting their early existence. Both were established quite deliberately because their sites were usable as harbours. Phaselis was founded by an expedition led by Lakios of Lindos in Rhodes about 690 BC,[1] that is, during the second phase of the Greek colonization movement, after the early, extended expeditions which reached to Syria and Italy. The first settlement was placed on a small but steep hill projecting into the sea, facing east into the Pamphylian Sea and west towards the mountainous land across a low peninsula (Plates 13, 14). The site is steep and awkward, only about six hectares in size, and it is connected to the mainland across a valley which is low, sandy, and in one part, marshy. The hill itself is uncultivable, and the valley, alternately marsh and sand, is unsuitable

---

[1] Eusebios, *Chronographia* VII.1.93.2 and Dionysios of Tell Mahre, *Epitome* 22 agree on 691/690; cf. M. Miller, *The Sicilian Colony Dates*, Albany NY 1970. The date is calculated from the fact that Lakios was the brother of the founder of Gela in Sicily which is dated about 690 also; contemporaneity is assumed, but the Sicilian colony dates are hardly set in stone, so '690' for Phaselis is obviously an approximation.

for arable farming. This situation means that the low isthmus forms a harbour on both sides, to north and south; a third harbour, small and roughly circular, and referred to at times as the naval harbour, but nominated more suitably as the *Stadthafen* by the German team which surveyed the site (as opposed to the larger and presumably mercantile harbours) also existed.[2]

Side was also established on a rocky promontory, but one which is low-lying. It is at the eastern end of the Pamphylian Sea, where the coastal plain narrows almost to nothing. Somewhat sheltered waters exist on either side (to north-west and south-east of the city site), but the real harbour was a shallow sandy bay on the end of the promontory, bounded in part by rocks which formed a natural breakwater, which was later artificially improved.[3] As at Phaselis the connection with the mainland was a low sandy waste.

In many ways these two cities had very similar situations, and were obviously developed above all as maritime settlements which could be defended against hostility from the landward side. Phaselis' hill is clearly easily defensible, at least from the land, while Side is at the end of a flat and sandy approach, across which any attacker's advance would be long visible, though defences would need to be, and were, constructed. Above all, however, the situations of both cities relate to the sea. They were both established at points which were very useful for shipping. They are the best harbours along the whole coast of Pamphylia, and each can tap the resources of extensive inland territories, Phaselis with forested hills, Side close to the entrance to the Melas River route inland. There is no doubt that the cities were founded mainly for commercial and mercantile reasons.

This is confirmed by the stories attached to the foundations of both cities. Side recorded a sort of foundation story, though this is in need of some interpretation. A party of colonists from Kyme is said to have landed at Side, but then immediately forgot their Greek and started talking in the local 'barbarian' language.[4] The story is recorded late, by Arrian in the second century AD, and refers to the background to the campaign of Alexander the Great in the fourth century BC; it also clearly needs to be understood as having been adjusted somewhat in the past. If it is accepted as having some basis in fact, which seems likely enough, we have to understand it as being a recollection of the arrival at Side of a small Greek group, not necessarily colonists, which was rapidly swallowed up into the much larger native population. They adopted the language of that city and abandoned their original Greek. This seems to be a

---

[2] Schäfer, *Phaselis*.

[3] P. Knoblauch, *Die Hafenenlagen und die Anschliessenden Seemauer von Side*, Ankara 1977.

[4] Arrian, *Anabasis*, 1.26.4.

reasonable situation if the group of Greeks was small, and the population they joined much larger.

A number of issues arise from the story, and need to be addressed. The first is the origin of the Greek 'colonists'. This has been attributed to Kyme in Aeolia, on the coast of western Asia Minor. This was an early Greek city of some importance, well attested in the eighth century BC with contacts in Phrygia and in mainland Greece.[5] It is also one of the cities which is thought to be the source of the Greek colonial settlement at Cumae in Campania, one of whose founders, Hippokles, is said to have come from the Aeolian city.[6] An alternative Kyme has been suggested in Euboia,[7] but grave doubt has been cast on the very existence of this Euboian Kyme,[8] and it seems best to stick with the Aeolian Kyme as the source of the men who went to Side. It was the source of the early Greek settlers on Ischia in the Bay of Naples, and of the settlers who moved to the Italian mainland to give their name to Cumae. The numbers of people involved was clearly small at both Cumae and Side. At Cumae Hippokles agreed that it should be reckoned a colony of Chalkis in Euboia, if it could be named for his home city, so implying that the Chalkidians well outnumbered his own Cumaians;[9] at Side the number of people involved was few enough for them to be swallowed up by the native population. It seems reasonable to assume that they were actually traders, not 'colonists'.

The reference to Kyme, therefore, implies that the Aeolian city was active in wide-ranging trading in the eighth century BC. At Side the Kymaians arrived at a community which already existed, and which was sufficiently large to absorb without trace a party of Greeks. The site of Side is an inhospitable place, exposed to storms, the land flat, sandy, and waterless. It is not a place which would be settled for any reason but to maintain contact with the sea. The Greeks who arrived were therefore joining an established urban community, which was already in existence by the later part of the eighth century BC. This fits in well enough with the known chronology of the eastward enterprise of the early expeditions from the Aegean, which reached north Syria in the eighth century, as is shown by the settlement at al-Mina on the Syrian coast among other sites;[10] Side would be a useful place to call at on the journey.

---

[5] King Agamemnon of Kyme married his daughter to King Midas of Phrygia (Pollux, 9.831); the father of Hesiod the poet lived at Kyme for a time (Hesiod, *Opera*, 636); both of these events were in the eighth century.

[6] Strabo 5.4.4.

[7] D. Ridgway, *The First Western Greeks*, Cambridge 1992, 32–33.

[8] K. Broderson, 'The 'Urban Myth' of Euboean Kyme', *Ancient History Bulletin*, 15, 2001, 25–26.

[9] Strabo 5.4.4.

[10] J. Boardman, *The Greeks Overseas*, London 1973, 38–47; the dating of the Greek presence at al-

Side, therefore, was a fully organized urban community before the Greek colonization movement began, and it was the first city to develop in Pamphylia. Already a considerable settlement, it was contacted by the Kymaians, and this happened during the eighth century BC – Cumae in Campania was founded by about 730 BC,[11] and the Euboians appear to have reached out to both east and west simultaneously. At Side a basalt cauldron made in North Syria in the eighth or seventh century BC has been found, and may be taken as an example of the sort of trading goods being transported. It is the oldest artefact found in the excavations which took place in the 1950s.[12] A reminder that it was not only Greek sailors and merchants who frequented this coast comes from the discovery of a fairly lengthy Phoenician inscription at Cebel Ires Daği, in Rough Kilikia, some way inland from Side and Korakesion. It is dated to the later seventh or early sixth century. Along with the Syrian stone vase from Side, this is a sign that Side was in contact with the east independently of the Greeks.[13]

Whereas Side was an indigenous development, Phaselis was founded from outside as a colony of Lindos, in an expedition headed by Lakios about 690 BC.[14] The date is no doubt an approximation, or a later calculation, but Lakios' brother's foundation of Gela in Sicily is dated to 688 BC,[15] and so the date for Lakios at Phaselis cannot be very far distant from 690. Pottery of the Archaic period has been reported from Phaselis' acropolis, and this would tend to act as confirmation of the reputed date.[16] When inscriptions were made in the city later, the Rhodian dialect of Dorian Greek was used,[17] so the Rhodian origin seems thus to be confirmed; and the name of Lakios survived as the founder, the *ktistes*, maybe even with a cult to his memory. The foundation of Phaselis

---

Mina is less than precise, but the eighth century will encompass its main activity: cf. M. P. Popham, 'Precolonisation: early Greek contact with the East', in G. R. Tsetskhladze and F. de Angelis, *The Archaeology of Greek Colonisation, Essays dedicated to Sir John Boardman*, Oxford 2002, 11–34; J. Boardman, 'Greeks and Syria: Pots and People', in G. R. Tsetskhladze and A. M. Snodgrass (eds), *Greek Settlements in the Eastern Mediterranean and the Black Sea*, BAR S1062, 2002, 1–16, dates the Euboian pottery in the Levant as beginning in the tenth century BC.

[11] Ridgway, *First Western Greeks*, 32–36.

[12] A. M. Mansel, 'Ein Basaltkessel aus Side', *Anadolu* 7, 1958, 1–13.

[13] P. G. Mocsa and J. Russell, 'A Phoenician Inscription from Cebel Ires Daği in Rough Cilicia', *Ep. Anat.* 9, 1987, 1–28; the stone is exhibited at Alanya Museum.

[14] Stephanos of Byzantion, 'Gela'; Eusebios, *Chronicle*, ed. Karst, 184; cf. Blumenthal, *Siedlungscolonisation*, 129–132.

[15] Thucydides, 6.4.2; Boardman, *Greeks Overseas*, 174–175; Miller, *Sicilian Colony Dates*, 187–188.

[16] D. J. Blackburn, 'A Brief History of the City, based on the Ancient Sources', in Schäfer, *Phaselis*, 31, n. 2.

[17] Inscriptions from the city are in *TAM* II.1.413–416, and others are in Schäfer, *Phaselis*, ch. 7.

would seem to connect with another outreach from Rhodes to Soloi in Kilikia[18] as well as to Sicily: so these colonies mark stages in the development of a Rhodian trade route system to the east and to the west, in the same way as the Euboian cities and Aeolian Kyme had done a generation earlier.

The Phaselite foundation story includes the information that Lakios had to buy the city's site from a local shepherd, paying for it with a quantity of dried fish. The name of the shepherd was given, Kylabras, and is a good Lykian name.[19] The land thus acquired was presumably the hilly peninsula, the later acropolis, a small area of little importance to a shepherd, but which was just the sort of place chosen by Greeks and Phoenicians as a defensible site for their new settlements overseas. It is likely that both sides in the deal thought they had gained a bargain; the Phaselites certainly thought so, and they commemorated the deal with a sacrifice of dried fish annually. From the historian's point of view, however, the story shows clearly that the area was already inhabited when the Rhodian settlers arrived, even if at that moment only by a shepherd and his sheep. Few if any archaeological remains can be expected of pre-Greek settlement, since the shepherd was presumably only selling grazing land, not his home. The expansion of the city from its early peninsular site was therefore at the expense of other lands of the aboriginal inhabitants. The small size of the original settlement, if, as I suppose, it was on the peninsula, means that the settlers would almost certainly become cramped quickly, and expansion onto the adjacent mainland would soon follow. Conflict certainly ensued, and, since early warfare is associated with the name of the founder Lakios, it began soon after the city's beginnings.[20]

Phaselis' date of 690 BC therefore means that the colony was probably established at a time when Side already existed, and when the Rhodians, or at least the Lindians, were emulating the Euboians by despatching expeditions to Sicily and to Kilikia; the difference was that the Euboians were mainly traders, while the Rhodians were also colonizers. The two places were therefore used differently: Side was clearly a port at which to call on the way to Syria, one which already existed; Phaselis, on the other hand, was established as a new port-of-call on the way from Rhodes to Kilikia (where a Rhodian colony was also established at Soloi) and to Egypt. The Egyptian connection remained strong

---

[18] Strabo 14.5.8; Livy 37.56; Pomponius Mela 1.13, giving Rhodians, Argives, and Achaians variously as founders; the Rhodians are specifically said to be of Lindos.

[19] Athenaios, *Deipnosophistai* 7.297E–298A.

[20] *Lindos Temple Chronicle*, ed. Blinkenberg, 24, a reference to spoils taken from the Solymoi by 'the men of Phaselis under Lakios', which were dedicated at the temple.

at Phaselis for centuries. The city took part in the foundation of Naukratis, the pan-hellenic trading centre in the Nile delta, in the early sixth century. It was thus a fairly important maritime and trading city within less than a century of its foundation.[21]

In neither case did the local inhabitants resist the new arrivals; indeed they appear to have been welcomed, at least at first. In fact, whereas the site of Phaselis was effectively uninhabited – though the land was purchased by the colonists – Side would seem to have been substantial enough to be considered a city-state when it was contacted by the Kymaians. Both sites, however, were fairly small. From their situation close to mountainous areas, they had only limited hinterlands, without extensive local markets. Indeed, at Phaselis, the mountains begin within half a kilometre of the acropolis, and rise very steeply (Plate 14). They were both minor ports established at places where natural harbours already existed, and whose harbours needed little improvement to make them usable (though Side's harbour needed constant dredging). They were both therefore products of the Greek and Phoenician search for trade, and neither was selected as a place to which people would normally be attracted to settle; both were oriented towards the sea rather than the land. This inevitably changed with time, but their origins were as ports-of-call, not colonies of settlement. Indeed, the period of their early existence – by the mid-eighth century for Side, the early seventh century for Phaselis – was at the very beginning of the time of Greek emigration, which went mainly to the north and west, rather than to the east. Neither community was much concerned with the Pamphylian hinterland, and both were situated on the very margins of the Pamphylian plainlands. Phaselis, however, did soon develop into a place of settlement, with a numerous enough population to make war on the nearby Solymians; similarly, Side's relations with its landward neighbours were not good.

Phaselis and Side are located at the western and eastern extremities of Pamphylia and they were carefully sited to provide harbour facilities for passing ships. The coasts of Pamphylia are of three types, and the differences help to explain the locations of these cities by the sea. From Side eastwards, the hills of Rough Kilikia come close to the sea, there is only a narrow passage along the coast, now holding a road and not much else, and only small sites are available in which towns and cities could develop; Side is sited at the last reasonably spacious coastal plain (going eastwards), where the Melas River breaks out of the hills to flow through a plain for half a dozen kilometres.

---

[21] Herodotos, 2.176–180; Blackburn, 'Brief History', referring to Robert, 'Un pierre à Phaselis et une inscription de Cilicie', *Docs*, 42–44, on the trade in timber.

To the west of Side the coast is low-lying and sandy almost as far as Antalya. This coast has continued to accumulate and to move south since the Ice Age, reinforced by deposits from the land by the rivers, and from the sea by the westward current. There are no settlements directly on the coast in this section. From Antalya to the southern Cape Gelidonya, however, the third section of the coast is steep mountains and cliffs and estuaries of mountain streams strewn with boulders. This is the coast which was the first part of Pamphylia seen by the Greek sailors conning their small ships from landing to landing at the end of the 'dark age'.

Along that western coast there were a string of small settlements, usually with Greek names – Korykos, Olympos, Idyros, Phaselis, Olbia, Magydos. The last three can be reckoned as cities, at least for part of the time; so was Olympos later, but none of them were ever large. The main point about them as a group is that they all share the same geographical character. They are all founded at points where a northward sailing ship's master would come to the end of a cliff-bound mountain coast and find a beach on which he could draw up his ship. Some are at, or close to, fresh water. Olympos, for example, is at the mouth of a mountain stream, with a shelving shingle beach curving invitingly to the north from the river mouth, which itself is just to the north of a mountainous coast. Magydos is at the eastern end of a line of vertical coastal cliffs. It was founded where a projecting reef of rock forms a lee against the westward current, and where there is the first beach for fifteen kilometres. The same may be said of Korykos and Idyros, and probably of Olbia, if it is placed at modern Gurma (and if that is not Olbia, it is a place of similar characteristics to the other places noted here). Korykos, Olympos, Phaselis, and Idyros have little or nothing in terms of hinterland on which to settle, though Olbia and Magydos are different.

These places mainly remained small. Only Phaselis, with its greater harbour space, and Magydos, with a more open hinterland of some size, developed into cities with a lasting future. But the situations of all of these places, with their Greek names and their coastal sites, were clearly the result of discovery and naming by sailors. They all existed by the time of the first surviving listing, in about 360 BC, by the sailor now called 'Pseudo-Skylax'. This was a man who would certainly notice these places, since his purpose was obviously maritime and nautical. Their positions and existence are evidence of the explorations and requirements of the Greek sailors who sailed the Pamphylian Sea. They are also evidence of the early years of that maritime enterprise. It is likely that they were all named, located, and settled at about the same time as Phaselis, in the early seventh century BC.

Olbia and Magydos were later to be overshadowed by the city of Attaleia, which was planted close to them in the second century BC. Magydos is a little to the east of Attaleia, between two of the mouths of the Katarrhaktes river, at the point at which the cliffs end (the river falls over the cliffs half a kilometre to the west). Its rocky reef-jetty was improved into an artificial harbour.[22] Olbia's location is a problem; it has been located most convincingly close to the coast at the village of Gurma, a few kilometres west of Attaleia, about where the coastline turns due south, near the mouth of the Çandır river, and just north of a stretch of mountainous coast.[23]

Magydos survived as an independent community into the Roman period, when it issued some coins,[24] but it was by then overshadowed by Attaleia. The site of Olbia (at Gurma) has produced a terracotta head of a woman dated to the Archaic period, late seventh or early sixth century BC,[25] and the city also appears to have issued some coins in the fifth or fourth century BC, but they are few and their attribution to Olbia is by no means certain.[26] We may assume that Olbia also survived (it is recorded as existing by Ptolemy in the second century AD, though it is not clear what his source was).[27] These two towns were always small, and had restricted territories – a matter I shall return to.

The origins of the cities and smaller places on the western coast, and of Side, therefore may be attributed above all to mercantile requirements, and to the needs of sailors for landing places which provided security and shelter. One city, Side, was founded by local inhabitants at least as early as the mid-eighth century and perhaps earlier; another, Phaselis, was certainly of Greek, specifically

---

[22] M. Adak and O. Atvur, 'Epigraphische Mitteilungen aus Antalya III: Die Pamphylische hafenstadt Magydos', *Ep. Anat.* 31, 1999, 53–68.

[23] Strabo 14.4.1; N. Cevik, 'The Localisation of Olbia on the Gulf of Pamphylia', *Lykia* 1, 1994, 90–95, and id., 'Antalya-Hurma, Koyu'nde Bir Ciftlik Yerlesimi', *Lykia*, 2, 1995, 39–61; this is not definitive, in that no written confirmation of the site's identity exists, but there is sufficient in the way of remains to demonstrate a fairly substantial settlement, and the only known place in the area was Olbia; S. Sahin, 'Olbia und einige andere küste norte bei Kemer in Westpamphylien', *Ep. Anat.* 33, 2001, argued for the site near Kemer, but the one farther north seems best, taking the written documents into account; Idyros would be only a kilometer away, and two Greek sites so close together is extremely unlikely. Strabo says Olbia was 367 stades north of Cape Gelidonya, and Gurma is just about that distance.

[24] *BMC Pamphylia* lxxvi–lxxvii; Head *HN* 701.

[25] H. Metzger, 'Tête en terre cuite du Musée d'Adalia', *REA* 54, 1952, 13–17.

[26] *BMC Pamphylia* lxxvi calls the coins (attributed to the town by only one student) 'uncertain', and Head (*HN* 701) used the word 'doubtful'. There is a small set of coins with an indecipherable inscription, or with the letters LBI (written right to left). They are dated to the fifth century BC, and the inscription is suggested to have been the name of a dynast. Maybe it was simply a matter of near-illiteracy. Strong doubts on all this are clearly still required.

[27] Ptolemy, *Geography*, V.1–7.

Rhodian, origin; the smaller places on the west were probably also Greek, and probably also founded for maritime reasons.

These explanations, however, will not apply to the other cities of the region. The three inland cities, Perge, Sillyon, and Aspendos, are all sited on isolated flat-topped hills with steep, even in places vertical, sides. Perge and Aspendos both later expanded off their hills, but the original cities were confined to the hilltops, which became their *acropoleis*, and Sillyon scarcely expanded at all beyond its hilltop site. All three cities are situated within the Pamphylian plain, but several kilometres from the coast. Perge and Aspendos are close enough to the Kestros and Eurymedon Rivers respectively to rank as minor ports; Sillyon's river is no more than a stream. Their hilly sites, though in the plain, are inconvenient, for they would force a farmer into an awkward climb at the end of a hard day spent working in the fields, and they are some distance from their rivers. For the same reason they are distinctly awkward for visiting merchants, despite the rivers' proximity to Perge and Aspendos. The only possible justification for the occupation of such sites is for defence (see Plates 8, 11, 19).

The existence of Parha/Perge in the Bronze Age is attested in the Hittite document discussed in the last chapter, but no physical remains of that period have been found, except some 'prehistoric' potsherds which will be contemporary with the Hittite reference. Considerable survey work and excavation has taken place on the Pergean acropolis, and at the sites of the other two cities, but again there is no other sign of inhabitation in the Late Bronze Age, and none in the Early Iron Age. Excavation has been extensive enough to suggest that any substantial occupation of that time would have been detected. This is only an indication, of course, which could be upset by more excavation, but I will argue on other grounds that the absence of earlier material is due to the absence of settlement at the city sites, that the cities were founded more or less simultaneously, and that, as with the arguments for the foundation of overseas Greek colonies elsewhere, the earliest pottery is a good sign of the approximate foundation period. Pottery of the seventh century BC, described as 'Rhodian', has been found in the Perge acropolis excavations, and some potsherds of about the same age have turned up at Sillyon.[28] This tends to rule out the foundation of any of these cities during the two or three centuries after 1100 BC. By 500 BC all three cities were certainly fully organized and properly established, so that the latest date for their foundation may be pushed back some time before

---

[28] Reports by J. Inan and W. Martini in 17, 18, and 19 *Kazı* (on Perge) and by M. Küpper in XIV *AST* II 451–462 (on Sillyon); summaries by S. Mitchell in the British School at Athens, *Archaeological Reports* for 1999, 171.

that date, say by, at the minimum, a century. These hilltop sites were thus in all likelihood first occupied between about 800 and 600 BC, and this is the period which will be examined. For, if such a drastic development as a change from a rural to an urban community is made in a society, there must be a reason, or reasons, for it, and discovering reasons is part of the historian's task.

This period, the eighth and seventh centuries BC, includes the foundation of Phaselis (690 BC) and the somewhat earlier emergence of Side as an urban community (by c.750 or earlier), the dates of the Archaic terracotta head from Olbia (c.600 BC), of the Archaic pottery from the Phaselis acropolis, and of the rather earlier Geometric sherds from Sillyon (c.825 BC). The identification of the sherds from Perge as 'Rhodian' suggests contact with the coast and with traders from Greece, though it does not imply that the city was a Rhodian foundation.[29] These coincident dates show that the foundations of the inland cities are in all probability connected in some way with the foundations of the coastal cities, at least those on the western part of the Bay.

The eighth and seventh centuries was a period in which Anatolia as a whole went through a widespread series of upheavals, and these led to major political changes. These have to be considered as the essential background to the foundation of all the Pamphylian cities, for although Pamphylia was somewhat isolated by its surrounding sea and mountains, it was not out of touch with other lands – apart from the Rhodian pottery, Attic black figure pottery has also been found at Perge,[30] and the Olbia head is regarded as being at least influenced by Cypriot work.

The great powers operating in interior Asia Minor in the eighth and seventh centuries – the kingdoms of Phrygia, Assyria, and Lydia – do not seem to have impinged directly on Pamphylia until the very end, when the Lydian King Kroisos (ruling c.560–546 BC) extended his power into the country (see next chapter). The Assyrian empire reached as far as the eastern borders of Rough Kilikia, and Assyrian armies campaigned into central Anatolia in the second half of the eighth century, but the Assyrian state's main concerns were always elsewhere, and it remained separated from Pamphylia by the Kilikian and Taurus mountains. But it was brutal in its methods, and in 696 the city of Tarsos in Kilikia was destroyed after a rebellion.[31] Tarsos is only two or three days' sail from Side: the sack of the city surely provoked apprehension in Pamphylia.

---

[29] These seem to be suggested by H. Abbasoğlu, 'Founding of Perge', 177.
[30] Inan and Martini (note 28).
[31] Eusebios, Chronicle, 1.4–5.

The Phrygian kingdom was based entirely in north central Anatolia, centred at Gordion, and it also clashed with Assyria.[32] In neither case would these states have found it a simple matter to reach into Pamphylia; for Assyria, whose foreign policy seems to have been based entirely on scotching apprehended and presumed threats at ever greater distances from the homeland, the Pamphylians posed no serious threat, and moreover were behind a formidable barrier of hills and mountains; these factors made them difficult to get at and at the same time prevented them from reaching out, a difficulty reinforced by the political division of the Pamphylian tribes. For the Phrygians, the Taurus Mountains were also a barrier, but it seems that, in addition, their kings were considerably less aggressive than the Assyrian rulers. This does not mean that these powers had no influence on Pamphylia; direct effects seem to be absent, but indirect effects there surely were, for these were formidable states.

The Assyrian Empire went down to destruction in the late seventh century, to be replaced by a whole set of competing kingdoms: the Babylonians in the Fertile Crescent, the Medes in Iran and the eastern half of Anatolia as far west as the Halys River, independent pharaonic Egypt, and the new kingdom of the Syennesids in Kilikia.[33] The Phrygian kingdom had gone earlier, damaged by the Assyrians and then destroyed in the invasion of the nomad Cimmerians in about 680 BC;[34] it was in part replaced in western Anatolia by the Lydian kingdom, which was based around Sardis and the fertile river valleys which lead to the Aegean, and which earned its reputation and power by fighting successfully against the invading Cimmerians.[35] The more westerly basis for this kingdom's power, as compared with the Hittites or the Phrygians, meant that it had much easier access to Pamphylia, if it wished, than any earlier Anatolian power, for it commanded the northern ends of the western routes into western Pamphylia, by way of the Golcuk Beli and Gubuk Beli passes.

There is no indication at all that Pamphylia was involved in any of the tremendous activity of the fall of kingdoms and empires, of warfare and destruction, but that does not mean that it was unaffected. The kings of Assyria and Phrygia may not have actually penetrated into Pamphylia, but they were certainly close enough to do so had they wished, and they were obviously a threat. I would suggest that it was these apparent threats, and the turmoil they generated, which was one of the elements which persuaded the Pamphylians to

---

[32] A. R. Burn, *The Lyric Age of Greece*, rev. ed., London 1978, 50–51.

[33] *CAH* III.2.646–649; see map in A. J. Toynbee, *A Study of History*, XI, *Historical Atlas and Gazetteer*, London 1959.

[34] Strabo 1.61.

[35] Burn, *Lyric Age*, 103–105.

disintegration of the cliffs below the theatre (Plate 11). This was built on the very edge of the site, and the audience had a view out over and beyond the *scena* into the surrounding plain, for the *scena* seems to have been built close to the edge of the cliff. Since then, however, great cracks have formed in the rock so that parts of the theatre have broken away, leaned out, and then fallen into the lowland; other sections have broken away and are now leaning outwards, waiting for ice or a storm or an earthquake to complete the process.[36] Below the theatre, the collapse has produced a confusion of great rocks, with fragments of the theatre visible here and there. This is the situation round a good deal of Sillyon. The other two cities are not so dramatically breaking up, but they do have vertical cliffs which were obviously formed in the same way. At Perge, for example, the gaping remains of originally underground cisterns are visible in the cliff face, revealing where sections of the cliff have fallen away (Plate 8).

The result of these natural conditions was that only a little work was needed to make the hills fully defensible. At Aspendos the hill is divided into two parts (or the site is formed of two hills, if you will), with the smaller section separated off from the larger by a small valley (Map 5). The mouths of that valley are easily blocked by walls and gates so that both hills are included to form the city acropolis; at Perge and Sillyon the problem was the reverse, no easy access of this sort being available. Access ways had to be constructed, for relatively easy paths from the surrounding farmland to the upper city were necessary. At Perge there is a steep zigzag climb from the lower, later, part of the city to the acropolis, the track zigzagging up the hillside: the walk takes perhaps a quarter of an hour (if you don't get lost on the way) (Map 7). At Sillyon the cliffs were continuous all around the hill and the approach is now so steep and rubble-strewn that getting to the top is extremely difficult. There are two ways in, both of them a good half-hour's struggling climb today (Map 6). The solution at Sillyon in the ancient world was a long artificial ramp, parts of which are still in place, though not, unfortunately, continuous enough to be used now.[37] The difficult climb up the steep sides to the hilltop illustrates just how necessary the ramp was, and how easily defensible the whole site had been. (The ramp is, in effect,

---

[36] M. Küpper, 'Sillyon: Research Work 1995', XIV *AST*, II, fig. 4, p. 457, has a photograph of 'freshly fallen rock 1995'; from Bean's description of the theatre (*TSS*, 63), it is evident that parts of that building have fallen since his visit in the early 1970s. Between my visits in 2003 and 2006 more has fallen away, and little more than half the theatre is left. T. M. P. Duggan, 'A Short Account of Recorded Calamities (Earthquakes and Plagues) in Antalya Province and Adjacent and Related Areas over the past 2,300 years – an incomplete list, Comments and Observations', *Adalya* 7, 2001, 123–162, tends to make earthquakes responsible, but there is no evidence for this, and the geology of Sillyon in particular is clearly conducive to progressive wear.

[37] Bean, *TSS*, 39–42.

also a fortification; it was roofed and gated and its existence did not make the city any more vulnerable to attack.)

Water supply would be a problem at all three cities, for none of the hilltops had a source; at Perge, the only construction still standing on the acropolis is a 'cistern' now used as an animal shelter. At Perge, the main source later was brought to the city along a canal-cum-aqueduct to below the acropolis, where it later enclosed and formalised in a nymphaeum (Plate 4). At Sillyon a survey has located many cisterns, and a casual stroll around both Perge and Aspendos reveals many underground cisterns on their *acropoleis* also.[38] (Aqueducts were only built in the Hellenistic and in the Roman periods, and not at all the cities.) Water was also a problem at Side, a city site with no immediate local supply, and it must also have been difficult on the hill of Phaselis; no underground cisterns seem to have been located at either city, but Side certainly paid detailed attention to its water supply all through its history. This frequent difficulty emphasizes again the element of desperation in the choice of these inland sites.

The three inland cities, when confined to their hills, were thus very similar: Sillyon had the largest surface area, twenty-eight hectares, but the most difficult access; Aspendos was somewhat smaller, with a surface area of about twenty-three hectares including the valley; Perge's hill is still smaller, about fifteen hectares, and this is presumably the explanation for the city's later considerable expansion on to the lower land to the south. Sillyon never really expanded off the hilltop at all, except to establish a few large public buildings on the lower land to the south, and Aspendos did so only on a fairly small scale, though at neither Aspendos nor Sillyon has much in the way of excavation been done on the lower land, and such a conclusion is subject to change. Virtually all of the surface areas of all three cities were usable since the hilltops were only gently sloped. The most level was Perge, though the surface is undulating; the surface of Sillyon slopes more or less evenly upwards from south-east to north-west; the most awkward was Aspendos with its valley separating the two hills. None of them was difficult to occupy or build on, and all three were clearly used and inhabited all through the ancient world from their formation as cities into the Byzantine period.

These three inland cities had all-round defences, and the two main coastal cities are also placed with a view to defence, particularly from the landward side. Side's promontory, for example, could be easily walled off; Phaselis was founded on its isolated hill. All five were roughly the same size, taking into account their

[38] Küpper, 'Sillyon: Research Work 1995', 452.

sites. The area within Side's present walls is about fifty hectares, but this marks the widest extent of the city, which was reached in the Hellenistic period, and it is certain that it was a smaller city for much of its existence before that. The promontory on which the city was built had roughly parallel sides, about 550 metres long, with the harbour at the seaward end (Map 9). The point where the coastline widens out was in all likelihood the boundary of the original city, and the line of its earliest fortification: all the buildings beyond that line are Hellenistic or Roman. This was where the 'later city wall' was built in the Byzantine period, when the Arab threat developed; it is in fact the most logical place for a city wall. In that case the area of the first city was about twenty-two hectares (including the harbour), about the size of Aspendos. It was not on a hill, but the land beyond the walls is open, partly sandy, uncultivated, and slopes gently up and away from the city; with a wall as protection and wide visibility inland the city was defensible so long as a secure supply of water was available.[39] This was provided, it seems, by wells; much later, after the site had been long deserted, a British visitor in the early nineteenth century reported that 'there is no water whatever on the site'.[40]

Phaselis was founded on a hill connected to the mainland by a low valley. The hill is obviously defensible, with steep sides, but it is small in area, no more than about six hectares, and the area available for building was much less than that, given the hill's steep slopes. The city expanded onto and over the low sandy valley connecting the hill to the mainland. This was separated from further inland by a marsh, but another area beyond the marsh was also a later suburb, separately walled. The first expansion, called by the German excavators the *Weststadt*, roughly tripled the city's habitable area, to perhaps twenty hectares, and the second suburb to the north, named the *Nordsiedlung* by the investigators, increased it again by perhaps another six or seven hectares (Maps 10, 11). Despite these extensions, Phaselis clearly always remained a somewhat smaller city that the cities of the plain.[41]

It is difficult to say anything even of this level of detail about Olbia and Magydos. The first has not yet been definitively located, but it is probably on level ground near a hill on which later buildings have been noted; this sounds

---

[39] The 'later city wall' uses a series of existing buildings, such as the theatre, as its basis; no excavation seems to have been made and perhaps no remains of an earlier wall exist, but this is the most obvious line for the earliest defensive wall to take.

[40] C. R. Cockerell, *Travels in Southern Europe and the Levant 1810–1817*, London 1903, 175.

[41] Schäfer, *Phaselis*, has a large plan; chapter 8, 'Bemerkungen zur baugeschichte der Stadt', mainly by Schäfer, sketches the broad outline of the city's development at the successive periods.

like an acropolis.[42] The site of Magydos is known, and a surrounding wall has been discerned; it is on low ground and there is no sign of any acropolis.[43] It can be said quite certainly of both cities, however, that they were smaller than all the others, and also that they probably never grew beyond their original sites.

(As a comparison with these areas and sizes, the surface of the acropolis at Athens is about two hectares, while Athens itself, within the circuit of the later walls, is over three hundred hectares; Rome of the Servian Walls contained over four hundred hectares; the Ortygia part of Syracuse – founded in the same generation as Phaselis – was about seventy hectares. These Pamphylian cities were all fairly small, and in general they always remained that way.)

The areas of the early cities can be estimated, based on the published plans, but that does not give any clear notion of the sizes of their populations. It is quite unclear what proportion of any city's people actually lived within the walls, or what proportion of the sites was occupied by housing, rather than by public buildings. The *acropoleis* were apparently always fully inhabited, as excavations at Perge show; at Aspendos and Sillyon the hilltops themselves were the cities; public buildings later occupied the acropolis at Phaselis, and this part of the city was probably uninhabited in the city's heyday. (For the statistics on which this part of the argument is based see Appendix 2.)

Nor do the varying sizes of the cities give any real indication of their power or importance. It is clear that Phaselis was in many ways one of the most important of these cities in the early years, yet it was one of the smallest; the historical record, the remains, and the indications of wealth all imply that Perge was a more important city than Sillyon and Aspendos in the Roman period, yet its original area was only half theirs'. Aspendos was the richest and most important of the cities in the Akhaimenid and early Hellenistic period, but it was probably no larger than Sillyon; in the Byzantine period Sillyon proved eventually to be the most effective city, considered as a defensible site. The importance, political, strategic, economic, religious, of the various cities changed over time.

The cities founded on the hilltops eventually extended themselves onto the nearby lowlands. Aspendos had done this by the time of Alexander's visit in 334, for its suburb was evacuated when relations with the king turned unpleasant.[44] Perge expanded away from its original hilltop site, more than doubling its size.

---

[42] Bean, *TSS*, 86, mentions the buildings on the hill; cf also Cevik, 'Localisation' (note 23).

[43] Adak and Atvur (note 22); their plan (p. 56) enables an estimate to be made of the extent of the site.

[44] Arrian, *Anabasis* 1.27.2–3.

Side, if its original wall was on the line of the 'later city wall', expanded onto the land beyond that line in the Hellenistic period, when the later wall was built to enclose and protect the expansion. Phaselis expanded in two stages, across the valley onto the *Weststadt*, then across the marsh onto the *Nordsiedlung*. Sillyon shows no real evidence of any expansion; the city built a stadium and a gate to control entry to the access ramp, but there is little sign of anything else other than a few buildings below the hill until the last phase of the city's life.

The expansion of all the cities took place mainly in the Hellenistic period or even before, and only minimal expansion took place in the Roman period. At Perge the area of the lower walled city, where the walls are Hellenistic in date, is double that of the acropolis; the only later extension is marked by a small triangular enclosed section area at the main South Gate, amounting to an expansion of no more than five per cent of the whole (Map 8). (I exclude the stadium and the theatre, which are outside the walls; this area was probably not inhabited.) Much the same can be said of Aspendos, where the expansion had begun in the preceding Persian period. At Side, like Perge, the Hellenistic walls were only modified slightly at the main gate by enclosing a small area. At Phaselis the detached suburb to the north, the *Nordsiedlung*, is apparently Hellenistic, but the city had certainly expanded into the first suburb (the *Weststadt*) next to the southern harbour well before then: its original site was so small as to insist on it (Map 10). In all, the Roman period saw very little urban expansion in any part of Pamphylia, though there was clearly a good deal of reconstruction within the cities.

A traditional method of estimating population has been to calculate the capacity of theatres, and since these are generally Roman in date, when little growth took place, such estimates might be expected to provide some guidance. In this case figures of 14,000 for the capacity of Perge's theatre, 20,000 for Aspendos', and 22,000 for Side's have been suggested, based on a space of sixteen inches for each seated spectator,[45] but others have suggested smaller capacities. Side's theatre was larger than that of Aspendos, but it has fewer rows of seats, while that of Phaselis is smaller and Sillyon's even smaller still. Any figures are clearly only approximations, since estimated needs vary, and most theatres are partly ruinous, but the real problem with this method of calculation is that there is no guarantee that these theatres were built with the sizes of the cities' populations in mind, nor that the whole populations ever attended, or were even expected to. All this sort of calculation does is to roughly confirm the rank-sizes of the cities: Side, Aspendos, and Perge were the largest; Phaselis and Sillyon

---

[45] Bean, *TSS*, 39 and 49–50.

smaller. On the whole this does not seem to be a particularly useful means of establishing city populations.

A different approach is to apply a uniform standard of population density to each city area. A recent discussion has come down in favour of a suggested density of 200 persons per hectare, both for villages and towns.[46] On this basis, which has the advantage of being based to some degree on reality, the populations of the cities – the urban areas, that is – would have ranged from 5,200 at Phaselis and Sillyon to about 10,000 at Side and 12,000 at Attaleia. In their early phases, however, the cities were much smaller: Side's original area suggests a population of 4,400, growing to 10,000 in the expanded urban area; Perge's acropolis would have held about 3,000 and its later larger area 9,800; Phaselis' small acropolis might have held 1200 people (though its steep sides probably mean it had fewer than that) and the later enlargement would have had room for perhaps 5,200; Aspendos' original site held about 4,600, which the expanded area would enlarge to about 7,000. (It will be seen that the theatres seem to be planned for much larger numbers, generally of the order of twice as many – if the estimates are correct.)

These city-sites were, of course, only parts of the city territories. The extent of the *chora*, the rural territory of the *polis* which was also part of the several cities, is never defined. This bring us to the second element in the founding of the cities, which is their overall geographical situation, and particularly that of the three cities of the plain, and the two smaller cities on the coast. There is, of course, no historical source which gives us any indication of the extent of the *chorai* of these cities, but their geography provides a setting in which some conclusions can be drawn. Evidence from inscriptions will also provide confirmation. (See Maps 1, 2 for this section.)

It seems reasonable to assume that geographical features formed the boundaries for the cities' territories where possible. Phaselis was close to mountains inhabited by the Solymoi, a Pisidian people with whom they were at war soon after the foundation of the city. One of the Solymians' villages was attacked by Alexander in his march north from Phaselis, and has been located at Marmara (now Mnara, a hill fort beside the Çandır valley, twenty kilometres north of the city.[47] This attack was in part carried out at the request of the Phaselites, so it would seem that Phaselis was still attempting to gain control of the upper part of that valley three centuries after the city's foundation. Its expansion elsewhere

[46] G. G. Aperghis, *The Seleukid Royal Economy*, Cambridge 1004, 13–14.
[47] Stark, *Alexander's Path*, 248–253.

was blocked by the inland mountains or by the lands of the Lykian cities to the west; only a short distance to the south were other towns – Korykos and Olympos – which Phaselis certainly never controlled. These restrictions would suggest that the city had a maximum territory of about twenty kilometres by twelve, something less than 250 square kilometres. Again, most of that land was mountainous and forested.

The territory of Side was as affected by its mountainous background as Phaselis's, and its local situation was very similar. The Kilikian mountains are less high or steep than those of Lykia, but they were the more heavily populated for that very reason, and almost as rugged. The city had a longstanding enmity with the Etenneis, a Pisidian people inhabiting the hills. Their centre, Etenna, was perched above the valley of the Melas River, the valley which formed the only practicable route from Pamphylia into central Anatolia.[48] Side in fact had villages on either side of Etenna in its *chora*, so its territory surrounded Etenna on three sides. Side's territory was also bounded on the east by several small places spread along the coast as far as Korakesion, none of which Side ever controlled. That does mean, however, that Side controlled that section of the eastern end of the Pamphylian plain which was also the lower course of the Melas River, part of the hill country inland, and a section of the plain westwards towards Aspendos as far as as the modern site of Güvercinlik, where a fort put up by the Aspendians marked the boundary.[49] This was a reasonably substantial and productively varied land.[50] It is worth noting that Side's territory was something more than four hundred square kilometres in area. This would depend on the extent of its control of the hills, which no doubt varied with the fortunes of the disputes with both Etenna and Aspendos.

In the plain the three inland cities are spaced fairly regularly: Perge and Sillyon are eleven kilometres apart, Sillyon and Aspendos seventeen, measuring in straight lines. Since these cities are all situated on similar hills, it was obviously the hills which determined the cities' location; in other words the choice was dictated by the geography. But there are other hills, and other possible sites for cities; the fact that these particular hills were developed as cities means that the founders were deliberately utilizing those particular sites, and that the locations

---

[48] Side and the Etenneis were on opposite sides in Akhaios' war on Selge (Pol. 5.72.4–5), and when Antiochos III helped Side against the Etenneis in 193 (Livy 35.13.5).

[49] See below.

[50] J. Nollé, 'Zum Landbau von Side', *Ep. Anat.* 1, 1983, 119–129; Blumenthal, *Siedlungscolonisation*, map p. 123.

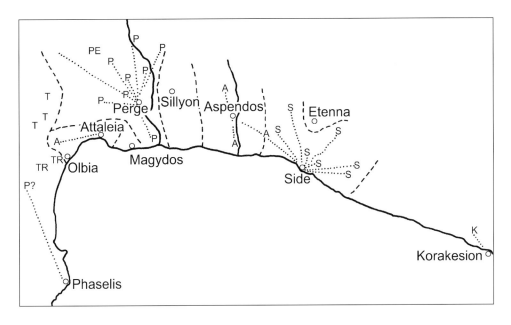

LINKS BETWEEN CITIES AND VILLAGES   (PE – Pednellisos)
SUGGESTED CHORAI BOUNDARIES   (TR – Trebenna)
                                                       (T – Termessos)

Map 2. The Cities' Territories

of the cities were determined in part by their distribution across the Pamphylian plain; it was not merely a matter of environmental dictation.[51]

So their similar distances apart of these three would seem to be significant. In addition all three are located with some regard to the rivers flowing south out of the Taurus mountains, and it would seem that it was the valleys of these rivers which formed the bases for the cities' territories. Perge lay about three kilometres west of the Kestros; Sillyon was about two kilometres from a stream which was the source of a small river now called the Aci Su; Aspendos was less than a kilometre from the Eurymedon. These locations mean that the valleys were their territories, not the rivers their boundaries. Each of these rivers flows through an alluvial plain, which they have been instrumental in forming, and between each river valley a finger of hills stretches southwards. These 'fingers' are not very high, but they are limestone rather than alluvium, rough rather than smooth, stony rather than soil, and are even now mainly wooded and pastoral

---

[51] The discussion by Blumenthal, *Siedlungscolonisation*, 45–80 is particularly useful for these cities.

rather than arable. They clearly divide the plain into three sections. Each city dominates one of these sections (Map 1). [52]

The territories of these cities thus each included a section of the plain, and their boundaries obviously lay along the summits of the 'fingers' of hills between them, giving them some of the upland as well. They also stretched inland into the mountains to the north, but how far is not so obvious; these northern hills are steep and forested, and the boundaries in that direction were no doubt always vague. One clue may lie in the aqueduct of Aspendos. This was built in the Roman period; its source is in the mountains at about 500 metres above sea level, and about fourteen kilometres inland from the city. [53] This would put the city's boundary about halfway up the mountain slopes, leaving the higher peaks uncontrolled. Similarly Side's *chora* excluded places at about the same height.

So far can geography take us. Epigraphy provides a cross-reference. A substantial number of recorded inscriptions from rural areas note which *chora* or *polis* the villages are in. The record is particularly good for Perge and Side, minimal for Aspendos, Phaselis and Attaleia, and non-existent for Sillyon. The findspots and the limestone hills are plotted on Map 2. The inscriptions tend to be of Roman date or later, but there are only a few indications that any of the cities' boundaries ever changed. The correlation of the geographical indications and the inscriptions is quite convincing. [54]

The two cities with the most extensive territories were Perge and Side. The area subject to Perge reached west to the foot of the hills, but does not include some villages at the edge of the plain, which are in Termessos' territory. To the north it borders on the territory of Pednelissos, and to the east it crosses the Kestros River to include the eastern bank. The city's coastline is short, but it includes the mouth of the Kestros, where much later an outport, Emporion, developed.

For Attaleia, one village in the Çandır valley is claimed as in the city's *chora*, and an imperial estate of the Byzantine period became the site of a small monastery; it was exempt from local taxation, and for that very reason it was noted as within the city's *chora*. [55] Attaleia would seem to have taken over Olbia's

[52] This division would have been even clearer in the ancient world if Blumenthal's estimate of the position of the coastline at the time is anywhere near correct. Based on a comment by Strabo (14.4.2) on the distance of Sillyon from the sea, he estimates that the sea has retreated up to four kilometres. This would bring the 'points' of the 'fingers' close to the coast.

[53] A. P. M. Kessener and S. A. G. Piras, 'The 1998 Campaign of the Aspendos Aqueduct Research Project', XVII *AST* 1999, 263–269.

[54] I have used the references collected in *TIB*.

[55] *TIB*, vol. 3, 'Çakirlar'.

chora – Olbia was certainly defunct as a *polis* by the fourth century AD, and probably earlier. Attaleia's village lay to the west of Olbia, in the Çandır valley, which implies that Olbia had been engulfed. When this happened is not known, but it could well have been as early as the foundation of Attaleia in the second century BC.

Sillyon has not a single reference to its *chora*; indeed its prescribed territory is almost a blank on the map of Late Antique settlements. Perge's lands extended a little way east of the Kestros, and Aspendos presumably held the whole valley of the Eurymedon. Only Kadriye and the anchorage of Kynosarion may be Sillyonian.

Aspendos has two references to its *chora*, and the line of its aqueduct and its source may be added, as may its bridge over the Eurymedon. One reference is to its later outport, at Bogazak, near the mouth of the Eurymedon, and the other is to Güvercinlik, where there was a border fort, built by the Aspendians in the Hellenistic period, and facing Side's territory. This is the one border within Pamphylia which we know was in dispute: Alexander was involved in trying to settle it, when Side accused Aspendos of aggression.[56] We do not know what judgement was made, if any, but the fort at Güvercinlik was built after his reign, so the dispute went on.[57] Since the Aspendians were responsible for the fort, it follows that Side was still disgruntled, Aspendos having been responsible for seizing lands which Side claimed as its own. This gives us the one fixed boundary point in the whole region. Note that it is within the extensive limestone area separating the two cities, at a low pass between awkward hills; the modern highway uses the gap in the hills even now.

The site at Güvercinlik fort implies that Side had claimed land still further west than that. Side already existed many decades (at least) before Aspendos was established as a city, and the dispute may have begun at Aspendos's very foundation. Side's territory is extensive, no doubt in part because it was originally the only *polis* in the region, and its territory was no doubt at first indefinite. The foundation of Aspendos will then have imposed a limit in that direction for the first time; hence the dispute. It is noticeable that no obvious limit to Side's territory to the east, towards Kibyra or Korakesion, can be located. Side's *chora* stretches up the Melas valley as far as the latitude of Lyrbe (which is high above the valley), and included the valleys of smaller rivers to east and west. The city was able to build an aqueduct along the Melas valley.

---

[56] Arrian, *Anabasis* 1.27.4 (not naming Side).
[57] *TIB*, vol. 3, 'Güvercinlik'.

A single reference for Korakesion's *chora* is not very helpful, and a single reference to the *chora* of Phaselis, as far north as Hisançandır, is difficult to accept – it is an inscription on a sarcophagus, and may have been moved.

The sizes of the territories of Side, Perge, and Aspendos can therefore be estimated, though their precise boundaries are not known, nor is the extent to their control into the hills. But the plains were the most important elements, forming the basic agricultural land of each city. These can be measured very approximately, taking in also the slopes of the hills all round. On that basis Perge's territory was about six hundred square kilometres, Sillyon's about 200, and Aspendos' about 370. But both Perge and Aspendos, lying as they did on the major rivers, had access to the valleys of those rivers leading inland, and these were and are agriculturally rich. Sillyon, between them, whose river was much smaller than the others', did not have this extra land. This factor, combined with a distinctly smaller section of plain, plus the city's greater distance from the sea, was part of the geographical basis for Sillyon's minor role in affairs for most of the history of Greek Pamphylia.

The northwest corner of the bay where Attaleia was established in the second century BC also contains two smaller areas of alluvial soil, each with its own river, and these valleys are separated by areas of stony hills and cliffs from each other and from the eastern areas of alluvial land, in the same way as the main cities of the plain. These were the lands chosen as the *chora* of Olbia and Magydos, just as the greater plains to the east were by the inland cities. The Duden-chai, the ancient Katarrhaktes, flows to the sea over a waterfall to the west of Magydos, and another branch reaches the sea in a more conventional way to the east; between these mouths lies the site of the city. Further west, the Karaman-chai flowed through an even smaller alluvial plain, reaching the sea through an area of sand dunes, which was perhaps under the sea in the first millennium BC;[58] it is here that Olbia was established.[59] Antalya, by contrast, is built on the tongue of travertine limestone which reaches the sea between these small plains, and which forms one of the 'shelves'. This is a much wider section of limestone than those separating Perge and Sillyon, or Sillyon and Aspendos, and no doubt it formed the frontier area between Olbia and Magydos. The basic weakness of these two small cities is thus to be explained by the very limited area of plain they controlled, and the wide area of limestone separating them later provided the opening for the founding of Attaleia.

---

[58] Cf. the map in Blumenthal, *Siedlungscolonisation*, 50; the movement of the sea level is confirmed at Olympos, where Bean (*TSS*, 71) notes that the 'quay now stands ... high above the stream', and at Phaselis (Schäfer, *Phaselis*, 70–85).

[59] Assuming Gurma is the correct site.

These geographical situations shed light on the foundations of the several cities, and to some degree on the dating of the whole set. Olbia and Magydos are centuries older than Attaleia, which was clearly established where it was because its territory was an area the existing cities shunned. Perge's territory occupied the land behind all these cities, but did not control the small but useful plain of Magydos, which suggests that its territory was organized and defined *after* the two coastal cities were founded. Being on the coast distinguished these from the three greater cities of the plain; their geographical situations linked them with Phaselis and the smaller Greek cities on the west of the bay. They remained small because they had only small alluvial plains behind them, and so small *chorai* (only about forty square kilometres for Magydos, a small area for Olbia).

The geographical distribution of the three cities in the plain implies that the whole scheme was organized by the inhabitants of Pamphylia as a collective act. It is clearly artificial. The distribution could only have come about by an agreement among those who established the cities. There are other sites which could have been the sites of urban centres, and founding cities away from rivers in the drought-prone Mediterranean lands is unusual. The sizes of the several alluvial plains are such that other cities could have developed, particularly in Perge's area; the one-city-per-section spread is hardly spontaneous. This pattern of cooperation established from the beginning is something which will be found to exist also in later times.

These various geographical and epigraphic indications, and the earlier argument from the political situation in Asia Minor, indicate that the sequence of urbanization in Pamphylia was as follows. Side existed as an urban community in the eighth century and probably even earlier, based on trade with both east and west and on its location as a useful port-of-call for voyagers going in both directions. Phaselis, founded in about 690 BC, was next, again a mercantile and maritime city, originally small, but able to grow to dominate its inland rural neighbours. The two small Greek cities, Olbia and Magydos (both with Greek names, note), together with the smaller posts along the western coast of the Bay, were founded round about the same time as Phaselis. The three cities of the plain, Perge, Sillyon, and Aspendos, were founded during the quarter century or so after Phaselis, by mutual agreement among their inhabitants, and in response to the threat from the sea (the Greeks) and from inland (the collapse of the Phrygian kingdom).

The cities' geographical distribution in the several alluvial valleys, and the indications of their territories in the epigraphic evidence, provide some basic data upon which to base calculations about population. I have already done so with respect to the urban centres themselves, and now it is possible to do the same for the *chorai*, using a rural density of one hectare to one person. This is a scale suggested by several surveys.[60] All sorts of special considerations could be discussed – the mountains, the limestone areas, differential fertility – but we are only considering comparisons, not accurate or precise figures. Accordingly I shall use the same suggested density for all the cities. (See Appendix 2 for the full list).

On these bases I calculate that Pamphylia had a total population of about 250,000 people.[61] This will not have been a constant size, but only the maximum, which was reached perhaps in the early Roman period. (And it includes Attaleia and Korakesion, founded in the Hellenistic period.) At the start the original cities were small, probably with less than 5000 for the largest – Sillyon, Aspendos, and Perge were about the same, with Side in the same league. As their populations expanded so the urban centres grew. Perge and Side were the largest in area, but Aspendos was clearly more important, and probably therefore larger, than Perge until the later Hellenistic period; the large territory Perge had may well have taken some time to become fully inhabited and developed. The later foundation at Attaleia, though it will have had a smaller *chora*, may have rivalled the others fairly quickly. Including the *chora* and *polis* together none of the cities were greater than 77,000 in population (Perge), and the smallest of the cities – Korakesion and Olbia – will have had total populations of less than 10,000. These were all small cities; their populations added together were probably less than that of Athens alone at its height.

---

[60] Aperghis, *Seleukid Royal Economy*, 13–14.

[61] The census figures of the last century of the Ottoman Empire give some comparisons. The administrative area was larger than the Pamphylia used here, including the hills to the north and part of Lykia to the east, an area called Teke, and later Antalya. The five censuses taken between 1830 and 1914 produced the following population figures for this enlarged Pamphylia:

1831:	Teke (including the hills and half of Lykia) – 35,839
1877/8:	Teke 80,394
1881–1893:	Teke 194,132
1906/7:	Antalya 236,754
1914:	Antalya (including part of Lykia) 249,686

Even supposing that there was under-recording in all censuses, and very great under-recording in 1830, it is clear that the population increased with the administrative improvement of the Ottoman regime during the period covered. By 1914, after three generations of this internal peace, the population of our Pamphylia was clearly less than 200,000. In 1881/1893 the population of the districts of Antalya and Alanya (Attaleia to Korakesion) was 115,000; in 1914 that of Antalya, Alanya and Manavgat was 132,000; to these figures must be added the populations of the Phaselis area. 200,000 would seem to be the very maximum in pre-industral times, and perhaps even that estimate is too high. Figures are from K. H. Karpat, *Ottoman Population 1830–1914, Demographic and Social Characteristics*, Madison WS 1985.

This theory of the origins of the cities of the Pamphylian plain is, at present, unproveable. It depends on arguing from geographical conditions, and on the occurrence of much later inscriptions, as evidence. It does, however, fit what few facts there are, and has a certain consistency with the history of other areas. It was also outside areas which were to have most effect on the cities in the future.

3

Intruders: Kroisos and the Persians

The development of the three inland cities in Pamphylia was due, according to the theory put forward in the last chapter, to the apprehensions of the people, the 'many tribes', that they were under threat from outside. By combining into *poleis* they were simultaneously presenting a defensible face to those threats and forming themselves into a new society. This process took place in the early seventh century, and the new centres then had a century or so to settle down as working cities before facing an actual threat from outside. The coastal cities had different origins, indigenous at Side, Greek colonist at Phaselis and Magydos and the western towns. The division tended to persist, but in the sixth century forces from outside emerged to threaten both groups. And it was only when intruders from outside reached into Pamphylia that the effectiveness of the defensibility of all of them was tested.

As it happened, neither the Greeks from the sea nor the Assyrians or Cimmerians from the lands to the east and north penetrated into Pamphylia; one might therefore argue that the constitution of the people of the plain into cities was effective – though this is a circular argument. The first recorded intrusion in any strength from outside did not come until the mid-sixth century BC, a century after the foundations of the cities, but once such interventions began, they continued, and for the next five centuries there were repeated invasions and interventions. Pamphylia ceased to be a quiet backwater; it had become part of the greater political world. This chapter considers the earliest intrusions, and the effects they had on the region.

The first of these intrusions – apart from the Greek settlers along the western coast – was by King Kroisos of Lydia in about 550 BC. The kingdom of Lydia emerged in western Asia Minor, out of the ruin of the Phrygian kingdom, as a vigorous military state bent on expansion. It was one of a new constellation of powers which now encircled Pamphylia, if from a distance: Egypt, presently confined to the Nile valley; Babylon in the Fertile Crescent, controlling the Mediterranean coasts of Syria and Palestine; Media in Iran and eastern Anatolia; and Lydia in western Anatolia. There was also a relatively minor kingdom in

Kilikia, and in southern Iran the Persian kingdom was another minor power. Of all these, Media was individually probably the most powerful; the other powers formed an alliance in response. Lydia and Media fought an inconclusive war and then made a peace in 585, fixing their boundary at the Halys River.[1] This proved to be a most successful peace arrangement, lasting for four decades. As a result Lydia was able to impose its rule on all western Anatolia north of the Taurus Mountains, including the Greek cities of the Ionian coast.[2]

By the time of the accession of King Kroisos to the Lydian throne, in about 560 BC,[3] conditions were changing, and the peace of 585 had begun to fray. The Median kingdom was taken over by Cyrus the Persian in 559,[4] and a dozen years later he was challenged by Kroisos. In the war which followed in 547 – 546 the Lydian kingdom fell to Cyrus.[5] This decisively upset the diplomatic balance which had been maintained throughout the whole Near Eastern area since the peace of 585. Kroisos had maintained close and friendly contacts with Egypt and Babylon;[6] the main Lydian enemy was the Median kingdom, the largest and most powerful of the kingdoms and the only one with which Kroisos had a common boundary. His alliances with the other powers thus made a diplomatic balance. Cyrus' *coup* in seizing the Median throne did not at once destroy that diplomatic balance, but it certainly increased the pressure on the others.

Kroisos is the only Lydian king who is credited with ruling in Pamphylia,[7] and it is reasonable to assume that the earlier kings had been unable to reach so far south because of their more local preoccupations on the Aegean coast and with the Medes to the east. Kroisos ruled only from c.560 to 546, so any Lydian domination of Pamphylia can only have been a very brief episode, no more than a decade in length at the very most, and it is probable that it happened at least in part as a result of the Lydian involvement in the great power contest.

Lydia under Kroisos was clearly expansionist, and, given that his avenue to expand eastwards was blocked by the Medes, and that his predecessors had mopped up the Ionian coastal cities, southwards was the one direction left. This was obviously one source of Kroisos' intrusion into Pamphylia, but it is also a fact that by moving into Pamphylia he was providing himself with a better means of contacting his allies.

[1] Herodotos 1.74.
[2] A. R. Burn, *The Lyric Age of Greece*, rev. ed. London 1978, 103–105 and 210–214.
[3] Herodotos 1.92–94.
[4] A. T. Olmstead, *History of the Persian Empire*, Chicago 1948, 34; J. M. Cook, *The Persian Empire*, London 1983, 25–26.
[5] Herodotos 1.76–76.
[6] Herodotos 1.77.
[7] Herodotos 1.28.

Regular contacts between the three allies were clearly necessary if the alliance was to be maintained. For Lydia this meant being able to exchange embassies with Egypt and Babylon, and the Pamphylian cities were well placed to facilitate relatively swift contacts between them. Contact by sea through the Aegean cities might have been as quick, but the Aegean coast is dangerous, the Aegean islands were not under Lydian control and were the haunt of pirates, and Lydia and the Lykians were at enmity, all of which would render the sea route past the Ionian and Lykian coasts dangerous for Lydian ships. On the other hand, a message sent by land from Sardis to Pamphylia could then go by sea to Egypt or Syria quickly, and with much less hazard. In this it would be the coastal cities of western Pamphylia which were especially involved, and it is clearly Olbia, Magydos, and/or Phaselis which would be the most convenient ports to use, in particular the latter, because of its established trading relations with Egypt, and because they, and perhaps Perge, were the easiest of the cities to reach from Lydia.

Magydos was the most convenient city for messengers from Lydia – Phaselis' land connection to the north was always poor, and Olbia was always small – but it was only a small city. In terms of sheer geography, for an authority entering Pamphylia from the north and intent on seaward communications with Egypt and Syria, however, Magydos would surely be the first target. Perge was a minor port, as was Aspendos, but both were some distance from the sea; Magydos was on the coast, at the end of a route along the Katarrhaktes River. But Phaselis was the main sea-power in the area, and if Phaselis was hostile, Magydos, Perge, and Aspendos would be unusable as bases for packet-boats. Hence Phaselis, with good connections overseas, which the others probably did not have, would be Kroisos' main target. Yet Phaselis' land connections with the rest of Pamphylia were, and are, poor – it is only in the last few years that a motorable road has connected the area with the lands to the north, and Alexander's army had either to wade neck deep in the sea to get through when invading along the shore or climb a difficult mountain path. So it is most likely that Kroisos aimed to dominate both Magydos and Phaselis, the one to provide a maritime link to Phaselis, the other to the lands of his allies overseas.

Phaselis was an important and wealthy enough city to participate in the foundation of the joint Hellenic trading city of Naukratis in Egypt within a century of its own foundation.[8] The original purpose of the Rhodians in founding Phaselis may have been to provide a safe haven for Rhodian (and no doubt other) ships sailing along the coast, but it certainly developed into a

---

[8] Herodotos 2.178–180.

wealthy town fairly rapidly. Trade on Phaselis' own behalf was clearly one of the original purposes of the first colonists as well, and contact with both Syria and Egypt may be presumed from the start – these were the obvious trading targets for any southern Asia Minor city. When it began minting coins, in about 550 BC (during Kroisos' reign) the city's symbol was the prow of a galley, and this was retained as the city's emblem until well into the Hellenistic and even the Roman periods.[9] It was thus both an active and wealthy trading city and one with some pretensions to sea power, for the emblem was a galley – that is, a warship – and not a merchant ship.

For an inland power like Lydia, which wished to keep in contact with its overseas allies, Phaselis was therefore well placed to act as a conduit for diplomatic messages, and so a connection between Kroisos and Phaselis is a reasonable supposition; Kroisos is recorded as having some power in Pamphylia; he and the Phaselites both had connections with Egypt. Furthermore, the first coinage from Phaselis is dated to the very time (c. 550 BC) that Lydian power reached the area; and Lydia is reputed to have been the scene of the invention of coinage; all this taken together provides a context for the Kroisan intrusion into Pamphylia.[10] A further element may be Phaselis' enmity towards its neighbours, the Solymoi; Kroisos was hostile towards the Lykians, so the city and the king had enemies as well as friends in common. These similar policies might have commended themselves to each other as allies.

Whether Kroisos penetrated much further into Pamphylia than Magydos and Phaselis is not known (if, indeed, these were Kroisos' destinations). Herodotos lists the 'Pamphylians' as one of the peoples Kroisos ruled, but this is scarcely specific, and it occurs in a summary list of peoples with no further concrete detail. It may simply mean some Pamphylians. Given Kroisos's obvious preoccupation with the Medes, it would be a waste of Lydian strength to devote much of his resources to the cities of the Pamphylian backwater. If, as I have suggested, Kroisos's purpose was mainly to open up easier communications with Egypt and Babylon, by way of the land route into Pamphylia and the sea route onwards, he would not have needed more than the occasional use of one of the ships of Phaselis. On the other hand, there were several cities, notably Perge and the Pisidian city of Termessos, which might be thought to threaten that line of communication. From the point of view of the Pamphylians themselves, the intrusion of Lydian power into the area – which certainly occurred, no matter

[9] Hiepp-Tamer, *Phaselis*.
[10] V. Sevin, 'Kroisos ve Pamphylia', *Belleten* 40, 1976, 185–193, does not discuss the individual Pamphylian cities.

what conclusion is reached concerning my hypothesis as to his reasons and extent – was surely unwelcome.

This was just the beginning of the intrusions from outside, but it was quite typical of later similar events. Pamphylia of itself was always of little interest or value to outsiders. Its sequence of fortified cities was, at least minimally, formidable; its lack of easy communications out of the region meant it was a cul-de-sac, both geographically and geopolitically speaking. It was thus not really worth conquering; it was of use to an outsider only if it led elsewhere, and it did so all too rarely.

The overthrow of Kroisos' regime by Cyrus the Persian in 547–546 BC is generally assumed to have meant that Pamphylia thenceforth formed part of the Persian empire, though the issue is not usually given any discussion. Scattered notices in the sources do support this, but they are either vague or late, or both. None of them, for example, states in so many words that Pamphylia fell to the Persians, though the later sources show that it did come under Persian power at some point.

Herodotos, writing in the mid-fifth century, put the Pamphylians, along with several other peoples, in the 'first' satrapy of the empire,[11] and in describing the fleet which Xerxes sent against Greece in 481, he notes that 'the Pamphylians' contributed thirty warships[12] – though Queen Artemisia of the Karians was scathing in her assessment of them later. She included them with the Egyptians and others as Xerxes' 'confederates', implying a certain voluntarism in their participation.[13] In 469, 412, and 388 Persian fleets used the mouth of the Eurymedon as a forward base. In 334 BC, Alexander found a Persian garrison in occupation of Sillyon, according to Arrian.[14] That is all the direct written evidence for Persian involvement in Pamphylia: it is clear that Pamphylia was under Persian authority, and it is reasonable to assume that it became so soon after 546. If Queen Artemisia's words can bear any weight, the cities had perhaps submitted without argument, perhaps even before they were asked. There was, after all, little point in resisting. Each of the later instances of Persian presence, however, has implications which need to be teased out.

The first concrete reference is Herodotos' description of the reorganization of the empire by Dareios after his victory in the Persian civil war of 522–521, and this is the first reference to Pamphylia since Kroisos' intrusion in the

---

[11] Herodotos 3.90.
[12] Herodotos 7.91.
[13] Herodotos 8.68.
[14] Arrian, *Anabasis* 1.26.5.

550s. During that thirty year period war had raged along the Aegean coast for several years as the generals of Cyrus first suppressed Lydian rebellions and then conquered the Greek coastal cities, the Lykians, and the Karians. It would be surprising if the Pamphylians escaped involvement in these events, particularly since Kroisos had power and/or influence in the country before his death. The area was clearly not a priority for the Persians, so all that can be said is that at some point between 546 and 522 they became Persian subjects. When, after his victory in the civil war, Dareios organized, or perhaps reorganized, the satrapal system, the Pamphylians were put into the same satrapy as all those former enemies – whom the Persians would have referred to as rebels – Ionians, Lykians, and Karians. This grouping may or may not be significant. It would not be safe to conclude that the Pamphylians had had to be reconquered like the others. Other explanations are possible, in particular the geographic, for Pamphylia was close to the Lykians and the Milyas, and the Milyas commanded the route from Lykia to Pamphylia. A better explanation might be social-political. All these areas were urbanized, with many more or less small cities dividing up the land. The neighbouring satrapies – Lydia, North-West Asia Minor, Kappadokia – were by contrast largely rural. Differing governmental strategies were clearly needed for the two types of society, and the cities were obviously more difficult to rule and control than rural areas, particularly in view of the resistance the Aegean communities had made to Persian rule. The Pamphylians thus, on this view, were put into the satrapy of the urban communities because of their organization into cities. No conclusions at all can be reached, however, concerning the attitude of Pamphylians towards Akhaimenid rule.

The accuracy of Herodotos' list of satrapies is doubtful, and even if correct at the time he wrote, it is not safe to assume that it represented a permanent governmental scheme; it may indeed be his own work and only a partially understood version of the Persian system; the westernmost satrapy was only the 'first' from the Greek point of view, not from the Persian.[15] It may, in fact, have been no more than a record of the allocation of tax dues rather than a scheme of provinces. The record suggests that the 'first' and 'second' satrapies of Herodotos were in practice often combined, which would make better geographical sense – but then later it seems that a greater subdivision also took place.[16] That is,

[15] There is, of course, a Persian version, in the Behistun inscription of the deeds of Dareios, but this is rather a list of the peoples he ruled; the empire was clearly more bureaucratic than that.

[16] The changing administration is discussed by Olmstead, *Persian Empire*, and Cook, *Persian Empire*; C. Huart, *Ancient Persia and Iranian Civilisation*, London 1927 and J. Weisehofer, *Ancient Persia*, London 1996, are very brief on this and do not notice changes.

the Persian system was one which responded to needs and events, and was adjustable to cope with changes. This is surely something to be expected in an empire which lasted for two centuries. Later Roman attempts to fit Pamphylia into imperial schemes (and those of the Hittites and Alexander at other times) show frequent puzzled changes of mind: no doubt the Persians had the same difficulty. Pamphylia was rarely big enough to constitute a province by itself, but it was also too isolated to be easily attached to a neighbouring area. If it was so attached, it tended to be neglected, for the other area was usually larger, or richer, or more troublesome, or otherwise more important. In all probability it was transferred from one satrapy to another at intervals, as required, no doubt to everyone's confusion. Neglect, of course, was not necessarily something to be complained of by the subjects of an empire.

In Dareios' visit to Lydia after the elimination of his rival Oroites in 521, he was accompanied by a fleet, which, according to Herodotos, was recruited from the Ionians and other Greeks from north-west Asia Minor;[17] again, the Pamphylians are not mentioned; they were, by implication, not involved. All these absences of mention are not conclusive of anything, but we must assume that the Pamphylians were at some point visited by envoys from the Persian kings, both Cyrus in or after 546, and Dareios in or after 521, and summoned to submit. An area which had been associated with Kroisos will not have been ignored, particularly one which had relations with Syria and Egypt, still enemy countries to Cyrus, and a land in which there were Greek cities and Greek ports at a time when the kings were facing trouble among the Greek cities of Ionia and Lykia. Yet the main conclusion we may draw is that the Pamphylians did not cause any trouble. Going a little further, it seems very likely that, had there been any serious problem for the Persians from the Pamphylians, Herodotos would have noted it; not a good argument, of course, but one worth making nonetheless, given Herodotos' tendency to include everything. It seems reasonable to assume that the several Pamphylian cities submitted without argument to the suzerainty of the Persian Empire.

Herodotos provides one concrete reference to Pamphylians taking an active part in events in the expedition of Xerxes against Greece. They do not appear in the account of the earlier Ionian Revolt (504–499 BC), nor in that of the expeditions of Mardonios and Datis in 492–490 into the European lands of the Greeks, but Xerxes called up all available forces in 482, and the Pamphylians are reported to have supplied thirty ships to the Persian fleet.[18]

---

[17] Herodotos 4.90.
[18] Herodotos 7.91.

It is not known which Pamphylians were involved. Phaselis and Side may be presumed to be contributors of ships, being ports, perhaps Magydos also, though Phaselis may have been included in the Lykian contingent. Perge and Aspendos were river ports, and could possibly also provide some ships, though it seems unlikely that they had many warships, which were the vessels required. The ships all carried troops, and it is likely that all the cities would be expected to contribute soldiers, and so this would probably be the contribution of the inland cities. The whole group of cities, from Phaselis to Side, was obviously treated as a set ('Pamphylians'), and the ships were presumably brigaded together.

There are other problems here. For one thing, it seems that Pamphylia was addressed by the Persian government as a single entity, and this implies that it was treated as such in the Persian administration, but just exactly what did 'Pamphylia' mean? Was Phaselis counted as Pamphylian, or as Lykian? The number of ships, thirty, is surprisingly small for an area of Pamphylia's size, however it was defined. The manpower provided can be roughly calculated. The ships were of a type which was decked in order to carry more soldiers, and each would seem to have had thirty to forty of these men on board. The crews were at least as numerous, probably more so. Each ship may thus be thought to have had at least a hundred men on board; the manpower contribution from Pamphylia would thus be about three thousand men. The maximum population of the area in a pre-industrial economy was perhaps 250,000, though in 480 it is probable that the population was considerably less than that, so this was a fairly substantial contribution.[19]

Herodotos' mention of this naval force is the only time the Pamphylian forces appear in his account of the war, with the exception of Queen Artemisia's scornful dismissal of them, along with 'Egyptians, Cyprians, Kilikians', as 'a miserable lot'. This was a slanderous description at least of the Egyptian naval forces, who fought extremely well at Artemision, and were detached to special duty at Salamis, not a task which would be given to an incompetent squadron. Her depiction of the others may thus be equally wrong. The small Pamphylian force would no doubt be attached to a larger group in battle. If they survived the various disasters and battles in Greece, they will not have survived the defeat at Mykale next year. Xerxes sent his Egyptian and Phoenician ships home after Salamis, and the fleet he retained at Samos was overwhelmingly made up of Greeks of Asia, and that fleet was destroyed. Any Pamphylians who had survived

---

[19] Half the population were women; half the male population was too old or too young; 3,000 would be five per cent of the eligible males; it is comparable with the proportion of the population in the armed forces of Britain in the Napoleonic War.

Salamis and the other fights will probably have been included in the Samos fleet; after Mykale most of the men who did not die in the battle were killed in the pursuit, and the ships were either captured or burnt.[20] We may assume that very few of the Pamphylians recruited in 481 returned to their homes in 479.

In the campaigns between the Greeks – latterly the Athenians – and the Persians which were conducted from 478 to the peace of 449, Pamphylia became a frontier area. The war came close in the year after Mykale, when a Greek expedition sailed to Cyprus and liberated most of that island,[21] but it seems that the Greek forces by-passed Pamphylia. The Pamphylians therefore remained Persian subjects, and were clearly not regarded by Athens as likely to rebel. It was only in the 460s that Pamphylia was again directly involved in the war, when a new Persian expeditionary force was despatched from Syria westwards. The troops were commanded by either Pherendates or Ariobandes, and the fleet by Tithraustes; as a son of Xerxes, Tithraustes was in overall command. The fleet advanced in two sections: the first, of uncertain size, camped at the mouth of the Eurymedon river to await the second part, of eighty ships.[22] As they waited a Greek fleet under Kimon arrived from the west.

The story of the campaign is told, in the only extended treatment which makes much sense, in Plutarch's biography of Kimon, from the Athenian point of view; that of the Persians is, as usual, ignored. It is possible, however, to glean some information about Pamphylia from the events. Kimon abandoned earlier operations in Karia because the Persian army and fleet were perceived as a threat to his force. But he did not sail directly to intercept the Persian fleet; instead he attacked Phaselis, which resisted. He was, that is, in the first place reacting to the Persian move, which would seem to have been intended to drive him away from Karia, but then by his siege of Phaselis he placed his force in such a position as to invite attack. The first part of the Persian fleet was not strong enough to do this, however, so Kimon, having now located the enemy, extricated himself from the siege of Phaselis,[23] and sailed to meet it. When the Greeks arrived the Persian troops from the fleet were already camped near the mouth of the Eurymedon, in Aspendian territory, and the ships were in the river.

---

[20] Herodotos 9.100–107.

[21] Thucydides 1.94.

[22] Plutarch, *Kimon*, 12.1–13.3 is the main source for this campaign; less important are Thucydides 1.100.1, Diodoros 11.60–61, Nepos, *Kimon* 2.2, Pausanias 1.29.14 and 10.15.4, Frontinus, 2.9.10 and 3.2.5, and Polyainos 1.34.1.

[23] It is said that Chians in Kimon's fleet, 'old friends of the Phaselites', intervened and brought about Phaselis' surrender. This looks very like a later excuse. With a fleet of some two hundred ships (the lowest estimate) Kimon should have had no trouble in taking Phaselis on its small peninsula.

The size of this first Persian naval contingent is uncertain. Various numbers are given in the sources, two hundred by Thucydides, 350 by another source, six hundred by yet another, though no figures are given for the land force. It seems best to assume that the force camped on land was composed of soldiers carried by the first part of the fleet, and that this fleet was no larger than the Greek fleet which attacked it, about two hundred ships.

The Persian fleet had sufficient warning of the Greeks' approach to be able to come out to fight – that is, the men were able to man the ships, and the ships to be rowed to the mouth of the river, if not out to sea. Then the fleet rapidly retreated, as though the true size of the Greek forces suddenly became clear. Kimon's ships were of a heavier type of trireme, and this could have been another reason for the Persian retreat. Having beaten the fleet, Kimon landed his hoplites, who then defeated the land force in the camp. All this implies that the Greek fleet was larger, or at least stronger, than the Persian fleet – Plutarch claims that the Athenians captured two hundred ships – and that the hoplite force was larger, or stronger, than the Persian land force. We may assume that Kimon deliberately attacked while the enemy forces were divided, before the arrival of the second naval contingent. This second fleet was no doubt intended to bring the total Persian force up to a strength sufficient to take on Kimon's force.

Having won the dual battle at the Eurymedon, on land and sea, Kimon then took his fleet further east and intercepted and destroyed the second Persian force. This took place at 'Hydros', according to Plutarch's manuscript, but such a place is not otherwise known – the name suggests a river mouth, which is likely enough, but it is now unlocatable; the mouth of the Melas is possible, but there are many rivers along that part of the coast, and the name does not appear again.[24]

The political position of the Pamphylians is made somewhat clearer by this episode. The camp of the Persian land force at the mouth of the Eurymedon put it in Aspendos' territory, and we may thus assume that the city accepted Persian authority. The Persian ships at the river – the first contingent – had sailed past both Korakesion and Side, which were thus in all likelihood also under Persian authority. When Kimon's force, coming eastwards, passed the Chelidonian Cape he found that Phaselis was also a loyal Persian subject. He had to besiege the city, which only submitted after some time. The city had to pay ten talents in order to secure peace.[25]

---

[24] If a river is not meant, then the word may be corrupted: 'Syedra' is suggested by B. Perrin in the Loeb translation of Plutarch (p. 445); in *I. Side*, 2.658–659, Nollé suggests the same; it cannot be Idyros, which was to the west.

[25] Plutarch, *Kimon* 12.3–4.

The timing of events thus becomes rather curious. The story as described is a series of moves by Kimon's forces: first he sailed to Phaselis from Karia, then his attack at the Eurymedon, then his defeat of the second naval force. But if the Persian force was already in Pamphylian waters when Kimon sailed east, he was acting very dangerously in allowing himself to be tied down to a siege at Phaselis. This in fact might be Kimon deliberately trailing his coat, inviting the Persian fleet to attack him while the first Persian section was still unreinforced. Phaselis was not a very strong city. It was defensible in the face of an attack by land by the local Solymian tribesmen, but to an attacker with overwhelming sea power only the city's acropolis could hold out for any length of time. In the end the city was persuaded to give in suspiciously easily. It could be that Kimon spun out the siege, occupying the city's lowland suburb, the *Weststadt*, to increase the cries of pain, hoping thereby to entice the Persians to attack.

On the other hand, it could also be that Kimon's move to Phaselis was the first move in the campaign, and so the arrival of the first Persian force at the mouth of the Eurymedon was the beginning of a relief of the siege at Phaselis. In this view the Persians were expecting Phaselis to hold out longer than it did. The city's surrender was therefore the event which permitted Kimon to sail off to victory.

Phaselis' resistance, and the apparent acquiescence of Aspendos and Side, and perhaps Korakesion, together with the contribution of ships to Xerxes' force in 481, all show that Pamphylia as a whole had remained loyal to Persia since the wars had begun. There was, indeed, little or nothing to attract these cities to the Greek side. The lunge at Cyprus by Kimon in 478 roused that island to join the Greeks, but then the Greeks withdrew and the Cypriots were left to fight on alone; the Persians successfully reconquered the whole island. Kimon's expedition to Pamphylia did not promise to produce results any more permanent, and indeed he sailed away again, back to the Aegean, immediately after his victories.

The reasons for Pamphylian loyalty to Persia are therefore not far to seek. Their ships and men had been destroyed and killed by Greeks in the wars provoked by a rebellion in which they had not taken part. The Persian victory over Kroisos had removed Lydian authority, which may or may not have been a burden. Of all the cities, only Phaselis and perhaps Olbia and Magydos were pure-Greek cities; the rest were either not Greek at all, as Side, or only partly Greek in population, as Perge, Sillyon, and Aspendos. There was nothing in their past, or in the political situation in the early Persian period, which would persuade these cities to join the Greek side in the conflict in the Aegean. Persian military and naval power was clearly capable of reaching Pamphylia, both by land and sea, as the fleet of Tithraustes demonstrated, whereas that of Athens could do so only briefly, as Kimon's swift withdrawals in 478 and 468 showed. To join the Greek cause would only invite Persian attacks, so that Pamphylia would be a battleground.

We do not, of course, know much about the internal affairs of any of these cities, but it is a reasonable assumption that the surrender of Phaselis to the Greek forces had been accompanied by a change in its governing regime. Those in control before Kimon's arrival had resisted him; the surrender implies that the regime was changed. The fact that the city then remained within the Delian League also implies that the new government system remained in place; given Athenian prejudices, it seems probable that the new regime was a democracy, but one in which the foreign policy of the government was under Athenian 'guidance'. Phaselis was enrolled into the Delian League, by Kimon, presumably, and remained in that alliance as it evolved into an Athenian empire. The city began by paying six talents a year as its contribution, which is recorded for 453 (the earliest surviving tribute list), 451, and 450.[26] By this time the treasury of the league had been moved from Delos to Athens.

In 450 Kimon led another expedition to Cyprus (and a force went also to Egypt), during which he died.[27] Again, there was nothing in this to persuade any of the Pamphylians to leave the Persian Empire and plenty to deter them from any sympathy for Greece or Athens. The prospect of this renewed warfare, after some years of relative quiescence, was enough, it seems, to persuade both Athens and Persia to seek peace, which was probably concluded next year; Plutarch attributed the negotiations to the Athenian Kallias; the Persian negotiator is not known, but was clearly equally responsible, if direct negotiations actually took place. The terms can only be deduced but it appears that Pamphylia was divided, and so became the frontier of the two powers, as it had been, in effect, for decades already. The peace terms allocated the Aegean and its coastal cities to Athens, by forbidding Persian warships to pass the Chelidonian Cape or the Bosporos.[28] Phaselis, though it was on the Persian side of the cape, remained within the Athenian empire, and so was in a somewhat ambiguous situation. The city went on paying its reduced tribute of three talents to Athens for the next fifteen years (recorded for 449, 447, 442, and 440),[29] so the idea that the

---

[26] *Athenian Tribute Lists* I, years 453, 451, 450.

[27] Thucydides 1.112.1–4; Plutarch, *Kimon* 18–19.2; Diodoros 12.3–4.

[28] Meiggs, *Athenian Empire*, 129–151 and appendix 8; D. Stockton, 'The Peace of Kallias', *Historia* 8, 1955, 61–79; G. Cawkwell, *The Greek Wars*, Oxford 2005, 136–138.

[29] *Athenian Tribute Lists* I, years 449, 447, 442, 440.

Cape was a formal boundary is not correct. A prohibition on Athenian warships passing the Cape would leave Phaselis vulnerable; and at the other extreme, the Athenians did not hesitate to sail into the Black Sea. The peace terms are in fact largely guesswork.

The rest of the Pamphylians, apart from Phaselis, by implication remained subject to Persia. There is no record of any payments to the Delian League or the Athenian empire by any Pamphylian city other than Phaselis. It has been supposed that, just as Phaselis was enrolled before the Eurymedon battle, so Aspendos, Perge, and Sillyon must have been enrolled after that battle.[30] The evidence, however, is thin to the point of invisibility. It is based on the possible mention of these cities in the list of cities from which the Athenians hoped to collect tribute in the re-assessment of charges they made in 425.[31] But this is not evidence of actual collection, or of the actual subjection of the cities, and none of the Pamphylian cities, except Phaselis, ever appears on any of the lists recording actual payment. Further, none of the other Pamphylian cities, even on the re-assessment list of 425, appears in the inscription clearly; all the names have had to be 'restored'. Aspendos, for example, has only its last three letters surviving.

There is no real reason to dispute these restorations, but neither is there any reason to believe that including these cities' names was anything other than Athenian wishful thinking; there are other places in the 425 list which never paid contributions. It is necessary for there to be further evidence before we can accept that these cities were part of Athens' empire; in its absence we must conclude that the Pamphylian cities were never members. The inclusion of Phaselis in Athens' sphere and the exclusion of the rest of Pamphylia from that sphere in the Peace of Kallias in 449 was thus a recognition of the political position in the area as it had been since the battle of Eurymedon twenty years before. Pamphylia as a whole was never a part of the Athenian Empire.

Aspendos appears again in the historical record in 412–411, when it was once more the base near which the Persian satrap Tissaphernes assembled a fleet, said by Thucydides to be of 147 ships, with accompanying soldiers;[32] the assembly point was presumably the mouth of the Eurymedon, where Tithraustes' fleet had camped in 468. Tissaphernes minted coins, probably at Aspendos, to the Rhodian standard, suggesting that his target in the campaign might be Rhodes

---

[30] Meiggs, *Athenian Empire*, 58 and 102, assumes that Aspendos was in the empire, but can adduce no evidence other than the mention of the city in the revised assessment of 425.

[31] *Athenian Tribute Lists* I, year 425.

[32] Thucydides 8.81 and 87–88.

and Karia.[33] Aspendos, and no doubt the rest of the cities of the Pamphylian plain, was thus under Persian control at that time, which is what one would expect.

The choice of the same site for the Persian base by both the Tithraustes and Tissaphernes does not mean it was a permanent Persian military/naval base, as has been inferred.[34] It was, instead, a convenient halting place, a reprovisioning centre, a source of fresh water, and a place where the crews and soldiers could disembark and the ships be cleaned – and a place at which intelligence could be gathered. It does imply, of course, that the city was loyal and cooperative. Given that Aspendos was obviously the most important of the inland cities at the time, it is probable that Perge and Sillyon were equally loyal.

Phaselis, on the other hand, was in Spartan hands in 411, the commander of the city being a man called Hippokrates.[35] It had presumably fallen to the Spartans fairly recently, since Athenian control of the coast of Asia Minor had not faltered until a year or so before, but it does not seem likely that the Spartans kept the city for long. The Athenian commander Alkibiades is described as sailing for Kaunos and Phaselis in 411, supposedly to meet Tissaphernes, and he is similarly described as returning from those places a little later;[36] there is no account of any meeting, which, if it did take place, will have been at Aspendos, Tissaphernes's base. Alkibiades did claim to have persuaded Tissaphernes not to move west. He had sailed with just thirteen ships to persuade Tissaphernes, who had 147, to turn back from his intended expedition westwards. When Tissaphernes did turn back, no doubt for his own reasons, Alkibiades blithely claimed the credit. The size of Tissaphernes's fleet in comparison with that of Alkibiades indicates quite clearly where real power lay in the Pamphylian Sea.

The defeat of Athens in 406–404 did not change the situation in Pamphylia, though no source records what happened there as a result. Phaselis began minting coins once more about 400 BC, reviving the old type which the city had produced before the Athenian conquest, which showed the prow of a galley on the obverse and the stern on the reverse, and reverted also to the 'Persic' weight standard.[37] This suggests that the city regarded its return to the Persian Empire, which took place soon after 411, as a liberation from Athenian or Spartan control.

---

[33] Head, *HN* 699–700.
[34] By Cawkwell, *Greek Wars*, 45, n. 16.
[35] Thucydides 8.99.
[36] Thucydides 8.88 and 108.
[37] Hiepp-Tamer, *Phaselis*.

In the wars in which the Spartan hegemony was tested and overthrown, Pamphylia appears only once. The Athenian commander Thrasyboulos attempted to extort money from Aspendos in 388. This return to Athenian imperial behaviour was unpopular. Thrasyboulos did manage to compel the Aspendians' submission (so showing there was no Persian camp in the area, and probably no Persian garrison either), but then a small group of citizens penetrated his camp at night and assassinated him. The reason for this, as given by Xenophon, was the misbehaviour of some of Thrasyboulos' soldiers; the real reason, surely, was the behaviour of Thrasyboulos himself, and through him Athens.[38] The Pamphylians of Aspendos, like those of Phaselis, had no wish to be extracted from the Persian Empire. Athens, since its emergence as a major power, had never been attractive as a friend to any Pamphylian city, and both Phaselis and Aspendos had decisively rejected Athenian pretensions. The Pamphylian cities, so far as we know, were contented Persian subjects for the next half-century.

Thrasyboulos' action in raiding Aspendos is a tribute to the prosperity of that city, which is also indicated by the Persian use of its territory as their base, and by the production and distribution of its abundant coinage.[39] Athens maintained its hold on Phaselis from its capture in 468 to its loss in about 411, but failed to extend its authority into any other part of Pamphylia. This was a political fact throughout the fifth century; Thrasyboulos' exploit is thus not to be seen as an attempt to resurrect the former empire, which had never extended so far to the east, but purely as a raid for money and booty. To the Pamphylians it was perhaps seen as an event typical of their relationship with Athens, which had been characterized by hostility for the whole of the previous century.

The Pamphylian cities, from Phaselis to Side, were therefore content to remain within the Persian Empire all through the wars between Greeks and Persians, and to pay their taxes and to provide accommodation and sustenance to Persian forces; Phaselis had to be forced into the Athenian Empire, and apparently it was relieved to be released from it. At the same time the meagre evidence for the social and cultural history of the cities indicates a steadily increasing acceptance of Hellenic culture. The evidence is partly artefactual, in the form largely of coins and some pottery, but there are also other indications, often indirect. The locally made artefacts which survive and which have been studied are the coins produced by the coining cities – Side, Aspendos, Sillyon, and Phaselis.

---

[38] Xenophon, *Hellenica* 4.6.29.
[39] *SNG* Paris 3, 'Aspendos'.

Phaselis had, of course, produced coins since the mid-sixth century, and Side began to do so early in the fifth;[40] Aspendos minted from the middle of that century, and Sillyon produced a small coinage in the fourth century. (Perge did not mint until the middle of the third century.) Phaselis' galley returned when the city returned to Persian suzerainty. Aspendos began with coins showing a warrior backed by a triskeles, and replaced this with a horsemen backed by a wild boar. This is connected by some with the story of the horsemen Mopsos who is credited with killing a boar.[41] It may be that this is a sign of the prevalence of the Mopsos foundation legend by the end of the fifth century. But comparing the coins of the two cities, it would perhaps be more appropriate to consider the types as representing the cities' contributions to the Persian imperial system: ships from Phaselis, horses (and cavalrymen) from Aspendos; it is known that Aspendos' tribute included horses.[42]

Side began producing coins about 490 BC – though all coin dating is very approximate. They showed a head at the god Apollo with a pomegranate on the reverse.[43] This combination is curious, in that it is totally Hellenic: Apollo was the quintessentially Greek god, and the pomegranate's name in Greek was *side*, so its appearance on the coins was a pun – but it was a pun in Greek. These coins were therefore directed above all at Greek speakers. No doubt there were by that time plenty of people in the city who knew and spoke Greek, but the city had its own language and script which was still in use at the end of the fourth century. The coins were therefore intended to be understood by non-Sidetans, no doubt particularly Greek merchants.

Sillyon did not mint until the fourth century, and then produced only a few coins. The city's first coins show an armed and bearded man, interpreted as a 'hero', or as Ares; the reverse has a figure which is probably Apollo. And the coins were inscribed with the city's name in the local dialect – 'Selyviiys'.[44] Again there is the combination of a warlike figure with a Greek god. Aspendos had also indicated its local name on the early coins either in full, 'Estwediiys', or as an abbreviation.

These early coins were replaced, at Aspendos and Side, and perhaps at Sillyon, by new types which became the standard coins of the cities. Aspendos in the

[40] Hiepp-Tamer, *Phaselis*; C. M. Kraay, 'Notes on the Mint of Side in the Fifth Century BC', *Num. Chron.* 1969, 15–20.
[41] Hero: Head, *HN* 700; Mopsos: L. Robert, *Hellenica* XI-XII, Paris 1960, 177–178, and *SNG* Paris 3.
[42] Arrian, *Anabasis* 1.25.3.
[43] *SNG* Paris 3, 'Side'; Kraay, 'Notes'.
[44] Head *HN* 703; *SNG* Paris 3, 'Sillyon'.

fourth century produced coins showing on the obverse either two wrestlers, or, more rarely, the Gorgon, and on the reverse either the city's name and a sling, or the head of Athene. Bronze coins also showed Athene, in one case on the obverse and in another on the reverse; other coins had a horse or a shield or a Gorgon and a sling or a slinger. The triskeles which had been so prominent before was now reduced to a single bronze issue, or to an appearance in the field on the reverse of the stater. A similarly complete change took place in Side's coins. Instead of the punning pomegranate, which had been the normal obverse in the fifth century, the city now put the head of Athene on the obverse, with one issue showing a lion's head, a type retained from the past; reverses now had Apollo standing clothed; Athene was on the reverse of the lion's head issue. In the city, the dual temples overlooking the harbour were of Athene and Apollo.[45]

The weight standard of the coins of all these cities remained the same as before, that is, the 'Persic'. The designs, however, had become less local and more decidedly hellenic. The appearance on both Aspendian and Sidetan coins of Athene (and even her palladium on some of Phaselis') are obvious signs of the acceptance of Hellenic culture. It was also done, no doubt, for more obviously prosaic reasons. The most widely accepted currency of the time was Athenian, and the head of Athene had become a sign of its quality. The use of that same symbol clearly aided the acceptability of the coins outside their cities of production. And yet all three are also concerned to proclaim their individuality, with Phaselis' ship, Aspendos' wrestlers, and Side's use of its peculiar script. But where trade and currency go, so goes culture. Side's Apollo was a local version of the Greek god, but he was Greek all the same.

The coins of Aspendos which depict a pair of wrestlers, a design which appears from about 400 BC or so and is repeated until replaced by the Alexander coins in the 320s, is interpreted as showing a well-known statue, presumably one in the city. The earliest of the wrestler coins, in fact, give their names, Menetus and Elypsa.[46] Wrestling is, of course, one of the contests of Greek games, and a famous statue such as this – for it is used as a symbol of the city – implies that the city held games. The date 402 has been suggested for the inauguration of the games,[47] no doubt penteteric (that is, every four years).

---

[45] Kraay, 'Notes'.

[46] At first it was thought this inscription was an obscure slogan, or a magistrate's name, for the early finds had 'Elypsomenetus', which looked like a word; then versions inscribed 'Menetuielypsa' appeared, and it was realised that it was two names: Head *HN* 700, for the early interpretations; G. F. Hill, 'Greek Coins acquired by the British Museum in 1919', *Num. Chron.*, 20, 1920, 97–116, at 115–116. A lesson to us all.

[47] Radet and Paris, 1886, 161.

It has to be said that this interpretation of the coins is only one of several possibilities. These are detailed briefly, with references, by C. Brixhe,[48] who approaches the problem as a language student, but without seriously considering the layout of the design. In every case the double name clearly refers to the wrestlers, being written beneath the figures on the coin. There are also letters which can be interpreted as the signatures of the mint masters and which are clearly separate. On the reverse is a slinger in action, a triskeles, and the name of the city in the local dialect, 'Estwediiys'. The wrestlers are always in the same pose, whereas the pose of the slinger varies, so one must assume that the first is a static figure, the second one in action: hence the interpretation of the wrestlers as a statue, and so as a statue commemorating a notable contest. And so we arrive at the Greek games.

The institution of such games carries with it some major implications. A regular games will have required a substantial investment by the city. A stadium of some sort was needed, of a size sufficient to hold several thousand spectators and capable of being used for several sports. The city would need to have at least one gymnasium for its own citizens, some of whom would be contestants. Also required was a performance area, such as an odeon or a full theatre, since there were also musical contests involved in most of these festivals. All this implies the acceptance of a whole set of Greek attitudes, an education system, Greek values, and so on, by the community as a whole. The coins showing the wrestlers' statue therefore are in this case indications of a rather more than superficial hellenization; they imply a whole-hearted acceptance of it, and this at the very time when the city was at times acting as the local Persian headquarters – which the fleets of Tithraustes and Tissaphernes indicate – and actively rejecting political and military advances by the contemporary cultural powerhouse of Hellenism, Athens. The city, of course, still has a magnificent theatre, virtually complete (which is also still in use, for, amongst other things, wrestling contests[49] – and for concerts as well). The theatre is in fact of the Roman type, the gift of two brothers whose names are on the building; it must be assumed that an earlier Greek type was on the site, and was obliterated by this new building.[50] There is also a stadium whose remains lie in the plain below the fortified wall which crowns the cliffs around the city, and so outside the city. Alongside and beyond the stadium there is a road lined with tombs of Hellenistic date, and this would suggest that the

[48] Brixhe, *Dialecte grec*, 197–199.
[49] Bean, *TSS*, 49–50.
[50] There is an indication of an earlier building at the modern entrance to the theatre, where a line of stones, of a different petrology and aligned in a different way from the present structure, can be seen. There are only half a dozen of them, but their existence demonstrates an earlier building on the site.

stadium was already in place by that period, for the tombs are placed beyond it and respect it. This may also be the site of the original statue.[51]

Aspendos was also the home of a fourth century Pythagorean philosopher, Diodoros, whose chosen lifestyle was to be unshaven and uncombed, vegetarian, wearing a worn cloak, and affecting a beggar's staff and bowl. This was clearly an individual choice, his personal variation on Pythagoras' teaching. He had obviously had a good Greek education at home, before making his choice. It is confirmation of the hellenization of his city.[52]

The progress of the hellenization is also shown in the other cities. Side's non-Greek origin is demonstrated above all by the city's use of its own individual script. This was a purposely designed script for use with the city's own language, a version of Luwian. The script used letters taken variously from the Phoenician alphabet, from the Cypriot syllabic script, and from Luwian hieroglyphic writing. In other words, the Sidetans had selected a variety of letters from all available scripts, to express their local Luwian dialect, but Greek was not amongst them.[53] During the fifth and fourth centuries, the Attic Greek script did begin to overtake Side's own script, so that by the time Alexander campaigned through Pamphylia, Side was ready to use the now near-universal Greek alphabet. It retained its own letters on the coins for rather longer,[54] just as the cities of the Pamphylian plain continued to refer to themselves by their old names on their coins, even though it is clear from the inscriptions in stone from their city sites, that their citizens were now using the normal Attic script for these purposes.

It had been thought that the Sidetan script was confined to that city, but an inscription using it has been discovered at Lyrbe, in the hills to the north, dated to about 300 BC.[55] This suggests that other places may well have also

[51] Bean, *TSS*, 49–50. The Pisidian city of Selge also produced coins showing the two wrestlers, though without ever naming them. This clearly implies a relationship with Aspendos, which is at the base of the road leading to Selge. Were the wrestlers from the two cities? If the statue was in one city, it would be odd if another should use the same unusual symbol; if the men symbolised both cities, this would make some sense.

[52] Diogenes Laertius 6.13; Athenaios, 4.163c–f.

[53] The peculiar Sidetan script has attracted a considerable amount of scholarly attention (rather more than it perhaps warrants). See the articles by G. Neuman, 'Zur Entzifferung des Sidetischen Inschriften', and S. Atlan, 'Die Münzen des Stadt Side mit Sidetischen Auschriften', both in *Kadmos* 7, 1968; C. Brixhe, 'L'Alphabet épichorique de Side', *Kadmos* 8, 1969; J. Faucounau, 'Remarques sur l'Alphabet des inscriptions 'Barbares' de Side', *Belleten* 44, 1980; F. C. Woudhuizen, 'Origins of the Sidetic Script', *Talanta* 16/17, 1984/1985. There are others, but the general conclusion is that the script is a local development designed to accommodate the local language (as was, at much the same time, Greek, Etruscan, and a little later, Latin).

[54] Head, *HN* 703, but the dating of the city's coins is difficult, cf. Kraay, 'Notes'.

[55] C. Brixhe and G. Neuman, 'Die Griechische-Sidetische bilingue von Seleukeia', *Kadmos* 27,

used it, perhaps the Etenneis above all, who had an occasionally violent – and therefore close – relationship with Side. The Lyrbean stone is in fact bilingual, which implies that the old script was no longer legible for all those to whom the inscription was addressed. It is therefore not only a mark of the wider use of Side's invented script, but a sign that, as at Side itself, it was being replaced by Greek, and that this was taking place while these places were part of the Akhaimenid empire.

At Perge there was a major temple of Artemis, noted in the *periplus* of 'Pseudo-Skylax', of about 360 BC, which, since this was a document describing a coastal voyage, suggests that the temple was especially notable even then.[56] This is another element in the evidence of the slow hellenization of Pamphylia, but also of the powerful native non-Hellenic element in the local culture, and of the population. The temple was clearly well known already in the mid-fourth century, but a rather earlier record, in an inscription of about half a century earlier, indicates that the goddess of the temple was not really Artemis at all. In that inscription, the goddess is simply the 'Lady of Perge' (*Wanassa Preiia* on later coins), and as such was honoured by a man called Klemutes son of Lvaramos, a pair of distinctively local (that is, Luwian) names.[57] Thus the goddess is obviously local, and by the mid-fourth century was being identified by Greeks from abroad (as by the author of 'Pseudo-Skylax') with the Greek Artemis. The goddess's image, as it is shown in various ways, is distinctly un-Greek, being a solid near-conical block, with, apparently, a series of images carved on the lower part, perhaps on the plinth, and a face above. Even in later years, when it appears to have been replaced by a new statue, the form was the same;[58] on the other hand, she was also portrayed as Greek Artemis on the coins of the city later.

The apparent ease with which Perge's 'Lady' was identified with Artemis suggests that she had similar attributes, but the identification with Artemis did not change the goddess, and her chief votary was always a priestess. The age of the cult is by no means obvious, though no doubt it was locally claimed to be of great age, even indefinite, and there seems no reason to doubt she was a

1988, 35–43. Seleukeia is now thought to be Lyrbe: J. Inan, *Eine Antike Stadt in Taurusgebirge, Lyrbe? – Seleukeia?*, Istanbul 1993. It has to be said that this is one of the most delightful sites to visit in the region, with some of the most interesting remains, and set in a fragrant pine forest; but the road up to it is very rough.

[56] Ps. Skylax, *GGM* 100.

[57] *I. Perge* 1, published originally by I. Kaygusuz, *Belleten* 40, 1980, 249–256; *SEG* XXX, 1980, 1517.

[58] T. S. MacKay, 'The Major Sanctuaries of Pamphylia and Cilicia', *ANRW* II.18.3, at 2072–2074 ('The Cult Statue').

survival from the Bronze Age, or even earlier. The limits of hellenization were, in religion, fairly clear, and apart from acquiring a Greek name, the 'Lady' did not change as a result of her identification with a Greek deity.

The furnishings of burials in Perge's territory, however, did not reject Greek goods. Presumably the contents of tombs were for the use of the dead, and that cutting a good figure was as important in Hades as on earth, so the furnishings are indicative of local values. In Perge's territory, two *necropoleis*, at Varsak to the north of the city and at Karacalli near the river to the south, have produced well-made kraters of Greek manufacture of the late fifth or early fourth centuries BC.[59] The Lady of Perge might resist hellenization in her own person, but her subjects did not, and wanted its products with them also after death.

It may well be at this time that the attribution of Greek origins to the various cities began. Phaselis was, of course, Rhodian. When Alexander arrived, so Arrian noted, Aspendos claimed to have been an Argive colony, while at Side the odd story of the Kymaians who arrived and lost their language was related and picked up later by Arrian; Selge in the mountains later claimed a Lakedaimonian origin.[60] Indeed the Kymaian story from Side is noted a generation earlier by 'Pseudo-Skylax'.[61] Aspendos' claim to an Argive origin was especially cunning, for Alexander's dynasty claimed descent from three brothers from Argos; one might suspect the story to have been developed for the occasion of Alexander's visit. The other two claims were, however, scarcely helpful to their cities at that time: to claim a Spartan affiliation in 334 could have been a dangerous matter – if these claims were taken seriously – for Sparta was the one Greek city which had obstinately remained outside the Hellenic League which Alexander headed, and Selge's claim to that relationship might have been a statement of intent to remain outside Alexander's empire. There is no sign that, in Alexander's time, these claims had any effect; indeed Aspendos, supposedly by its Argive claim to be a sort of cousin to the Macedonian royal family, was the city in Pamphylia which was most heavily punished by Alexander.

The fact that all the cities of Pamphylia were loyal subjects of the Akhaimenid Empire did not, therefore, prevent them from accepting the culture of the Greeks, even if, like Side, they were emphatically non-Greek in origin. In religion, in education, in language, if not in political allegiance, the three cities of the plain were only partly Hellenic, but became more fully so during the fourth century

---

[59] The vases were found in rescue excavations and are exhibited in Antalya Museum; two are illustrated in the Museum Guide.

[60] Arrian, *Anabasis* 1.26.4; Polybios 5.76.11; Strabo 12.7.3.

[61] Ps.-Skylax, *GGM* 100.

BC. Side, which had no Greek ancestry, became hellenized, and by the end of the Persian period, was putting Greek inscriptions on its coins. And yet all of these cities were quite firmly and apparently contentedly within the Persian Empire until Alexander's passage.

The Pamphylians are recorded as taking part in the Satraps' Revolt in the 360s, though it looks more as though they were included willy-nilly, because their satrap was involved.[62] One of those satraps, Mausolos of Karia, did manage to penetrate Pamphylia's isolation, though he got no further than had Athens or Sparta. An inscription from Phaselis, unfortunately incomplete now, records an agreement between the city and Mausolos, largely, as far as can be seen, on legal matters.[63] Mausolos had no actual power in the city, for the two dealt with each other as equals, not as master and subject. The Great King was invoked at one point in the agreement, in a formal way, but no doubt also as a way of limiting Mausolos' aspirations. Phaselis had been subject to attack by a Lykian ruler, Perikles of Limyra, who objected to the city providing a refuge for a man he regarded as an enemy.[64] Perikles himself was an enemy of Mausolos; it may be that the agreement was between the two authorities because they had the same enemy. Mausolos' intrigues thus stopped at Phaselis, as had those of Athens and Sparta. The rest of Pamphylia remained undisturbed by all this.

The account of Pamphylia by 'Pseudo-Skylax', dated to about 360 BC, is particularly useful in providing an outline picture of the country in the later Persian period, just before the overwhelming cultural and political change which followed the conquest of the area by Alexander.[65] The author was concerned to provide a guide to the places along the coast, but he also notes the occasional notable place inland – the temple of Artemis at Perge, for example, and the Chimaera above Phaselis. Coming towards Pamphylia from Lykia he reckoned the coast was still Lykian until the mouths of the Katarrhaktes. He included in Lykia, therefore, all the Greek cities and towns along the western coast as far as Magydos. For him Pamphylia then stretched as far as Korakesion. This was a sailor's judgement, perhaps based on the trends of the coast, and perhaps on the mountainous nature of the western regions, but it also marks the division between the Greek settlements and the partly- or non-Greek towns and cities to the east. He classified certain places as *poleis*, which is probably not a reliable political guide, but it certainly gives an indication of the relative sizes of the

---

[62] Diodoros 15.90.
[63] *TAM* II.3.1183; also in S. Hornblower, *Mausolus*, Oxford 1982, 267.
[64] Polyainos, *Stratagems*, 4.8.
[65] Ps.-Skylax, *GGM* 100.

settlements. Phaselis, Perge, Sillyon, Aspendos, and Side are all noted as *poleis*, but so also are Idyros on the west, and Kibyra and Korakesion in the east, which were added at the end of the list almost as an afterthought. Kibyra has been located at Kara Burun, near the mouth of the Alana-chai, a small river flowing out of Rough Kilikia, about halfway between Side and Korakesion. Neither Idyros nor Kibyra has left substantial remains on the ground, and calling them *poleis* was a clear exaggeration of their size and importance.[66] Yet, since the term is to some degree a cultural one as well as political, this might suggest that they were well hellenized by that time.

Several other places are named, but not described as *poleis*, and so they can perhaps be safely assumed to be of only minor importance, Olbia and Magydos among them, though Magydos at least should perhaps be ranked as a *polis* at this time. Apart from the Katarrhaktes, the only river the author names is the Eurymedon, with a note about its navigability as far as Aspendos. The mentions of the Chimaera and the temple at Perge, both inland, and neither of relevance to a sailor, suggest that travellers using the *periplus* were likely to need to know of their existence, and that people were making special journeys to those places. Sillyon, without a navigable river, and with no other obvious maritime connections, no doubt had control of part of the coast, hence requiring a mention.

The account by 'Pseudo-Skylax' is thus a confirmation, before the campaign of Alexander, that the period of the Persian domination had also been one of the penetration of Hellenic culture in all its forms into the Pamphylian cities, and that this penetration came by sea. People went to see the Chimaera, and visited Artemis the Lady of Perge, and to Aspendos, and they did so by ship. Since the *periplus* author is writing in Greek, he understands that it is Greeks who made these journeys; he remarked on Side's distant connection with Kyme. The hellenization he is witness to meant not just games and language and education and philosophy and so on, but trade and pilgrimage as well, and honouring the dead. It also included political forms and attitudes. This is indicated by the affiliation of some of the cities to Greek 'parents', historical or invented, which appears about this time, but also by their general attitude to political affairs.

For it seems clear that the cities had a vigorous tradition of local autonomy and that the Persian yoke upon them was relatively light. Aspendos' tribute to the Great King included horses for his army; no doubt the other cities paid a tribute also, and there is no sign that this was seen as unfair or onerous. Their

---

[66] Idyros is in Kemer; the site is now fenced off and overgrown, with no sign of any development, though it is almost surrounded by buildings.

autonomy was clearly real and the cities were left largely to themselves, no doubt so long as the tribute was paid. The imperial government, however, did not provide much in return. Phaselis clearly did not get, nor perhaps did it expect, protection from the satrap Mausolos or from the adventurer Perikles. Aspendos was in dispute with Side, its neighbour, but this was a continuing problem which the Persians had not solved, and perhaps did not even know about; alternatively they might have been happy enough to see the dispute continue, as a local distraction. Indeed by the fourth century it is not at all clear which satrap had authority in Pamphylia, and certainly no responsible satrap is known by name, though the area's participation in the Satraps' Revolt might suggest that the Lydian or Ionian satrap was in charge. The autonomy of these cities thus had its negative side, in that they had to fight their own battles. Aspendos had to fend off Thrasyboulos, and Phaselis had treated with Perikles and Mausolos. The cities were thus clearly autonomous and to some extent self-reliant. The acceptance of Hellenic culture thus occurred by virtue of its innate attractiveness, but the local civic society also provided a fertile social ground for its reception. Alexander's arrival was thus unwelcome because, though he was in his way a carrier of Hellenic culture, he also clearly aimed to restrict the cities' autonomy more than the Persians had, while proclaiming the propaganda of liberation, which the Pamphylian cities did not require. And he left a satrap behind.

The intrusions from outside which took place into Pamphylia, between that of Kroisos in about 550 and that of Alexander in 333 BC, revealed the rather limited possibilities available to these outsiders. There was the approach from the north, taken by Kroisos and probably by the Akhaimenids, presumably by way of the pass at Gubuk Beli and directly towards Perge and Magydos. The Akhaimenids also used the approach by sea along the coast from the east. In 513, 490, 482, and 481 Persian fleets had sailed from Syria to the Aegean; in 468 and in 411 large fleets had advanced as far as the Eurymedon mouth, but not further. In both cases the Persian fleet had been met there by Athenian fleets, which had approached along the coast from the west. By seizing Phaselis, Athens had provided herself with a base from which she could dominate the Pamphylian Sea, though in fact it seems to have been more useful as a defensive post to block further moves westwards by the Persian fleet. Thrasyboulos in 388 managed to reach the Eurymedon from the west, to his ruin. Athens was clearly incapable of advancing its power beyond Phaselis other than for brief campaigns: Kimon, Alkibiades, Thrasyboulos, all in effect recoiled, leaving all Pamphylia except Phaselis untouched. The third approach was out of the west by land. Mausolos and Perikles had made attempts on Phaselis along that route, from

Karia and from Lykia respectively, but with little success; Alexander, carrying a greater punch, had better fortune.

The distribution of coins minted at the Pamphylian cities reflects some of these routes, and provides information on the external economic relationships of the cities. Aspendos' coins circulated over a considerable area, and have been found in hoards in Kilikia and in at least three places in central Asia Minor;[67] Sidetan coins on the other hand, were spread by sea, having been found in hoards in Egypt, Cyprus, and Kilikia, and in the Black Sea area.[68] The contrasting distributions emphasize the geographic situations of the two places, Aspendos inland, Side on the coast.

The Sidetan distribution shows the city as a trading centre, with contacts all round the eastern Mediterranean. The reputation of its hard bargaining merchants was proverbial in Athens.[69] The Aspendian distribution into the Anatolian interior shows that the city had important contacts in that region. The coins will have moved inland by way of the old Hittite route along the valley of the Melas, and along the Eurymedon valley to Selge. What was traded is unclear, but the city bred horses for tribute and no doubt exported more; it was later a producer of salt[70] and an exporter of oil, which cannot be produced in the lands north of the Taurus Mountains; its imports are not known, perhaps silver which was later minted.

The production of Aspendian coins is surprisingly large, and this recurs in the Hellenistic period. One might suppose that the city had a silver mine, and that has been suggested,[71] though there is no evidence for one. The theory that coins were manufactured in order for governments to have a handy means of paying wages, for soldiers, for example, and to collect taxes, might be the origin of the city's production, if it was known that it had a garrison.[72] The soldiers who held Sillyon in the face of Alexander's attack would certainly have to be paid, and paid in coin, and Tissaphernes minted distinctive coins at Aspendos in 411, but it would only be a guess that the city had a garrison in the Persian

---

[67] Aspendian coins were found in the following hoards: *IGCH* 1244 (Karaman), 1245 (Karapinar), 1246 (Kayseri), 1259 (Cilicia), 1254 (Selimiye), all dated to between c.400 and c.340 BC

[68] *Coin Hoards* I.15 (Black Sea area), II.17 (Asyut, Egypt), VI.10 (Cyprus), VIII.91 and 100 (Cilicia), dating to between c.425 and c.370 BC.

[69] Athenaios 8.349–350.

[70] Bean, *TSS*, 47, suggested that the salt was collected from the periodic drying of Lake Kapria, which is mentioned by Strabo (14.4.2). If Kapria was a salt lake, it was presumably originally a sea inlet; if it was refreshed periodically, the connection with the sea will have been re-established on occasion.

[71] O. Mørkholm, *Early Hellenistic Coinage*, Cambridge 1991, 143.

[72] C. M. Kraay, 'Hoards, Small Change, and the Origin of Coinage', *JHS* 84, 1964,76–91; much discussion on the theory has ensued.

period. This explanation does not account for the continuing production of coins at Phaselis and Side, where commerce is surely the explanation. At Aspendos, therefore, a certain governmental contribution may have occurred, but the main explanation for the coinage must be commercial. It is, as with Side and Phaselis, an indication that the city was, at least by local comparison, wealthy.

The evidence from the Persian period, and before, is that the cities were on the edge of Greek political and social influence. Phaselis was the city with the closest contact with Hellenic culture. The others were apparently reasonable facsimiles of Greek cities, both in their culture and in their political systems, though Side is referred to in Arrian quite roundly as a barbarian city.[73] The Lady of Perge retained her non-Hellenic shape, but her subjects used Greek pottery and called her by her Greek name. At Aspendos the city's wealth had permitted a more whole-hearted acceptance of Hellenic culture than elsewhere, with its regular games and its Pythagorean philosopher. Phaselis, a Greek city, could also point to having produced a well-known philosopher in Theodektas, a pupil of Aristotle,[74] a clear mark of the availability of a Greek education. So there was a gradation of Hellenism in the area, from the wholly Greek Phaselis through the hellenized Aspendos to the less hellenized Sillyon and Perge, to the only partly affected Side.

It might be argued that the organization of the communities into city-states showed another aspect of Hellenism. Yet such a political *schema* is by no means distinctively Hellenic: one may mention the Phoenicians and other Syrians, the Kilikians, the Italians – to go no further afield than the Mediterranean basin – and the first city state in Pamphylia had been Luwian Side. The evolution of Pamphylia into a group of city-states was, as argued earlier, an independent reaction to outside threats. It was only after this political development that the area became irradiated by Hellenism, which was adopted only fairly slowly, and in some cases with some reluctance, but whose adoption was surely facilitated by the existence of *poleis* in Pamphylia – just as, later, the Phoenician cities were able to adopt much of Hellenic practice and culture, while remaining distinctively Phoenician. The pressure of Persian authority, even if it was distant, as seems to have been the case, would tend to retard the Hellenic influence, but only marginally, and this would enable the Pamphylians to be selective in their choice of the elements of the culture they chose to adopt.

Pamphylia was thus originally almost on the edge of the influence of Hellenic culture. The independent origin of the local city-states came about by the

---

[73] Arrian 1.26.5.
[74] Plutarch, *Alexander* 17.

decisions of the local communities, who were a mixture of Greeks and Luwians. During the sixth to fourth centuries, the cities came to be seen as the sort of *poleis* Greeks knew at home, but their origin owed little or nothing to Greek influence – unless it was threatening. As a result, by the time of Alexander, the arriving Hellenes could recognize the cities of the plain as Greek in some aspects, and Side as a *polis* with barbarian speech. The influence of Hellenic culture is shown by the publication of Side's Kymaian origin story, but this also emphasizes the city's difference.

To a Greek traveller in the fourth century, such as 'Pseudo-Skylax', or Alexander a quarter of a century later, Pamphylia will have seemed to be a cultural and political borderland. Coming from Greece he would find that Phaselis was a typical Greek *polis*, but one which was under threat from barbarians in the nearby mountains, as it had been since its foundation. The cities of the plain seemed familiar also, but with considerable barbarian elements, notably in their religion, where the goddess of Perge might be called Artemis in Greek, but did not look remotely like any Greek goddess; these cities also use a distinct dialect of Greek, and a local set of personal names, which emphasized their 'provincialism'. At Side he would see these proportions reversed, a barbarian city with Hellenic elements where a peculiar and local language and script were in use, and proud to relate a story in which Greeks faded into the general population. In the mountains Hellenic influence was minimal. The fading out of Greek culture in this way, from west to east and from south to north, made Pamphylia a classic frontier region, an area where one culture insensibly gave way to another; this, of course, was similar to its political situation as a region within the Persian Empire but affected and periodically threatened by Greeks' actions.

4

The Effects of Alexander

Alexander approached Pamphylia from Lykia, the same direction as Mausolos and Perikles, but with a good deal more power at his command. He brought a detachment of the Macedonian army, and was sufficiently threatening and overwhelming that the initial reaction of all the Pamphylian cities was to surrender without a fight. Attitudes soon altered, however, shifting towards defiance in some cases, and to exploitation of his presence in others. The reports of Alexander's campaign in Pamphylia provide a good deal of information about conditions in the region. It is worth dwelling on these accounts, since the details are revealing (see Map 3).

Phaselis was the first city he encountered, and, well warned of Alexander's expectations, it surrendered before he even arrived, providing him with gifts of gold crowns, no doubt understanding well in advance his need for money. The city then played host to the king and his army for several days, and saw the king moderately drunk, when after a party he and his fellow drinkers crowned the statue of Theodektas in the city centre, saying that he and Theodektas were both pupils of Aristotle.[1] Friendship was evinced all round.

The Phaselites requested Macedonian assistance against a people whom they claimed were raiding their farmlands, but the actual result of the request is odd. Whatever was his initial reply to this request, Alexander did not apparently intend to comply, but on his march north his baggage train was attacked by the enemies in question, the Marmares, whose village may be identified with the modern village of Mnara on the Kauk Dagh.[2] If the Marmares had stayed put, Alexander would presumably have ignored them, despite the Phaselites' request. They accused the Marmares of threatening the lands of some of the city's farmers, but it may be that it was the Phaselites who coveted the Marmares' lands, and hoped Alexander would so damage their enemy that the lands could be taken

---

[1] Plutarch, *Alexander* 17.
[2] S. Sahin, 'Olbia und einige andere küste norte bei Kemer in Westpamphylien', *Ep. Anat.*, 33, 2001; F. Stark, *Alexander's Path*, 73–88.

easily. It seems that the lands in dispute were at the head of the Çandır valley, where the Phaselites had colonized, or were attempting to colonize, the southern part. It is clear that, before 333, the Çandır valley was not under the control of Phaselis. Having been attacked, Alexander turned back and punished the raiders, who are reported to have been largely eliminated.³ If this can be taken literally, then one may perhaps assume that Phaselis quickly benefited, though the only evidence is from a much later sarcophagus inscription suggests that the village of Hisançandır, some distance to the north, was in Phaselis' territory.⁴

Alexander had accomplished one of his spectacular marches on the way. Faced by either climbing a mountain pass or braving the sea, he had opted to defy both. Part of the army climbed the mountain, presumably along the route later used by the Roman and Byzantine road along the Kesme-chai, a pass called Klimax, where the troops hacked out a path for themselves: they then had to march along the Çandır valley, which is a difficult route in itself. The rest of the army, led by the king himself, went along the shore, presumably past Kemer and the headland called Koca Burun, having to wade in the sea, which obligingly receded for him.⁵ He must have visited Idyros on this march, but the sources make no mention of it.

Having reached the main Pamphylian lowland, Alexander's army camped at Perge, which apparently submitted readily, possibly, like Phaselis, in advance of his arrival. It has been supposed that this city became Alexander's headquarters,⁶ but no source actually claims that. Indeed, his headquarters were always wherever the king was, and never seem to have been at a fixed spot, except when he stopped for a time. He may well have left a force at the city to guard his rear and his baggage while he went on to try to subdue the rest of Pamphylia.

Another supposition has been made that Alexander was searching for a route out of Pamphylia in his marches about the country, and that it was only later that the Selgians revealed the best way north, by way of Sagalassos,⁷ but this is clearly nonsense. The routes north and north-west were hardly secret from either the Phaselites or the Pergeans, or anyone else in the area for that matter, and if Alexander was uncertain no doubt the Pergeans would be able to explain the local geography to him. If they did not, his men could easily find out from the inhabitants. As an explanation for his campaign this is a non-starter.

³ Arrian, *Anabasis* 1.24.6; Diodoros 17.28.1–5;
⁴ C. Anti, *Monumenti Antichi* 39, 1923, 735–738, no. 3; Robert, *Docs* 42, n. 4.
⁵ Arrian, *Anabasis* 1.26.1–2; Strabo 14.3.9.
⁶ A. B. Bosworth, *Conquest and Empire, the Reign of Alexander the Great*, Cambridge 1988, 51.
⁷ P. Green, *Alexander of Macedon*, 2nd ed., Harmondsworth 1974, 206–209.

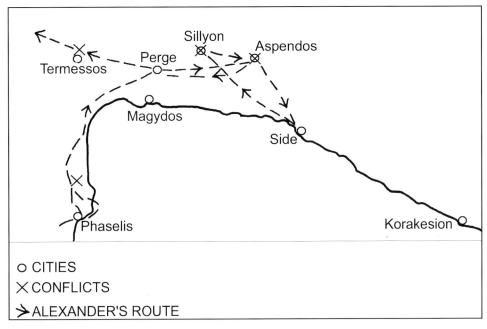

Map 3. Alexander in Pamphylia.

From Perge eastwards there were, in order, the cities of Sillyon, Aspendos, and Side. Envoys from Aspendos brought their city's submission to him soon after he left Perge. They requested only that he refrain from posting a garrison in the city. Why they should have made this condition is not explained, for he had not left a garrison anywhere since leaving Halikarnassos. It could be that there had been a Persian garrison there earlier, which the Aspendians expected Alexander to replace with one of this own. Alexander agreed to the condition, but the city was instructed to supply fifty talents for the army, and to hand over the horses that were bred as tribute for the Great King.[8] Again Aspendos stands out as different. Other cities may have given the king gifts, as Phaselis did, but none of the rest had tribute imposed on them.

In the process of dealing with Aspendos, Sillyon, off to the side of his route, had been ignored, though Alexander must have passed the city on his way from Perge to Aspendos. He then went on to Side, which submitted at once, so it seems, and accepted a garrison, the first to be mentioned in any source since Karia.[9] The city was a potential base for the Persian fleet sailing west, as was

[8] Arrian, *Anabasis* 1.26.2–3.
[9] Arrian, *Anabasis* 1.26.4–5.

Phaselis, and it has been suggested that Alexander was concerned to deprive that fleet of possible bases. This is only an inference, made by Arrian earlier,[10] but it is unconvincing as a strategy, for the Persian fleet later reached the Aegean without trouble even though Alexander had seized most of the ports along its route, and he made no attempt to gain control of any of the many other harbours further along the coast, including Korakesion.

This concept, of seizing the ports, has become a major point of interpretation among modern historians.[11] It ignores, however, the ease with which a major fleet could capture such ports – Phaselis was repeatedly captured from the sea – as well as the fact that the Persian fleet evidently did not need them. Alexander surely knew all this, or could easily find it out. Added to this is the fact that he did not garrison Phaselis, nor did he impose a garrison on Aspendos, whose territory had been used twice by Persian fleets as a base for a westward campaign. It would be better to seek out another explanation for Alexander's strategy.

Alexander turned back from Side to deal with Sillyon, which was held by a garrison of mercenaries and 'barbarians from those parts', presumably a group hired by Persia from the available Greeks and the local Pisidians;[12] it is possible that this had been the garrison which the Aspendians had so disliked that they asked Alexander not to replace it. Before he could make a second attempt on Sillyon – the first failed – Alexander discovered that Aspendos was now refusing to accept his original terms. He had repassed Aspendos on his way to Sillyon from Side, and the Aspendians may have therefore assumed that he had left altogether, or was locked into a siege at Sillyon. He left Sillyon still untaken, and occupied the lower suburb of Aspendos. The suburb's inhabitants had been removed to the upper city, but clearly no-one felt safe even there. Aspendos is a less difficult prospect for an attacker than Sillyon, and Alexander could threaten to begin by destroying the suburb, where part of the population had their homes. His threat to do this persuaded the Aspendians to submit once more, though Alexander doubled the fine he had imposed on the city to a hundred talents, ordered the payment of a regular tribute, and made the city subject to the authority of his satrap. This must mean Aspendos' autonomy was restricted, and presumably more restricted than that of the other cities, for it implies that the other cities in Pamphylia were not so subject. There is no sign that he imposed

---

[10] Arrian, *Anabasis* 1.24.3.

[11] A German interpretation, as pointed out by Bosworth, *Conquest and Empire*, 49–50, who did not like it. It is a good example of a historian's preoccupations assisting in interpretation, for 'Kontinentalsperre' was in fact the German grand strategy in two European wars – and that of Napoleon with his Continental System.

[12] Arrian, *Anabasis* 1.26.5.

a garrison; but he did take hostages from the city for the performance of the terms. After all this there was probably no need for a garrison.[13] There was no second attempt on Sillyon, and Alexander moved west back to Perge in order to head north towards Phrygia, using the route westwards past Termessos, and then northwards along the Taurus valley.[14]

This Pamphylian episode of Alexander's was hardly a military triumph. None of the cities he attacked were taken: Aspendos and Sillyon had both defied him, the latter successfully; Side, Perge (presumably), and Phaselis had surrendered in advance, as had Aspendos originally. It would seem that Alexander was not really interested in conquest, only in submission, for had he wished, he could surely have carried through any of the various attacks he started. Submission would do, otherwise. He even marched off without dealing with the one place, Sillyon, which had seriously defied him, and which was still held by a Persian force. At the same time the cities were scarcely vitally concerned to preserve their independence. Aspendos' change of mind is unexplained; Sillyon's defiance was the result of being controlled by the Persian force; the rest gave in rapidly. Two centuries of Persian domination had no doubt accustomed the citizens to submission rather than defiance.

This is, in fact, reminiscent of other conquerors who operated in and near Pamphylia. All found that a serious effort at conquest was not worth the effort involved. Several of the cities could be compelled to submit, to be sure, but then there was nothing else. The conquests would need to be controlled, leaving useful troops holding a small area which was isolated from the rest of the world, while, since the Pamphylians had submitted easily, a garrison would seem redundant. The Pamphylians presumably understood this when they proffered their timely submissions. It was not glorious, but it was eminently practical and sensible in their situation. None of their cities, for example, was ever sacked until the very end of the Greek presence, when strategic conditions had changed. Phaselis was captured by several conquerors, and damaged by Kimon, but survived without real difficulty.

The record of Alexander's campaign, such as it was, throws a good deal of light on Pamphylia, another snapshot of the region a generation after that of the Pseudo-Skylax, but like that view it was all rather one-dimensional, and raises as many problems as it provides items of information. Only one place, Sillyon, had a Persian garrison when he arrived, but we cannot tell if this was normal or permanent; the make-up of the garrison, mercenary soldiers, might imply

---

[13] Arrian, *Anabasis* 1.26.5–27.4.
[14] This route is explicated by R. Syme, *Anatolica*, Oxford 1995, 193.

that it was a recent installation, gathered at the strongest and most defensible place in order to provide resistance which would delay Alexander as long as possible; the Persian strategy at this point was to delay Alexander until King Dareios could gather an army; Aspendos' curious insistence that it did not want a garrison rather suggests that the city had recent unpleasant experience of one. Side, Aspendos, and Phaselis all acted as independent communities – as did Perge, presumably, and as did Sillyon, in effect; this may be because the Persian satrapal authority was absent – no satrap appears in Arrian's account, which is not to say that such an official was not there – or it may be because these cities really were capable of making, and entitled to make, their own political decisions; but Sillyon was surely coerced into resistance, just as Aspendos was into submission.

There is also some information about the individual cities embedded in the accounts of Alexander's campaign. Aspendos in particular is described as having a suburb below the hill, on which the main city was built. That suburb was walled, though not very effectively, for the citizens did not venture to defend it. They evacuated it when threatened, and moved to the top of the hill, which by then became an acropolis.[15] Phaselis' statue of Theodektas was in the *agora*,[16] which implies that the low stretch of land between the original settlement and the mainland, and which also connects the north and south harbours, was already laid out as a civic centre. Sillyon's cliff face was clearly a very effective defence, though whether the city would have survived if Alexander had launched a second assault is not clear; in Central Asia even more formidable rock fortresses were taken. A garrison placed by Alexander in Side implies that the town was defensible, and so it will have been walled by then, for there is no sign of an acropolis there.

As Alexander continued his erratic journey, Aspendos was accused by a neighbouring city of seizing some land by violence.[17] Which city this was is not stated, but it can only have been Side, Selge, or Sillyon. The king heard of the matter from the aggrieved party. Aspendos will not have mentioned it, for the complaint had originated with the Aspendian seizure of the disputed land. He heard about it after he had visited and garrisoned Side; at the time he had no relations with Selge, and Sillyon was under Persian occupation. Side was thus Aspendos' victim, which might well be one of the reasons for Side's rapid acceptance of his authority – just as Phaselis clearly hoped that Alexander would assist with the removal

---

[15] Arrian, *Anabasis* 1.27.1.
[16] Plutarch, *Alexander*, 17.
[17] Arrian, *Anabasis* 1.27.4.

of the Solymian nuisance if he was greeted in a friendly and generous manner. It is likely that this Aspendos-Side dispute was never settled, each decision by an outside authority only leading on to an appeal to the next. We may in fact locate the disputed area, for there is a fort part way along the old road from Aspendos toward Side at Güvercinlik, ten kilometres from Aspendos. The remains of a fortified building, dated to the Hellenistic period, are still visible today, and a substantial building was seen by Evliya Celebi in the 1670s.[18] It marks the Aspendos-Side border, fortified by the Aspendians, no doubt to discourage Sidetan ventures and claims. It is placed in a gap through the limestone hills, a region identified in chapter two as the frontier area between the two cities. This was the area over which, no doubt, the cities were in dispute, and the 'castle' of the Aspendians would control the road and the gap, as well as marking, with unusual definitiveness, the boundary.

It follows from this that Aspendos had been using its wealth and strength against at least one of its neighbours. Alexander promised to have the matter investigated, and this would be one of the problems his first satrap, Nearchos, would have to deal with. It does not necessarily follow that the decision would go against Aspendos, whoever the other party was. If the accusation was unjust, a finding against Aspendos would only make the situation worse;[19] at the same time, a little later Side was the site of an important official mint, possibly a mark of power, possibly a consolation.[20]

The prominence of Aspendos in this Alexander episode fits in with other items to suggest that during the Persian period that city was the most important of those in Pamphylia. The 'Pseudo-Skylax' itinerary has already shown that some places were clearly more important than others, being distinguished as *poleis*, whereas others were simply named. A wider consideration brings out the prominence of Aspendos among the group of the more important cities. It was the site of the Persian naval camp in 468 and in 411; it was the most prolific minter of coins in the region; it was the target of Thrasyboulos' extortion raid in 388; it was the only Pamphylian city to have a cash contribution levied from it by Alexander in

[18] *TIB* 2.552–553 (with a full list of sources); H. Crane, 'Evliya Celebi's journey through the Pamphylian Plain in 1671–72', *Muqarnas* 10, 1993 (Essays in honor of Oleg Grabar), 157–158: 'a high castle with a single wall', occupied by Turkmen nomads in winter. The compilers of *TIB* report its continued existence, though I confess I could not find it.

[19] Green, *Alexander*, 208, is unnecessarily cynical about this; we do not know the result, but a century later Side was said still to harbour enmity towards Aspendos (Polybios 5.73.4). The border castle is of Hellenistic date, so it was built *after* Alexander and Nearchos.

[20] M. J. Price, *The Coinage in the Names of Alexander the Great and Philip Arrhidaeus*, London 1991, 362–386.

334 (though Phaselis, and perhaps other submitters, gave him gold crowns); it was singled out by 'Pseudo-Skylax' as having a navigable river; it had expanded from its original site onto the lower land, in a suburb that was vulnerable; it held regular games of some international significance. It is clear that in the fifth and fourth centuries this was the most important city in Pamphylia. We may thus rank the settlements of Pamphylia more precisely as follows:

1. Aspendos.
2. Other notable poleis (Side, Sillyon, Perge, Phaselis).
3. Smaller poleis (Idyros, Kybira).
4. Non-poleis (Olbia, Magydos).

It must be borne in mind, however, that much of this is based on one man's view, and is accordingly idiosyncratic; the lack of identification of Olbia and Magydos as *poleis* seems especially awkward.

As he left Pamphylia, Alexander appointed Nearchos the Cretan as satrap, adding the area to his responsibilities as satrap of Lykia. Nearchos had to collect the fine from Aspendos, to deal with the dispute between Side and Aspendos, and reduce the Persian garrison still in Sillyon; he would need to be on the lookout for activities by the Persian fleet as well. This was the pattern of Alexander's campaigning at this time; he had left forts at Halikarnassos untaken, and was to do the same in Phrygia at Kelainai.

Nearchos remained as satrap till called forward to Alexander's headquarters in 330. It may be presumed that he had succeeded in controlling Pamphylia, and this would include the reduction of Sillyon. If he had failed and lost control of his satrapy, he would scarcely have been employed again.[21] He was, however, noticeably absent from the (admittedly thin) record of fighting in Anatolia during 332, when the Persian forces made a determined attempt to cut Alexander's landward communications with Macedon, and retake his conquests. Antigonos had the responsibility of leading the resistance, and he had the help of the satraps of Hellespontine Phrygia and Kilikia;[22] Nearchos is never mentioned. This could be because he was still busy with Sillyon, or because he had to be on the defensive along the coast against the large Persian fleet operating into the Aegean. No doubt the re-invasion of Anatolia by the Persian forces would invigorate the troops in Sillyon, if they still resisted. There

---

[21] Arrian, *Anabasis* 3.6.6; E. Badian, 'Nearchus the Cretan', *YCS* 24, 1975, 147–170, is sceptical about the degree of his success in Pamphylia, but he does not consider what tasks he had to undertake while there.

[22] R. A. Billows, *Antigonos the One-Eyed*, Berkeley and Los Angeles, 1990, 43–45.

is no sign that Nearchos had been left with many soldiers under his command, so he would need to rely on local levies (and on the guard Alexander had left at Side), who may not have been enthusiastic. Antigonos' victory, on the other hand, will have correspondingly dejected the Sillyonian soldiers, but it may not have been until late in 331 that the city surrendered. Nearchos' summons to Alexander's headquarters in 330 must certainly imply that resistance at Sillyon had ended by that time. No replacement for Nearchos is known, and by 323 Pamphylia, and probably Lykia as well, was attached to the great Phrygian satrapy of Antigonos Monophthalamos.[23] He had established his headquarters at Kelainai, once he had taken it, and Kelainai is a much more suitable base from which to exercise control over both the Pamphylian area and central Anatolia than any of the cities further north.

The Macedonian visitation to Pamphylia had been fairly brief, less than a month, and it caused very little damage. Yet the transit of Alexander and his large army was surely a shock to the Pamphylians after nearly two centuries of Persian rule. For all his acquisition of Greek culture, Alexander is unlikely to have done much to further that cause in his brief campaign. His homage to Theodektas at Phaselis was casual, at the end of a party; his placement of a garrison, presumably of Greek-speaking soldiers, in Side may have had some effect on language-use in that city. But his treatment of Aspendos was hardly encouraging, he appears to have ignored the Lady of Perge – in fact, Perge is never mentioned in the only account of the campaign; it is only conjecture which puts him there. He failed to tackle seriously the Persian garrison at Sillyon.

Antigonos' combination of the greater and more important satrapies of Phrygia and Lykia with Pamphylia was confirmed to him in the redistributions at Babylon in 323 and at Triparadeisos in 321;[24] it relegated Pamphylia to unimportance. The language of the imperial administration was perhaps different from that used in the Persian Empire, and Greek was probably more congenial to most citizens (except perhaps for those of Side), but the demands of the governors were similar, and no doubt similarly capricious and onerous. The direct effect of Alexander on the area was thus fairly small. Once again the region was subject to a governor who remained at a distance, and there is no evidence that the Akhaimenid governing system was changed.

Little or nothing is known, as usual, about any events in Pamphylia during the three decades of Antigonos' rule (330–301). Side was the site of a very

---

[23] Antigonos was confirmed in the three provinces in 323 (Diodoros 18.3.1); cf. Bosworth, *Conquest and Empire*, 230–231.

[24] Diodoros 18.69.6; Curtius Rufus 10.10.2.

active mint in the latter years of Alexander's life, and this continued through the joint reign of his brother Philip III Arrhidaios and his son Alexander IV. A prolific coinage of 'Alexander tetradrachms' was produced, but it is clearly an odd place for a large mint. Maybe the guard Alexander had left there was one of the factors, since the mint would need guarding, and the soldiers would need to be paid. Presumably the metal came from the Persian treasure acquired by Alexander during his conquest. The mint ceased to produce these coins about 317 BC, which was just the time when Philip III was murdered, and when the great armies had marched off to the east in the great contest between Antigonos and the Eumenes. The city reverted to the production of its own coins thereafter.[25]

Antigonos actively recruited troops in his satrapies, and his forces are several times noted as containing a contingent of 'Lykians and Pamphylians', a force of hoplites three thousand strong in Iran at the Paraitakene campaign in 317.[26] This is the largest number recorded, but his son Demetrios had a contingent of five hundred in Syria in 314,[27] and a thousand two years later at the battle of Gaza.[28] Right at the end, in 302, a group of eight hundred who were in Lysimachos' service deserted to Antigonos because they had not been paid, though how Lysimachos had acquired their services in the first place is not known – perhaps as deserters from Antigonos.[29] It is reasonable to assume that these were all the same men, a force which was divided at times, and which diminished in numbers as the campaigns passed.

This is the first time Pamphylians are recorded as soldiers since the troops who sailed on the thirty ships called up by Xerxes in 481, unless there were Pamphylians in the force holding Sillyon in 334. This is not to say that there had been no fighting in Pamphylia: Phaselis was clearly fighting the inland Solymoi before Alexander arrived; the Aspendians adopted an effective defensive posture in their second encounter with Alexander, and had previously exercised some military power to take over the boundary territory which they disputed with Side; some Sillyonians were presumably involved in the defence of their own city against Alexander. There was obviously a considerable reservoir of (probably fairly amateur) soldiery in Pamphylia from which Antigonos could recruit his three thousand men. As in the case of Xerxes' forces (also, note, three thousand in number), it seems unlikely that many of Antigonos' recruits survived to return

[25] Price, *Coinage* (note 20); cf also M. Thompson, 'The Cavalla Hoard', *ANSMN* 26, 1981, 33–49.
[26] Diodoros 19.29.3.
[27] Diodoros 19.69.1.
[28] Diodoros 19.82.4.
[29] Diodoros 20.113.3.

to their homes – assuming that the successive appearances of these men in the years between 317 and 301 is the same group, getting smaller. They started as a unit of three thousand men; the last group, survivors of the original contingent perhaps, was only eight hundred strong; and these changed sides in 302, just in time to be on the losing side in the final battle of Antigonos' life at Ipsos. If they were the survivors of the three thousand, it seems unlikely that Lysimachos showed them any mercy after his victory, if they had survived it.

Antigonos' enemies had been chipping away at his kingdom for years, and in 309 Ptolemy of Egypt, Antigonos' rival, having seized control of Cyprus, conducted a raid along the Pamphylian coast, during which he captured Phaselis.[30] It is generally assumed that the city was besieged,[31] but this is not what Diodoros, the only source for the episode, says: his account is simply that Ptolemy 'took' the city. Indeed, given the long connection between Phaselis and Egypt, it is much more likely that the city gave in at once than that Ptolemy had to resort to a siege. In a contest between the ruler of Asia Minor and that of Egypt, the Egyptian connection was much more potent for Phaselis, especially if Antigonos was preoccupied elsewhere at the time, as he generally was. An attack on Phaselis from the landward side would be difficult to mount, given the steep and forested nature of the land, and the lack of roads, and it seems likely that Antigonos did not react to its loss. (Once again Pamphylia is seen to be a frontier area with respect to both internal Asia Minor and Egypt, but in a reverse of the situation postulated with Kroisos.)

Ptolemy had seized parts of Rough Kilikia the year before, and after Phaselis he went on to capture other ports and islands in Lykia and the Aegean. One of the places he seized was, in all likelihood, Korakesion, whose rock he then fortified, probably for it to be the local headquarters of his representative. The place grew much in importance as a result, whereas earlier the only reference to it had been a mention by 'Pseudo-Skylax'. In that document it is, to be sure, referred to as a *polis*; it was presumably autonomous at the time, though subject, of course, to Persia, but it was surely small; Alexander had not bothered with it, though Nearchos might have taken it over while he was satrap.

How long Ptolemy and his successors continued to hold Phaselis is not clear, but there is no sign of any other power being capable of taking the city for the next century. It would require seapower to do so, and only Ptolemy had such power in the area for the time being. Later Antigonos' son Demetrios Poliorketes could have had an effect in the area, notably after his naval victory at Salamis

---

[30] Diodoros 20.27.1.
[31] As by Blackburn in Schäfer, *Phaselis*, 83.

in 306, but he did not show any interest. It is thus probable that Ptolemy I retained control of Phaselis and Korakesion, and that his son, Ptolemy II, did the same. Antigonos, so far as we can tell, continued to exercise authority in the rest of Pamphylia until his death. His proclaimed willingness to respect the freedom of Greek cities will have limited his authority over the Pamphylian cities, but that freedom also required that the cities be subservient to his wishes. The cities thus governed themselves, but their foreign relations conformed largely to Antigonos' policy. It was no different from their situation under Persia.

It cannot be pretended that a connected narrative history of Pamphylia is possible for the period of Alexander and his successors. And yet, as with Alexander's brief campaign, items of information do exist which can be used to shed light on the situations of the cities. Their overall situation was, after all, not by any means enviable. Any city which chose the wrong side in these wars risked its very existence. It took some nimbleness of policy to evade the heavy military feet of the magnates and kings and war-lords.

Three inscriptions in particular, and the establishment or renaming of three towns, are revealing of elements of the situation; none of them can be accurately dated, which is why they cannot be used to reveal precise events, but in combination they reveal something of the conditions of the time. The earliest is a decree of Argos found at Nemea, in which is recorded an alliance of Argos with Aspendos, and an exchange of privileges between the two cities. This fits in with similar connections developed by Argos with Rhodes and Kilikian Soloi. This is dated after Alexander's death, but before 300 BC.[32] The second inscription is from Aspendos itself, recording the city's acceptance of a group of Ptolemaic soldiers into citizenship as the result of the help they had provided to the city.[33] The third is from the city of Termessos, west of Pamphylia, recording honours given by the city to the 'Pamphyliarch'.[34]

The connection of Aspendos with Argos is claimed in the inscription to be ancient, but the precise occasion was the international position in the late fourth century. The initiative for the alliance of the four cities (Argos, Rhodes, Aspendos, Soloi) may have come from either Argos or Rhodes, but it is best interpreted as a search for allies in the new world produced by Alexander's

---

[32] R. S. Stroud, 'An Argive Decree from Nemea, concerning Aspendos', *Hesperia* 53, 1984, 193–216

[33] M. Segre, 'Decreto de Aspendos' *Aegyptus* 14, 1934, 253–263; the date, the enemy and the identification of the commanders in this decree are all disputed; Segre argued for 301–298, Demetrios and two well-known Ptolemaic generals, but Bagnall, *Administration*, 111–112, among others, systematically demolished his reasoning.

[34] Robert, 'Décret héllénistique de Termessos', *Docs*, 56–58.

conquests and the disintegration of his empire. The involvement of Rhodes also connects it with Ptolemy, whose friendship Rhodes particularly valued, but it seems to predate the attack on Rhodes by Demetrios in 305 – 304, and perhaps also the expedition of Ptolemy to the Aegean in 309.

The most likely enemy of Aspendos was, of course, Side, but neither city had ever been strong enough to dominate the other except with the help of a powerful friend. We do not know the outcome of the hearing by Nearchos on their dispute, but the existence of the fortified frontier post at Güvercinlik, dated to the Hellenistic period, is sufficient indication that the quarrel went on. The help given by the Ptolemaic soldiers, who were then rewarded with Aspendian citizenship, may thus have been against Side, though the inscription is unspecific.

It is relevant to this issue that a place called Seleukeia was established partway between Aspendos and Side, and not far from Güvercinlik. For a long time the exact position of this place was unclear, but it is now accepted to be about fifteen kilometres beyond Side, at the mouth of a small stream. It is, in fact, midway between Side and Aspendos, and so in the borderland of the two cities,[35] but, given the boundary fort at Güvercinlik, actually in Sidetan territory. The date of its foundation is not known, but it must be between 294, when Seleukos I acquired neighbouring Kilikia, and 190 BC, when Antiochos III was expelled from Asia Minor; the reign of Seleukos I seems to be the most suitable time. The Melas valley provides a useful communication line from Seleukid territory in Kilikia and Central Asia Minor; Side was a regular Seleukid ally, whereas Aspendos was a Ptolemaic friend, and on the other side of Side, Korakesion was developed as a Ptolemaic base from 309 onwards. Seleukeia is thus best seen as a Seleukid watchtower placed in friendly Sidetan territory with the object of keeping an eye on Ptolemaic activities, and perhaps to remind local cities that Ptolemy was by no means the only power in the region (see Map 4).

From Seleukos' point of view Seleukeia was no doubt considered to be a response to the Ptolemaic position at Korakesion; from Side's point of view it would be a useful protection against Ptolemy, but also a helpful friend against Aspendos. The establishment of the Ptolemaic soldiers in Aspendos would fit well as a Ptolemaic response to the Seleukid-Sidetan alliance. Or possibly it should be seen the other way round, with Seleukeia being established as a response to the Aspendian-Ptolemaic friendship. This is speculative, of course, though the basic facts are there and connections between them are highly likely.

---

[35] *TIB* 2.835; G. M. Cohen, *The Hellenistic Settlements in Europe, the Islands, and Asia Minor*, Berkeley 1995, 340–342.

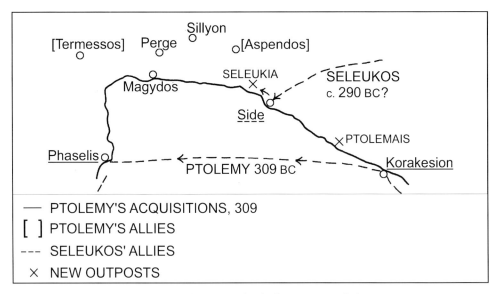

Map 4. Ptloemy I and Seleukos I in Pamphylia

From the point of view of Aspendos the putative alliance of the four cities may have been an attempt to free the city from dependence on the new lords and kings of the east. The mythological basis for the grouping was the supposed Argive foundation of the other three cities, a theory convenient for all of them, but of little relevance at any other time. After 309, however, and the intrusion of Ptolemy's presence at Phaselis and Korakesion, it became clear that the protection of one of the great men was of more use, particularly if they were serious in their repeated proclamations of regard for 'the freedom of the Greeks'. The soldiers' inscription from Aspendos indicates that the city had certainly accepted Ptolemaic protection, for Ptolemaic troops had been sent to assist in the defence of the city in a local crisis. It would seem, therefore, that Aspendos' relationship to Ptolemy was that of an ally, not a subject, and so the city's search for security had, for the moment, succeeded. The settlement of the Ptolemaic soldiers in the city may also be seen as one of the origins of the willingness of Aspendians to be recruited into the Ptolemaic forces, so it would seem that Ptolemy gained as much as Aspendos from the friendship.

The decree giving citizenship to the soldiers may also be seen as an indirect way to honour the king, but it cannot be seen as admitting his suzerainty. In the same way, a Termessian decree honouring the 'Pamphyliarch' Philippos son of Alexander[36] is just that, not a sign of the city's subjection. There is, in fact,

---

[36] Note 34.

no other evidence of either city being subject to Ptolemy, or any of the other kings of that family, at any time; in particular neither of these inscriptions has any mention of a Ptolemaic official posted to them, notably not of an *epistates*, and this tilts the balance of probability away from any direct control of the cities and towards an alliance between the king and the individual cities. Also this is the only record of a Pamphyliarch. Others may have been appointed, but apparently made little mark. From Ptolemy's point of view there was little or no advantage in direct control where his influence would suffice to encourage trade and provide access to recruiting, since he already had a firm base in the area by his control of Korakesion and Phaselis.[37]

One clear result of the jostling for power in the period after Alexander was the permanent presence of Ptolemaic power in Pamphylia, in a combination of direct control and alliances with cities. The direct control was exercised at the two extremes of the bay. One sign of this is that Phaselis ceased minting its own coins for half a century after its capture, and there is evidence of a good deal of infrastructure construction at the city during the time of Ptolemaic control, including work on the quays.[38]

Korakesion's fortifications are sited on top of its steep hill, two hundred metres high, on a rock which takes a good half-hour to climb using a road which hairpins back and forth to minimize the gradient – a steep path of many steps is available for the descent. The city – as a *polis* – is recorded in the mid-fourth century BC by Pseudo-Skylax. The purpose of the fortification was clearly defensive, though the defended area is too large for the mere protection of its own population; it would seem probable that it was developed as an administrative centre as well, and so as a fortress, aggressive as well as defensive.[39] At the same time the rock, projecting as it does into the sea, creates two sheltered bays, to south-east and north-west, the first forming the modern (and medieval) harbour, and presumably the ancient one as well.[40] Its position at the far south-east corner of Pamphylia made it the first city of the region to be reached by travellers from Egypt and Cyprus, which helps explain the attention given to it by the Ptolemies.

---

[37] For a different view, arguing for full Ptolemaic control, but not remarking the absence of evidence for it, see Bagnall, *Administration*, 111.

[38] Schäfer, *Phaselis*, 164–174.

[39] There is no direct evidence that Ptolemy I fortified the place, but it was still in Ptolemaic hands in 197, and in 309 Ptolemy I seized Phaselis, coming from Cyprus; he is the likeliest person to have taken Korakesion, and if he held it, he will have fortified it.

[40] The medieval remains include the great Red Tower and the covered dockyard at sea level; there are many more remains, Byzantine and medieval Islamic, on the rock itself; it became the capital of a Seljuk principality for a time in the thirteenth century.

At some point a town on the eastern part of the coast, was named or renamed Ptolemais,[41] and there was another with the Ptolemaic name of Arsinoe.[42] These are west and east of Korakesion respectively, clearly establishing the range of Ptolemaic control along that coast. The names indicate their establishment during the early part of the reign of Ptolemy II, between 282 and 270 (when Arsinoe died). Perhaps they might be seen as a response to the intrusion of Seleukid interest at Seleukeia and the alliance with Side. The sequence of events and buildings would therefore be:

1. Ptolemy I's seizure of Korakesion and Phaselis in 309.
2. A local crisis in which Aspendos is assisted by Ptolemaic forces, probably against an attack by Side.
3. Alliance of Seleukos I and Side, leading to the establishment of the Seleukid post at Seleukeia (after 294).
4. Firm alliances of Side with Seleukos and of Aspendos with Ptolemy bring an end to the local crisis; that is, the principals exert control to prevent the problem spreading.
5. Ptolemy II extends his physical control over the coast to the east and west of Korakesion at Ptolemais and Arsinoe (between 282 and 270).

It follows from all this that the minimal intrusions from outside of the centuries before Alexander were long past. Not only had Alexander campaigned through Pamphylia, his successors – Nearchos, Antigonos, Ptolemy, Seleukos – had intervened repeatedly since his death. In this, of course, Pamphylia was only conforming with the experience of all other lands of Asia Minor, not that this would be any comfort. After 280, however, the wilder gyrations of power ceased, and in the eastern Mediterranean the conflict was between Seleukid and Ptolemaic kings. In this Pamphylia was necessarily involved, since both dynasties had footholds in the region, but the land was never a central issue in itself. The Ptolemaic hold on the coastal areas, indeed, tended to relax as time went on. This permitted a new development in the political affairs of the land.

---

[41] Strabo 14.4.2; Cohen, *Hellenistic Settlements*, 339.
[42] Cohen, *Hellenistic Settlements*, 335–337.

5

Hellenistic Growth

The passage of Alexander and his army through Pamphylia had been deceptive in its lack of immediate consequences. The next half-century produced more interventions with greater local effects, so that by the time the last of the Successors of Alexander, Seleukos Nikator, was murdered in 281, Pamphylia had felt the full effects. The kings had intruded their power into the area from all directions, so that at least three of the cities, Korakesion, Phaselis, and Aspendos, were part of, or attached to, the Ptolemaic kingdom, and Side was an ally of the Seleukid state. Indeed in at least two sources from the reign of Ptolemy II (282–246 BC), Pamphylia was noted as a Ptolemaic province.

'Pamphylians' are listed as Ptolemaic subjects by Theokritos in one of his *Idylls*,[1] and in the same way on the 'Adulis inscription' copied down much later by the ship's captain Cosmas *Indikopleustes*, but originally of about the same date as the *Idyll*.[2] In the same way, 'Kilikians' and 'Lykians' are also recorded as Ptolemaic, but all these statements are less than specific. We know that in neither Lykia nor Kilikia did Ptolemaic control extend much beyond certain coastal holdings, so there seems no reason to assume that Ptolemaic control of Pamphylia was any more complete. The two records are a praise-poem by a sycophantic poet, and a royal boast designed to impress; in both cases one expects exaggeration, but not accuracy, modesty, or even precision. Nevertheless it seems reasonable to assume that Ptolemaic influence, to put it no stronger, was also present at the other cities, Perge, Sillyon, and Magydos.

The Ptolemies had three main interests in holding on to a foothold in Pamphylia. Strategically the two ports of Korakesion and Phaselis provided them with well-placed bases for their naval power. Along with Cyprus, they allowed the Egyptian kings to dominate the sea-route along the south Anatolian coast and into the Aegean. In economic terms supplies of wood, of which Egypt is notoriously deficient, were available, and Phaselis has been suggested as a good

---

[1] Theokritos, *Idyll XVII*.
[2] *OGIS* 54.

source for it;[3] Rough Kilikia, next to Korakesion and Ptolemais, is another, and indeed the whole coast of southern Asia Minor could provide wood in abundance. The recruitment of soldiers as mercenaries for the army was another reason for the Ptolemaic presence. During the third century Pamphylians who became soldiers abroad did so overwhelmingly in the Ptolemaic forces, and several of them rose to high command, while other men entered the Ptolemaic bureaucracy. Occasional soldiers are noted in other armies, but it is in the Ptolemaic that most Pamphylians are recorded. One man, from Arsinoe and buried at Alexandria, provides the proof of the very existence of his home town.[4] They came from all of the cities from Side to Phaselis, but the largest number came from Aspendos – at least fifteen are known by name; an equal number came from all the rest of the cities combined.

Some Pamphylians achieved high positions in the Ptolemaic government, and this would have a bearing on the attitude of their home cities: Artemidoros of Perge was honoured at Thera where he retired after a long career,[5] Andromachos of Aspendos was in joint command of the phalanx at the Ptolemaic victory at Raphia in 217 and was then appointed governor of Phoenicia and Koile Syria,[6] Thraseas of Aspendos became governor of the city of Tamassos in Cyprus.[7] These men were not uncultured soldiers, for a display of education as well as intelligence was required in their positions.

Many of these men are known because they settled in Egypt, apparently as veteran soldiers after their service. Given the reputation of the Pisidians for militancy, it is worth noting that there are twice as many Pamphylians as Pisidians known in the Ptolemaic service. It is also significant that all but three of the Pamphylians are recorded with their civic origin, whereas most Pisidians are simply 'Pisidian'. The civic identity of Pamphylians was clearly much stronger than that of their Pisidian neighbours.

The cities were, of course, largely left to their own autonomous affairs. Phaselis, for example, was taken by Ptolemy I in 309, but actual later evidence of Ptolemaic control is remarkably thin: the worship of Isis and Serapis, which is hardly good evidence of political control, and a single issue of coins with the heads of Ptolemy IV and his wife, and so from some time between 221 and 204. And yet these heads were only small images, added to the normal coin,

---

[3] Robert, 'Une pierre à Phaselis et une Inscription de Cilicie', *Docs*, 40–46 (especially the notes).

[4] The basic research for all this which follows was done by M. Launey, *Recherches sur les Armées Héllénistiques*, Paris 1948, rev. ed., 1987, to which I refer readers in search of the detailed sources.

[5] *IG* XII.1333–1350; Launey, *Recherches*, 468–469.

[6] Polybios 5.64.4; 65.4; 83.3; 87.6; Launey, *Recherches* 469.

[7] L. Robert, 'Hellenica', *Revue Philologique* 13, 1939, 154–155.

and the reverse of the coin has the city's usual emblem, the stern of a galley, the city's abbreviated name, and the name of the supervising magistrate.[8] The issue looks more like an honorary one directed at an ally than a mark of Ptolemaic control, perhaps a gesture of support during the fourth Syrian War (221–217), or congratulations on the victory which ended that war, the battle of Raphia, when the two monarchs exercised joint command of the army, or, more likely, simply a gesture of honour at their accession. By this time Phaselis had been issuing its own coins for a generation, which, given the lack of issues between 309 and about 250, implies its return to effective independence.

Aspendos and Side had never ceased minting their own coins, and Perge began to issue its own in the middle of the third century, about the same time that Phaselis resumed doing so.[9] These actions are signs of autonomy in all the cities, and we have some evidence, at last, that some of the cities had standard Greek constitutions. The decree from Aspendos conferring citizenship on the Ptolemaic soldiers was in the standard Greek civic form, referring to a *boule* and the *demos*.[10] The title of the eponymous magistrate was *damiourgos*, also attested by two other inscriptions of the third and second centuries BC, in which men who have just completed their terms in the office commemorated it by gifts of cash to the city for the building of a gate and a tower.[11]

An extremely difficult inscription from Sillyon, incomplete and in the difficult local dialect, provides unusual evidence for an internal political conflict. (The stone survived because it was reused as a doorpost in a church, but it has been damaged by having a hole cut into it.) It appears to commemorate the conclusion of internal peace in the city, where there were two factions, led by Manes and Mheiales (that is, Megalos). The troubles had lasted fifteen years, and the inscription was set up to mark the ending of these disturbances. In the process two civic offices, *dikastai* and *argyrotai* – 'judges' and (perhaps) 'treasurers' – are mentioned. The date of the inscription is in the third century BC, but nothing more precise is available.[12]

The internal organisation of the cities took the normal Greek form of assigning each citizen to a tribe, or maybe a deme. At Perge these were named for divinities: Hermes, Athena, Hephaistion.[13] At Sillyon just one is known, the Megaleitidai

[8] Head, *HN* 697.
[9] H. Seyrig, 'Monnaies Héllénistiques', *Rev. Num.* 2nd serie, 5, 1963; Hiepp-Tamer, *Phaselis*; O. Mørkholm, *Early Hellenistic Coinage*, Cambridge 1991, 143.
[10] M. Segre, 'Decreto di Aspendos', *Aegyptos* 14, 1935, 253–268.
[11] Brixhe, *Dialecte grec*, nos 17 and 18, pp. 200–205.
[12] Brixhe, *Dialecte grec*, no.3, pp. 167–167, a very useful discussion.
[13] L. Robert, *Hellenica* VII, 19 ,194–196.

(spelt Mealiteidai, in the Sillyonian dialect); this is in fact called a tribe (*phyle*), specifically.[14] One is known from Side, the Lukomitarai, from a bronze tablet thought to be a judge's shingle.[15]

Examination of the physical remains of the cities shows that they all had active local governments which were attentive to the needs of the city and its population, and generous rich citizens prepared to pay of amenities. This, of course, was also the Hellenic way, to gain personal renown by civic generosity, by participating in the city's affairs, and by acquiring honours by service. So it is by examining the city's structures, layouts, and buildings that some further indication can be gained of the cities' histories. For the tormented and vigorous period which we call the Hellenistic was also the time when the cities were, by all appearance, at their most prosperous and vigorous, and it is this period which saw the expansion of the existing cities to their full size. The main evidence for this conclusion consists in the dating of the walls of the main cities, and in the apparent absence of later extra-mural expansion, but there are also several other indications of local prosperity at the time.

Pamphylia, given attentive cultivation, can be an agriculturally productive land, as any visit there today will show, and the major cities all had relatively large territories, with access to the sea. Agricultural production and trade, the necessary bases for prosperity, were thus present. There had been indications that the area was prosperous in the Persian period, as noted in the last chapter, and at the time of Alexander's campaign, Phaselis, Aspendos, and Side all showed signs of some prosperity, based on their coin issues; for Perge and Sillyon, it seems likely that the same sort of quiet prosperity was also present.

Aspendos had already expanded from its hill onto the nearby lowland during the Persian period.[16] The suburb was walled, but the main city was still in use and would seem to have been fortified sufficiently strongly to deter an immediate assault by Alexander's army. Aspendos's hill is less difficult of access than Perge's or Sillyon's, and there was less incentive to move off it for mere convenience. The suburb occupied by Alexander is said to have been towards the river, which is likely enough since the city was reckoned a river port by Ps.-Skylax in about 360 BC. There is little or no sign of it now, but it may have been in the area

---

[14] Count Lanckoronski, *Die Städte Pamphyliens und Pisidiens*, Vienna 1890, 655.

[15] C. Brixhe, 'Une tablette de juge d'origine probablement pamphylienne', *BCH* 90, 1966, 653–664; the tablet was purchased in the bazaar of Istanbul and given to the Cabinet des Medailles in Paris in 1965. The names of the owner – 'Ouwragweis son of Kedeiwas son of Ouwragweis' – are wholly Luwian-derived, and the whole may well be, as Nollé, in *I. Side* p.60, suggests, from Side.

[16] Arrian, *Anabasis* 1.26.

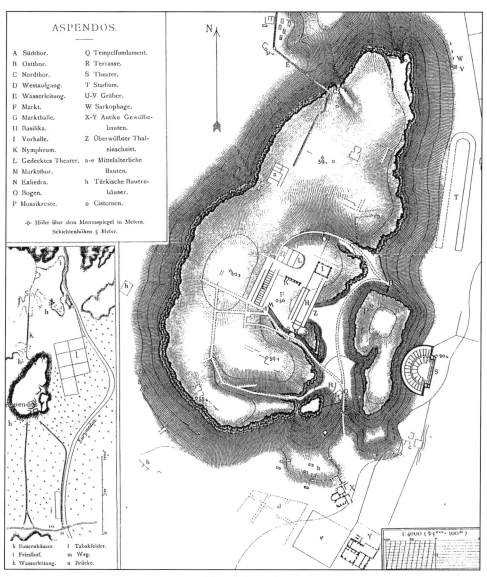

ASPENDOS.

A Südthor.
B Ostthor.
C Nordthor.
D Westaufgang.
E Wasserleitung.
F Markt.
G Markthalle.
H Basilika.
I Vorhalle.
K Nympheum.
L Gedecktes Theater.
M Marktthor.
N Exhedra.
O Bogen.
P Mosaikreste.

Q Tempelfundament.
R Terrasse.
S Theater.
T Stadium.
U-V Gräber.
W Sarkophage.
X-Y Antike Gewölbe-
    bauten.
Z Überwölbter Thal-
    einschnitt.
a-e Mittelalterliche
    Bauten.
h Türkische Bauern-
    häuser.
o Cisternen.

-0- Höhe über dem Meeresspiegel in Metern.
Schichtenhöhen 5 Meter.

h Bauernhäuser.
i Friedhof.
k Wasserleitung.
l Tabakfelder.
m Weg.
n Brücke.

Map 5. Aspendos

lying east and south-east of the town (Map 5). A street which was lined with Hellenistic-era tombs lies beyond the present stadium – that is, away from the city – and this implies that that particular area to the north-east was not inhabited, except by the dead (Plate 19). The stadium and the theatre were both outside the city to the east, and so the Persian-period suburb which Alexander occupied was in all likelihood somewhat to the south; in the Roman period there were certainly buildings in that direction, for two substantial baths have been found

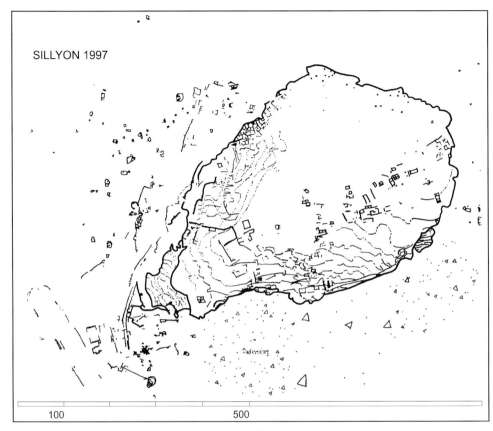

SILLYON 1997

100	500

Map 6. Sillyon

there, and there are several other prongs of masonry visible. But the interior of the main city remained well built-up all through from the Persian to the Byzantine period; large building remains stand to this day: a council chamber, an arch, a *basilica*, an *agora*, the foundations of two temples; this part of the hilltop was clearly the centre of the city throughout its history.

Most of these buildings are Roman in date, but the *agora* is Hellenistic,[17] as is the stadium (outside the walls), whose layout determined the positions of the Hellenistic tombs.[18] The line of the walls and gates already existed in the Persian period, and no doubt those temples which have been located are on ancient sites. Both the *agora* and the stadium are substantial buildings, and the present theatre, Roman in its plan and construction, was surely preceded by an

[17] H. Lauter, 'Die Hellenistische Agora von Aspendos', *BJ* 170, 1970, 77–101.
[18] Bean, *TSS*, 54–55.

earlier building. The city's games, perhaps founded in 402, required the full set of Greek educational and artistic institutions. The fate of the suburb below the hill in the Hellenistic period is not known, but since it existed in the Persian and the Roman periods, and had been walled already in the Persian, if not earlier, it will have continued to exist, and, given the apparent prosperity of the city and the region, it will presumably have expanded. Certainly Aspendos appears to have been seen as the main city of the country during both the Persian and the early Hellenistic periods, and Livy refers to 'the Aspendians and the others' in a communication made to the Roman commander Manlius Vulso in 189.[19] However, given the lack of evidence for many buildings below the main city, it may be that the city's main period of expansion was in the Persian period.

Sillyon never developed much of a lowland suburb at all (Map 6, Plate 12). Occupation stayed on the hill throughout its history – the most substantial building there is Byzantine. Instead of moving to the lowland, where the inhabitants would be vulnerable, a tremendous stone-built ramp was constructed to provide a fairly gentle incline from the plain to the city, over three hundred metres long. (It is a great pity it is no longer continuous.) The ramp is Hellenistic, from the apparent date of the masonry of the outer wall.[20] The problem then arose that the entrance to the ramp had to be protected, so a city wall with towers and a gate, with a semi-circular entrance between two towers – the type is found also at Perge and Side – was constructed to enclose the lower entrance to the ramp; a stadium was built just outside these walls. Since the ramp was Hellenistic, so the city wall was of that date as well; the stadium may be of Roman date, given the way it lies very close to the main gate, making access to it difficult, and also rendering it vulnerable; no city which feared attack would permit a building to be placed so close to its most vulnerable spot, and so we must date it to the period of the Roman peace. The wall and gate also imply a serious defence. Only at this western end is the hill at all vulnerable; not only the wall, but also towers and two bastions were built to block that access. A single substantial building was later built across the line of the wall; a Late Antique date seems most likely. The wall had therefore gone out of use by the time this building was constructed, and so presumably had the ramp, for the wall protected the ramp.

The hilltop has standing remains of all periods from the Persian to the Turkish, including baths, a theatre (now falling into the valley, as the neighbouring odeon already has) (Plate 11), and houses. From the rubble, which impedes

---

[19] Livy 36.15.6.
[20] Bean, *TSS*, 40–42.

any exploration of the centre of the site, or any walking – it threatens a broken ankle to any visitor at just about every step – it seems that the greater part of the hill was always covered in buildings, among which some of the older ones were preserved. It does not have the signs of expansion and wealth which are detectable at its sister cities; the whole place has an air of withdrawn privacy, though that may be mere imagination. And yet, even in the long Roman peace, the city colonized the lowland around it only with farms, several of which have been recently located in surveys.[21]

Recent archaeological work – a survey and some clearing – has located several of the more important public buildings and has revealed an area of private housing. Much of the dating material is Roman or Hellenistic, both on the hilltop and in the farms nearby, as one would expect. The houses were partly cut out of the rock, and partly built up with (presumably) the resulting stone; indeed much of the surface is rock-cut, with the streets and house-foundations cut from the rock's surface (Plate 10). Every house had a cistern: the survey has located seventy-eight of them, and there were certainly more; the city never had an aqueduct. The foundations of the only house which could be dated would seem to have been pre-Hellenistic, but many of the visible and excavated buildings are of Hellenistic date. There is no depth of archaeological material: the rebuilding was clearly done by reusing both the original foundations and the old building stone. The city may have been prosperous in 'classical' times – which is, for Sillyon and Pamphylia, the Persian period – but it was in the Hellenistic that its prosperity was translated into permanent buildings.

Rather more important signs of expansion and prosperity come from Perge and Side. Perge did not produce coins until well after Alexander's visit, but minted a set from c.255 to c.241 BC,[22] and it resumed minting twenty years later (see, on this, the next chapter). The city's coins commemorate not the city, however, but the temple of Artemis. The 'Lady of Perge' is clearly the local description, though for wider Greek consumption she was described as Artemis, or, on some coins, *Artemidos Pergaias*, with the head of Artemis on the obverse, usually backed by a standing figure of Artemis as a Greek goddess, as a huntress or warrior, on the reverse. A sphinx is also portrayed, and in some cases the cult figure from the temple is shown.[23] Already in the Persian period

---

[21] M. Küpper, 'Sillyon: Research Work 1995', XIV *AST* II 1996, 451–457, and 'Sillyon, Bericht über de Arbeiten 1996', XVI *AST* II 1998, 475–496. Dating material has not yet been published; the coin evidence in particular would be welcome.

[22] H. Seyrig, 'Monnaies Héllénistiques: Perge', *Rev. Num.* 2e Serie, 5, 1963

[23] Head *HN* 699.

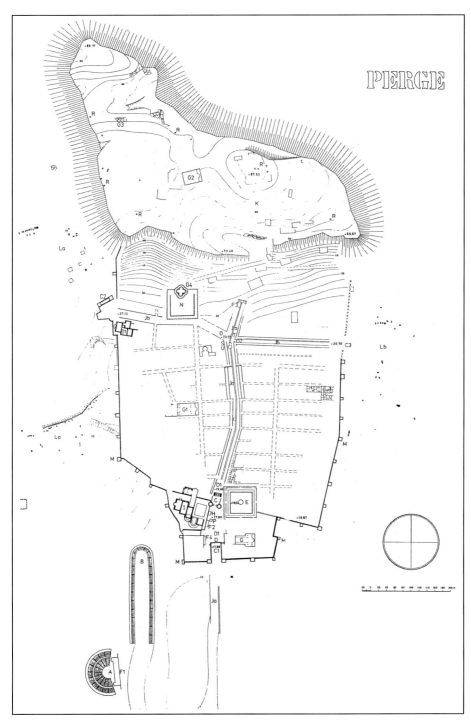

Map 7. Perge

the temple had been prominent enough to be mentioned by 'Ps.-Skylax' in his description of the Pamphylian coastline, and the worship of the goddess spread abroad to some extent later, in the normal Hellenistic fashion. There are records of devotions to her throughout the eastern Mediterranean, the worship of the goddess going where Pergaians traded and settled, in Egypt, the Aegean, north-west Greece; the distribution looks very like a result of the influence of Ptolemaic power in Pamphylia.[24]

The city itself now for the first time developed a suburb on the lower land, below the hill on which it was first founded, and which then, when the lower city had developed, became the city's acropolis (Map 7). The lower city was walled in the Hellenistic period, producing a rectangular space of about thirty hectares, which tripled the city's area; these walls still stand. The date of this expansion is shown by the plan of the southern gate, which is of the same type as at Sillyon and Side, with two circular towers flanking a semi-circular entranceway; like that at Side, it was altered later in the Roman period to make it monumental rather than practical[25] (Map 16, Plate 9). Since the gate is at the furthest part of the city from the acropolis, and is of Hellenistic date, so were the city walls. The plan of the city, as it has been discovered, shows clear evidence of deliberate pre-planning, but it may also suggest that the expansion took place in several stages.[26]

The main street of the city leads southwards from the entrance to the acropolis to the new southern gate (Plates 3, 4). The starting point is a Roman *nymphaeum*, whose water source was a nearby stream brought by an aqueduct; the acropolis has many cisterns, which may be early (Plate 8). A major cross street at right angles to the main street runs parallel to the base of the hill, at a distance of about hundred metres. The main street bends quite noticeably at that point, and again two hundred metres further south, as though it was a realization in stone of the original lane leading south out of the acropolis; the street leading to the west below the acropolis is also rather winding; that to the east is straight.

The plan suggests an urban history in four stages: the acropolis first, occupied in the threatening period in the seventh century, the original city (Map 8). Then a suburb developed directly below that hill to the south, centred on the

---

[24] T. S. McKay, 'The Major Sanctuaries of Pamphylia and Cilicia', *ANRW* II.18.3, 2048–2082.

[25] H. Lauter, 'Das Hellenistischer Südtor von Perge', *BJ* 172, 1972, 1–11.

[26] The most accurate published map seems to be in XV *Kazı* II, 1993, 601, drawn in 1991; see also N. Abbasoğlu, 'The Founding of Perge and its Development in the Hellenistic and Roman Periods', in D. Parrish (ed.), *Urbanism in Western Asia Minor, Journal of Roman Archaeology*, Supplement 45, Portsmouth RL 2001, 173–188.

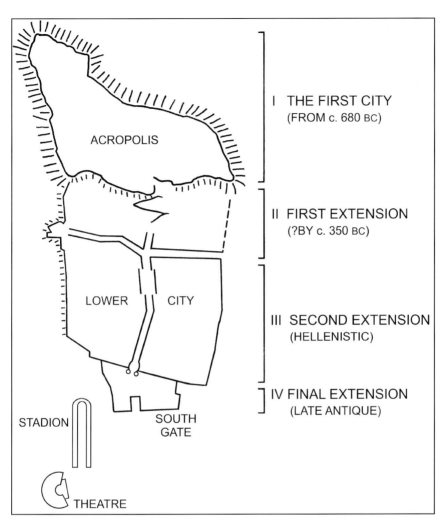

ACROPOLIS

I THE FIRST CITY
(FROM c. 680 BC)

II FIRST EXTENSION
(?BY c. 350 BC)

LOWER   CITY

III SECOND EXTENSION
(HELLENISTIC)

IV FINAL EXTENSION
(LATE ANTIQUE)

STADION

SOUTH
GATE

THEATRE

Map 8. Perge: stages of expansion

water source, and spreading east and west along the line of the cross streets. The cross streets lead to city gates at either end, and there are cemeteries outside both gates. This will be expansion of the Persian period, like that at Aspendos, though there is no dating evidence for it as yet. The city submitted suspiciously quickly to Alexander's advance, which would make sense if this suburb was unwalled at the time. The third stage of the city's growth was the planned extension southwards along the main street as far as to the Hellenistic South Gate. Within this large area, a rectilinear grid of streets has been detected, and the whole area was enclosed by the city wall; two other gates are the ends of the cross street. On the west, the wall utilises a slight rise in the ground level; on the east this does not occur, and a modern irrigation channel parallels the wall. The fourth stage was an extension of building outside the South Gate, part of which was subsequently walled in the Late Antique period. Beyond that area were the stadium and the theatre, both outside the city proper.

In general terms it is probable that the first expansion off the acropolis came in the Persian period; the walls and gates of the lower city were Hellenistic; the southern expansion beyond the South Gate was certainly Roman and was walled in the Late Antique period. That is to say the greater part of the city was Persian and Hellenistic, with only a relatively small growth in the Roman period. The last (Roman) expansion contains only large public buildings, a baths, an *agora* of shops which destroyed part of the Hellenistic wall, and a Christian *basilica*. The renovated and altered South Gate was decorated with busts of the 'founders' of the city in the process. Outside the walls much of the available space was taken up by the *necropoleis*, and by the theatre, originally Hellenistic and rebuilt in the Roman period, and the stadium, whose construction is Hellenistic; all these would prevent any further urban expansion near the city; any other suburban development would have to take place well away from the walls and the city. There is no sign that such further expansion was needed.

There was also the temple. The location of the temple of *Wanassa Preiia* is a famous puzzle. It is usually sought on one of the two hills south of the city which flanked the road leading away from the main gate but, despite repeated searches, it has not been found (Plate 3). Below the western hill, Koca Belen, the theatre and the stadium were laid out; the present buildings are both of Roman date; possibly they were close to the temple, which would suggest that Koca Belen was the site; but possibly these buildings were placed to the west of the road to balance the temple to the east, and so the other hill, Iyilik Belen, might be it. So one goes on. The only answer is to dig. Extensive surveys and some excavation on the acropolis, the earliest city, have not found it, though an area on the very northern tip of the high city has been tentatively identified as a '*tempelterrasse*'; a small Doric temple has been located, with some Late Antique buildings, on Iyilik Belen.[27] One would certainly have expected the temple to be on the acropolis, if anywhere. The real surprise is that this great temple, renowned far and wide in its day, and surely a very substantial building with plenty of ancillary buildings attached to it, should have vanished so completely.[28]

---

[27] N. Abbasoğlu and W. Martini, 'Perge Acropolisindi 1996 Yilinda Yapilan Çalısmalar', XIX Kazı II, 1997, 102.

[28] Bean, *TSS*, discusses the matter at 35–38; cf. McKay, 'Major Sanctuaries', 2066–2072.

The acropolis has recently received some renewed archaeological attention, a survey and some sondages having been reported in 1999.[29] The expansion of the city onto the lower land did not lead to a desertion of the hilltop, and fourth century BC fortification towers and a peristyle of the third century have been located, as well as other buildings of the main period. Streets on the acropolis have been located, laid out in a grid pattern; this grid was clearly a result of re-planning, at some unknown date, but probably Hellenistic. A similar grid layout has been detected also in the lower city, on either side of the main southward street, but the grid does not conform to that street's bends. The main street is therefore earlier than the grid, and the grid may be contemporary with the Hellenistic walls. Like Aspendos, therefore, the Pergean acropolis continued to be occupied, re-planned, and repeatedly rebuilt, but in this case the greater part of the city was now situated below the hill. Given the greater convenience of the lower city, it must be assumed that most of the population would choose to live there rather than on the acropolis.

These three cities of the plain thus developed in somewhat different ways in the Hellenistic period, though all of them showed both apprehension at the surrounding dangers and encouraging signs of accumulating wealth. It appears that the most prosperous of the three was Perge by the later Hellenistic period. Aspendos was certainly still a reasonably wealthy place, but it had been the richest of the three in the Persian period. Sillyon remained in third place, as before, but was still able to afford to build its great fortified ramp and its city wall. The differences between these cities, in size and wealth, are to be ascribed to the size and wealth of their territories; Perge had much the larger *chora*, which had perhaps been progressively organised and settled in the Hellenistic period. For Perge there was also the temple, whose visitors brought wealth, and for Aspendos there were its regular games; Sillyon had no such extra income-producing institution, its territory was smaller, and it had no access to a navigable river; it is not surprising that it did not produce coins until a few in the last years of the third century.

In the eastern part of Pamphylia both Side and Korakesion flourished in the Hellenistic period, according to the standing remains. Side had a constant connection with the Seleukid dynasty, and this was presumably reciprocated in some way, perhaps by trading privileges in Syria. It had a vigorous mint, as earlier, producing the standard silver coins, now showing the head of Athene with the figure of Nike on the reverse, with the names of the supervising

---

[29] W. Martini, 'Die Acropolis von Perge: Survey und Sondagen, 1994–1996', *AMS* 34, 1999, 155-161.

magistrates, as well as the punning pomegranate.[30] The city had now discarded its own script, which it had used until Alexander's time, and even its bronze coins, which were only intended for local circulation, were now inscribed in Greek 'Of the Sidetans' (*Sideton*).

The remains of the city have been extensively excavated, but the majority of the visible buildings and other remains are of Roman or Late Antique date (Map 9). The original city wall may be assumed to be on the line of the Byzantine wall, laid out at the point where the city's space begins to widen out landwards; the locations of the various temples, all of which were within the smaller area close to the harbour, would tend to confirm this. The suburb which developed on the landward side was walled in the Hellenistic period.[31] This expansion of the city added almost thirty hectares to the older city's area – an increase of about the same scale as at Perge; the area within the walls more than doubled as a result. The new suburb shows no major temples at all, but it does have several large public buildings of the normal Roman type. These include a large *agora*, perhaps containing a Tyche shrine, which will have supplemented an older market place which was presumably near the harbour. The extension also contains private housing, mainly along the street leading from the triumphal arch which replaced the old North Gate to the new North Gate; some of the houses were continuously occupied from the Hellenistic to the Late Antique period. The gate is of the Hellenistic semi-circular type, similar to those at Perge and Sillyon.[32]

The city's temples are a singular collection: a double temple for Apollo and Athene by the harbour, which would provide a helpful marker for sailors – these are also the two deities who appear most commonly on the city's coins; Dionysos beside the theatre, just inside the old North Gate; possibly a temple for Men, an Anatolian deity, in the southern corner near the shore.[33] There was also at least one altar to Zeus, somewhere in the southwest section, for it gave its name to that area of the city: 'the Quarter of the Altar of Zeus';[34] the other sections of the city were named for 'the Quadriga', which is assumed to have crowned the

---

[30] Head, *HN* 704; M. Arslan and C. Lightfoot, *Greek Coin Hoards in Turkey*, Ankara 1999, shows the type clearly.

[31] The date of the great city wall is given as second century BC by several authorities, but all rather uncertainly. The walls are a kilometre in length and will have taken a considerable time to build; it is quite possible that they are third century in part. Cf. A. M. Mansel, *Die Ruinen von Side*, Berlin 1963, 27–39, and 'Bemerkungen über die Landmauer von Side (Pamphylien)', in *Mélanges Offerts à K. Michalowski*, Warsaw 1966, 541–551.

[32] A. M. Mansel, *Die Agora von Side*, Ankara 1956, 339–347.

[33] A suggestion by Bean, *TSS*, 95, which is not always adopted by other researchers.

[34] *I. Side*, 410.

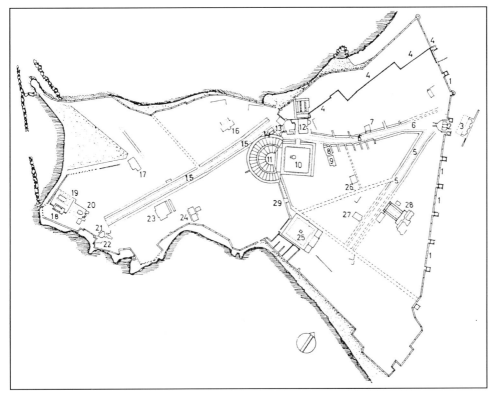

Map 9. Side

old North Gate, the Great Gate, that is, the new North Gate, and 'the Great Factory', which is otherwise unexplained.

In the city there is not much in the way of the remaining construction which can be dated to the Hellenistic period, though many of the excavated Roman buildings clearly had Hellenistic or earlier origins. The harbour, however, shows evidence of reconstruction – and presumably improvement – in the Hellenistic period, which fits well with the other indications of the city's prosperity in that time.[35] The harbour needed constant attention due to silting, even becoming proverbial as a task which was never finished.[36]

At Side there are three main streets, all of which were colonnaded in the Roman period, though each is slightly different. A consideration of the city plan and these streets is revealing. The main street in the old city was laid out diagonally from the harbour to the old North Gate, but its final, Roman-period,

[35] P. Knoblauch, *Die Hafenlagen und die Anschliessienden Seamauern von Side*, Ankara 1977.
[36] Bean, *TSS*, 74–75.

line looks artificial. It has a very slight bend about halfway along, and most of
the excavated buildings alongside it do not quite conform to its line, as though
they existed before the present street was laid out as a straightened version of
the original street. It was colonnaded, and so the present line is of Roman date,
and it was obviously desirable that it be built in straight sections, if possible.
The difference in alignment is only a few degrees, but this does suggest that
the former street, before it received its colonnade, was not so straight. In the
extension of the city, between the original wall and the Hellenistic wall, two
more streets have been excavated. That leading from the old to the new North
Gate is distinctly curved, and it would seem that it is a realization in stone of
the former lane whose line was fixed by the houses which lined it before the
street itself was paved; some of these houses are of Hellenistic date, and will
have determined the street's alignment. The third street was laid out quite
straight from the new North Gate towards a group of large buildings (Plate
20). This is clearly the last addition to the street system, in an area which was
developed later than the rest, and quite separate from the lanes which had been
laid out closer to the *agora*; it was thus probably laid out at the same time as
the buildings along it. At Side, as at Perge, in other words, the street layout
displays a simplified version of the site's development and reveals the several
stages of that development.

There is, of course, a certain paradoxical quality about this city. It had a
considerable *chora*,[37] which included the narrow coastal plain, the lower valley
of the Melas River, and, judging by the rural epigraphic records where there are
mentions of the city, considerable sections of the nearby hills. This is a well-
varied territory, capable of producing an equally varied set of saleable goods:
wood and forest products from the hills, fish from the sea, olive oil, wheat,
flax, and wine from the lowlands.[38] It also had access to the trading route along
the Melas valley into the Anatolian interior, but given the periodic hostility of
the neighbouring Etenneis, this may not have been altogether safe or reliable.
The city clearly prospered, as its expansion, its coins, and its walls show, and
the basic reason for this was its trade. Its position between Syria, Egypt, and
the west allowed it to be a link in the coastwise trade route.[39] Ships sailing
east would need to avoid the Pamphylian Sea, with its westward current, so

[37] J. Nollé, 'Die Landbau von Side', *Ep. Anat.* 1, 1983, 119–129; see also chapter 1.
[38] Nollé in *I. Side*, 1.29–24.
[39] H. J. Drexhage, 'Die Kontackte zwischen Side, Alexandria und Ägypten in der Römische Kaiserzeit (1–3 n. Chr.), *AMS* 3, 1991, 75–90; this contact will not be new in the Roman period, and probably went back to the foundation of the city.

Side, with the tall temples of Athene and Apollo at the harbour mouth, with their gleaming columns and red roofs visible from a long distance, would be an obvious port of call for supplies and refreshments. Its usefulness thus lay in the limitations of the sailing qualities of the ships of the ancient world. The harbour was largely an artificial construction, though based on the more or less convenient rocky outcrops. The coast as a whole was not particularly easy to navigate, and shipwrecks were not unknown; the harbour would be a welcome resort for tired sailors.[40]

Korakesion's fortifications, of Hellenistic date, and probably Ptolemaic construction, were concentrated on the summit of the great rock. This is unlikely to have attracted much more than military and administrative occupation, because of the sheer inconvenience of having to climb the hill: the civilian population surely lived nearer to sea level, as it does now, though no remains have been located to demonstrate this, no doubt because the whole area is now built over, and archaeological work has been largely concentrated on the summit, mainly in order to study the Seljuk remains. It may be assumed that many of the walls as they now exist are based on Hellenistic foundations, since there is one obvious line for them to follow, and at least part of the present walls have obviously Hellenistic footings. No doubt Korakesion had a fluctuating sense of prosperity. As the centre of the Ptolemaic presence in Pamphylia in the third century it would benefit from spending by its garrison and the officials. It was also a wine exporter, as is indicated by a record of the sale of Korakesian wine in Alexandria in 259 BC.[41]

Phaselis, the other Ptolemaic base in the area in the third century, cannot be so decisively characterized. The city's two extensions, the *Weststadt* and the *Nordsiedlung*, were developed in that order, and the *Nordsiedlung* seems to be Hellenistic[42] (Maps 10, 11). The city's peninsular situation gave it two large bays, to the north and south, to be used as harbours. There was also a smaller bay, the *Stadthafen*, close under the acropolis, which was perhaps the first harbour of the city – apart from the open beaches of the two greater bays. All three harbours were improved at various times. The *Stadthafen* could be relatively easily developed with walls linking the existing reefs, and with quays along the shore. The southern bay was the next most useful, and a breakwater

---

[40] Knoblauch, *Hafenenlagen*, details the phases of the harbour's history; J. Nollé, 'Stürme auf dem Pamphylischen Meer', Pamphylischen Studien, *Chiron* 19, 1989, 209–212, notes an oblique reference to this in a poem of Melegros of Gadara in the *Palatine Anthology* (XII, 157), and lists the (fairly few) records of storms in the Bay.

[41] Cf. V. Grace, 'Imports from Pamphylia', *Études Déliennes*, BCH Supplement 1, 1973, 197–198.

[42] Schäfer, *Phaselis*.

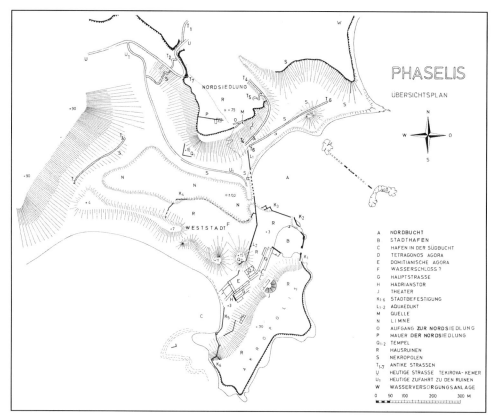

Map 10. Phaselis

has been detected, laid directly out from the land. The northern bay also has a breakwater linking two rocky islets, and this provides a large potential area as a sheltered harbour. In the nature of things it is difficult to date this work, but one would expect that the south bay would normally be the next to be worked on after the *Stadthafen*.

Fortification and marine development were both essential to the city, for Phaselis had a fairly violent history. Yet the city's expansion in the Hellenistic period happened despite its troubles, a good indication of the vigour of the times, but also under the shadow of Ptolemaic occupation and influence. The recent investigators have dated a number of significant constructions to the third century BC – a quay and a sea wall in the *Stadthafen*, walls on the acropolis, and the whole *Nordsiedlung*.[43] The responsibility for at least some of the work may well have lain with the Ptolemaic government, which implies a

---

[43] *Ibid.*

considerable financial investment in the city, comparable with that which took place at Korakesion.

It is not clear how long the direct Ptolemaic control of the city lasted, but the city began producing its own distinctive coinage at some time in the third century – 'mid-century' is the most convincing dating.[44] This implies an ending of Ptolemaic control about that time, perhaps from 250 BC at the latest. Some sort of connection with the Ptolemaic kingdom may have continued until at least the accession of Ptolemy IV in 221, judging by the coin of the city commemorating that king. This dating would concentrate the Ptolemaic contributions to the city's fabric into no more than half a century or so. The coins of this city, which name the responsible city magistrates, presuppose a local autonomy, but this does not exclude strong Ptolemaic influence.

The Hellenistic period was clearly the time when the cities of Pamphylia grew most vigorously. The new walls and new suburbs at Perge and Side, the ramp at Sillyon, the fortifications at Korakesion, the expansion of Phaselis into the *Nordsiedlung*, the buildings at Aspendos, all attest this. Although the buildings we can see, therefore, are almost entirely of Roman date, many of them were obviously built on the sites of older buildings and older versions of themselves. The theatres and stadia will have been on Hellenistic or earlier sites; the theatres are usually of the Greek type, with seating slightly greater than a semi-circle. Aspendos had a well-established tradition of games, and its stadium was certainly of pre-Hellenistic date. Within the walls all the cities had the usual complement of civil institutions, with some interesting exceptions. Gymnasia are known at Side, on a large site in the southeast section, and are implied at all the other places which had stadia – Aspendos, Perge, Sillyon. No stadium has been located at Phaselis, and this city would be a difficult site for such a building, but there is a gymnasium in the city. These institutions are the crucial educational establishments; without them a city was scarcely reckoned to be a city by the Hellenistic period. They were also necessarily supported by an array of more junior schools. Side produced a doctor of some note, Mnemon, who also edited a work of Hippokrates;[45] he can be added to the philosophers Diodoros of Aspendos and Theodektas of Phaselis as notable products of the region's cities and their educational establishments.

There are no temples located within the walls of Perge, but then the city had the great Artemis temple somewhere; one temple site has been suggested

---

[44] Hiepp-Tamer, *Phaselis*, says mid-century; Head, *HN* 697, has '276'.

[45] Noted by J. Nollé, 'Die "Charaktere" im 3 Epidemienbuch des Hippokrates und Mnemon von Side', *Ep. Anat.*, 2, 1983, 85–98.

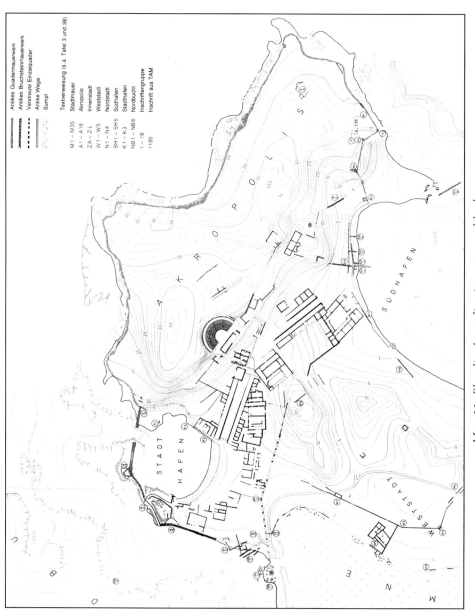

Map 11. Phaselis: Acropolis, city centre and harbours

on the acropolis, but proof is lacking; until excavation we must accept that the city contained none.[46] Strabo refers to the temple as being 'near' the city; if he considered the old and new cities as separate this can be explained.[47] But his words do not suggest personal knowledge. Every other city had at least one temple, and most had several: Side had at least four, Phaselis and Sillyon at least two each, as did Aspendos. The lack of temples in the main city at Perge is thus exceptional and in need of explanation.

A consideration of the coins of the cities reinforces this difference. Those of Perge showed only Artemis (in one case along with Apollo). The other cities are more liberal in their religious allegiances, though it is Apollo and Athena which are the most popular deities, and these appear on the coins of Phaselis, Aspendos, and Side. In the Roman period, however, all the cities commemorated a wide variety of gods and goddesses, and it was surely during the eclectic Hellenistic period that these deities arrived in the cities.[48] In Perge, therefore, the city was clearly devoted exclusively to Artemis, as the coins suggest, and this is reinforced by the apparent absence of other temples from the interior of the city. It may be that such temples have simply not been found, but this is a site which has been generally well explored. It may be that the Lady of Perge was so dominant that other temples were simply not permitted within the city walls.

The municipal equipment of the cities – streets, water supply, baths, *agorai* – is evident everywhere. The main street at Perge was also the main water channel, and side streets on a regular grid plan, a characteristically Hellenistic development, have been located in a survey. The city plan, as noted earlier, also suggests that in earlier periods planning did not take place. A series of streets, or at least ancient tracks, has been located at Phaselis, though given the hills and marshes of the site, a grid layout was scarcely possible. The main street of the city is a most impressive and well-paved central street (the present remains are of Roman construction, of course, but the layout is Hellenistic) (Map 11). At Aspendos a paved street leads up the hill from the main gate of the city centre, and there seems to be another from the southern gate, heading uphill for the same destination; the rest of the street layout has not yet been located, but the central part of the city shows careful and long term planning control, and some streets have been suggested leading to that centre (Map 5). The difficult plan of the site rather prevents much of a regular grid layout being organised. At Sillyon

---

[46] Martini, 'Akropolis von Perge', 158, tentatively suggests a large site at the northernmost part of the acropolis; see map in XIX *Kazı* II, 1997, 102.

[47] Strabo 14.4.2; if Strabo decided that the 'city' was the walled lower city, he might assume the acropolis was not part of the city. It was one of three hills, after all, the other two being clearly outside the wall.

[48] See the lists of types in Head, *HN*.

the main public buildings are rather scattered; in the excavated area there are narrow alleys between houses leading to larger streets – the sort of layout one would expect in an urban area which had developed without initial planning.

The positioning and supervision of the *agora* was one of the responsibilities of the city administration, and the examples we have show clear evidence of planning. At Perge, the most obvious *agora* is a Roman building laid out four-square close to the main city gate; this was clearly not the original position for such an important and central institution – it overlays in part the Hellenistic city wall – and there must have been one on the acropolis when it was the only area of settlement; published plans do not suggest one, but there are several 'peristyles' of Hellenistic and Roman date, one of which could well be the original site; one of these is next to the Roman *basilica*, a building which was often placed next to an *agora* (Map 7). Another is to be expected in the lower city, fairly close under the acropolis, in the first extension of the city off the hilltop; the crossing of the two main streets would be obvious place. That main street doubles in width halfway through the city, and this may a sort of elongated *agora*. (This is the place where the local hucksters offer their lace and jewellery today – no doubt a coincidence.) The one *agora* now visible is clearly placed less for the convenience of the inhabitants, for it is right at the edge of the city, and more for that of the municipality, which could direct supplies from outside straight into it without their having to travel the length of the city, and street cleaning could perhaps the more easily be accomplished – as well as rents charged for the shops.

Aspendos' *agora*, by contrast, is in the very centre of the city, and surely kept its original position all through the city's history; it is dated to the Hellenistic period by the latest investigator.[49] In its present condition the *agora* is flanked on three sides by the Hellenistic and Roman period *basilica*, by a (Roman) *nymphaeum*, and by a splendid 'market hall' of small shops, which is also of Hellenistic date. The *basilica* utilized a good deal of the Hellenistic walls of the *agora* as part of its building. If nothing else the permanence of the *agora* in its present site demonstrates the continual occupation of the hilltop site of the city throughout its life.

At Phaselis also the positioning of the *agora* – or *agorai*, for there seems to be more than one – shows both a continuation of use, and the commercial orientation of the city's life. The low-lying peninsula between the acropolis and the *Weststadt* holds three or four buildings which have been identified as

---

[49] Lauter, 'Hellenistische Agora'; also H. Cuppers, 'Getriedemagazin am forum in Aspendos', *BJ* 161, 1961, 25–35.

agorai, one close to the small harbour, which is called the 'rectangular *agora*' in an inscription.[50] Another is near the southern harbour, and a possible market hall is at the midway point. The two *agorai* next to the harbours are named the 'Domitian' (the southern) and the 'Hadrian' (the northern), but these are only late names of convenience, imposed when they were rebuilt. There were surely market places next to the harbours from the very start of the city. The market hall in the centre was later converted into a church and three other intercommunicating halls; its description as originally a market hall is generally agreed, and the building itself is no doubt Roman with a later conversion; it may be a specialised market place: the harbourside *agorai* were no doubt there from the start, and will have dealt with the exchange of goods brought by sea.

The positioning of the later *agora* at Side emphasizes that section of the city which contains a large proportion of the public buildings: the theatre, a large bath building (now the town museum), a temple, and a fountain are all close together (Map 9). There was a large and regular *agora* close to the theatre and just outside the old city gate, just the place where an informal market would develop for local produce to be bought by the inhabitants of the city. There was also another rectangular building, called by the excavators the 'official *agora*', in a similar position on the southern side of the Hellenistic extension, where another gateway existed, though it has more the appearance of a gymnasium than a market place.[51] The *agora* by the theatre was a sensible place for a market – central, and with good access – but there was surely another *agora* in the older part of the city, and the logical place for it would be beside the harbour, where a fish market could exist, and where overseas goods, such as the slaves captured by the pirates in the heyday of their careers, could be landed and sold.

No *agora* has been located at Sillyon, but a Roman-period *basilica* is known,[52] and next to it is an irregularly shaped open space without obvious buildings, though a Byzantine structure occupies part of it (Map 6). This would seem to be a reasonably obvious place for the *agora*; it is fairly close to the entrance to the city by way of the great ramp, and to some of the Hellenistic and earlier buildings, and it is fairly central to the whole city. This is only speculation, of course.

None of the cities shows signs of much expansion after their Hellenistic growth, with the exception of the small areas at Perge's South Gate and at Side's North Gate. All these cities, that is to say, reached their maximum sizes before

---

[50] Bean, *TSS*, 131–132.
[51] As Bean, *TSS*, suggests.
[52] Küpper, 'Sillyon. 1996'.

the Roman period. The only city to show any serious re-planning later is Perge, and this is perhaps to be ascribed to the wealth brought to the city by the renown of its temple – the Roman was Perge's greatest period. Even so this growth was only minor. All the cities put their *stadia* outside the city walls, and at Perge and Aspendos the theatres were outside as well. The overall planning of the several cities is always individual, and only at Perge is there any real evidence of the 'hippodamic' grid layout of streets which is so common in other areas. But the hilly sites do not lend themselves to such planning, and the cities themselves are generally much older than the grid layout idea.

6

The Effects of Antiochos III

The written sources for Pamphylian history are, as will have been appreciated by now, only irregular and occasional. This leaves considerable stretches of time for which little or no information about the region has been preserved. These blanks can be partially filled by other sources, but epigraphic material is often even less forthcoming, and numismatic information is often intractable and subject to drastic revision when a scholar takes a hard look at the material; it can also be arcane beyond the understanding of ordinary mortals.

The mid-third century BC is one of those nearly blank areas. Ps.-Skylax and the records of Alexander the Great provide useful information for the second half of the fourth century, but the information from the following period is thin and difficult, as the last chapter will have suggested. But for the reign Antiochos III (223–187 BC) parts of the *History* of Polybios provide useful information, while a startling set of coins from six of the cities supplement his work. Needless to say, the relative abundance of source material is accompanied by difficulties of interpretation.

It is just about possible, however, to make some sense of the situation in the region in the generation before Polybios' material becomes available. The Ptolemaic domination of Pamphylia, which began with Ptolemy I's pass along the coast in 309, faded during the mid-third century. The signs are faint, but compelling, with the resumption of coining at Phaselis, and the beginning of coining at Perge. In Phaselis' case most of the coin issues showed no reference to the Ptolemies, and the one issue which does has the heads of the king and queen in a small version, clearly added as an extra detail to the regular image; Perge's coins have no Ptolemaic references at all, and there is in fact never any indication of Ptolemaic presence there. The reason for the decline of Ptolemaic pressure and presence was no doubt the relaxation of international tension at about that time, as Seleukid power declined drastically. In 246 Ptolemy III captured the great Seleukid city of Seleukeia-in-Pieria, and soon afterwards the Asia Minor province of the Seleukid kingdom was detached into independence by the rebellion of Antiochos Hierax, the brother of King Seleukos II. So, for a generation from 246, Ptolemy III did not need to keep up his guard quite so strenuously, and this Seleukid debacle coincides almost exactly with the apparent decline in Ptolemaic power and interests in Pamphylia. Korakesion remained a Ptolemaic centre, along with its satellites at Ptolemais and Arsinoe, but the assertion of Ptolemaic authority waned in the rest of Pamphylia.

In fact it seems that the relaxation began even before Ptolemy III's successful war. The new coining by Phaselis is said to have begun about 255 BC. This is only an estimate, of course, but it is based on the internal evidence of the coins, which are validated by magistrates' names, even though not otherwise dated.[1] Perge's coining began about 241 BC, according to Seyrig's study,[2] which fits well with the end of the Third Syrian War – and 255 is also the year in which the previous Ptolemaic-Seleukid war ended. It would not do, perhaps, to rely too much on such chronological coincidences, but in general terms it seems clear that the fading away of Ptolemaic interest in the region is a large part the result of its successes in the wars – over-confidence leading to neglect, perhaps. It may be noted that Aspendos continued to coin all through the time of Ptolemaic power, with no sign on its coins of any Ptolemaic authority or influence.

When Hierax died in 229, the area of Asia Minor he controlled fell to King Attalos I of Pergamon, who was soon driven back into his ancestral principality by Akhaios, fighting on behalf of the Seleukid King Antiochos III. But then Akhaios moved into independence as king in 221/220. So from the 240s until 212, when Antiochos captured Akhaios' last stronghold at Sardis – and Akhaios himself – Pamphylia did not normally need to be concerned about being a battleground between Ptolemy and the Seleukids. The Seleukid civil wars from 241 to 212 BC suited the Ptolemies admirably, and they were discreetly encouraged to continue by Ptolemy III and IV. But in 221/220, Akhaios, who was in effective control of western Asia Minor, found a reason for an armed intervention in the south (see, on what follows in this chapter, Map 12).

Akhaios was looking for local support and perhaps for soldier recruits when he intervened in Pamphylia. He was responding to an appeal from the Pisidian city of Pednelissos, Perge's northern neighbour, which was threatened by the Pisidian city of Selge, Aspendos' northern neighbour. Akhaios was no doubt intending to use this dispute to extend his own authority; it is significant that the commander of the expedition was a Pisidian, Garsyeris. Extending his control into Pamphylia would enhance Akhaios' power, and would also ease his connections with Egypt. He was, in fact, in much the same strategic situation

---

[1] Hiepp-Tamer, *Phaselis*,
[2] Seyrig, 'Monnaies Héllénistiques: Perge', *Rev. Num.*, 5, 1963.

as Kroisos three centuries earlier, and his solution to the problem was similar. It may be noted in passing that this presupposed that Ptolemaic control, or even dominance, in the area was no more.

Akhaios' army entered Pamphylia,[3] even though in order to fight Selge it did not need to. The purpose was clearly to use the crisis to extend at Akhaios's authority into the Pamphylian cities. Perge, which commanded the southern end of the road out of the north, and Aspendos were quickly involved, and no doubt their governments quickly appreciated Akhaios' and Garsyeris' deeper purposes. Garsyeris marched his army south through the pass which Polybios calls Klimax,[4] the modern Gubuk Beli, into Pergean territory, leaving a guard at the pass.

Perge was occupied, possibly by agreement between Garsyeris or Akhaios and the city, and the city may have contributed soldiers. Aspendos also joined in the war on Selge, contributing four thousand men to the joint army. Side refused to participate, citing an attachment to Antiochos III, the legitimate Seleukid king, a refusal whose terms were not good news for Akhaios. Side's own neighbouring Pisidians, the Etenneis, whose territory also bordered on that of Selge, and who are noted as Sidetan enemies, thereupon joined Garsyeris, sending him eight thousand troops. (Garsyeris had begun with an army of six thousand, some of whom were left to guard the route back into Lydia north of Perge, and others were probably left at Perge; the army he led against Selge was thus overwhelmingly Pamphylian and Pisidian in personnel).[5]

Garsyeris required alliances such as these partly to provide the military manpower for his attack on Selge, but at the same time he had to ensure Pamphylian participation so as to guard his southern flank. Indeed he needed not only their troops, but supplies from them as well. Marching from his base at the head of the pass, Garsyeris was able to relieve Pednelissos and to defeat a Selgean attack on the city and on his own camp, but he was unable to capture Selge itself, even after being reinforced by Akhaios in person.[6] Nor could he be said to have established Akhaios's power either in or south of the mountains. There was certainly an extension of Akhaios's influence into Pamphylia, in much the same way that Ptolemy's influence had been extended earlier, or Kroisos's three centuries before, but it was still no more than influence.[7] Akhaios was in diplomatic contact with Ptolemy – both were enemies of Antiochos III – and the whole expedition may well have been concerted with the Ptolemaic government.

---

[3] Polybios 5.72.1–10.
[4] Polybios 5.72.4.
[5] Polybios 5.72.10–73.3.
[6] Polybios 5.73.4–76.11.
[7] Polybios 5.77.1, exaggerates Akhaios' power in Pamphylia.

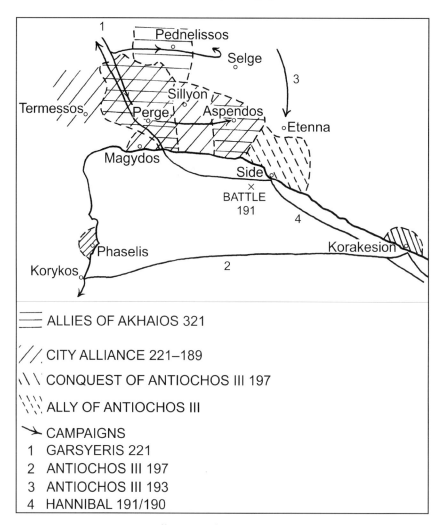

Map 12. Alliances and campaigns 221–189 BC

It cannot be claimed to have been a success, except in the minimal sense that Pednelissos was saved.

It is in part as a result of this intervention that the Pamphylian cities jointly produced a set of alliance coins: Perge, Sillyon, Aspendos, Phaselis, Magydos, and Termessos were all involved. To appreciate the significance of these coins not just as coins, or as indications of international connections, but in terms of Pamphylia and its cities, it is necessary to take a long look at the historical relationships between the several cities, and to do this it is necessary to go back to the beginning, to the very foundations of the cities. For I contend that the production of the sets of coins by the cities of Pamphylia from 221 onwards was the latest manifestation of a pattern of political behaviour which can be traced right through the history of the Pamphylian cities from their origins into Roman times and even beyond.

In the first instance it is evident that at the very foundation of the three cities of the plain, Perge, Sillyon, and Aspendos, their distribution and location, each in a well-defined part of the plain, argues that they were established by a concerted and deliberate agreement (chapter 2). This joint action is an early indication of the good relations between the three cities, and there is no evidence of any fighting between these cities at any time. This is difficult to justify, as is any negative conclusion, but a survey of the military history of the whole area will provide the background for it.

At either end of Pamphylia, both Side and Phaselis are recorded as being involved in more than one local war. Side was at odds with the Etenneis two or three times to our knowledge, and at least once with Aspendos, which responded by fortifying their common border. Phaselis was fighting its neighbours, the Solymoi, soon after the city was founded, and was still at odds with the Solymian Marmares when Alexander passed through, over three centuries later. Given the thinness of our sources for Pamphylian history this is an impressive record of conflict by these two cities. By contrast, Perge, Sillyon, and Aspendos are never recorded as fighting each other, though this does not mean that they were unarmed, nor that they did not face conflict with others – Aspendos was at odds with Side, and, as noted, provided troops to Garsyeris to fight Selge, and both Sillyon and Aspendos will willing to fight Alexander.

Xerxes called up thirty ships and their crews and soldiers from 'the Pamphylians', taking the area as a unit. During the Peloponnesian wars, neither Athens nor Sparta penetrated further east than Phaselis, except for brief expeditions at the end of which both cities swiftly retired. Phaselis itself was a tribute-paying member of the Delian League, and was later occupied for a time by Sparta, but the three cities of the plain were loyal to Persia all through. Aspendos repelled Athens in 388, and refused to cooperate with Kimon in 468, and Phaselis returned speedily enough to the Persian Empire after half a century under Athenian control.[8]

The arrival of Alexander and his army was the first occasion a major military power reached into Pamphylia – with the exception of the Persians, who do not seem to have needed to do any fighting to establish their control – and the three cities reacted differently. Or so it might seem. Perge submitted, apparently in advance of Alexander's arrival, just as Phaselis had. Aspendos submitted, but then

---

[8] For references, see chapter 3.

reneged, perhaps as a result of hearing that Side had appealed to Alexander to assist in the 'recovery' of Sidetan territory taken by Aspendos. Sillyon, occupied by a Persian mercenary force, resisted when Alexander got round to dealing with it: we have no information about the attitude of the citizens. No doubt the Persian governor, if there was one, was in Sillyon, and no doubt also Sillyon was chosen as the place to make a stand because of its great inherent strength. This was not the last time the city would play that role. Aspendos was forced into a second submission.

In all this, however, there is in fact a certain consistency. The cities which were free to choose, Phaselis, Perge, Aspendos, and Side, submitted to Alexander quite readily; it was the treatment they received from the conqueror which produced differing conduct by Aspendos. So far as we know, Sillyon might have submitted just as quickly, but the Persian force there scarcely permitted it. In the end, Alexander did not take either Sillyon or Aspendos; Aspendos was assessed at double the tribute it had resisted paying earlier, but we do not know if it ever actually paid. And, apart from Aspendos' 'rebellion', all the fighting was between Macedonians and Persians; unless some of the Sillyonians took part, none of the Pamphylians took up arms.

So, when, a century after Alexander, Akhaios sent his army into Pamphylia under Garsyeris to attack Selge, Perge and Aspendos cooperated with him, and Sillyon was ignored. Thirty years later still, in 189, when the army of Cn. Manlius Vulso approached from the west, Aspendos 'and the other people of Pamphylia sent their submission',[9] which can only mean that at least Perge and Sillyon participated along with Aspendos.

In all this there is never any indication that the three cities of the plain were ever on different sides, with the sole exception of Alexander's passage, which, because of the presence of a Persian garrison at Sillyon and the presence of Alexander's army, an unusually sizable force, was clearly an exceptional case. The cities were apparently sufficiently friendly under normal circumstances to be referred to simply as 'Pamphylians', or 'the Aspendians and the other people'. The intrusion of Alexander allowed Phaselis and Side to try to enlist him in their local quarrels, but this did not happen with Perge, Sillyon, or Aspendos. These three were not at odds, it seems. It is to be noted, however, that Sillyon and Aspendos, at least, and no doubt Perge as well, had armed citizen forces, but never, at any point where we have information, were those forces used against each other. Armed conflicts were quite noticeably restricted to the extremities of Pamphylia.

---

[9] Livy 38.15.4.

Despite the expedition in 221/220, when Aspendos contributed to Garsyeris' force in the war against Selge, there is some indication of friendly relations between those two cities, provided by the coin designs of both cities: Aspendos' type showing a pair of wrestlers, probably based on a famous statue in the town, and it was copied at Selge.[10] Selge and other Pisidians were often reported to be belligerent, but their bellicosity was usually indulged in relation to other Pisidians or the rulers of central Anatolia – Kyros the Younger, Akhaios, Antiochos III – not Pamphylia, and generally the fighting was provoked by threats to their independence.

Much of this is, of course, no more than suggestive, given the great gaps in our knowledge, and it is based on an absence of evidence, and so is not a good argument, but it does lay the groundwork for other evidence which is rather more positive. The coinages of Aspendos and Selge, showing the same statue, surely imply generally good relations, and there are other indications in the various coin issues also. In the Akhaimenid period the only cities to coin in Pamphylia were Side, Aspendos, and Phaselis. The Aspendian coins showed the two wrestlers, but another common device was the so-called 'triskeles', three legs running and set in a circle.[11] The term is a modern neologism, but the symbol appears on other coinages here and there in the ancient world, particularly on coins of an early version of the Lykian League, which was Pamphylia's neighbour to the west. It has been suggested that in Lykia the triskeles – or a four-legged alternative – was a symbol of the league, interpreted as signifying Apollo as god of light, with the circle representing the sun.[12] Aspendos' coins with the triskeles are later than those from Lykia, and the city was never a member of that league, but if the device was a federal symbol in Lykia, it may have been regarded in Pamphylia as having a similar significance. Lykia was an area where Apollo was not so important a god (and at Aspendos Apollo appears on the city's coins only in the Roman period). I suggest that the triskeles at Aspendos was also a symbol of an association of a group of peaceful cities, representing the friendly relationship of the three cities of the plain with one another.

I freely admit that none of this is definitive, but I do contend that it suggests very strongly that there is a pattern here of political behaviour: the three Pamphylian cities of the plain began their existence in concerted action, and remained at peace and associated with each other afterwards. Their reaction to Alexander's passage is consistent with this, given the constraints on Sillyon's policy; the triskeles

---

[10] Head, *HN* 700 and 701; F. Imhoof-Blumer, 'Münzen von Selge und Aspendos', *Zeitschrift für Numismatik* 5, 1878, 133–142.

[11] *BMC Pamphylia* 94.

[12] *BMC Lycia* xxvii–xxx; E. Babelon, *Les Perses Achemenides*, Paris 1893, xc–xci; Head, *HN* 688.

coins of Aspendos might earlier reflect this whole attitude as well. None of this is proof, for it is all negative evidence – but the absence of hostility between the three neighbouring cities is worth commenting on in itself. It contrasts with the active hostility of Phaselis and Side towards their own neighbours.

This peaceful relationship probably had its origins even earlier than the cities' foundations, in the early centuries of the first millennium BC when Greeks and Luwians intermingled. The various ethnic groups clearly cooperated in founding the cities, as indicated by the persistence of both Greek and Luwian terms and personal names in the local dialect. Initial hostility between communities is always difficult to eradicate; its later absence suggests strongly that it was never present at all.

So I return to the situation which was produced in Pamphylia by the expedition of Garsyeris against Selge, in which he was defeated. In its immediate aftermath, a new set of coins began to be produced at three of the Pamphylian cities, Phaselis, Perge, and Aspendos; later issues were also produced at Sillyon, Termessos, and Magydos, though not as frequently nor as consistently. The obverses of all the issues bore a head of Alexander the Great – numismatists accordingly describe them as 'posthumous Alexanders' – in an identical design. The reverses, by contrast, were all different: Zeus for Phaselis, Artemis for Perge, Zeus or a helmeted head for Sillyon, Zeus and at times a sling for Aspendos, and each city was identified by the initial letter or phrase of its name – PHA for Phaselis, AS for Aspendos, PE for Perge, SIL for Sillyon, M for Magydos.[13] What links them, besides the head of Alexander on the obverse, and the two- and three-letter abbreviations of their names, is a sequence of numbers, beginning with one, on all sets. The numbers go up to 33 on the coins of Phaselis and Perge, to 29 for Aspendos (with a probable counterfeit of 31), but Sillyon's have only 3 to 6 and 11, Magydos only 14, and Termessos only 13;[14] Termessos is also reported to have issued bronze coins of years 1 to 12[15] (see Chart I).

Considerable discussion has, of course, ensued as to the dates and significance of these coins, for the numbers are clearly years of issue. It might be assumed

---

[13] The single coin presumed to be from Magydos used an obverse die of Aspendos of 'Year 10': Price (next note), 358.

[14] The most significant examinations of these coins are by H. Seyrig, 'Monnaies Héllénistiques: Perge', *Rev. Num.* 2nd serie, 5, 1963; G. Le Rider, 'Les Tetradrachmes Pamphyliens de la fin du IIIe siècle et du debut de IIe siècle avant nôtre ére', *Rev. Num.* 2nd série, 14, 1972, 253–259; O. Mørkholm, 'The Era of the Pamphylian Alexanders', *ANSMN* 23, 1978, 69–75; M. J. Price, *The Coinage in the Name of Alexander the Great and Philip Arrhidaeus*, London 1991, 346–367; C. Boehringer, *Zur Chronologie Mittelhellenistischer Münzserien 220–160 v. Chr.*, Berlin 1972, 52–68; cf. also Hiepp-Tamer, *Phaselis*.

[15] Price, *Coinage*, 362–386; no further details, nor a reference, are given; the bronze coinage of Pamphylia is an unstudied area.

Year	Date	Pe	Ph	As	Sil	Mag	Ter	Comments
1	221/220	X	X	X			B	Garsyeris' War
2	220/219	X	X	X			B	Fourth Syrian War
3	219/218	s	X	X	X		B	
4	218/217	s	X	X	X		B	
5	217/216		X	X	X		B	Antiochos' War against Achaios
6	216/215		X	X	X		B	
7	215/214	X	X	X			B	
8	214/213	X	X	X			B	
9	213/212	X	X	X			B	Death of Akhaios
10	212/211	X	X	X			B	Antiochos in the East
11	211/210	X	X	X	X		B	
12	210/209	X	X	X			B	
13	209/218	X	X				X	
14	208/207	X	X	X		X		
15	207/206	X	X	X				Antiochos Returns
16	206/205	X	X	X				
17	205/204	X	X	X				
18	204/203	X	X	X				Antiochos in Asia Minor
19	203/202	X	X	X				
20	202/201	X	X	X				War with Egypt
21	201/200	X	X	X				
22	200/199	X	X	X				
23	199/198	X	X	X				Defeat of Ptolemy Antiochos in Asia Minor
24	198/197	X	X	X				
25	197/196	X	X	X				
26	196/195	X	X	X				
27	195/194	X	X	X				
28	194/193	X	s	X				
29	193/192	X		X				
30	192/191	X	s					Roman War
31	191/190	X	s	?				Battle of Side
32	190/189	X	s					Vulso's campaign
33	189/188	X	s					Treaty of Apamea

As – Aspendos   Ph – Phaselis   X – silver issue (probably bronze also)
M – Magydos   Sil – Sillyon   B – bronze issue
Pe – Perge   Ter – Termessos   s – small issue
    ? – questionable issue

Chart I. The issues of 'Posthumous Alexanders' in Pamphylia

that the missing numbers have not yet been found, but this assumption is not actually necessary, for there was no necessity for every city to issue a set of coins every year. The similarity of design, the coincidence of the numbers, and the geographical and social proximity of the cities, all require us to accept that the coins were issued in conjunction, that they were all contemporaneous, and that they used a chronological era common to them all.

Experts on these coins fall into two groups, those agreeing with the notion of the use of the same era by all cities, and those who detect different start dates.[16] We may start by recognizing the sheer unlikelihood of different eras being used in neighbouring cities which issued similar coins. Then one must consider that the few issues from Sillyon, Termessos, and Magydos are very odd if they are using different start dates, for enough examples exist to make it obvious that these cities did not issue coins in other years. Why should Termessos issue just one set of silver coins, and date that set to 'year 13'? Sillyon issued coins in years 3 to 6 and year 11; there seem to be no others, so why those dates, and why begin with 3? And Magydos' one issue was of 'year 14'; why bother dating a single issue at all if it was not a coordinated issue with the other cities? Further, Magydos' coins reused a die brought from Aspendos. The conclusion must be then that all the cities were using a single era.

The argument for staggered era starts rests essentially on their incidence in coin hoards, and the supposed demonstration in those hoards that 'there must be a difference of some ten years between the base dates of the eras used at Perga and Aspendos'.[17] But there is no such difference; or rather the differences are there but, of the six hoards quoted in support, the differences are 13, 9, 10, 9, 11, and 7 years; this is not 'a difference of some ten years'. The same argument is used to argue a gap of three years between the starts of the eras of Perge and Phaselis, but the hoards show differences between the two of 24, 11, 3, 4, and 0 years. The assumption is, of course, that the hoards are random collections of coins in circulation when they were buried, but all they show is that coinage in circulation is far too varied to be able to rely on it in such specific terms. And no convincing argument is put forward to explain why the cities should all copy each other, produce similar coins, and yet start their local eras on different years; and above all no explanation is given for the odd coins of Termessos and Magydos of the years 13 and 14. It is more reasonable to assume a common era.

---

[16] In the first: Seyrig and Mørkholm; in the second: Price and Boerhinger (note 14).
[17] Price, *Coinage*, 346.

Furthermore this range of years can be pinned down to a set of external events, linking the issues to major political developments, and even the fluctuations in the internal histories of the issues can be similarly linked. The end date of the issues has been located most convincingly at 189/188 BC ('year 33'), when the Seleukid kingdom was deprived of all its territory west of the Taurus mountains at the Treaty of Apamea. Pamphylia was included in the lands from which the Seleukids were to be excluded by the treaty, and at that time (189/188) the Roman army of Cn. Manlius Vulso marched past and collected the submissions of 'Aspendos and the other peoples of Pamphylia'.[18]

There are in fact only very small issues in years and 32 and 33 from Perge, and gaps in year 29 at Phaselis and after 29 at Aspendos. On this dating this reduction and these gaps cover the years 193/192 (year 29) to 189/188 (year 33), which, as I will argue, saw much political disruption in Pamphylia. Counting back, this end date would locate the beginning of the coinage in 221/220 BC, and this in turn is the year of the intrusion into Pamphylia of Garsyeris's army and the power of Akhaios. This event, the first intrusion of a major armed force into Pamphylia since Alexander, was obviously a serious political crisis for the cities.

This linked coinage, using a common era across a geographically contiguous set of cities, was necessarily the result of a political decision made by the several cities individually: it is, that is, the monetary manifestation of a political association, which can only be termed an alliance. The three central members were Perge, Aspendos, and Phaselis, to which we may add Sillyon, whose need for coinage was clearly less than its partners', and Termessos, at least until 'year 13'. Magydos was associated with the allies in their monetary activity only briefly, though it was presumably politically involved, from its geographical situation.

The participation of Termessos may be explained by the crisis in Pisidia. Garsyeris and the Selgeans fought initially at the Klimax pass, which is close to Termessian territory, and Termessos was surely concerned that the power of Akhaios was approaching. The city may indeed have been involved in the war, for Selge is said by Polybios, more than once, to have had allies, though none are specified.[19] Whether actually involved or not, Termessos was surely apprehensive; participation for a time in the alliance of the cities is hardly surprising. Note also that Side, which was at odds with Aspendos, and had refused to participate in the war on Selge, did not join in the joint issues at all.

[18] Polybios 5.73.4.
[19] Polybios 5.73.10 ad 74.3.

The perception of an active political alliance of the cities goes some way to providing an explanation for both the failure of the intrusion of Akhaios in 221/220, and for the later action of Antiochos III in by-passing Pamphylia during his sea campaign along the south coast of Asia Minor in 197. Antiochos had been fighting and winning yet another war with Ptolemy since 202; he had conquered Syria and Palestine and defeated Ptolemy's main army; in 197 he mounted a joint land and sea expedition into Asia Minor to mop up the remaining fragments of Ptolemaic power which were spread along the Asia Minor coast from Rough Kilikia round to Ionia. He himself commanded the fleet which sailed from Syria along the southern Anatolian coast. The first serious problem was Korakesion, which he besieged for a month before it was surrendered. Then he took the fleet across to the Lykian coast, where he halted at Korykos, south of Phaselis. Then he sailed on round the Lykian coast and into the Aegean.[20]

One of the oddest omissions from the list of Antiochos' conquests in this campaign is Phaselis, the best harbour on the west coast of the Bay: he used the minor anchorage of Korykos instead, and the conclusion must be that the better facilities and anchorages (and supplies) at Phaselis were not available to him. This had not been the case for any other conqueror who needed a base on that coast – the city and its harbours had been seized by Rhodes, Athens, Sparta, and Ptolemy I from the seaward side in the past with ease, and from the land the city had been threatened by local lords such as Perikles and Mausolos, and occupied by Alexander; it was clearly a desirable prize, and in the future it would be used by Zeniketos, P. Servilius Vatia, Cn. Pompeius Magnus, and the Byzantine navy. It was clearly valued by these rulers, commanders, states, and conquerors, and if Antiochos III did not seize it, it is reasonable to assume that he was deterred, or otherwise prevented, from doing so.

If Phaselis was allied with the other Pamphylian cities, as the joint issues of these coins imply, then it became a more formidable political and military proposition than before, when it had usually fought alone. Antiochos' main purpose in his voyage was to remove such Ptolemaic outposts as Korakesion, and to establish his power in the Aegean and the surrounding lands; if he became entangled in a local war in Pamphylia, this would fatally delay him. He had already been delayed by the need to take Korakesion, and ahead lay an awkward passage past Rhodes, which was unhappy at his approach and had already strongly suggested that he stay away. A siege of Phaselis might just

---

[20] This is a much simplified version of what happened, which has to be sorted out through two sources, Livy 33.20.4–5 and Hieronymos, *In Danielam* 11.15; for the full argument see my book, *The Roman War of Antiochos the Great*, Leiden 2002, 37–42.

persuade Rhodes, Phaselis' mother city and still officially neutral, to join in against him. Speed and audacity were requisites in this campaign. So Phaselis and its allied cities were ignored. If he really wanted to establish control over them, he could do so later, and more effectively from inland, as Akhaios and Garsyeris had attempted to do.

It is also noticeable that, when Antiochos campaigned against the Pisidians four years later, he did so in alliance with Side, and none of the four allied cities was mentioned, nor did any of them participate in the campaign.[21] Their alliance may thus have been effective again; the Pisidian campaign also shows the effectiveness of the longstanding Seleukid-Sidetan alliance. Antiochos' victims in this campaign are only specified as 'Pisidians', but the involvement of Side makes it all but certain that he was fighting the Etenneis, which would not only gratify Side, but might well also allow him to rack up good points with Selge. The city-alliance was thus in full working order in the 190s. It is time to look at its beginning.

The origin of this presumed six-city alliance in 221/220 coincides with the intrusion of Akhaios' army into Pamphylia. Garsyeris carefully pointed out the threat to the Pamphylians which he claimed was posed by the Pisidians;[22] this was obviously a redundant comment, since if the threat had really existed, it would be surprising that the Pamphylians had not already noticed; it may therefore have been invented by Garsyeris for the occasion – there is no other evidence for trouble between the Pisidians and Pamphylians, except that between Etenna and Side – which Garsyeris' diplomacy may well have exacerbated – and several indications of friendship and association. Garsyeris camped at Perge and made an alliance with Aspendos, which provided four thousand hoplites to join his assault on Selge.[23] Here are the essential basic components for the alliance – Perge and Aspendos – active on the same side in the Selgean war. Perge and Aspendos lay on either side of Sillyon (and Magydos); Phaselis was the fifth member, and had its own Pisidian problem with the Solymoi; Termessos perhaps felt threatened by the proximity of Akhaios' forces. The city which stood out against Akhaios was Side, supposedly because of a wish to please Antiochos III, Akhaios's enemy by that time, and Side is also absent from the cities' alliance; its antipathy towards Aspendos was blamed,[24] but we may also note that Etenna had been recruited by Garsyeris, which would hardly please Side. The casual remark of Polybios at

---

[21] Livy 33.13.2.
[22] Polybios 5.72.–10.
[23] Polybios 5.73.3.
[24] Polybios 5.73.4.

the end of his account of Garsyeris' campaign, that Akhaios had subjected the greater part of Pamphylia,[25] is vague, and, in that the term which Polybios used implies overlordship, inaccurate, but it could be understood to cover the idea that Akhaios's 'subjection' of the area was in reality the alliance he had formed with the several cities which had joined Garsyeris.

It seems very likely that the cities' alliance was formed as a result of Garsyeris' campaign, possibly by Garsyeris himself (he certainly worked with Perge and Aspendos), or possibly in reaction to his presence – that is, after he left. The intrusion of a foreign army into Pamphylia was obviously upsetting, and it was highly unusual. It would not be at all surprising if the cities reacted to it. If '221/220' as the start date of the coinages is correct, then the withdrawal of Garsyeris' army in that year would be a good moment for the alliance to be formed, or if it already existed, for it to be extended to other cities, and for it to be detached from Akhaios' influence. By participating in Garsyeris's expedition Perge and Aspendos might bring down the wrath of the Pisidians or that of Antiochos III upon the region, so defensive measures were clearly called for, at least in the short term. Other intrusions of armed forces would hardly be welcome, and a firm alliance might well deter them. If the Pamphylians had had good relations with the Pisidians earlier, Garsyeris' expedition might well have soured that relationship, though the Aspendians might argue that the troops they contributed had not been volunteered but conscripted, or that they were helping Pednelissos rather than fighting Selge. (The Etenneis' contribution of eight thousand men, double Aspendos' contribution, shows that city as a much more enthusiastic participant.) Garsyeris's intrusion thus stirred up a very dangerous brew, quite threatening enough to inspire an alliance amongst those in fear, especially if the core cities – Perge, Sillyon, and Aspendos – had an old tradition of association and peaceful relations.

The alliance of the six cities was a defensive measure against present and future intruders. Antiochos III in 197 found it still in operation, and respected it, by avoiding Phaselis; no doubt an embassy had gone to him, perhaps at the Korakesion siege, as the Rhodians did, to point out the situation of the alliance; maybe friendly gestures were mixed in with the deterrent threat. There was no point in Antiochos attacking the members of the alliance, for the defensive alliance of these cities was no threat to him; it was also not a potential enemy; Phaselis had been in Ptolemy's power, but was now free; the capture of Korakesion removed the last of Ptolemaic influence from the region; Phaselis would hardly rejoin Ptolemy's empire, which was Antiochos'

---

[25] Polybios 5.77.1.

immediate enemy, just as Antiochos was mopping up the last non-Egyptian elements of that empire. Nor would the alliance of four small cities be a threat to the ruler who could put an army of 70,000 men in the field. In 189 Manlius Vulso also conspicuously avoided Pamphylia, though he found a garrison of Seleukid troops in occupation of Perge on his second visit in 188,[26] a matter to be considered shortly.

The alliance may well be defensive – it could hardly be anything else – but in the political conditions of the time, it has to be considered above all in relation to the Seleukid kingdom. It began amid the attempted extension of the power of Akhaios, a Seleukid dissident and rebel; its termination was connected to the expulsion of Seleukid power from all Asia Minor after Antiochos III's defeat at Magnesia in 190. But between those dates the nature of the Seleukid power in the local area changed. After Garsyeris' withdrawal Akhaios ruled in Asia Minor north of the mountains undisturbed until 216, in which year Antiochos III began a campaign to suppress him. This war lasted four years, until Akhaios' last citadel, Sardis, was captured and he was killed in 212. In those years Pamphylia was obviously in danger, and some nimble diplomacy was clearly needed to avoid trouble. Then in 211 Antiochos III vanished from the scene when he went off to the east on his great expedition as far as India; he stayed in the east for five years, returning to Syria in 206/205.

The alliance coinages show interruptions or additions at three points in their sequences (see chart I). In years 3 to 6, Sillyon issued coins (for the first time) each year, while in years 5 and 6, Perge ceased to do so, and for the two preceding years (3 and 4) Perge's issues were only small. On a common era calculation this covers the years 219/218 to 216/215 BC. A second hiatus came in years 11 to 14. In these years Aspendos did not mint in year 13, Sillyon produced a set in year 11, for the first time since year 6 (and for the last time), and Termessos and Magydos produced one set each in years 13 and 14 respectively; this would be 211/210 – 208/207 by the common era used by the cities. The final years of the coinages saw them come to a stuttering end. Aspendos coined its last set in year 29 (a 'barbarous' coin in minted in year 31 was probably not an official issue); Phaselis did not coin in year 29; only Perge coined through to year 33. However, the issues from Phaselis in years 28 to 33 were not numerous, since there were only three obverse dies used in that six-year period: thus the three main coinages came to an end over a period of several years, which by the common era would be 194/193 to 189/188 BC.

---

[26] Livy 38.37.11; Polybios 22.26.

These three interruptions in the emission of the coins can be co-ordinated exactly with important developments in the history of Antiochos' reign. In 219–217, Antiochos III was busy with a war with Ptolemy IV, the 'Fourth Syrian War', campaigning in Syria and Palestine; Akhaios was quiet, having been prevented by his own army from venturing outside Asia Minor;[27] the need to enforce the alliance's objectives of defence may have seemed less urgent while the two main neighbours were preoccupied. The opening of the mint at Sillyon may have been in response to the slackening and then ending of production at Perge. Either way, the pressure of international events was clearly less during those years. The second set of interruptions, between 211/210 and 208/207, can similarly be related to Antiochos' actions. His absence on his great expedition to the east will have reduced any pressure on the cities from the Seleukid government. Antiochos' return began in 207, and the news of this could be the cause of the resumption of coining during 208/207. Termessos does not seem to have done so; presumably it dropped out of the alliance after year 13 (211/210). The stuttering end to the collective coinage after 194/193 is clearly to be connected with the activity of Antiochos in Pisidia (in 193) and his war with Rome (from 192). The continued coining by Perge may well be connected with the presence of a Seleukid garrison, which was there until 189. After 189/188, with the expulsion of Seleukid power to the east of the Taurus Mountains, there was no further need for the alliance and its coinage; and Phaselis was included in the Rhodian dominion in Lykia from 188, by an arrangement made by Rome. There is also some evidence that Antiochos finally managed to gain some control over Pamphylia in these last years, which would obviously affect the coin production.

Such a city-alliance as I have postulated could only be effective where the greater powers, in particular Antiochos III, were not seriously interested in the area, or were too busy to enforce their control. Pamphylia was still, in international terms, a backwater, largely isolated from the surrounding lands; the few routes out of the region did not lead to any place which was unattainable from elsewhere; its cities were small and of little account. So Antiochos did not bother with the area, even in the later 190s when it was evident that he was expanding his power and control into areas such as Karia and Lykia and Pisidia, but not into Pamphylia. That changed in 191, when Rhodes joined the war against him which was being waged by Rome.

The Rhodian fleet attempted to block the advance of Antiochos' second fleet, commanded by Hannibal, which was sailing from Syria towards the Aegean. The Rhodians were based at Phaselis for a time and were given information about

---

[27] Polybios 5.57.6.

the Seleukid fleet's location by the Aspendians.[28] It would thus seem that the allies were taking Rome's side, unless Phaselis had no choice in being used as a Rhodian base, and the Aspendians were simply being anti-Sidetan in passing on the information. In either case, the alliance had come to be identified as anti-Seleukid by these actions. In this the cities were, of course, adopting the same policy as most of the cities of Asia Minor which were free to choose.

Near Side, the two fleets fought a drawn battle, and then the Rhodians withdrew westwards; the Sidetan fleet had come out to join Hannibal, thus honouring the city's obligation to Antiochos.[29] The seaway was thus blocked at the island of Rhodes, but by their withdrawal from the bay the Rhodians had left Pamphylia exposed to Hannibal's fleet and army. By now, for the first time, the routes north from Pamphylia into Lydia were vital to Antiochos, whose army was in Lydia and Ionia, and Hannibal's best means of reaching Antiochos was through Pamphylia. An occupation of Pamphylia by Hannibal's forces, which may well have occurred, would not actually end the alliance. It is probable that Antiochos (and Hannibal) were only concerned for their communications, not to exert control over the cities themselves.

It is just at this point that there is evidence for a Seleukid military presence in Pamphylia. The region had become subject to recruiting into the Seleukid army. At the battle of Magnesia in late 190, a contingent of 'Pamphylians, Pisidians and Lykians' fought on Antiochos' side.[30] They were only four thousand in number, and were described as *caetrati*, translated as 'targeteers' – light infantry, in other words. The number is small, seeing that Aspendos alone had been able to produce that many hoplites thirty years before, and light forces are much more likely to come from Pisidia and perhaps Lykia than from the cities of the alliance. The alliance of cities had been marginal to Antiochos' interests, and then hostile to him; Antiochos could not have got many reliable troops from its cities – Side would be the obvious source; indeed he might have had to leave a force in the area as a guard. The Pamphylian contingent fought at the battle of Magnesia where it was overrun by Roman cavalry early in the fight; probably few of them survived.[31]

---

[28] Livy 37.23.3–4.
[29] Livy 37.23.6–34.5.13; two years later Antiochos' ambassador to the Achaian League noted that the Sidetans' fleet was joined to Antiochos' own fleet (Livy 35.48.6); this is not surprising since it was only in 193 that Antiochos had campaigned against Side's Pisidian enemies on the city's behalf; on all this, see my *Roman War*, 296–301; in that book, however, I ignored Pamphylia.
[30] Livy 37.40.13–14.
[31] Livy 37.42.1–3.

During the truce which followed the Seleukid defeat, a Roman army commanded by the consul Cn. Manlius Vulso marched through northern Lykia, skirted the edge of Pamphylia, and eventually went on to defeat the Galatians in central Anatolia.[32] This expedition was designed to subdue the remaining allies of Antiochos, exploiting a loophole in the truce terms. Vulso followed a route deliberately designed to avoid all Seleukid forces and Seleukid-held cities, while at the same time he aimed to collect allies for Rome and to deprive Antiochos of his own allies. Vulso carefully avoided entering Pamphylia on this march; he reached Termessos, taking a tribute of fifty talents from the city and compelling it to desist from attacking its western neighbour Isinda, but then abruptly turned north towards Phrygia.

Livy claims that 'the people of Aspendos and the other peoples of Pamphylia were similarly treated', referring, it seems, to the treatment of Termessos.[33] This appears to mean that they paid him to go away, though the whole sentence is notably unclear, and no sum of money is mentioned, which is at variance with everything else in the rest of this section. It may only mean that Vulso *claimed* that they were similarly treated. There is no mention of any Seleukid authority in the area at the time, and yet Vulso did avoid Pamphylia, as he had earlier always avoided Seleukid-occupied cities elsewhere. It very much looks as though the alliance of the four cities was still in place, as is implied by the reference to 'Aspendos and the others', but it might also be that Seleukid forces were in occupation in Pamphylia, the legacy of Hannibal's exploits.

After defeating the Galatians, Vulso returned to the Aegean coast to winter quarters for 190/189. In the spring of 189 he marched back to Pamphylia, this time by way of the Maiandros valley and the route south from Apamea in Phrygia. His purpose was to collect 2,500 talents of silver, which was due to be handed over to the Romans as a part of the truce terms. Pamphylia had been designated as the transfer place, no doubt for its convenience as a midway point between the two sides; this would also argue that it was a region where Seleukid forces could still operate – they would need to mount guard over such a large treasure until it was handed over to Vulso. Vulso collected the silver and then marched away past Perge, but where the silver was actually handed over is not clear. Vulso had taken three days to march from Apamea-Kelainai to reach the handover point, and that point must therefore have been considerably north and

---

[32] Everything about the activities of Vulso in Asia Minor is confused in Livy's account. It seems evident that he was combining two sources, one a diary of the march, and the other a more literary composition. The result is repetition and a lack of clarity, combined with much specific detail; see my article, 'The Campaign of Cn. Manlius Vulso in Asia Minor', *Anat. St.* 54, 1995, 23–42.

[33] Livy 38.15.6.

west of Pamphylia proper, perhaps at the Gubuk Beli pass ('Klimax' to Polybios). He then marched on through Pamphylia in part to assist his brother by sending a detachment of troops to Oroanda to collect unpaid tribute. This time he was informed that there was a Seleukid garrison at Perge, whose commander asked for a local truce of thirty days to allow him to seek instructions from the king in Syria. Vulso is said to have agreed to this truce, and then he marched away northwards to Apamea once more to attend the peace negotiations, ignoring the Seleukid forces.[34]

A Seleukid garrison at Perge in 189 suggests that there had been one there the year before. Livy makes the point that it was the only such force in the area on Manlius' second visit. The garrison commander's request for a local truce was quite unnecessary, for Vulso had no intention of attacking him, and the main overall truce between Rome and Antiochos was still in force. One is drawn to the conclusion that Livy did not really understand the Pamphylian situation. He clearly abbreviated his description of events, in part to emphasize Roman grit and determination, as personified in the blunt and unpleasant Vulso. He ignored the fact that the general truce covered the whole situation, but he clearly got some sort of a reference to a thirty-day delay from his source or sources. It was the Roman contention that Pamphylia lay outside Antiochos' new boundary, as negotiated later at the conference at Apamea. It is perhaps reasonable to assume that this was the burden of Vulso's communication to the garrison commander, perhaps to try to frighten him into a premature evacuation.

If the Seleukid troops had been in occupation since before the Magnesia fight, they were surely put there in 191/190, and by Hannibal, after the Rhodian fleet's withdrawal from Side and evacuation of Phaselis. Alternatively they may have only recently arrived as an escort for the silver payment. The need to protect the silver, which was delivered through Pamphylia, having come from Syria by sea, was a good reason for Antiochos to keep troops in the area. This would also explain why his troops only occupied Perge, and not any of the other cities, since Perge was the one city on the route from the sea to the Klimax pass. Once in occupation, he would be unlikely to leave, and his troops would no doubt stay at Perge until the peace was agreed. In the past year Vulso's whole conduct in Asia had been designed to remove all Antiochos' allies, and deprive him of local resources of food and money. In the process he had put the king into such a situation that he was unable to resume the war at the expiry of the truce except at a heavy disadvantage. In this Vulso was wholly successful, and the attempted removal of the Pergean garrison may have been another of the

---

[34] Livy 38.37.9; Polybios 32.26.

elements involved. But one may note that it is not known just when the garrison left, nor whether the thirty-day period had any effect on anyone's actions. By then Vulso had long left the area.

So far as can be seen, Pamphylia as a region was otherwise ignored in the peace settlement, though by implication. if anyone was to be in control it was to be the Pergamene king, Eumenes II: he was awarded various territories, including Phrygia,[35] though Pamphylia was not specified as one of them. Yet his family's activities in the country later suggest that the Attalids did acquire some rights there. Phaselis fell once more under the control of Rhodes, which was awarded control of Karia and Lykia, which are otherwise undefined. Phaselis's coinage appears to cease for the next two decades,[36] which is a good sign in the circumstances that its autonomy had also ceased.

The victory of Rome, and the 'liberation' of the Greek cities of Asia Minor, marked the point at which the close association, or alliance, of the Pamphylian cities was no longer necessary. The joint coinages ceased in 189/188, and the cities separated. Phaselis was put under Rhodian control for twenty years, and the three cities of the plain resumed their independence.[37] With Antiochos confined to his lands east of the Taurus Mountains, the need for the defensive city-alliance ceased. The association of some of the cities did not end, however. When the Romans again became involved in an eastern war, the Pamphylian civic connection is again detectable. In 169 BC a delegation of 'Pamphylians' went to Rome to present to the temple of Jupiter a crown made out of 20,000 gold coins of Macedon, with which kingdom Rome was at that time at war, a present of neat appropriateness in the circumstances. It could also be seen as a gesture of gratitude for having removed Seleukid pressure from the cities twenty years before. In return Rome renewed the former friendship with these 'Pamphylians'.[38] They are not otherwise specified, but in the context of the time they can only be the three cities of the plain. Phaselis was still within the Rhodian sphere, a city with which Rome was just then rather annoyed, and Side and Korakesion were acting most independently, the former insisting on

[35] Livy 38.38.14–17; Polybios 23.29; for discussions, which generally ignore Pamphylia, ses E. Bikerman, 'Notes sur Polybe: Le Statut des villes d'Asie après la paix d'Apamee', *Revue des études grecques* 5, 1937, 217–239, and D. W. Baronowski, 'The Status of the Greek Cities of Asia Minor after 190 BC', *Hermes* 119, 1991, 450–463.

[36] Hiepp-Tamer, *Phaselis*.

[37] There is no justification for the repeated assumption that 'Pamphylia' became a part of the Attalid lands.

[38] Livy 44.14.3–4.

its friendship with the Seleukid king. The 'Pamphylians', acting together, were thus still recognized as a political group by Rome, and the term must refer to the three cities of the plain.

The source information on Pamphylia, so relatively abundant in the reign of Antiochos III, ceases to flow in the decades following the Treaty of Apamea. In international affairs the major local players were now the Attalid kings, with Rome intervening, but neither was directly involved in Pamphylia for some time, though the Attalids were in expansionary mood.

The removal of great quantities of silver from the Seleukid kingdom by Rome as part of the peace terms in 188 left a dearth there. To fill it considerable numbers of coins flowed east out of Asia Minor, including large numbers of the posthumous Alexanders which had been minted in Pamphylia. These no doubt were used to purchase goods from Syria, but there they were countermarked in many cases with the Seleukid symbol of an anchor.[39] This may be not unconnected with the political need in Pamphylia to fend off Attalid attentions; friendship with the Seleukids could be a useful counterweight. In the same way the very public gift of the gold crown to Rome in 169 may be seen as, in part, an anti-Attalid gesture – Eumenes II was not happy about Rome's war with Macedon, and dithered about expressing his support.

Attalid relations were established with Perge, at least, for the city honoured a member of the Attalid family with a statue;[40] it will have been one of the later kings, Eumenes II, Attalos II, or Attalos III, since only these three had any influence in the area. Perge's neighbour city Termessos was given a *stoa* by Attalos II.[41] Geographically this is significant, since it was between these two cities that Attalos founded his new city of Attaleia.

The city was founded where a line of rocks projected out into the sea from the limestone cliffs, and so where a reasonable, but small, port could be organized, though the cliff itself at that point made the site awkward. The rocks formed a bay which could be improved by artificial breakwaters, and the city was placed where a road could connect the city with the routes leading north to Apamea-Kelainai and the nearby cities, and on to the Maiandros valley (see Maps 1, 2). Attalos II succeeded his brother as king at Pergamon in 159 BC; the city would

---

[39] *I. Perge*, 43.

[40] *TAM* III.1.4.

[41] O. Mørkholm, *Early Hellenistic Coinage*, Cambridge 1991, 23 and Boehringer, *Chronologie*, who suggests that there were also, or instead, a communal agreement between the cities and Antiochos III (and presumably his successor Seleukos IV). The heavy presence of Pamphylian coins in Syrian hoards lasts till about 160 BC. The contents of coin hoards from Syria are listed in *IGCH* and *Coin Hoards*.

thus have been founded a few years after that date, probably in the 150s.[42] The city had only a small territory, since there were fully established communities all around it – Magydos, Perge, Olbia, Termessos, and Trebenna (Map 2). Some of its territory may have been taken from some or all of them. (Olbia is an obvious possibility, and it certainly ceased to be a *polis* at some time.) An inscribed stone found at the modern village of Çakırlar in the Çandır valley, states that the area was in the *chora* of Attaleia *polis*.[43] This is west of the supposed site of Olbia, and if Olbia still functioned, its lands were now extremely constricted. Even so, Attaleia's lands did not reach very far even if some or all of Olbia's lands had been taken.

To the north two other villages, Neapolis and Eudokia, were in Termessos's territory in the Roman period.[44] However, there is, further west in the valley leading to the Golcuk Beli pass, a fortified wall which evidently formed a boundary. It has been dated to the second century BC, and was built so as to be controlled by a political authority to its east. It lies just at the point where the path leading up the mountain to Termessos city leaves the valley, and the valley to the west was part of Termessos' lands.[45] That is, it blocks off Termessos from the lands of the valley to the east, which epigraphic evidence at Neapolis and Eudokias shows to be Termessian territory later. The boundary between Termessos and whoever controlled the eastern end of the valley was thus clearly unstable. The only time when a really major political upheaval took place in the area in the second century was when Attaleia was founded. It seems reasonable to conclude that there was conflict between Attalos and Termessos at the time of the city's foundation. (Attalos was at war with Selge for a time and this may have spilled over into war with Termessos, and have been the origin of his move into Pamphylia; this had been what happened with Akhaios; it would then be a case of similar situations resulting in similar actions.) The result was the acquisition by the newly founded city of some lands formerly belonging to Termessos, which lands were later returned to Termessos. The wall was perhaps part of the peace terms; the gift of a *stoa* to Termessos by the king could then be a pacifying gesture.

The wall itself looks formidable, but it has been pointed out that it can be easily outflanked.[46] This is not a serious drawback, for it was mainly designed to

---

[42] The exact date is not known, and is not to be connected with his campaign against the Selgians, which probably took place in 159 or 158. It is conventional to apply the date of 159 to the foundation of the city, but it seems most unlikely that this was the first thing Attalos did on his accession. The mid-150s are perhaps the earliest possible date.

[43] *TIB* 2.493.

[44] *TIB* 2.533–535 and 744–745,

[45] F. E. Winter, 'Notes on Military Architecture in the Termessos Region', *AJA* 70, 1966, 53–58.

[46] Pointed out by Bean, *TSS* 136, who credits Freya Stark with noting this drawback.

channel traffic through the gate, no doubt in part for customs revenue purposes. Its position meant that the Termessians could seize it at any moment, simply by advancing down their valley from the south. It was never going to be attacked from the front. It is a boundary, not a fortification.

Attaleia was laid out as the largest urban community in Pamphylia, no doubt quite deliberately. The bounds of the city are those of the walls which, repaired and improved, still surrounded it in the late nineteenth century. The area inside the walls, ignoring the harbour, is a little over sixty hectares, making it by far the largest city in Pamphylia, half again as big as Perge or Aspendos, and even larger than the expanded Side, whose great walls are also Hellenistic. There is no obvious site for an acropolis. The medieval citadel area enclosed the landward side of the harbour on the north, and this was perhaps the site of the original 'acropolis'. It was, after all, as a harbour city that Attaleia was established, and the harbour and the citadel together would be a power statement of substantial proportions.[47] The size would imply an ultimate population within the walls of about 12,000 people, according to the formula used for the older cities. The *chora*, at least in the early days, was very limited and probably added relatively few to the city's population. It would, of course, take some considerable time for the population to reach its maximum possible, if it ever did.

Examination of the street layout of the old city suggests that it was partly organized on the grid pattern (Map 13). The city walls indicate that the city was roughly circular, and the interior appears to separate into three parts: the fort-acropolis on the northwest, an area of lanes and streets on various alignments behind the harbour; and in the southeastern half two major streets linked by narrower lanes which imply a regular pattern. One of the main streets leads off from the Hadrian Gate, and terminated close to a great tomb of Roman date by the shore, the Hıdırlık Tower. The Kesik Minare, which was originally the Panaghia Church, is aligned on that street. It is paralleled to the north by another street which can also be traced in an almost straight line right across the old city. To either side of these two streets fragments of streets running parallel to them can also be found.

The positions along the streets of the gate, the tower, the Kesik Minare and some smaller remains provide some confidence that the original grid layout has been preserved. The city has been in continuous occupation since its foundation,

---

[47] This is not a definitive description, but in the absence of a serious investigation which can get below the modern city and its medieval remains, this will have to do. In support I might add that all the major ancient remains are within the suggested area within the ancient walls; cf. B. Pace, 'Adalia', *Annuario* 3, 1916–1921, 3–21.

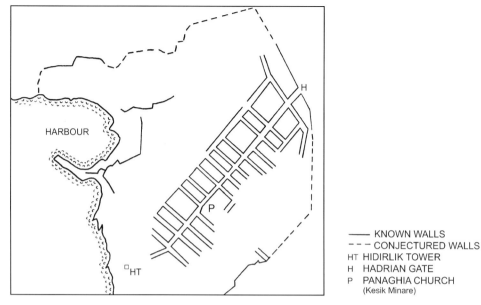

KNOWN WALLS
CONJECTURED WALLS
HT HIDIRLIK TOWER
H HADRIAN GATE
P PANAGHIA CHURCH
   (Kesik Minare)

HARBOUR

H

P

HT

Map 13. Attaleia: traces of grid street pattern

which provides another index of confidence. The northern section of the city, between the streets and the fort-acropolis, does not show such evidence, and the lanes are at all angles. This is close to the harbour area, and an open space for the *agora* and the harbour works and storehouses must have been there; it looks very much as though the southeast quarter was laid out separately from the rest. Note that between the gridded area and the south-east city wall there are lanes on various lines; no doubt an open area was left behind the wall, later occupied by casual residents.

The new city was primarily a port, giving the Attalid kingdom access to the eastern Mediterranean separate from the local cities, and which avoided the many, and possibly hostile, cities of the Aegean coast, and the rocky and dangerous coasts of Karia and Lykia, which by that time were no longer under Rhodian control. In other words, much the same strategic considerations as I have imputed to Kroisos in his intrusion four centuries before were also operating in the 150s. The city's coins, which were produced from its earliest days, powerfully emphasized the sea-connection, on which the main deity being portrayed was Poseidon, sometimes on both sides of the coin and sometimes backed by the similarly maritime image of a dolphin. A certain martial quality is visible also, in the portrayal on several obverses of Nike – a possible reference to the presumed defeat of Termessos. The impression of a seaward orientation of the city is overwhelming.[48]

At the same time as he founded Attaleia, Attalos took control of, and fortified, Korykos, the anchorage which had been used by Antiochos III's fleet in 197.[49] Its only historical use has been as a naval station – it was so used much later by the Byzantine navy – and along with Attaleia this means that Attalos was organizing a naval presence in the Pamphylian Sea, with two bases, one of them a fortified city, the other a fortified anchorage.

The new port was not therefore designed solely for trading purposes, though this was certainly one of its main functions. Given the costs of land transport it would probably be cheaper for merchants to sail past Rhodes and into the Aegean to trade with western Anatolia. On the other hand, Attaleia did become the only sizeable port in Pamphylia. Phaselis is separated from the Pamphylian plain by difficult hills, and Side, which was friendly with, if not allied to, the Seleukids, was distant from the Pamphylian centre. Perge and Aspendos, both substantial cities, were river ports, but their capacity was limited. Attaleia as a port city was clearly a success – it is the only Pamphylian city with a continuous history of occupation and activity since the second century BC.

The foundation of Attaleia permanently altered the local political situation. It was, from the moment of its foundation, physically the largest city in the area, and once it was built and populated it became one of the most powerful. Its growth shifted the urban balance in Pamphylia. Before it was founded, the urban centres were evenly spread across the land, from Phaselis to Side and Korakesion, more or less according to the availability of arable land – a basic consideration which had affected even the port cities of Side and Phaselis. Attaleia was the first to be planted for reasons other than access to farmland. It was a different type of city.

By the time the new city was founded, Phaselis had escaped from Rhodes' control. We have no indication of the city's attitude to its position under Rhodes, but it seems clear that it was pleased to be free even of the Lykian League, of which it was briefly a member after Rhodes' continental lands were removed from it by order of Rome in 167. The evidence for this is, once more, numismatic. Phaselis and its neighbour to the south, the small city of Olympos, produced similar coinages, on the same pattern as the league coins, but inscribed with their own names instead of 'Lykion'. This would indicate that they were

---

[48] N. Baydun, 'Die Münzen von Attaleia in Pamphylia', *JNG*, 26 1975, 33–75 and 1976, 37–78.
[49] Strabo 14.4.1.

no longer in the league, but that they were still using the old coin dies, and in the first minting of these independent coins (called 'pseudo-league coinage' by the numismatists) the two cities in fact used the same obverse die.[50] Olympos produced one set of these coins, and Phaselis three. This indicates a period of only a few years, surely no more than five; Phaselis was probably out of the league by 160 BC. The episode of Rhodian and Lykian domination is reminiscent of those by Athens and Ptolemy earlier. The city submitted, endured its fate for some years, and as soon as the controller's strength waned, shook itself free. Minting a new set of autonomous coins is a sign of its freedom, and by this time it was a traditional gesture which had been used several times. The only change to the pattern this time may have been a lack of resistance to the imposition of Rhodes' dominion, but Rhodes may well have exerted force; we do not know. The independence of Phaselis came not long before the intrusion of Attalos at Attaleia and Korykos; these changes profoundly altered the political situation in this corner of the bay.

The need for careful and nimble diplomacy by such small powers as single cities and small alliance groups, in order to survive in a world of ruthless and heavy-handed powers, has been commented on already. The city of Side had, separately from the rest of the Pamphylians, pursued its own path. In 220 and in 193 it had publicly proclaimed its attachment to the Seleukid cause, as it probably had back in the 290s. Later the city was to show it retained that attachment. After 188, however, the city seems also to have developed a friendly attachment to the Attalid monarchy, for its coins circulated widely in Attalid territory, though being subjected to validating countermarking at various places, just as those of Aspendos and Perge were countermarked in Syria.[51]

---

[50] H. A. Troxell, *The Coinage of the Lycian League*, New York 1982, 68, suggests that Phaselis and Olympos became members of the Lykian League in 'the latter part of the [second] century', but any precise date is not available. It seems most likely that the cities' brief membership was in the 160s directly after the end of Rhodian control; even if their membership was a generation later, it was still only brief.

[51] Countermarks of ten cities in the Attalid sphere are listed in Head *HN*, 704, and are interpreted as:

ADRA – Adramyttion
APA – Apamea
EPHE – Ephesos
LAO – Laodikeia
PER – Pergamon
SALE – Sala ?
SAR – Sardes
STRA – Stratonikeia
SUN – Synnada
TRA – Tralles.

Side's coins of the second century BC show Nike – 'victory' – holding a wreath, with Side's pomegranate in the field. There is no indication of over whom the victory was won, but the excavation of the south gate in the Hellenistic walls revealed that it was decorated with a relief showing weapons and armour.[52] The walls themselves have been dated to the second century. Linking these two items is probably reasonable, for they are of roughly the same period, but the identification of the enemy who was beaten and against whom the walls defended the city is problematic. The only fighting on land in which we know Side was involved was in alliance with Antiochos III in 193 against the Etenneis.[53] Since this was certainly a victory, and friendship with the Seleukids is a constant in Sidetan affairs, this is the event most likely commemorated.

By about 150 BC the number of Pamphylian cities had increased to eight (assuming Olbia no longer existed as a *polis*). Apart from the promotions of small towns in the Roman period this was to be the maximum number. Not only was Attaleia a large new city, most of the others had expanded substantially in the previous two centuries. Perge's lower city, Korakesion's walls, Phaselis's *Nordsiedlung*, Side's expansion and its new walls, had all been laid out and built in that time, and no doubt investigation will eventually show growth at Sillyon and Aspendos also. This was a major process of urbanization, in a time when terrifying threats – Ptolemaic fleets, Seleukid armies and fleets, Roman consuls, Attalid kings – approached and invaded. To have come through such turbulent times, to have survived and prospered and grown, argues a confidence and resilience and determination among the citizens which is surely wholly admirable. Needless to say, such success and survival was soon threatened, and the black cloud in the west, the Roman Republic, soon grew to overshadow the whole scene, affecting it increasingly for the next century and more.

---

[52] Bean, TSS 62 and plate 30.
[53] Livy, 35.13.6.

7

Pirates and Romans

The Pamphylians had been relatively fortunate in their relations with the great men of the Hellenistic world. They had not been in the way of any of the great warriors' destructive marches. Alexander might be seen as an exception, but his passage was brief and not seriously damaging. Ptolemy I affected the margins only. Antiochos III had more effect, and his defeat brought a Roman army close, but his and its visits were brief and again little or no damage had been caused to any of the cities. The intrusion of Attalos II to found his new city at Attaleia was, however, much more dangerous, since it seemed to signal a permanent foreign presence in the heart of the region. Then in 133 Attalos III bequeathed his kingdom to the Romans.

For the Pamphylians this marked the beginning of a new and dangerous time. New threats developed simultaneously in western and southern Asia Minor: the approach of Rome from the west and north became more threatening and slowly came closer; the pirate menace at sea off the south coast became increasingly a problem. These two menaces eventually clashed and Pamphylia for once was in the midst of affairs. During the century after the death of Attalos III in 133 the country was slowly, and at times painfully, brought into the Roman Empire, and this was in part a result of the proximity of the pirates. Once again a relatively brief period of time contains a set of events which created sources which shine a revealing light on the area.

Pamphylia's geographical situation between the sea and the mountains had been echoed repeatedly by its political situation between the seaward powers (Athens, Sparta, Ptolemy I and II, Antiochos III, Hannibal) and the landward rulers (Kroisos, the Akhaimenids, Antigonos, Akhaios, Antiochos III again, Attalos). From 133 BC that landward ruler became Rome, firmly established in the Lydia of Kroisos and Akhaios, which now became the province of Asia. Whereas most of the preceding kings and governors had only tentatively reached into Pamphylia, Rome was more like the Akhaimenids, relentless, overwhelming, and long-lived.

Rome's intervention took a considerable time to develop, however. For a start, the transfer of the Pergamene kingdom to Rome took place over a period of several years. Rome at first hesitated to accept Attalos III's bequest, for its acceptance would have grave effects on internal Roman politics, and this hesitation gave time for a major 'rebellion' to develop under the leadership of a bastard son of King Attalos II, Aristonikos. The fighting did not end until 129, when the consul M'. Aquillius finally crushed the last holdouts.[1] Aquillius was then retained for three more years as proconsul in the new province of Asia[2] in order to see to its organization and government, in which task he was assisted by a commission of ten senators. The final settlement, by an act of Rome, was not completed even when Aquillius left in 126; it was perhaps not fully enacted until as late as 123.[3]

It almost goes without saying that no clear statement survives to indicate the fate of Pamphylia and its cities in this prolonged crisis, and so it is necessary to proceed by indirection as usual. First, it needs to be recalled that the preceding history of the country shows that the Pamphylian cities owed allegiance to a variety of authorities before 133. Attaleia and Korykos were Attalid possessions; Phaselis was a former member of the Lykian League and now independent; Side was, as ever, operating independently, but had been the refuge-city of the current Seleukid king Antiochos VII Sidetes (reigning 138 to 129), and was traditionally friendly towards the Seleukid royal family; Perge, Aspendos, and Sillyon were probably allied to one another, and had the status of friends of Rome, a status which had been resumed and recorded in 169. Aspendos was, of old, hostile to Side; Side was friendly both to the Attalids and to the Seleukid king. Its neighbour Korakesion had been a pirate base under the Seleukid usurper Tryphon (Antiochos VII's former enemy), and it was probably still a place hospitable to pirates, as it was to be half a century later.

The Roman measures thus fell most directly and immediately on Attaleia and Korykos. One source seems to indicate that these two cities were handed to the sons of the king of Kappadokia. Ariarathes V of that kingdom had been killed in battle during the war with Aristonikos, and this could be seen as compensation for his loss. The source is Justin, in his shortened paraphrase of the earlier historian Pompeius Trogus: he reports that Lykaonia and 'Kilikia' was given

---

[1] E. S. Gruen, *The Hellenistic World and the Coming of Rome*, Berkeley and Los Angeles 1984, 600–605; R. M. Kallet-Marx, *Hegemony to Empire, the Development of the Roman Imperium in the East from 148 to 62 BC*, Berkeley and Los Angeles 1995, 99–111.

[2] T. R. S. Broughton, *The Magistrates of the Roman Republic*, New York, 1951–1960, Vol 1, 509 and 503.

[3] Gruen, *Hellenistic World*, 607–608.

to Ariarathes' sons.[4] This is clearly wrong, for Kilikia at the time was Seleukid territory, though it could perhaps refer to Rough Kilikia, but this had not been part of the Attalid kingdom, and was not Rome's to allocate. The passage has therefore been interpreted as referring to the later Roman republican province of Kilikia, an indeterminate region which at one time included Pamphylia and Pisidia and even Lykia; it is thus argued, in this serpentine way, that Pamphylia was awarded to the Ariarathids.[5]

One has one's doubts. For a start, Kappadokia in the 120s was scarcely a stable enough kingdom for its king to take on any further responsibilities – it was at enmity with Mithradates V of Pontos, and there were disputes and murders inside the royal family, which made the kingdom thoroughly unreliable.[6] And then 'Pamphylia' had never been a single unit, except geographically; in the 130s it was a set of cities, some of them clearly and determinedly independent states. The Ariarathids, based far away in north-central Anatolia, would have as much difficulty in exercising control in Pamphylia as had the ancient Hittites. Giving Pamphylia to Kappadokia is not, that is, in the least likely. The Roman commission and Aquillius did not distribute the Asian booty quite so carelessly; nor did they do so with such a contempt for local opinion.

If the idea of the transfer of Pamphylia to Kappadokia is dismissed, then it is necessary to consider the situation of each city individually. Attaleia and Korykos certainly became Rome's to dispose of by right of both inheritance and conquest: they had been bequeathed by Attalos III and conquered from Aristonikos. These places were all that could be handed to the Ariarathids, if any were. The rest of the country was already friendly to or allied with Rome, and will have been left alone – with the possible exception of Side. There was no need to decide anything about Phaselis, since, having been freed of Rhodian control in 167, it was therefore automatically already a Roman client.[7]

The settlement commission, under instructions from the Senate, was clearly determined to restrict Roman responsibilities in Asia to the minimum. This means that most of Pamphylia remained independent; only Korykos and Attaleia were available for distribution. Independence in relation to the Roman Empire was a limited thing, however, and Pamphylia, like all the rest of western and central Asia Minor, was now regarded by Rome as part of the empire of the

---

[4] Justin 37.1.2.

[5] A. N. Sherwin-White, 'Rome, Pamphylia and Lycia, 133–70 BC', *JRS* 66, 1976, 1–14.

[6] Justin 37.1.3; but see B. C. McGing, *The Foreign Policy of Mithradates Eupator King of Pontus*, Leiden 1986, 73; Justin has mixed up the wives of Ariarathes V and VI; the former was Nysa, the latter Laodike.

[7] H. A. Troxell, *The Coinage of the Lycian League*, New York 1983, 68.

Roman people. As a visible testimony to this fact, M'. Aquillius ordered and oversaw the construction of a road from (probably) Pergamon into Pamphylia. The road, called the Via Aquillia, passed through a series of Anatolian cities and then south to the coast at Attaleia. This was clearly the main route, but a branch went off eastwards at least as far as Side, and this is marked by a milestone which has been found near Side. It has Aquillius' name and the distance 331 (Roman) miles, which is accurate for a measurement along the road from Pergamon, depending on the route followed.[8]

This road was one of three built in the 130s and 120s as highways of empire – the Via Domitiana from Italy to Narbo Martius in southern Gaul, the Via Egnatia from the Adriatic coast to Thrace and the Hellespont, and the Via Aquillia through Asia to the southern coast. They were organized and built in order to provide the Romans with the means of responding militarily to distant crises. The roads themselves were not, of course, actually new, but were old routes, even age-old, which were now marked out by Roman milestones. The stone at Side is inscribed in Latin and Greek, though probably no one in Pamphylia could read Latin; the stones were therefore guides for Roman troops. The road from Attaleia to Side surely already existed, though the section from Attaleia to Perge will have developed only since Attaleia's own foundation.

The organisation of this road and its designation with the consul's name is clearly a mark of Roman power, but it is not necessarily a sign of actual Roman rule. Many of the places through which it passed were, in formal terms, independent (Pergamon, Kolossai, Hierapolis, for example), and this category will have included the Pamphylian cities. There is no reason to suppose that these cities had concerned Rome at any time in the past. The 'Pamphylii' had renewed their friendship with Rome in 169, and their status as Roman 'friends' – whatever that meant in precise terms – implies their recognition as independent cities at the time; and their status had not changed since then. But that renewal of friendship had probably applied only to the three cities of the plain. The destination of the road was, so far as we can tell, Side, and this also suggests that Side fell into the category of Roman friend. As a friend of the former Attalid dynasty this would make sense, for the city would wish to maintain its economic ties with the area of the new province. That it was also a friend or ally of Antiochos VII had ceased to apply after his death in 129;

---

[8] D. H. French, 'Sites and Inscriptions from Phrygia, Pisidia and Pamphylia', *Ep. Anat.* 17, 1991, 51–58 at 53–54; this is also discussed by S. Mitchell, 'The Administration of Roman Asia from 133 BC to AD 250', in W. Eck (ed.), *Lokale Autonomie und römische Ordnungsmacht in den kaiserzeitlichen Provinzen von 1 bis 3 Jahrhundert*, Munich 1999, 17–46, though he ignores Attaleia; given the recent warfare it is surely likely that this city was the primary destination in Pamphylia for the road.

the subsequent disturbances in Syria were unsettling enough for Rome to wish for relatively easy access to the Syrian threshold; and the Roman road reaching its very gate would be an inducement for Side to consider its best interests. Yet Side being the target of the road did not necessarily affect the city's political status; it was still an independent state.

For Attaleia, one must begin with the fact that the city, being part of Attalos' kingdom, was clearly at Roman disposal after the war, and that the Via Aquillia was aimed directly at it, or close to it – the branch to Side was surely an extra. Geographically, however, the city was separated from that part of the former Attalid kingdom which eventually became the new province of Asia. Fifty years after the Roman conquest, in the 70s, the proconsul P. Servilius Vatia deprived the city of some of its territory[9] because it had become involved in the pirate problem. This suggests that the city was acting as an independent state until his arrival, and that, whatever Rome thought was the situation, in practice Attaleia had become an independent city state in the same way as the other Pamphylian cities. Its coins certainly show no recognition of Roman authority: the same types were minted from the origin of the city in the 150s till about 100, and were marked as *Attaleion*, 'of the Attaleians'.[10] No doubt Servilius' action in punishing the city was a sharp reminder that Rome's memory was as long as its arm, but he did not treat Attaleia any differently than he did Phaselis and Olympos, who also had lands confiscated, and for the same reason. This set of minimal evidence suggests that in the commission's settlement in the 120s Attaleia was put into the same category of independent-but-client cities as Phaselis, but both were able to act independently.

From the 120s, therefore, Pamphylia once more consisted of a set of independent cities, all the way around the bay from Phaselis to Korakesion. Some of them had friendship agreements with Rome; all of them, whether they realized it or not, were expected to do as Rome said, and were regarded, in a tenuous way, as parts of the empire of the Roman people. On the other hand, Rome did not show much interest in the area; in this the city adopted the attitude of neglect which all other great powers had taken towards Pamphylia.

During that same period, 130–78 BC, the pirates entered the power equation in the seas off Pamphylia. The origins of this problem are put in the 140s, specifically at Korakesion, which was used as a base for a time by the Seleukid usurper Tryphon. But piracy had never ceased in the Mediterranean; what was new was the unusual scale of the plague, as perceived above all at Rome – though

[9] Cicero, *De leg. agr.*, 5.10.
[10] N. Baydun, 'Die Münzen von Attaleia an Pamphylia', *JNG* 26, 1975, 33–72, and 1976, 37–78.

exaggeration was clearly involved, since the issue became entangled with the internal politics of the city.[11]

The actions and reactions of the Pamphylian cities towards the pirates who were their neighbours should have been affected by that relationship towards Rome. However, just as any modern estimate of that relationship is uncertain, so it was also probably uncertain to the citizens. Rome's relationships with other communities were defined by Rome herself, and it was rarely felt necessary to explain it to those others. To Greeks, being liberated by a great power was an old story, going back to the successors of Alexander, and they were generally comfortable with the distant suzerainty which that implied, but Rome was exceptionally negligent in failing to massage that mutual relationship. There is no sign of any contact between Rome and the Pamphylians for three decades after Aquillius, and it seems likely that the Pamphylians, ignored by Rome, themselves ignored Rome. They were compelled to act as independent cities by Roman negligence, and so became independent – but only until Rome chose, for its own reasons, to intervene in the area once more.

The problem of the Kilikian pirates is the source of most of the information about Pamphylia for the next fifty and more years. The first time Rome took serious measures against them was in 102, when the propraetor M. Antonius conducted a campaign against the pirate bases in Rough Kilikia. His naval force was largely composed of ships from several Aegean cities as far off as Byzantion, and he also used locally raised armed forces on land. His local base was Side, and from there he campaigned along the coast of Rough Kilikia,[12] by both sea and land (thus using what was in effect a prolongation of the Via Aquillia) (see Map 14).

Nothing in Pamphylia apart from Side is mentioned in this episode, though it has to be said that the sources are very poor and fragmentary. The implication of what we do know is that Pamphylia from Phaselis to Side was not involved in the pirate problem, and that Side itself was not yet the notorious pirate market it was later reported to be – or, of course, that this was not seen to be reprehensible. Strabo, a century later, described the city as the place where pirates had their ships built, where they sold their loot, and where they auctioned off their captives,[13] but none of this was necessarily regarded as wrong in contemporary terms.

---

[11] On the pirates cf. H. A. Ormerod, *Piracy in the Ancient World*, Liverpool 1926, and P. de Souza, *Piracy in the Greco-Roman World*, Cambridge 1999.

[12] Livy, *Epitome* 68 and *Obsequens* 44; *ILRRP* 1.342; Tacitus, *Annals* 12.62; De Souza, *Piracy,* 102–108.

[13] Strabo 14.3.2.

At the same time, a city with such a reputation as Strabo gives it was hardly the sort of place the Roman commander would have chosen as his anti-pirate headquarters, unless Antonius did so in order to put the fear of Rome into the citizens. However, Side was not punished, as far as we know, and Antonius mainly operated along the coast to the east of the city in his campaign. He was regarded at Rome as successful. What he achieved in concrete terms is unclear, but he was awarded a triumph, and elected consul for the year 99.[14]

This Roman campaign was just one of a series against the pirates at about this time. Athens sent an expedition as far as Kilikia, for which the city was thanked by Kythnos, Phaselis, and the Lykian League, all of whom may be presumed to have been victims of the pirates.[15] The Lykians, or at least the city of Xanthos, sent a fleet east under a local commander, Aichmon, who campaigned in the area of Cape Chelidonia.[16] Neither of these expeditions was decisive. Like that of Antonius they had some success but only in the short term; pirate activity was restricted only briefly as a result. All three expeditions are probably to be connected with a new law issued by Rome, *the lex de provinciis propraetoriis*, which pretended to encourage local authorities to mount their own anti-pirate measures. It seems unlikely that the Greek and Anatolian communities subjected to pirate attacks needed any such encouragement, still less that they would seek permission from far-off Rome to strike back. The inscription recording the Athenian expedition notes that it was reported to a Roman magistrate, L. Furius Crassipes, but there is nothing in it which can be construed as seeking Roman permission; the record of the Lykian expeditions of Aichmon have no reference to Rome at all.

The longer-term result of such measures was rather different. Rome's attention, when it was not directed to matters at home, was largely taken up by the activities of Mithradates VI of Pontus for the next twenty years, and then with the civil war and revolution in Italy. By the time Rome was sufficiently interested to take action against them, the pirates had become more widely active; it may be that Antonius' campaign had stung them into greater activity. The Romans, of course, tended to blame Mithradates. It is in this period, from about 100 to the 60s BC that we must see them as most threatening, and Side as so involved in their activities as to become notorious. The pirates also used Phaselis as another of their markets, and they are said to have gone on to form an alliance with the

---

[14] Broughton, *Magistrates*, 1.572 and 2.1.

[15] *IG* II.2.328; L. Robert, 'Hellenica XXI: Trihemiolies Athéniennes', *Opera Minora Selecta*, 3, 1377–1383.

[16] *OGIS* 552–554.

city, whatever that might mean.[17] Another supposed friend of the pirates was Zeniketos, a hilltop chieftain of the Solymoi, who had seized control of both Olympos and Korykos, and soon after of Phaselis as well.[18] Attaleia was also involved, or at least so the Romans believed.

The pirates, in fact, were not simply slavering barbarians; their activities were as much commercial as criminal. They were based in areas outside the sphere of any of the major states and those bases were political organizations akin to city-states. Some of them, such as Korakesion, were actually recognized *poleis*, others were smaller and more rural. The pirate personnel came from many areas. At Syedra in Rough Kilikia, just along the coast from Korakesion, an inscription of this time records the city's attempts to gain guidance from the oracle of Apollo at Klaros, in which Syedra is called 'the home of mixed peoples'.[19] The city seems to have wanted to resist the pirates, but its people were divided, both ethnically and politically, and were unable to reach a clear decision; hence the resort to the oracle. It may be assumed that their case was fairly typical, and that the response in Pamphylia – the country of 'mixed peoples' – and Lykia to the activities of the pirates based further east was similarly ambivalent; they were both a danger and a source of profit. At the same time, 'piracy' was a helpful accusation to make at anyone who was an enemy.[20] This is illustrated most clearly by what we know of Zeniketos and the cities the coast of western Pamphylia.

Because he was dealt with by the proconsul P. Servilius Vatia, who is said to have conducted a campaign against the pirates, Zeniketos is all too easily classified as a pirate himself. But his base was inland, apparently on a mountain behind Olympos, and an inland mountain is an unlikely base for a sea-going pirate.[21] Zeniketos's principality originated at a hill fort on one of the local hills, and he extended his grip to the small towns of Korykos and Olympos; Phaselis, a bigger city, was taken next. It is not clear just when Zeniketos took these places, but he was holding them in 78 BC, when he was the object of Servilius Vatia's attention. Zeniketos' career is not that of a pirate, though he probably controlled a war fleet, for Phaselis at least was a minor sea power. He was a conqueror, possibly to the citizens a barbarian; in all likelihood he was

[17] Cicero, *Verrines*, 4.21.

[18] Strabo 14.5.7.

[19] C. E. Bean and T. B. Mitford, *Journeys in Rough Cilicia in 1962 and 1963*, Vienna 1965, 21–23; P. De Souza, 'Romans and Pirates in a Late Hellenistic Oracle from Pamphylia', *Classical Quarterly* 47, 1997, 477–481.

[20] In the same way, 'terrorist' is a label pinned on any enemy in the early twenty-first century, partly as a means of enlisting the sympathy (and money) of the United States.

[21] Strabo 14.5.7.

a Solymian; he represented the latest stage in the continuing struggle between the cities of that coast and the people inland, a struggle as old as the Greek settlement at Phaselis.

Zeniketos' conquests produced a small principality which was fairly typical of the Lykian area at the time; another was constructed by a man called Moagetes based at the city of Kibyra, and had been suppressed by a Roman commander a few years before.[22] Zeniketos may have had dealings with the pirates, as is recorded separately for Phaselis, but he was actually expanding his principality at the expense of the nearby cities. Dealing with pirates was quite normal for the cities around the Pamphylian Sea, and Zeniketos is only linked with piracy by these dealings, and by the fact that his conqueror is said to have been sent to fight these pirates. It is worth noting that both Olympos and Phaselis had client relationships with Rome as a result of their being freed from Rhodian domination in 167; yet Rome had paid no attention to their capture by Zeniketos.

The Romans had enacted the *lex de provinciis propraetoriis* soon after the expedition of Antonius. One aspect of this law, as its name indicated, was to regularize the situation with regard to Rome and the pirates: the pirates were declared enemies, and all allies were directed to oppose them. Local forces were empowered to act against the pirates in Rome's name, apparently independently and without pre-arrangement. This was, after all, the only way to deal efficiently with what is best seen as a guerilla campaign at sea.[23] The *propraetor* of the province involved – Kilikia – was to coordinate the fighting. This may have been the origin of the dilemma the Syedrans faced, and which they attempted to resolve by consulting the oracle. But it all took time, and those allies were at times more in danger from Romans than from the pirates.

C. Verres was *quaestor* to Cn. Cornelius Dolabella, *propraetor* of Kilikia in 81–79, and he came from the north to the cities of the Pamphylian plain. Verres, whose Pamphylian activities took place in 79, is accused of plundering the temple of Artemis at Perge and another temple at Aspendos, though knowledge of his depredations in Pamphylia is rather overshadowed by his later activities in Sicily.[24] What Verres had been sent to do in Pamphylia is not stated, but the pirate war was the only issue concerning Rome we know of in the area at the

---

[22] Strabo 13.4.17; this was a principality which had existed for a century by the time it was destroyed, by the propraetor L. Licinius Murena. The current ruler, another Moagetes, had been too hospitable to the Roman enemy Mithradates.

[23] The law is published in its fullest form by M. Hassall, M. Crawford, and J. Reynolds, 'Rome and the Eastern Provinces at the end of the Second Century BC', *JRS* 64, 1974, 195–220, and by M. Crawford, *Roman Statutes*, London 1996, 231–271.

[24] Cicero, *Verrines*, 2.1.21.

time, and Dolabella had the Kilikian command, a region of southern Asia Minor which had no precise boundaries. Verres was thus in Pamphylia as Dolabella's subordinate and agent. Dolabella was almost as notoriously acquisitive as Verres, and it is tempting to assume that Verres was in Pamphylia merely to steal, and Cicero later asserted that that is what he did. But Dolabella had political duties which he could not neglect, and Verres, as his representative required an official reason for his journey to the south. The only reason for a Roman commander to be in Pamphylia in 79 was in connection with the pirates. Since Verres visited Perge and Aspendos, this probably means that Dolabella had sent him to take anti-pirate measures; any thieving he did was an extra, and his acquisitions may have actually been gifts from the cities; or he may have been appropriating treasures to use them to finance the fight against the pirates. Presumably his primary anti-pirate measures, perhaps no more than ensuring that the cities of the plain were not actively pro-pirate, were successful; at any rate if he had failed in his primary task one may have expected Cicero to comment on it later.

The next serious, specifically Roman, attempt to deal with the pirates after that of Antonius was the expedition of P. Servilius Vatia, consul in 79, and proconsular governor of Kilikia from 78 to 74 (and so Dolabella's immediate successor).[25] Verres's visit to Pamphylia will have reminded the cities there that the Roman intention was to deal with the pirates, and faced with this they will presumably have reduced any relations with them to an absolute minimum. Servilius' command was not an area of territory, but a task; he was able to go wherever he could find 'Kilikians' and 'pirates'.[26] He began by eliminating Zeniketos. He captured Olympos, a loss which drove Zeniketos to suicide, and went on to take over Korykos and Phaselis, which will have been a simple task once Zeniketos was dead. Then he dealt with Attaleia, which was also seemingly involved with the pirates, for Servilius deprived the city of some of its land, a punishment he also imposed on Olympos and Phaselis; the land became the property of the Roman people.[27]

Servilius can be traced from Olympos to Korykos to Phaselis and on to Attaleia, all of which places he is recorded as visiting or capturing; Verres in 79 had been in Perge and Aspendos on behalf of Dolabella, Servilius' predecessor, a

[25] Broughton, *Magistrates* 2.81 and 85.
[26] R. Syme. 'Observations on the Province of Cilicia', in W. C. Calder and J. Keel (eds), *Anatolian Studies presented to W. H. Buckler*, Manchester 1939, 299–332; P. Freeman, 'The Province of Cilicia and its Origins', in P. Freeman and D. Kennedy (eds), *The Defence of the Roman and Byzantine East*, BAR S297, vol. 1, 1986, 252–275.
[27] Strabo 14.5.7; Cicero, *De leg. Agr.*, 5.10, and *Verrines* 2.1.21, and several later references; H. A. Ormerod, 'The Campaign of Servilius Vatia against the Pirates', *JRS* 12, 1922, 35–56.

The pirates generally were never more than a nuisance, and were never a serious problem, at least for Rome, though for smaller communities by the sea they could be a danger. They had been cleared from Pamphylia easily enough, and their subjugation in their Rough Kilikian bases took only a couple of months in the end. The minor rulers who were aggressively expanding their principalities, men like Zeniketos, were also no more than subsidiary problems. Pamphylia, therefore, was only a peripheral area in these minor problems.

The real problem for Rome in Anatolia was always Mithradates, and again Pamphylia's involvement in the great contest between the two was only marginal. During his first war with Rome (88–85 BC), Mithradates gained control of much of the Roman province of Asia, but he did not have much success in the south, where a series of sieges (Patara, Stratonikeia, Rhodes) absorbed many of his troops and took up much of his time. Mithradates sent officers to the Pamphylian cities at the start of the war, and Appian claims that the land was 'subjugated',[32] but he says the same about Lykia and Ionia, and then goes on to discuss the fighting in both areas, so it is clear that parts at least of those countries were never in Mithradates' control. It does not seem as though he had much time or many resources to spare for Pamphylia, which was not really important to his Roman war, and was wholly marginal to his purposes. The absorption of many of his forces in the attacks on various cities, including one on nearby Termessos, will have allowed the Pamphylian cities to sit back and wait to see what resulted. Later, in 85, L. Licinius Lucullus is said to have formed a fleet of ships from 'Cyprus, Phoenicia, Rhodes, and Pamphylia';[33] in this company Pamphylia was suitably listed last, though it would be helpful to know just which cities were involved. (Phaselis and Side, of course, are the obvious candidates.)

Once again, the cities of Pamphylia had receded to the edge of events, and even when the Romans and the pirates fought each other in the Pamphylian area, they had not been the centre of attention for long. Only Korakesion was an active pirate base; Side and Phaselis and Attaleia, and perhaps the other cities, provided the pirates with markets in which to sell their loot, but this was no more than passive collaboration, not a full participation in their piratical deeds. They were providing no greater assistance to the pirates than did Rome itself, which was the greatest absorber of the slaves they captured and sold. The punishment meted out to Phaselis and Attaleia was only minor, and we hear of no punishment at all for Side, despite Strabo's accusations against the city.

[32] Appian, *Mithradatic Wars*, 20.
[33] *Ibid.*, 57.

Verres may have stolen from Perge and Aspendos, but his actual presence there was quite legitimate, whatever criminality he also undertook. The involvement of Pamphylia in the Mithradatic Wars was similarly minimal; there had been a visit by a Mithradatic officer and a few ships were contributed to Lucullus' fleet by the cities on the coast. The reality of Roman-Pamphylian relations was that each provincial governor had a different viewpoint and a different policy, different tasks and a different agenda, and each man required to be approached and negotiated with individually, while each also needed to negotiate separately with each city. It would seem reasonable to assume that the Pamphylian cities all had the same difficulty in accommodating themselves to the erratic Roman demands.[34]

The presence and actions of Verres and Vatia in Pamphylia made it quite clear that the region was part of the Roman Empire. The actions of Zeniketos, of the pirates, and the coining of money at the various cities, had earlier carried the implication that the cities and their neighbours were able to act independently – though the actions of Antonius, and the *lex de provinciis propraetoriis* (if the Pamphylians knew of it) might have given them all pause for thought.

This inclusion of Pamphylia and its cities within the Roman Empire had come about gradually and slowly, and without the disruptive conquest which damaged Asia and Hispania and so many other provinces. It was only after a century of involvement with Rome that the inhabitants became fully aware that the process of inclusion within the empire had taken place, and by that time it was too late to enter any objections. It is equally impossible for us to locate the decisive moment, the point of no return, after which imperial subjection was a reality. One could argue persuasively for one or more of several dates: for 188, when the Seleukid power evaporated from Asia Minor as a result of Roman actions; for 169, when several cities protested their loyalty to Rome with gifts and were referred to as the friends of Rome; for 133, with the bequest of the Attalid kingdom to Rome, if Pamphylia as a whole is to be regarded as Attalid territory; or for 129, when Asia was conquered and the great road was organised by M'. Aquillius as far as Side, and so right through Pamphylia; or even for as late as 76 BC, with the transit of P. Servilius Vatia and his forces and his confiscation of lands at Attaleia, Olympos and Phaselis. Indeed, by 76 BC it is certain that Pamphylia was Roman without any doubt, and the earlier dates by comparison look distinctly ambiguous. In reality, each of these events and dates marked a stage in the process of incorporation, though what was clearly definitive by 76 may still have been regarded as uncertain in 100 BC.

[34] Sherwin-White, 'Rome, Pamphylia and Cilicia'.

It is only with hindsight that this process may seem inexorable and inevitable. For most of the time the cities of Pamphylia pursued their own affairs in the same low-key fashion they had done through the previous several centuries. And indeed the most obviously decisive moments, 129 and 76, could be said to have affected only some of the Pamphylian cities. The three cities of the plain insisted on their coins into the imperial period that they were allies of Rome rather than her subjects; by then, of course, the distinction was minimal.

This gradual incorporating process was in the end far more effective than any of the earlier imperial adventures into Pamphylia had ever been and was perhaps all the more effective for the very negligence by which it was carried out. The intrusions of Kroisos and Akhaios and Ptolemy were scarcely conquests at all, so brief were they, and the 'conquest' of Alexander was no more than a superficial transit. The only real conquest of Pamphylia had been by the Akhaimenids, which, perhaps not by coincidence, is as undatable and perhaps had been just as slow, if not quite so prolonged, as was the Roman; certainly both Akhaimenids and Romans laid only light burdens on the area, financial and political. These empires endured because they were both large and all-enclosing, moving forward with a relentless, negligent, patience.

From the time of the bequest, conquest, and destruction of the Attalid kingdom in 133–129 there could be no doubt that Roman wishes were paramount in the conduct of Pamphylian affairs, and that from then on it would be necessary to take account of likely Roman wishes in any of the policies pursued by the cities – yet there is no sign, at least until Antonius in 102, that Rome had anything to do with the area. In the 70s Servilius Vatia had no compunction about punishing three cities for having commercial relations with the pirates. These cities were treated, that is, as contumacious subjects, and if any of them protested there is no record of it. But it is noticeable that two had been rescued from alien subjection – to Zeniketos – and that Attaleia had been an Attalid city: Rome had the rights of a patron over a client in all three places. It cannot have been unknown in those cities that this legal condition existed, and if both parties chose to ignore it for a long time, this did not mean it was unimportant, nor that it had expired. So we can say that Attaleia was definitely part of Rome's empire from 129, but Phaselis' citizens city may not have been realized their city's status as a Roman subject until then.

The real test for the cities of the plain had been Verres' conduct at Perge and Aspendos. If he really behaved as Cicero claims he did then the cities could have resisted, had they believed they were fully independent. They did not resist, which rather suggests that Cicero distorted what had happened, but also that Verres was operating in communities which already reckoned themselves within the empire of the Roman people. To those with eyes to see the region had been part of the Roman Empire for at least the two previous generations.

The expedition by Servilius Vatia in 76 made it all clear, from Phaselis to Side, even to those obtuse enough not to have noticed until then. Pompeius' conquest of Korakesion in 67 completed the tally. By 67 BC, all the cities had been fully integrated into the empire, and were subject to its laws and its governors. The cities were now unambiguously part of the Roman Empire and they were to remain within that empire until they died. Indeed their existence and that of the empire were now inexorably intertwined. They had existed for perhaps six centuries as independent cities; they were to be part of the Roman Empire for twice that length of time.

8

Imperial Subjects

The enclosure of the Pamphylian cities within the Roman Empire lasted, let us say, from 76 BC until AD 1207, almost 1300 years, twice as long as the cities had already existed. It is therefore as Roman subjects that the cities and their citizens mainly lived. Yet 'Roman' is a flexible historical term. The cities became 'Roman' during the Republican period, which collapsed into world-wide civil wars in the first century BC; the period following, the Imperial, also shifted its shape – in the form of the relatively lightly governed Principate until the third century AD, then the more tightly governed Dominate, now becoming called 'Late Antique'. Each of these periods is reckoned to last several centuries; finally, there was the Byzantine period, which coincides with the Arab and Turkish invasions, when the cities were driven to destruction over another period of several centuries.

The subject of this chapter is the first of these periods, the three centuries from the enclosure of Pamphylia into the Roman Empire to the late third century AD. This is a period in which very little in the way of political events happened in Pamphylia or to Pamphylia, so the information which can be used tends to throw light on the social situation rather than politics and warfare. It will be well to begin with the governmental system to which the area was subject.

The 'province' of Kilikia, which was used as a convenient term of reference in the Roman Republic in the first century BC as an area of authority for a proconsul in southern Asia Minor, was a variable geographical area, which did not include Kilikia itself. It existed from about 100 BC until Pompeius' conquest of Smooth Kilikia in 65 BC, after which it acquired a definite territorial aspect, and was applied to the historical Kilikia.[1] This temporary and variable province was actually therefore an area facing *towards* Kilikia, not Kilikia itself – a command against the Kilikians, that is, the pirates – in which Roman forces could defend the empire, or from which they could launch attacks. The inhabitants of the lands from Pisidia round to Rough Kilikia were regarded as

---

[1] See references in note 26, chapter 7.

hostile, or potentially hostile, to Rome, and this included the pirate bases. When Kilikia itself was finally acquired by Rome – Smooth Kilikia, at least – the large indefinite command ceased to exist.

Pamphylia had been included in the republican version of 'Kilikia' only because it bordered on the troubled and hostile regions of Pisidia and Rough Kilikia. Once the command vanished, it seems that Pamphylia was not included in any of the organised provinces of the empire for some decades; since it was composed of a group of self-governing cities, it may have been felt that a governor was not really needed. Its inclusion in the empire was therefore clear and certain from the 70s, but its provincial status remained undefined; this, of course, was partly because clear decisions on the organisation of provincial Asia Minor had not yet been made, and partly because it was marginal to Roman concerns once Mithradates and the neighbouring pirate problem were eliminated. Much the same neglect was offered neighbouring Lykia, but there the cities were mainly included within the Lykian League.

This is not simply a modern historian's problem resulting from the usual shortage of sources and authorities, as so often in the study of the ancient world; it was also a difficulty for the successive Roman governments as well, and no doubt for the Pamphylians. Once Kilikia and the pirates ceased to be an immediate problem, Pamphylia reverted to being a small unimportant territory once more. Cut off by the Taurus Mountains from its surrounding neighbours, it was far too small and isolated to be constituted as a province by itself. When territorial provinces were finally organized, under Augustus, Pamphylia was invariably attached to another area. As a sort of preliminary to this, under the triumvir M. Antonius part of the country was included in the kingdom for Amyntas, a Galatian. Antonius made him king over several Asian territories, and Augustus kept him on; he was a vigorous ruler until killed in one of his many small wars.[2]

In Pamphylia the extent of Amyntas's authority is not wholly clear. He minted coins at Side, and this might indicate that he controlled that city;[3] this would make geopolitical sense, because his main territories were to the north-east and east of Pamphylia, in Galatia, Lykaonia, and Rough Kilikia; Side would thus be a useful port for him and an anchor at the seaward end of his main route to the Mediterranean coast along the valley of the Melas. And yet it was not necessary for the mint to be situated within lands he controlled; Side could simply be his ally; the city certainly retained its normal autonomy, even if it was regarded by

[2] Strabo 12.6.3.
[3] R. Syme, *Anatolica*, Oxford 1995, 177–178.

Amyntas as inside his kingdom. The western cities, Attaleia and Phaselis, being Roman, were certainly excluded from Amyntas's direct rule.

The three cities of the plain are also unlikely to have been placed under Amyntas. Antonius had placed a king over a Greek city elsewhere,[4] but in Pamphylia there was no reason to do this; it would be sufficient for his needs if Amyntas merely had some sort of influence in Side. It was not necessary for him to control any more of Pamphylia, whose cities were quite capable of ruling themselves, and of paying the Roman tribute. Amyntas' purpose, in Roman eyes, was to establish his control over some turbulent territories along the Roman frontier and in the mountains of Pisidia and Isauria, without Rome having to do so. In other words he was a later version of the old Kilikian command. The Pamphylian cities were not in that category any longer since the active frontier had moved on eastwards; it may be assumed that they were left to their own devices.

When Amyntas died in 25 BC, Augustus annexed the whole of his kingdom, and made it into a new province;[5] in the process he also made an effort to tidy up the local political geography by adding to it various other territories. As a result, Pamphylia became part of the new province of Galatia, along with the mountain areas of Pisidia and Isauria.[6] This province formed a solid block of territory stretching from the Mediterranean coast in Pamphylia to Ankyra, a huge and unwieldy area for any governor, but one which nevertheless endured for some decades. It functioned as a wide frontier area – again – separating the rich Asian province from the threatening and disturbed east, but Pamphylia was clearly not integral to that purpose.

The individual cities retained the same legal and political positions as before, which in each case was the result of the city's previous history in relation to Rome. Attaleia, Phaselis, and Korakesion were certainly part of the province by virtue of their conquest by Rome and of Roman decisions earlier. The status of the old cities from Magydos to Side, however, is less clear.

The three cities of the plain were counted as 'friends' of Rome in 188 and 169, and there is nothing in their histories in the next century and a half – so far as it is known – to suggest that their political status had changed. All three cities survived the Roman civil wars intact. On coins of the imperial period, Aspendos, Sillyon, and Side,[7] all claimed the status of Roman allies (*symmachoi*),

⁴ Strabo 12.335; the Galatian Adiatorix ruled Herakleia Pontika.
⁵ Cassius Dio 53.26.3.
⁶ Syme, *Anatolica* 178–179.
⁷ Head, *HN* 701 (Aspendos), 704 (Side), 705 (Sillyon).

though Perge does not, concentrating instead, as ever, on the Lady of Perge. Cities will scarcely claim such a legal and political status without good reason, and we should accept their statements as accurate when made in such a public way. Attaleia simply put 'Of the Attaleians' on its coins,[8] though this does show that the city had a formal autonomous status.

The status of the cities as variously autonomous and free was obviously limited by the sheer power of Rome and its imperial governmental system, but it was in some important respects quite real. The cities had autonomy in matters of local criminal justice, city organisation and planning, building, entertainment, and so on, all matters which might concern the provincial governors, but which they were no doubt happy to leave to the local civic authorities; the apparent absence of a governor for Pamphylia was therefore of little importance. It was impractical for governors to supervise each city of their province in detail; an annual visit to the larger cities was probably the most they could manage, and for Pamphylia even this was unlikely when the governor had all Galatia to tend to as well. A governor's authority was thus in practice limited to major matters only, a situation which suited everybody. In practice, the cities' responsibilities were exactly those which had always concerned them most. For the cities of Pamphylia the inability to pursue foreign relations was hardly a deprivation: most of them had turned their attention to external affairs only when compelled to do so. Side and Phaselis had, to be sure, been fairly belligerent towards neighbours outside Pamphylia, and this was now forbidden them, as was any serious conflict between Side and Aspendos; the cities of the plain had always been largely peaceful, so their lives continued as ever.

The limited authority of the governors over the cities made it even less worthwhile for the country to be a separate province: it remained linked to Galatia and Pisidia until the reign of Claudius.[9] Lykia was technically an independent league until AD 43 but was then formally annexed by Claudius, and this was the signal for a provincial reorganisation in the region. Since Lykia was, like Pamphylia, apparently regarded as too small to form a province of itself, it was linked with Pamphylia and Pisidia into a triple province.[10]

This change took place at the time when a rebellion broke out to the east, among the people called the Kietai in Rough Kilikia, who were proving to be awkwardly difficult, having rebelled in 36, and did so again in 54. The sequence

---

[8] N. Baydur, 'Die Münzen von Attaleia in Pamphylia', *JNG,* 6, 1975, 33–72 and 1976, 33–78.

[9] R. Syme, 'Pamphylia from Augustus to Vespasian', *Klio* 30, 1937, 227–231.

[10] Cassius Dio 60.17.3; Syme, 'Pamphylia' (previous note); see also S. Mitchell, *Anatolia*, vol. 2, Oxford l989, 151–157.

of events is not clear, but it is hardly a coincidence that their second rebellion and the provincial reorganization took place in the same year. The commander who suppressed the rebels was Q. Veranius, who was the first governor of Lykia-Pamphylia after Lykia's annexation. He held the office for five years, 43–48, an unusually long tenure, and later he was governor of another militarily active province, Britannia.[11] It seems obvious that his long period of office, and the annexation of Lykia, were results of the rebellion.

The linking of the three sub-provinces, however, also looks like a typical bureaucratic measure, one which was determined from a distance, and which wholly ignored the long history of differences, even at times hostility, between the three lands, and their very different characters and populations. The Emperor Galba restored Lykia's separateness under its own governor in 68 or 69, though the reason is not known; Vespasian cancelled it again a year or so later;[12] in the process Pamphylia was switched back to Galatia briefly and then it was returned to link with Lykia once more.[13] This was the final change for two centuries. The rapid changes tend to confirm that the precise governmental arrangements had little effect locally. The joint province ceased to be an 'imperial' province in the 160s; it was apparently necessary, in the context of a Parthian war, that Bithynia-Pontus become 'imperial' – directly under the imperial government, that is, probably for logistical reasons – and handing over Lykia-Pamphylia to the Senate to provide its governors kept the balance of the provinces between Caesar and Senate. Lykia-Pamphylia was a good deal less valuable, strategically at least, than Bithynia-Pontus.[14] No doubt local opinion took due note.

It does not seem that, locally, the allocation of a particular province to Senate or emperor was very important. The direction in which complaints and compliments had to be directed was different, and it is just possible that being part of a province along with Lykia rather than Galatia meant that the governor could attend to Pamphylian affairs more often and in more detail, having less to do elsewhere, but that would be about all. The very ease and frequency of the changes between 43 and 70 implies that the precise province which Pamphylia was part of was unimportant; similarly the change from 'imperial'

---

[11] A. E. Gordon, *Q. Veranius, Consul 49 AD*, Berkeley CA, 1952; Mitchell, *Anatolia* vol. 2, 153–154; the Cietai had rebelled earlier in 36 and were to do so again in 52: Syme, *Anatolica*, 272–273.

[12] Tacitus, *Histories* 2.9.

[13] Mitchell, *Anatolia*, 2.154.

[14] *AE* 1927, 88 and 1929, 85; A. Birley, *Marcus Aurelius*, London 1966, 190–191; B. Rémy, *L'Évolution Administrative de l'Anatolie aux trois premiers siècles de Nôtre Ére*, Lyon 1986, 40–47, 62–63, 76–77, 93–95, 109; Rémy also lists the governors, pp. 167–172 an 191–193; the governor in 165 was Q. Servilius Pudens, who was *consul ordinarius* in 166, and the brother-in-law of the Emperor Lucius Verus.

to 'senatorial' was of minor importance on the ground, whatever may have been its significance at Rome. The change in 165 was the last for a long time, and 'Lykia and Pamphylia' was one of the few Asian provinces to continue unaltered through the second and third centuries.

The governors were of praetorian rank after Pamphylia was linked with Lykia in 43, but of consular rank when they had to govern Galatia as well. Those before AD 43 are therefore somewhat better known than those after that date, for men in the latter group did not always reach the consulship. They were generally commemorated in one city or another, but hardly in any enthusiastic way. It is possible to construct a list of governors for the first century and more, but accuracy in dating terms founders from the mid-second century onwards, and in much of the third century even the names of the many of governors are unknown. This fits well enough with the gubernatorial powers: throughout Lykia and Pamphylia and indeed Pisidia the cities were autonomous; governors are unknown because they had little to do. The province of Lykia-Pamphylia was still fairly small, even though it included a large part of Pisidia. It was well away from the imperial frontier, was virtually ungarrisoned, and was militarily of little or no importance, so all that was required was civilian administration and supervision. The system relied on local civic government and administration most of all, so that the governors did not need to be experts at anything, nor even present most of the time.

The cities were thus responsible mainly to themselves. They all had the usual complement of officials and magistrates, which are recorded on various inscriptions. The offices they filled were largely carried forward from the Hellenistic period. The cities all recorded their acts as of the council and people (*boule kai demos*);[15] some show the existence of a *gerousia*,[16] or a group of *dekaprotoi*.[17] The titular head of the city, probably an annual post, though there is no evidence for this, or for elections, was the *damiourgos* in most of the cities,[18] but at Attaleia it was the *strategos*.[19] This no doubt reflects the differing origins of the cities: *damiourgos* implies a magistrate working for the city and its people; a

---

[15] Attaleia: Bosch/Atlan 1, 4–8, 13, 15 and Bean 1958, 2–5, 7, 8, 10; Perge: Merkelbach and Sahin 5 and *I Perge*, 12; Phaselis: Schäfer, *Phaselis*, NIP 3 and pp. 151–154, *TAM* III; Sillyon, *BCH* 13, 1886, 2; Side:

[16] Attaleia: Bosch/Atlan 2, 15 and Bean 1, 21; Perge: Merkelbach and Sahin 16, 7, 36, 46, 57, 159; Sillyon: *BCH* 13, 1886, 1.

[17] Sillyon, *BCH* 13, 886, 1, 2.

[18] Korakesion: J. Nollé, S. Sahin and Ch. Vorster, 'Katalog der Inschriften im Museum von Alanyà, *Ep. Anat.* 5, 1985, 8, 9; Sillyon: Radet and Paris, 1, 2.

[19] Bean 9.

strategos is a commander, and the first holders of the office at Attaleia will have been commander-governors appointed and installed by Attalos II and Attalos III. Administrators of particular aspects of city life included *gymnasiarchoi* at most of the cities;[20] *agonothetai* organized festivals at three of them;[21] only one *agoranomos* is recorded, at Perge,[22] but it is an office which must be presumed everywhere. Where there are gaps in the lists it is usually because of a lack of record rather than the absence of the office. There are only four inscriptions from the city of Magydos, and the scarcity of inscriptions from Sillyon means that we are dependent on only three major documents of the second century AD for knowledge of the offices there.[23]

These local officials had real authority. They controlled the markets, the temples, the sacrifices, the buildings, and they paid for the privilege of doing so. In return for these public services, they collectively formed an oligarchic crust over the local society, which was successful in controlling the city and its unenfranchised population, and in deflecting too much imperial and gubernatorial interference.

The fighting against the Kietai will have required a military presence in Pamphylia in the 40s, for its governor was involved, but in normal times it was scarcely garrisoned at all. Side perhaps held a citizen cohort, the *cohors Apula CR*, for it was close to Rough Kilikia, the home of the Kietai. Pamphylia's link with Galatia early in the first century AD was no doubt also in connection with the still-unresolved problem of Isaurian enmity, of which the revived problems in Rough Kilikia was a continuation.[24] A successor for the regiment at Side was perhaps the *cohors Raetorum*, though the evidence, as with the *cohors Apula*, consists only of a tombstone found at Side,[25] and rather more evidence is really needed for an approach to certainty. A soldier's discharge diploma found

[20] Perge: Merkelbach and Sahin 7; Sillyon: Radet and Paris, 1, 2; Hereward 3; cities with stadia necessarily had such officials.

[21] Attaleia: Bosch/Atlan 23, 24 and Bean 19, 21–23; Korakesion *EA* 19, 7; Perge: Merkelbach and Sahin 52; theatres and odeons at all cities imply the existence of these officials.

[22] Merkelbach and Sahin 4; S. Sahin, 'Epigraphische Mitteilungen aus Antalya I, Bleige wicht des Agoranomen Crispus Didymus', *Ep. Anat.* 3, 1999, 41–42.

[23] R. van Bremen, 'A Family from Sillyon', *ZPE* 104, 1996, 43–56, with reference to the rather complicated publication history of the document.

[24] Based on a single gravestone (*AE* 1966, 478), so this is not certain; its commanding officer was active at Alexandreia Troas (P. A. Brunt, 'C. Fabricius Tuscus and an Augustan Dilectus', *ZPE* 13, 1974, 161–185); M. P. Spiedel, 'Citizen Cohorts in the Roman Imperial Army: new Data on the Cohorts Apula, Campana and III Campestris', *TAPA* 106, 1976, 339–341.

[25] M. P. Spiedel, 'The Roman Army in Asia Minor: Recent Epigraphical Discoveries and Research', in S. Mitchell (ed.), *Armies and Frontiers in Roman and Byzantine Anatolia*, BAR S156, Oxford 1983, 14 and 28.

at Laertes, inland from Korakesion, however, provides the concrete statement that in 138 the provincial garrison of Lykia-Pamphylia-Pisidia consisted of the *cohors I Musulaniorum*, from which the soldier Galba – no more than this of his name is preserved – had just been discharged.[26] He came originally from Kyrrhos in northern Syria, and had been stationed in Pamphylia long enough to acquire a Pamphylian wife and two sons, which suggests that his unit had been in Pamphylia for a couple of decades at least. A successor to this regiment was the *cohors I Flavia Numidarum*, attested in the province between 157 and 167,[27] and it seems likely that it remained until at least 238 when a tombstone implies that part of it at least was stationed at Perge.[28]

It seems likely that these regiments were spread through the province in small detachments, only occasionally being brought together into one place, perhaps for inspections or exercises. The soldier Galba's diploma was found at Laertes, which was perhaps the place he retired to, possibly his wife's home town. Side and Perge are both mentioned as places where soldiers were stationed, and it is reasonable to assume that the other cities held military detachments as well. The garrison was thus being employed essentially on police and internal security duties. Just south of Phaselis, at Olympos, we know of a *stationarius*, a road-patroller, commanded later by a *beneficarius*,[29] who may or may not be part of the provincial garrison. But one cohort of less than five hundred men was a small garrison for even part of the province. It seems a good indication of the peacefulness of the area once the Pisidians and Isaurians had been persuaded to calm down.[30]

The general absence of the governors from the scene in Pamphylia is reflected in the shortage of commemorations of such men in the Pamphylian cities, even in Perge, which has been fairly well explored. Nor is there much evidence for the presence of other officials. If governors were rarely present, then they would need to send junior officials to the cities, if only to collect the tax monies. The

[26] J. Russell, 'A Roman Military Diploma from Eastern Pamphylia', *AJA*, 95, 1991, 469–488.

[27] RMD 5.67; J. Nollé, 'Pamphylische Studien: 1. Ein centurio der cohors I Flavia Numidarum in Perge und Brundisium', *Chiron* 15, 1985, 199–202.

[28] *AE* 1966, 459; *I. Perge* II.47; Haensch, *Capita*, 610.

[29] *TAM* 2.3.953, 987, and 1185; Haensch, *Capita*, 610; three *beneficarii* are recorded, two of whom were buried at Olympos.

[30] It has to be said that this section on the supposed garrison is somewhat speculative. The regiments mentioned are not actually stated to have been stationed in Lykia-Pamphylia, and the evidence is no more than suggestive. The fact that a man of a regiment itself is buried in the province is not necessarily evidence that the regiment was stationed there. The diplomas are better evidence, but only for the single moment when they were issued. It must be assumed that, at the least, the list of garrison regiments is incomplete, and possibly inaccurate.

officers in command of the military detachments, such as the *beneficarius* at Olympos, or the centurion of the Numidian cohort at Perge, were available, of course, but there is little evidence of officials who must have been on the governors' staff.[31]

Pisidia, the land in the hills north of both Lykia and Pamphylia, was included in the joint province. The area involved reached north almost to the great east-west road through central Anatolia. The great cities along the road, notably Apameia-Kelainai, where there was a military base, were not included, though several of the Pisidian cities were, notably Sagalassos, Cremna, and Selge. When King Amyntas died, the area was still somewhat turbulent, and no doubt this was one major reason for it to be joined originally with Galatia, which was a well-garrisoned province. By the time it was linked with Lykia and Pamphylia, however, from AD 43, it was greatly changed.

Roman imperial policy in the years after Amyntas's death had been to contain the disaffection of the Pisidians by planting colonies of Roman citizens, mainly former soldiers, in and around the area. Pisidia was the object of one of the densest concentrations of such colonies in the Roman world. It was ringed and penetrated by half a dozen Roman *coloniae*, some in the Lykia-Pamphylia province, others outside it. Some of the existing cities also received contingents of such settlers – there will have been plenty of confiscated land, as at Phaselis and Attaleia, to which these colonists could be allocated. A *colonia* clearly received larger numbers of colonists than a city which just received some extra men, but even the *coloniae* were not wholly new urban foundations. Rather they were older cities whose civil constitutions were altered to conform to Roman ways, and whose Pisidian (and Greek) populations were swamped by the imposition of the new colonists.

The difference between the *coloniae* and the cities which were not *coloniae* but which received new settlers was perhaps less than we would suppose, since in most cases the original populations remained in place; and whereas the new *coloniae* had former soldiers as their city councillors from the start, cities which received contingents of soldiers or civilians found that these men soon came to take their places in the highest ranks of local society, though without the overwhelming numerical superiority which happened in the *coloniae*. The essential difference lay in the citizenship. In the new *coloniae* only Roman citizens were enfranchised, and in the older cities the Roman citizenship did not carry with it any special political privileges: the city councils, the *boulai* and

---

[31] What little there is has been collected by Haensch, *Capita*, 610–617, a collection which includes Lykia also.

the *gerousiai*, were still composed of the leading men of the city and the local oligarchs easily outnumbered the Roman citizens.

Within Lykia-Pamphylia full *coloniae* were established at Cremna, Comama, and Olbasa, forming a line of settlements dominating the central Pisidian area, and at Parlais in the north. Beyond the northern boundary, in the Galatian-Kappadokian province, there were *coloniae* established at Antioch-in-Pisidia, Iconium, and Lystra, controlling the main road to the east. In addition, several strategically important cities received colonists as reinforcements: Attaleia the port, Apollonia, just north of the provincial boundary, and Neapolis and Isaura to the east. In total we must envisage some tens of thousands of Latin-speaking Roman colonists and former soldiers being imposed on the area during a relatively short period of time, say ten to fifteen years (c.25 to c.10 BC).[32]

This dating means that the whole process was organised and supervised by the governors of the Galatian province, the successor to the kingdom of Amyntas. This is one of the reasons for the provincial organisation by which Pisidia and Pamphylia were included in that province. It was well garrisoned, by at least two legions, with a considerable number of auxiliary regiments also: one legion and five auxiliary units were stationed nearby for the whole of the period following Amyntas' death,[33] and to these may be added the colonists in the several cities. Pisidia was, in effect, swamped by the Roman army, both serving soldiers and time-expired veterans.

The only part of Pamphylia affected directly by the policy of colonisation was the city of Attaleia. This city was important as a port and it provided the shortest access to the Pisidian interior from the Mediterranean. It had Italian settlers imposed on it, though it was not converted into a full *colonia* until it was awarded the title much later.[34] The Roman state already owned land there, confiscated by Servilius Vatia in 77 BC, and the availability of this land may have been one of the reasons for the imposition of the colonists, though there is no evidence that similar settlements were made at Olympos and Phaselis, where land taken by Vatia was also available.[35] This may be taken to emphasise the strategic purpose of the settlement, for the aim was not simply to settle soldiers,

[32] B. N. Levick, *Roman Colonies in Southern Asia Minor*, Oxford 1967.

[33] W. F. Keppie, 'Legions in the East from Augustus to Trajan', in P. Freeman and D. Kennedy, *The Defence of the Roman and Byzantine East*, BAR S287, Oxford 1986.

[34] Mitchell, *Anatolia*, 74; the city is described as *colonia* in the fifth century AD: N. Gökalp, 'Epigraphische Mitteilungen aus Antalya IV: Inschriften aus Attaliea', *Ep. Anat.* 31, 1999, no. 1.

[35] S. Mitchell, 'Roman Residents and Roman Property in Southern Asia Minor', in *Proceedings of the Xth International Congress of Classical Archaeology*, 1, Ankara 1978, 31–318, and in his *Anatolia* I.90–91; T.R.S. Broughton, 'Some non-colonial Coloni of Augustus', *TAPA* 66, 1935, 18–24.

but to secure imperial control. The presence of Latin-speaking colonists, each of them provided with a substantial landholding, and with their purses full of their discharge pay, helped to make the city more prosperous and thus still more important. These men became part of the ruling group in the city as soon as they arrived, and, being Roman citizens as well, they will have had both the ear of the governor and further connections back to Rome, to their former military units, and to their original homes in Italy.

Several of these settler families at Attaleia emerged as members of the local aristocracy in the first century AD. The evidence in all cases is epigraphic, though dating is rather vague. At least three generations of two families, the Gavii and the Calpurnii, can be discerned, together with several clients who took the Gavius name. The first of the Gavius family we know of was L. Gavius Fronto who was commemorated by his 'friend' P. Gavius Gallicus and by his freedman L. Gavius Seleukos with statues whose inscriptions survive. Fronto was the son of a man of the same name, who may or may not have been the original settler. He was a *primipilarius* of the legion III *Cyrenaica* and *praefectus fabrum* in XV *Apollinaris* in a career spanning the reigns of Domitian, Nerva and Trajan. His son Aelianus reached the quaestorship at Rome; his grandson Clarus was a senator. At Attaleia Fronto was prominent in public affairs as *gymnasiarchos*, *agonothetes*, and priest of the imperial cult. M. Gavius Gallicus, who may well have been the brother of Fronto's friend, was honoured by his freedman M. Gavius Eirenaius. Gallicus' career included a post as *praefectus fabrum* of an unnamed military unit, and made him a member of the equestrian order. He was also a generous benefactor of Attaleia as *agonothetes*, priest of the Victorious Augustus, city high priest, *defensor*, and patron; in addition he was honoured in other cities for his services to them in relations with the emperor and the provincial governors. The family tree may be reconstructed as in Chart II, but the precise connection between the two branches is not known:[36]

The Calpurnii, who were also settled at Attaleia, emerge as an important family in the reign of Claudius, when M. Calpurnius Rufus was governor of Lykia and Pamphylia, probably as successor to Q. Veranius, that is, in 48–50 or so.[37] He was the son of M. Calpurnius and Caecilia Tertulla, who was priestess of the imperial cult at Attaleia. If Rufus really did govern his home province he was unusual. The third generation of the family was L.

---

[36] G. Radet and R. Paris, 'Inscriptions d'Attaleia, de Perge, d'Aspendos', *BCH* 10, 1886, no. 1; Bosch/Atlan 19, 20 and Bean 26, 27, 31; *IGRRP* III 78; L. Robert, *BE* 61, 1948, 201; R. K. Sherk, *The Roman Empire. Augustus to Hadrian*, Cambridge 1988, 129.

[37] Rémy, *L'Évolution Administrative*, 167, dates him to '48–53?'

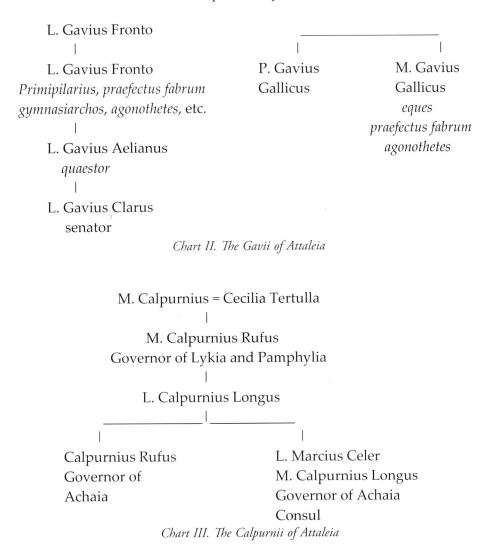

L. Gavius Fronto
|
L. Gavius Fronto
Primipilarius, praefectus fabrum
gymnasiarchos, agonothetes, etc.
|
L. Gavius Aelianus
quaestor
|
L. Gavius Clarus
senator

P. Gavius
Gallicus

M. Gavius
Gallicus
eques
praefectus fabrum
agonothetes

Chart II. The Gavii of Attaleia

M. Calpurnius = Cecilia Tertulla
|
M. Calpurnius Rufus
Governor of Lykia and Pamphylia
|
L. Calpurnius Longus
|

Calpurnius Rufus
Governor of
Achaia

L. Marcius Celer
M. Calpurnius Longus
Governor of Achaia
Consul

Chart III. The Calpurnii of Attaleia

Calpurnius Longus, whose two sons Calpurnius Rufus and L. Marcius Celer M. Calpunius Longus both governed Achaia, the latter becoming *suffect* consul (Chart III). The family was related also to an extensive network of Calpurnii those interests and properties spread through much of central Anatolia. Lucius was honoured at Attaleia as city patron, where he was commemorated by one of his freedmen with a statue. In the city the most prominent remaining building of the Roman period is the Hıdırlık Kalesi, overlooking the harbour (plate 16). This has been identified, a little tentatively, as the tomb of one of the Calpurnii, for it has the consular *fasces* carved on it; surely this makes it clear that it was the tomb of the consular Longus, though an earlier member of the family has been suggested.[38] This was a very wealthy, even distinguished, family, and the first from Pamphylia to have a member to reach the consulate at Rome. The size of the tomb – later used as a part of the city's defences – implies great wealth, and the tomb's placement, inside the city boundary, suggests very great political influence and renown.

At Attaleia, several other Latin family names are recorded in inscriptions: Paccius, Petronius, Favonius, Caesius, Rutilius, Sempronius. Some of these are fairly rare names, and in Italy they are often of very local distribution, so that the Italian origin of the families, or at least of the original emigrant – can thus be approximately located. It would seem, therefore, that these are records of some of the Italian families who were settled in Attaleia by the colonialist policy.[39] They are recorded because some of them became locally notable, such as Q. Rutilius, who may have held government offices in Rome, but whose broken inscription honours him as *agonothetes* and *philokaisar* and *philopater*, and Sex. Paccius Valerius Flavianus who was *agonothetes* and priest of the Goddess Roma.[40] These are the only members of their families to be recorded. The eminence of these Italian families above the general run of local oligarchs was only temporary and probably only partial. After the consul L. Marcius Celer M. Calpurnius Longus in Hadrian's reign, the Italians as a whole faded into the general population, if they had any descendants.

It is much more difficult to discern the non-Italian notables of Attaleia with whom the Italians competed. Individuals were certainly often honoured, or left other records, but their family connections are not so easily discerned, in part because of Greek naming conventions, which make it less easy to elucidate relationships than with the Roman system; also those of local origin who became Roman citizens left few records. Half a dozen or so could be listed, but only as individuals, not as families; and those who did not acquire the Roman citizenship all too often remain simply names. Yet there were certainly a considerable number of them, for the city council will have had a membership of several tens of men.

---

[38] Bosch/Atlan 10, 11, and Bean 21; Robert, *BE* 61, 1948, 199–200; R. Stuppich, 'Das Grabmal eines Konsularen in Attaleia', *Ist. Mitt.* 41, 1991, 417–422; also O. Salomies, 'Roman Nomina in the Greek East', *Arctos* 35, 2001, 139–174, for a recent general survey of these names; *SEG* II.696; W. Eck, 'L. Marius Celer M. Calpurnius Longus, Proconsul von Achaia und Suffektkonsul unter Hadrian', *ZPE* 86, 1991, 97–106.

[39] Paccius: Bosch/Atlan, 14; Petronius: *SEG* VI.650; Favonius: Bosch/Atlan 13; Caesius: *SEG* II.704; Sempronius: Bosch/Atlan, 33; Rutilius: *SEG* II.698; many are also listed and discussed by S. Jameson, *Lycia and Pamphylia under the Roman Empire from Augustus to Diocletian*, Oxford D. Phil. thesis, 1965.

[40] *SEG* II.698; Bosch/Atlan 14; another priest of Rome is at 16, but the name is gone.

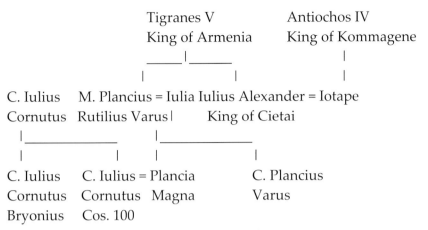

Chart IV. The Plancii of Perge

We have to accept that the vast majority of those men left no local record of their existence. And for the people below that social level – the vast majority of the population – virtually no record at all exists.

The other cities of Pamphylia display much the same erratic record of their inhabitants as Attaleia. None of them had Roman colonists foisted on them, but there are records of some incoming Italian families who arrived presumably as private immigrants or wealthy families who acquired local property. The recorded inscriptions provide evidence of such people at Perge and at Side, but not so much at the other cities.

At Perge one dominant family was the Plancii, again originally from Italy, which accumulated estates and connections in many parts of Anatolia, like the Calpurnii at Attaleia, and like them had political ambitions (Chart IV). M. Plancius Varus was a senator by AD 69,[41] and proconsul in Pontus-Bithynia in 70–72, so he had been praetor in Nero's reign. The family intermarried with the descendants of kings of other areas of Asia Minor, and with members of other Italian colonist families in other cities, including Attaleia, so that in total they and their connections formed a new aristocratic crust over much of Anatolia at the end of the first and into the early decades of the second century AD.[42]

[41] Tacitus, *Histories* 2.63.
[42] See the genealogy in S. Sahin, 'Studien zu den Inschriften von Perge III', *Ep. Anat.*, 27, 1996, 115–125; also S. Mitchell, 'The Plancii in Asia Minor', *JRS* 64, 1974, 27–39; C. P Jones, 'The Plancii of Perge and Diana Planciana', *Harvard Studies in Classical Philology* 80, 1976, 235 -

M. Plancius Varus was married to Julia, daughter of Julius Tigranes, Armenian king, whose son was king in Kilikia and married to the daughter of the last king of Kommagene. Varus' daughter, Plancia Magna, married C. Julius Cornutus Tertullus, son of a consul of 100, of a family dominant at Apollonia in Lydia. Her brother was consul in Hadrian's reign, and she herself was a friend of Hadrian's wife Sabina. Other relatives were from Ankyra in Galatia and Pergamon and Sardis in Lydia. The network also spread westwards, where a marriage connection with the Caeciia of Narbonensian Gaul was made, which also involved the Calpurnii of Attaleia.[43]

The Plancius family culminated in the extraordinary Plancia Magna, priestess of Artemis at Perge, daughter, wife, and mother of senators, relative of kings and consuls, who lavished gifts on the city of Perge, so that the family was acclaimed as equivalent of the old founders of the city.[44] Later, an allied family produced a wife for the Emperor Elagabalus,[45] but the Plancii faded away during the second century. It is notable that often the peak of achievement of these Italian-descended families came in the late first and early second centuries. None of them lasted much more than a century, at least in the records we have, though the evidence is mainly epigraphic and so more than usually erratic. There were also other Italian names recorded at Perge, just as at Attaleia – Caesius, Julius Cornutus, Feridius.[46]

One or two of the non-Italian families can be similarly traced, though not with full certainty. Apollonios, son of Lysimachos, was the city's envoy to Rome in connection with the defence of the status of the city as *asylos*. This was probably in AD 22/23. Another Apollonios, but this time a Roman citizen, Tib. Claudius Apollonios Elaibares, went to Rome three times for the same purpose in connection with the city's great temple. His name suggests the award of the Roman citizenship by Claudius, and so his visits would be in the 50s. This may or may not be the same man as the father of the brothers Apollonios and Demetrios, who paid for an arch honouring Domitian in the city. Their father is identified as '*Apolloniou Epikydrou*', which might be his name, or Epikydros

[43] I went into some detail on this in my book, *Nerva and the Roman Succession Crisis of AD 96–99*, London 2003, ch. 7.

[44] S. Sahin, 'Perge Kentenin Kuruculari ve Plancia Magna', *Adalya* 1, 1996, 45–52; *RE Supp.* XIV 378–379; the lady's gifts to the city, and her curious position, are discussed by M. T. Boatwright in an article in S.B. Pomeroy (ed.), *Women's History and Ancient History*, Chapel Hill, NC, 1991, 249–271.

[45] C. Settipani, *Continuité Gentilice et Continuité Familiale dans les familles Senatoriales Romaines à l'époque impériale*, Oxford 2000, chart p. 456.

[46] Caesius: *I. Perge* 51; Iulius Cornutus: *I. Perge* 16–21; Feridius: C. P. Jones, 'Old and New in the Inscriptions of Perge: I. The Foundation of M. Feridius', *Ep. Anat.* 31, 1999, 8–13; all three of these inscriptions record expensive work paid for by these men for the city.

might be his father's name. It seems possible, given the dating of the events, that we actually have two families – Lysimachos-Apollonios-Elaibares, and Epikydros-Apollonios-Apollonios and Demetrios.[47]

A few men with single Greek names also appear in the Roman period inscriptions, clearly rich, clearly local aristocrats, and continuing to take the same part in local affairs as their ancestors had, and as the Roman citizens among them were doing; no doubt they were in greater numbers than those with Italian names, though few are recorded.[48] The very insistence of the Italians on providing inscriptional evidence may be a sign of their small numbers, and hence one aspect of their need to assert themselves.

Aspendos, despite the fact that a very large quantity of epitaphs from there have been found and published,[49] shows only a little evidence of Roman or Italian colonisation. One inscription recording the building of the aqueduct in the second century AD commemorates the generosity of Ti. Claudius Italicus, who financed the project to the tune of two million *denarii* ('two hundred ten-thousands'). He had held a whole series of local offices: *dekaprotos* (city councillor), high priest, *damiourgos* (annual head of state in the city), *gymnasiarchos*, *agonothetes* at the quinquennial imperial games. The inscription was put up by his son, who had also been *dekaprotos* and *gymnasiarchos*. The son had the *cognomen* Kyreina, so either this is a Greek family which had gained the Roman citizenship from a Ti. Claudius, perhaps one of the emperors, or it was an Italian family – 'Italicus' would suggest so – which had begun to adopt Greek names, perhaps by intermarriage.[50]

Also in the second century the brothers A. Curtius Crispinus Arruntianus and A. Curtius Auspicatus Titinianus paid for the reconstruction of the city's theatre. From our point of view these men appear out of nowhere, but clearly they were immensely rich. Their *cognomina* ought to supply indications of their

---

[47] The rival interpretations are: S. Sahin 'Studien zur den Inschriften von Perge II: Der Gesändte Apollonios und seine Familie', *Ep. Anat.* 25, 1995, 1–23, and C. P. Jones, 'Old and New in the Inscriptions of Perge: II. The Asylia of Artemis of Perge', *Ep. Anat.* 31, 1999, 13–17.

[48] Trokondas: *I. Perge* 12; Kleobures: *I. Perge* 55; the brothers Demetrios and Apollonios: J. Inan, 'Der Demetrios und Apolloniosbogen in Perge', *Ist. Mitt.* 39, 1989, 237–244. Note that both Trokondas and Kleobures are local, Pamphylian, names.

[49] Most of the epitaphs are Hellenistic, with some Roman; many have been exploited for evidence of the local dialect. Cf. G. E. Bean, 'Epitaphs from Aspendos', *Jahrbuch für Klein-Asiatische Forschung* 2, 1952/1953, 201–266; D. Hereward, 'Inscriptions from Pamphylia and Isauria', *JHS* 78, 1958, 57–67; *SEG* XXXVIII, 1339–1392, XLI, 1304–1321, XLVI, 1684–1698, XLVII, 1778–1783, XLIX, 1876; Radet and Paris (note 36), no. 8.

[50] Radet and Paris (note 36); *IGRRP* III, 804.

ancestry – Arruntii, Titinii – but no connections can be discerned; nor is there any sign of their progeny.[51]

Another inscription of c. AD 100 from Aspendos, incomplete though it is, provides information about the mix of peoples in the city. It gives a list of local clerical officials, the *episphragistai*, whose office was a registration centre, sealing public documents. The officials and their assistants were a group of men both free and slave: Phereas son of Apollodoros, Markos Neikios and G. Ignatius Celer (the officials), Kendas son of Apollonios (a deputy), G. Mulvius Iustus (the secretary), and Charisenos, Eutychios, and one other man whose name is uncertain (the slaves). Of these men, two were Roman citizens (Ignatius and Mulvius), and both could be Italian in origin; Markos Neikios may be a Roman citizen, but he is more likely to be a Greek adopting a Roman-style name. Of the Greeks, two are identified by their patronymics in the usual Greek style (Phereas son of Apollodoros, Kendas son of Apollonios); the three slaves are identified by their names alone. In addition the inscription begins by dating the event by the name of the *damiourgos* in office, who was T. Flavius Poleito, a Greek who had gained Roman citizenship by a grant from one of the Flavian emperors during the previous thirty years.[52]

This group of names illustrates the integration of the Italian colonists into the local oligarchy (Ignatius and Mulvius), the spread of Roman citizenship into the Aspendian population (the *damiourgos* Flavius Poleito), and the aspiration of some Greeks to be thought Roman (Markos Neikios). The mixture of names in the personnel of a single municipal office, and the mixture of free and slave, is just what we would expect where Italian immigrants in small but wealthy numbers moved into an established Greek city; this same phenomenon of integration is visible at Perge, at Attaleia, and at Side. It was hardly a new development in Pamphylia, where there were still numbers of the old Luwian names in use, mixed with the Greek, though as far as can be seen the spoken Luwian language had died out by this time.[53]

In Aspendos there are two other local officials, both 'Ti. Claudius', and so given the citizenship under the Emperor Claudius,[54] and two epitaphs giving Roman names, L. Seius Akastos, a Greek *cognomen* on a Roman *nomen*, and

[51] *TIB* 2.466–467.

[52] S. Sahin, 'Epigraphische Mitteilungen aus Antalya I', *Ep. Anat.* 31, 1999, no. 6; *SEG* XLIX 1874.

[53] S. Colvin, 'Names in Hellenistic and Roman Lycia', in S. Colvin (ed.), *The Greco-Roman East, YCS* 31, 2004, 44–84, provides a list of names in use in Lykia, which are much the same in many cases as those in use in Pamphylia.

[54] The aqueduct men (note 50).

A. Geminius Firmus, clearly a Roman name.[55] In all, these names provide only thin evidence of Roman and Italian penetration into the city, and even the few clearly Latin names could have been adopted from Roman officials who were generous with the citizenship.

These three cities show a decrease in the Roman/Italian presence as one moves from Attaleia eastwards. Perge and Attaleia have the most such names, and there are many fewer in Aspendos; to reinforce this, it may be noted that Sillyon provides no evidence of Roman and Italian names at all – though it must be admitted that the number of inscriptions from that city is far fewer than from the others, even from Attaleia.

The names show only a very slow extension of the Roman citizenship into the Greco-Luwian population in the first century AD. At Side, there seems to have been some Italian immigration, for names such as Statorios appear,[56] but the pattern of only slow romanization is repeated; the appearance of a few Aelii and Aurelii mark the extension of the citizenship under the second-century emperors. A Sidetan, T. Licinius Mucianus, reached the consulship at Rome in 177/178, and was presumably the descendant of a man enfranchised by C. Licinius Mucianus, the able supporter of Vespasian, who had been governor of Lykia-Pamphylia about 58/60; if so, it had taken the family well over a century, perhaps four or five generations, to reach the consulship.[57]

It was necessary, as the case of Perge shows, that local privileges be maintained by contact with Rome. Men who held the local office of priest of the imperial cult were ideal for this. From Side T. Flavius Spartiaticus travelled three times to Rome as ambassador for his city to the emperor. It appears he was concerned with the Emperor Domitian's celebration of games at his Alban villa; no doubt his presence was duly noted as reflecting well on his city, and he was honoured in at least four surviving inscriptions at his home city.[58]

It might have been expected that Phaselis would show some evidence of Italian colonisation. Like Attaleia, some of its lands had been confiscated by Servilius Vatia in the 70s BC, so the Roman state could have allocated these lands to colonists, as it may well have done at Attaleia. But the records of the

[55] Seius: *SEG* XXXVIII 1346; Geminius: *SEG* XXXVIII 1361.

[56] *I. Side*, 131.

[57] *I. Side*, 59; G. E. Bean and T. B. Mitford, *Journeys in Rough Cilicia 1964–1968*, Vienna 1970, no. 19.

[58] C. P. Jones, 'Joint Sacrifice at Iasus and Side', *JHS* 118, 1998, 183–186, discussing inscriptions published by G.E. Bean, *Side Kitabaleri: The Inscriptions of Side*, Ankara 1965, nos 83, 111, 112, 127, 146.

city do not suggest any colonisation, and like the rest, there was only minimal acquisition of the Roman citizenship.

In all this the Pamphylian cities were really little different from the cities of the rest of the Roman Empire. The spread of the Roman citizenship was slow during the first century, and scarcely speeded up very much in the second. When in 212 that status became available to all, there still remained large numbers of men who could take it up. Some men were obviously keen to acquire the citizenship status, but the majority of those whose wealth and status at home made them eligible were apparently indifferent. It was, it would seem, an honour of minimal usefulness to most men. If one wished for a political career in the imperial service, citizenship was an essential first step, but to pursue such a career would necessitate leaving one's home town; a career in politics had to take place at Rome, was very strenuous and expensive, and there was no guarantee that one would get very far.

The usefulness of the Roman citizenship was thus only very limited for non-politicians. It was of little use in local affairs, where, as the inscription of the officials in the registry at Aspendos shows, magistracies went indiscriminately to local citizens, whether Roman or not. It was in this area, local affairs, that most men's political and social interests and ambitions lay; indeed, the great majority of cities in the eastern part of the empire had never been anything other than places with purely local interests. Their foreign relations had been limited for most of their existence, even when wholly independent, to contacts with their immediate neighbours. With kings of great territories looming over them, an adventurous foreign policy was both dangerous and foolhardy; and in the Roman Empire it was quite impossible. The cities' continuing foreign relations were now with their immediate neighbours, and with Rome, and these were mainly conducted through Rome's governor sent out to the area, whose presence was almost as distant as that of his city. Contact with the city of Rome need only be occasional and fleeting, and was expensive; it was only to be undertaken where a vital local interest was involved, as with the need to maintain the status of *asylos*, for which Apollonios son of Lysimachos travelled to Rome on Perge's behalf.

For cities which were ports, this sweeping generalisation has to be modified, but only in a small way. Side's foreign relations, for instance, were not only with Aspendos and the Etenneis, but with Syria and Cyprus and Egypt as well.[59] These lands were also its neighbours, in the sense that they were the

---

[59] H.-J. Drexhage, 'Die Kontackte zwischen Side, Alexandria und Ägypten in der Römischen Kaiserzeit (1–3 jh. n. Chr)', *AMS* 3, 1991, 75–90.

lands of its customers. The contacts the city had with such places were now overwhelmingly commercial and no longer political, as they had been in the Hellenistic and earlier periods. A similar comment could be made for Attaleia and Phaselis, and perhaps for Korakesion, though details are not available. Attaleia had more contacts with Rome than the others, but that was because of the colonists from Italy and because it was the government centre, in so far as there was one.

The field of political action for the local rich therefore consisted essentially in their home city, and since this had been the situation of their ancestors in Hellenistic and Persian and Archaic times as well, their life had not greatly changed with the arrival of the imperial system. The occasional man, such as L. Marcius Celer M. Calpurnius Longus of Attaleia, or T. Licinius Mucianus of Side, might reach the consulship at Rome, but there had always been men who left the cities for a career in the wider world, in the Ptolemaic army and civil services in the third century BC, for example. To their local contemporaries the construction of a bath for the city, or the proper conduct of the regular local games, or the correct performance of the priestly duties, was of more immediate concern. That is to say, the Roman imperial system had only a marginal effect on local affairs.

The economic basis for the wealth of the local oligarchies, and for the buildings which were put up by the cities (to be discussed shortly), remained what it had been for the previous several centuries and was for other areas around the Mediterranean: the production and export of grain, olive oil, wine, salt, wool, wood, horses, and similar items, the usual staples of trade in the ancient Mediterranean.[60] Phaselis, Attaleia, and Side were also trading towns on a smallish scale. None of this economic activity can have been particularly large, and Pamphylia was never a region likely to be a productive powerhouse such as Africa, or Egypt, or later, Syria. A story in a second century life of the wonder-worker Apollonios purports to condemn some Aspendians for hoarding grain in a time of shortage.[61] The story is unbelievable as it stands and has been roundly condemned[62] – but one does not invent a story and then set it in a particular place without using a degree of common knowledge, and so we may assume that grain was an Aspendian product, the city was known as a producer

[60] On this, see the exhaustive treatment by H. Brandt, 'Gesellschaft und Wirtschaft Pamphyliens und Pisidiens in Altertum', *AMS* 7, 1992 and Jameson, *Lycia and Pamphylia*.
[61] Philostratos, *Life of Apollonios* 1.15.
[62] J. Raeymaekers, 'The Grain Hoarders of Aspendos: Philostratus on the Intervention of Apollonius of Tyana', in L. Moore (ed.), *Politics, Administration and Society in the Hellenistic and Roman Worlds*, *Studia Hellenistica* 36, Leuven 2000.

Century	Side	Aspendos	Perge	Phaselis
5		?Walls ?Agora		
4		?Theatre		
3	Walls, Theatre Stadium		Walls	*Nordsiedlung*
2	Aqueduct *Nymphaeum*			Quays
1 BC				
AD 1	Vespasian Mon't		*Palaistra* Theatre	*Agora* *Agora*
			Gate Baths Arch	High Street Quays
2	*Agora*, Gymnasium Harbour temples Theatre	Theatre Aqueduct	*Nymphaeum*	Aqueduct
3	Gate 'Men' temple Aqueduct restored	Vestibule *Basilica* *Nymphaeum*		
4	Theatre repaired Walls rebuilt	Bridge Theatre repaired	Walls	
5	Baths *Basilica* Bishop's palace			Church
6				
7				
8	New Walls			Rebuilding

Chart V. City Buildings

of it, and that much of the trade was in the hands of the local landowners, those local oligarchs again.

The local wealth and the local affairs are manifested to us above all in the buildings whose remains are still often visible at the city sites. Again, in this the cities were acting in much the same way as all other cities in the empire, by equipping themselves with a range of buildings usually paid for by the local rich who took up the magistrates' offices. But these cities were already well equipped with such buildings. In the Roman period many of the older ones were replaced or repaired, but relatively few of the installations were wholly new (see Chart V). At Side, for example, the theatre and the stadium existed, the great walls had been built, and the aqueduct and the *nymphaeum* were constructed in the period between the Seleukid domination and the arrival of Rome. In the Roman period, the theatre was rebuilt in the second century AD and repaired in the fourth, while the aqueduct was restored in the third. Various additions, generally of a minor nature, were made between the Flavian period and the early third century, and these included the realigning of the major streets and their lining with colonnades.[63]

The buildings at Side are rather better dated than in the other cities, but the same overall pattern can be detected there, though again only in general terms, for exact dates for buildings are rare. New building at Perge perhaps started earlier than in the other cities with a large *palaistra* paid for by C. Julius Cornutus in Claudius' reign,[64] and the large baths by the southern gate dedicated to Vespasian.[65] The theatre, probably rebuilt rather than new, was renovated in Nero's reign and lavishly decorated with sculpture, now largely displayed in Antalya Museum,[66] while a *nymphaeum* was built alongside it later; another *nymphaeum*, perhaps earlier, existed just below the acropolis (plate 4),[67] and an arch honouring Domitian was dated AD 81/82.[68] Plancia Magna's gifts to the city included the new South Gate beside the baths, with its decoration of the names and busts of the old and modern founders of the city; it was remodelled to make the entrance to the city easier and more monumental in the first quarter of the second century;[69] perhaps it was this gift which allowed Plancia to be included in those counted as founders of the city (plate 9; Map 16).

Phaselis also embarked on a set of new and rebuilt works: the *agorai*, the aqueduct, new quays, the theatre, were all built in the first and second centuries

---

[63] I adopt the datings suggested in Bean, *TSS;* for this section and the following paragraphs on buildings.

[64] *I. Perge* 18–21.

[65] H. Abbasoğlu, 'The Founding of Perge and its development in the Hellenistic and Roman Periods', in D. Parrish (ed.), Urbanism in Western Asia Minor, Journal of Roman Archaeology, Supplement 45, Portsmouth RI 2001; 173–188; the inscription recording the Vespasian dedication is on p. 181 (and at I. Perge 54); the whole article is most useful for the sequence of development of the city.

[66] S. Mitchell, 'Archaeological Reports', *British School at Athens*, 1999, 171; J. Inan and E. Rosenbaum, *Roman and Early Byzantine Portrait Sculpture in Asia Minor*, Oxford 1966, and the Antalya Museum *Guide*.

[67] A. F. Mansel, 'Die Nymphaeen von Perge', *Ist. Mitt.* 25, 1975, 367–372.

[68] J. Inan, 'Der Demetrios- und Apolloniosbogen in Perge', *Ist. Mitt.*, 39, 1989, 257–294.

[69] H. Lauter, 'Das hellenistischer Südtor von Perge', *BJ* 172, 1972, 1–11; Plancia Magna lived on to honour Hadrian, which dates her work.

AD (Map 11).[70] Aspendos, where many of the surviving buildings are in fact Hellenistic in date, recommended building somewhat later, if a reasonably convincing theory of dates and sequences is accepted.[71] The great theatre was apparently the first of the new buildings, reconstructed by the architect Zeno for the Curtii brothers in the reign of Marcus Aurelius. It is an unusual case of a Roman type of theatre, which must have replaced an earlier Greek type on the same site. A gymnasium, the aqueduct (plate 17), the *nymphaeum*, the vestibule to the *basilica*, and then the *basilica* itself, were all built within the space of less than a century. The aqueduct, and therefore the *nymphaeum* as well, failed late in the third century and was not repaired; some of the material from the aqueduct and its piping was used to repair the nearby bridge over the Eurymedon early in the fourth century – the deposit on the pipes indicates that they had been in use for between a century and a century and a half.[72] At Sillyon it is difficult to provide any dates for the buildings, though the inscriptions commemorating Menodora and her family mention a temple of Tyche and a *plinthia*, presumably a block-like statue base supporting the statue of her son.[73]

These sequences of buildings are more often replacements for older buildings than new constructions, and in all cases the work was spread over a considerable period – perhaps eighty years at Aspendos, double that at Side, less at Phaselis, a century and a half at Perge. (There was no doubt similar work at the other cities, but even the approximations used here for these four cities are unreliable for the rest.) But it was all going on at the same time, between the reign of Claudius for the first building at Perge and the mid-third century for the Aspendian *basilica* and the restoration of the aqueduct at Side. There was then a break in construction during the troubles of the later third century, just as there had been an earlier break during the troubles of the first century BC, before the sequence resumed in the fourth century. The essential thing to note is that this building programme was subject to the economic resources being available, which were liable to be reduced if political troubles supervened. The finance came mainly from the private resources of the leading families, some of whom may well have bankrupted themselves in the process; they were, as *dekaprotoi*, also responsible for making up any tax shortfall, which might hit

---

[70] Schäfer, *Phaselis*, 175–176.

[71] M. Ballance, 'The Roman Basilica at Aspendos 1956 and 1992', *AST* XI, 1993, 453–457.

[72] P. Kessener, 'The 1998 Campaign of the Aspendos Aqueduct Research Project', *AST* 17, 1999, 263–269 (the second half of the article is about the bridge). There are discussions about the aqueduct in the *Journal of Roman Archaeology* for 2002.

[73] R. van Bremen, 'A Family from Sillyon', *ZPE* 104, 1993, 43–56; see, for this lady, the discussion later in this chapter.

them even harder. There was nothing specifically Roman about the programme of building, other than the fact that the Roman Empire existed at the particular point in the construction cycle: the process of building and rebuilding had been going on, as continuously as the economic situation allowed, since Akhaimenid times, and probably longer; it would resume in the fourth century. It has to be said, however, that the Roman-period buildings were larger and more solid and monumental in construction than the earlier ones; they might even be called coarse and brutal.

Water management produced ingenious work in many of the cities. The older cities, except Phaselis, all have large numbers of cisterns in their acropoleis, which were the basic resource for all of them. Side had an aqueduct from the Hellenistic period, for this was a city on low land, to which water could relatively easily be brought. It was only in the Roman period that the other cities acquired them, though Perge's southern extension may have been supplied earlier. The Pergean system involved tapping the local stream (now the Kalabaki) and constructing a channel for ten kilometres; in the city this supplied two large baths and three *nymphaea*. The overflow from the *nymphaeum* below the acropolis flowed along the centre of the main street in a carefully constructed channel.

The aqueduct at Phaselis was of Roman date, and was quite short, bringing water from (probably) the *Nordsiedlung* into the old city – though the line cannot be traced beyond the existing remains of the aqueduct; it was presumably only intended to supply the baths in the city. That at Aspendos employed a sophisticated siphon system to carry the water across the valley to the north and up to the level of the high city (plate 17); the first building the water reached inside the city was a bath. Other baths were later built below the acropolis on lower land to the south, no doubt using water from the river on that side of the city; these were built after the aqueduct seized up; one wonders if the aqueduct was really needed, or if it was built as a display of pride by the man who paid for it. Side, however, attentively repaired its aqueduct until the Arab attacks in the seventh century made it no longer feasible to do so; even then the new city wall was built to enclose a set of cisterns in the reduced city. Aqueducts also existed, though they are little known and were probably only short and perhaps low, at Attaleia and Magydos, which had convenient rivers nearby as sources. At Korakesion, some of the largest buildings on the summit of the hill are cisterns; they are now mainly Seljuk work, but no doubt the foundations are of Ptolemaic construction, if not earlier.[74]

---

[74] Not all of the aqueducts are well studied: P. Kessener and S. Pinas discuss 'The Pressure line of the Aspendos Aqueduct', *Adalya* 2, 1998, 159–187; the channel at Perge is noted by A. M. Mansel, 'Die

The existence of theatres and stadia is a reminder that several Pamphylian cities held regular civic festivals and games. Aspendos publicised its quinquennial games on its coins; the annual festival of Artemis at Perge was well known; Side also held regular games, though the only period they were celebrated on the city's coins is in the later third century: it may be they were only founded then.[75] It is odd that the stadium at Side has not yet been located; it is presumably somewhere outside the walls, though the immediate area is occupied by the necropolis.

There is evidence also for games at the smaller cities, such as Magydos. It had walls, baths, an aqueduct, and was a working port. The city had coined occasionally in the Hellenistic period,[76] and then more or less continuously from the early first to the later third centuries, just like every other city. The types are the usual variety of gods and goddesses, including a river god, suitably enough for a city positioned close to a waterfall and between the branches of the Katarrhaktes River. The coins also show a series of numbers, from five to forty-one, which may indicate a recurring games celebration.[77] If so, the event took place irregularly, possibly stimulated by some outside event – there were two in the reign of Philip the Arab, who celebrated Rome's millennium. These coins demonstrate the continued existence, autonomy, and vitality of this small city.

A more awkward group of coins relating to games comes from Aspendos and Perge in the third century. They show on the reverse a wreath and the legend '*themidos*' ('games', presumably) and a number, which should refer to the number of times the games were celebrated. Four are from Aspendos, numbered (in Greek) 369, 372, 374, and 375; two are from Perge, numbered 370 and 372. Since these inscriptions appear on coins with imperial portraits, an approximate dating can be made. '369' is backed by the head of Julia Domna, and so lay between 193 and 211; the highest number is '375', on coins of Gallienus and his wife Salonina (253–268). The interval between the celebrations, judging by

---

Nymphaeen von Perge'; for Attaleia some remains were note by W. M. Leake in his travels, *Journal of a Tour in Asia Minor*, London 1825, 133 and 193; the Magydos aqueduct is marked on the plan of the site in M. Adak and O. Atvur, 'Epigraphische Mitteilungen aus Antalya II: Die Pamphylische Hafenstadt Magydos', *Ep. Anat.* 31, 1999, 56.

[75] P. Weiss, 'Ein Agonostisches Bema und die isopythischen Spiele von Side', *Chiron* 11, 1981, 315–346.

[76] Head, *HN* 701; M. Adak and O. Atvur, 'Epigraphische Mitteilungen aus Antalya II: die Pamphylische Hafenstadt Magydos', *Ep. Anat.* 31, 1999, 53–68.

[77] Head, *NH* 701; J. C. Mossop, 'An Autonomous Coin of Magydos in Pamphylia', *Num. Chron.* 10, 1970, 319–320; *BMC* Pamphylia lxxvi–lxxvii.

the dates of the coins, was nine or ten years. This would put the first celebration in the third millennium BC, so a theory has been put forward that the initial letter of the number (always T) in the known examples is actually the definite article and that the numbers actually run from 69 to 75, thus allowing an initial date of 482 or 483 BC.[78]

The fact that some coins were from Aspendos and some from Perge detaches the games they celebrate from the individual cities, particularly since the postulated interval of nine or ten years does not correspond with Aspendos' four-year interval or the annual festival at Perge – though there was a nine-year cycle of games at Perge, founded by the Plancii. The coincidence of dating (both cities issued coins of 372 under Gordian III (238–244) suggests a regional celebration, possibly with the local city games designated as Pamphylian for the occasion. More information and more examples are really needed to sort out the meaning.[79] It is, for instance, curious that these coins were only issued in the third century. It is tempting to connect them with other coins of the period, which imply a mixture of civic competition and civic alliances (a subject to which I will return).

The peace and prosperity of the period from Augustus to the mid-third century permitted the growth of small towns in the countryside, or perhaps it would be better to say that the evidence for such places survives better for this period. The evidence may not be anything more than the discovery of Roman period inscriptions and Roman period building foundations, and these remains survive because little building has taken place in those town areas since the sixth century, until the modern period. But even those remains imply that the villagers had sufficient resources to put up more durable buildings and imitate the townspeople in their epigraphic culture.

The towns show the same architectural evidence as the great cities, but on a suitably smaller scale. At Lyrboton *kome*, in Pergean territory, to the north of the city, a series of richly carved sarcophagi indicate that some local families were wealthy, and this seems to have been founded on olive oil production

---

[78] SNG Paris 3, interprets the numbers as 'To B', 'To D', and 'To E' – second, fourth, and fifth.

[79] Head, *HN* 701; *BMC* Pamphylia lxxiv–lxxv; H. de Longprière, *Rev. Num.* 1869, 50–52; H. Graebler, 'Die Losurne in der Agonistik' *Zeitschrift für Numismatik* 39, 1929, 271–312; McKay, 'Major Sanctuaries', 2058, note 30. The new *SNG* Paris volume (3) (no. 166) has one of Geta marked '368', which spoils the argument; it certainly looks like a *theta* in the photograph, but it is perhaps really *eta*, which would make it another version of the Julia Domna coins. *BMC* reports that another coin of Julia Domna has been recorded as '319'. Two more examples of Salonina are in the Copenhagen and Austria, Leopold III, *SNG* volumes

and export.[80] Many of the sites surveyed in the *Tabula Imperii Byzantini* had Roman remains as well as evidence for later Roman occupation, and there are several cases of remains of olive oil production.[81] Olbia, supposing its site was at Gurma, shows evidence of Roman period buildings.[82]

Remains at Syedra east of Korakesion indicate a modest town, and there were several others along the coast east of Side. Syedra is beyond the eastern boundary of Roman Pamphylia, according to a naval diploma found at the site,[83] but this boundary was new, a line made for Roman bureaucratic convenience; earlier, places were allocated to Pamphylia or Lykia or Kilikia according to the writer's own ideas, and boundaries were not necessarily marked.[84] Along the coast to the east of Side, a number of small settlements have left reasonably substantial remains of the Roman period.[85] The towns of Ptolemais and Kibyra, midway between Side and Korakesion, may have been promoted to *polis* status in the Roman period. Coins of a city called Ptolemais have been attributed to the one in Pamphylia, but not definitively.[86] Kibyra, called a *polis* by the erratic Pseudo-Skylax about 360 BC, is also called that by Ptolemy the Geographer;[87] it was later an important naval base.[88]

The *TIB* survey has located a respectable number of villages, particularly in the *chorai* of Perge and Side, so the area of the cities of the plain is certainly beginning to produce evidence of rural life, in the form of either isolated farms, as in the survey by Küpper near Sillyon.[89] A number of *villae rusticae*, especially in the Çandır valley, have been located. This is an area in which careful systematic survey is clearly needed, and would certainly find more evidence.

There is one other site of particular interest in the rural area, the cave at Karain on the western edge of the plain which has produced evidence of occasional use and/or occupation at most periods between the Palaeolithic and the Byzantine.

[80] N. Cevik, 'An Olive Oil Production Center in Pamphylia: Lyrboton Kome', *Lykia* III, 1996/1997, 79–101; J. Keil, 'Das Lyrboton Kome in Pamphylien;', *Jahreshefte des Österreiches Archäologishen Instituts von Wien* 23, 1926, 89–106.

[81] *TIB* did not record Roman remains systematically, but notes the obvious remains.

[82] N. Cevik, 'The Localisation of Olbia on the Gulf of Pamphylia', *Lykia* I, 1994, 90–95.

[83] E. Rosenbaum, G. Huber, S. Onurkan, *A Survey of Coastal Cilicia*, Ankara 1967, 44–47 and 65.

[84] H.-J. Kellner, 'Zwei neue Flottendiplome: Zur Grenze von Pamphylien und Kilikien', *Chiron* 7, 1977, 315 -322.

[85] S. Sahin, 'Epigraphische Mitteilungen aus Antalya V', *Ep. Anat.* 33, 2001, marks a Lykia-Pamphylia boundary on his map.

[86] J. Nollé, 'Pamphylische Studien 7', *Chiron* 17, 1997, 235–250.

[87] *BMC*, lxxx, tentatively.

[88] Ps.-Skylax *GGM* 100; Ptolemy V.5.8.

[89] J. Nollé discusses some east Pamphlian towns in 'Karallia, Kibyra and Mylome (Justinianopolis)', Pamphylische Studien 6, *Chiron* 17, 1987, 235–250.

During the Roman period it was a shrine patronized by a guild of fishermen, who left a group of inscriptions recording their offerings to *Meter Oreia*, the Mother of the Mountain. The dates of the inscriptions are certainly Roman, and possibly Late Antique. It is a brief view of the less exalted parts of the local religion, which was largely controlled by the big men in the cities.[90]

The great temple at Perge was in fact the main religious centre for the whole of Pamphylia, and its influence stretched even further. An inscription found many years ago recorded an inventory of the temple's possessions, and who had presented them; it is no more than a fragment of a much larger record, and what remains cannot be regarded as representative of the whole, but it conveys useful information nonetheless. Gifts for the temple came from men and women of Side and Aspendos in Pamphylia, from Olympos in Lykia, and from people of Selge and Tarsos outside it.[91] No Pergeans are named – perhaps their contributions were listed separately – nor are any gift givers from any farther afield noted. The temple was clearly rich, as one would expect, and the evidence of the city's coins suggests that it was very influential, to put it no stronger, in the city's affairs. The changing depiction of the temple and of the image of the goddess as they appear on the coins might suggest changing methods by the moneyers. The engravers regularly showed the temple as distyle (two columns) in order to picture the baetyl within it; alternatively this might also suggest that building work and reconditioning took place fairly regularly.[92]

The coins of other cities also reveal aspects of their religious affairs. There is a great change from Hellenistic times, when types tended to be very restricted. In the Roman period many more gods and goddesses were depicted. Attaleia celebrated Poseidon on its coins, a suitable god for a port city, and no doubt there was a major temple for him there,[93] but in the imperial period the emperor took his place, and Poseidon only rarely appears on the coin-reverses. The coins of all the cities display images of many gods and goddesses, but one may doubt that all these deities had active temples in all the cities. The most prolific city in

---

[90] M. Küpper, 'Sillyon, Research Work 1995', XIV *AST* II, 1995, 451–462, 'Landliche Siedlungsplätze in Sillyon', *Lykia* II, 1995, 62–74, and 'Sillyon, Bericht über die Arbeiten 1996', XVI *AST* II, 1998, 475–496.

[91] S. Sahin, 'Bemerkungen zu Lykischen und Pamphylischen Inschriften; 5. Meter Oreia von Karain/Antalya: Eine Gottesgrotten in Sudkleinasien', *Ep. Anat.* 17, 1991, 126–132.

[92] *I. Perge*, 10.

[93] The cult has been the subject of several studies, including B. Pace, 'Diana Pergaia', in W. H. Buckler and W. M. Calder (eds), *Anatolian Studies presented to Sir W. M. Ramsay*, Manchester 1923, 297–314, L. Robert, 'La Sanctuaire d'Artémis Pergaia et la voilement des femmes', *Hellenica* V, Paris 1948, 64–69; S. Onurkan, 'Artemis Pergaia', *Ist. Mitt.* 19/20, 1969/1970, 289–298; R. Fleischer, *Artemis von Ephesos und Verwändte Kultstatuen aus Anatolien und Syrien*, Leiden 1972, 233–254.

this regard is Perge, on whose coins at least fourteen deities appear,[94] yet in the city no temples have been found (and, of course, the great temple of Artemis Pergaia still evades searchers). The Pergean temple in fact also appears on coins of Attaleia;[95] the Lady could have been worshipped in this city, but her temple was not there. It is therefore not reasonable to suppose that all the gods on the coins had cults in the cities which depicted them.

Phaselis, on the other hand, restricts itself to Athena and a female figure (presumably divine in some way), and still put its traditional galley on its coins at times.[96] At Aspendos, numerous gods and goddesses feature, but one in particular is singled out: Aphrodite Kastneites, honoured in an inscription on an altar, but she appears as a double goddess on the coins, and she also appears on an inscription at Sillyon.[97] On the other hand, at least a dozen other deities also appear on the city's coins, though only two temples have been located at the city;[98] the city's area is scarcely large enough for another dozen. At Sillyon we know that a temple of Tyche was built by Menodora out of her family's wealth, and Tyche is on the city's coins; but at least six other deities also appear, and for these no temples can be seen, though a temple of Zeus has been suggested.[99]

It is possible, however, that there were altars, without temples, for these gods and goddesses. A quarter in Side was named from an altar of Zeus, which implies that there was no temple. Yet the sheer number of deities commemorated on the coins is daunting. It is difficult to see that the cities were displaying their devotion to the gods or celebrating their own temples and cults. It is perhaps more likely that they were appealing to those deities for protection and assistance. Some of the deities – Artemis at Perge, Aphrodite Kastneites at Aspendos, the river gods at Magydos and Aspendos – are clearly local and it is significant that coins with these images and pictures of their temples are more common than the rest.

This ties in with the practice of cities throughout the empire in the second

---

[94] H. Chantaine, 'Schatzfund von Antalya', *JNG* 28, 1976, 89–106.

[95] Head, *HN* 699–700, for a list.

[96] SNG Paris 3, 279; M. Arslan and C. Lightfoot, *Greek Coin Hoards from Turkey*, Ankara 1999, 626.

[97] Head, *HN* 697.

[98] L. Robert, 'Monnaies et Divinités d'Aspendos', *Hellenica* XI–XII, Paris 1960, 177–188; H. Brandt, 'Kulte nach Aspendos', *Ist. Mitt.* 38, 1988, 237–250; Sillyon: D. Hereward, 'Inscriptions from Pamphylia and Isauria', *JHS* 78, 1958, 58–77, no. 10.

[99] Head, HN 701; a temple site has been excavated just above the main city gate; it has not been allocated to any particular deity; a second is suggested a little inside the South Gate in E. Ozgur, 'Aspendos Orenyeri 1991 Yili Kazı Onarim ve Cevre Duzenleme Calismaları', III *Muze* 1993, 251–255, marked as 'L' on the plan.

and third centuries boosting their images by acquiring honours and privileges from the emperors. The *polis* of Attaleia at some point became a Roman *colonia*. More locally, Perge, Aspendos, and Side put their local river gods on that coins. The temple at Perge successfully maintained its *asylos*-status when the Emperor Tiberius instituted an investigation of claims.[100] Several cities competed to acquire the title of *neocoros*, interpreted as a wardenship of the imperial cult, a competition which particularly enthused Side and Perge.

The imperial power was a rather distant matter for most Pamphylians. Only those few very rich men who took up political and administrative careers at Rome and in the imperial service would come into contact with the ruler. And yet the emperor, more as a force than as a person, pervaded everything: his head appeared on local coins. And yet it seems that the commemoration of emperors by statues and inscriptions in the several cities was no more than dutiful. Of the cities with relatively good collections of published inscriptions, the most numerous of these commemorations so far discovered – considering the period down to the late third century – is from Perge, beginning with Caligula and going as far as Tacitus, but there are no commemorations for Titus or Nerva, and few of the third century emperors, who were perhaps too ephemeral to be noticed;[101] Phaselis had a 'Domitianic' *agora*, and a 'Hadrianic' one, so named because of the monumental inscriptions found there – Domitian's name is excised – but there seems to be no imperial commemorations in the city before Vespasian and none after Caracalla, with a gap between Antoninus Pius and Caracalla. The quantity of inscriptions published from the city is substantial, and one would certainly have expected a longer period of imperial commemoration.[102] Attaleia, not a city with a large collection of inscriptions, has produced intermittent commemorations, from Vespasian to Philip the Arab.[103] Magydos, with only four published inscriptions, has produced one honouring Sabina, the wife of Hadrian.[104] Side was equally lacking in enthusiasm, with a statue for Claudius, commemorations of Vespasian, and then only occasional statues until Gordian III, but only a total of eight emperors were commemorated until 244 AD.[105]

---

[100] Menodora's gifts: Radet and Paris, no 3; coins: Head, *HN* 705.

[101] C.P. Jones, 'The Asylia of Artemis of Perge', *Ep. Anat.*, 31, 1999, 13–17.

[102] *I. Perge, passim*; this volume, arranged chronologically, only reaches as far as the Severi; the three Gordians and Tacitus are published by Merkelbach and Sahin, nos 15–17 and 22.

[103] *TAM* II.3. *passim*.

[104] Vespasian: Bean 1; Antoninus: Radet and Paris 1886, 2, Bean 3; Lucius Verus: Bean 4 and 5; Commodus: Bean 6 and 7; Julia Domna: Bean 8; Philip: Bosch/Atlan 9.

[105] Adak and Atvur (note 73), no. 2.

Neither Sillyon nor Korakesion have produced enough inscriptions to allow any conclusions to be drawn.

The imperial cult was also ever present, although, once more, it was hardly prominent – no temple of the cult is known anywhere in the region. Side and Perge competed for repeated honours as *neocoroi*, but neither has a temple, and both these cities are relatively well explored. There are signs in a few inscriptions of a cult at Attaleia,[106] and Menodora at Sillyon was the priestess of the cult there, but 'all the gods' and Demeter are a good deal more prominent in her activities.[107] There is nothing at Perge, not surprisingly, where the imperial cult could well have been absorbed into that of Artemis, though there were priests of the cult: the immensely rich Plancia Magna was priestess, and at the same time she was an acquaintance of Sabina, Hadrian's wife; if anyone would promote an imperial cult it would have been her. At Side Spartiaticus similarly was priest of the cult, but was honoured more for his embassies to Rome. All this looks as though none of the cities had any real enthusiasm for the empire or the emperors.

Most cities built a triumphal arch at one time or another, usually in honour of Hadrian as he travelled around the empire, though Side put up one for Vespasian (plate 21) and Perge one for Domitian. Attaleia had (and has) a splendid Hadrian gate (plate 15), as does Phaselis, now much reduced. At Perge the stumps of the arch put up by the brothers Demetrios and Apollonios in honour of Domitian are at the central street crossing.[108] Side decorated the southeast gate with a statue of Vespasian, and put up a triumphal arch at the civic centre beside the theatre. This was, much later, incorporated into the reduced fortifications as a new city gate; Aspendos had a triumphal arch and has produced an inscription honouring Germanicus, who may have visited the region,[109] and one recording a letter received from Hadrian.[110] There is no obvious monument of this type at Sillyon.

One of the reasons for this relative indifference must be that so few people in Pamphylia had any imperial connections; and there are very few indications that any imperial family members had any interest in Pamphylia – indifference may be said to be mutual. Even the travelling emperor Hadrian is not actually known

[106] *I. Side, passim.*
[107] Listed by S. Jameson in *RE*, Supp. 12, 122–123.
[108] H. van Bremen, 'A Family from Sillyon', *ZPE* 104, 1996, 43–56.
[109] J. Inan, 'Der Demetrios- und Apolloniosbogen in Perge', *Ist. Mitt.* 39, 1989, 237–244.
[110] S. Sahin, 'Bemerkungen zu lykischen und pamphylischen Inschriften', *Ep. Anat.* 17, 1991, 133–134, correcting the attribution to Drusus by Brixhe and Hodot (next note); on the possible visit of Germanicus see the articles by Sahin and Jones (note 47).

to have visited the area;[111] otherwise the only emperors who visited Pamphylia were Lucius Verus (probably),[112] and Tacitus;[113] the inscription concerning Germanicus at Aspendos may indicate that he visited that city.

Only Perge, through the Plancius family, had a direct link with an emperor. A descendant of the Plancii, Julia Aquilia Severa, married the strange emperor Elagabalus, though only briefly. She was related to a whole series of rich families in central Asia Minor, and included in her ancestors kings and tetrarchs,[114] while Elagabalus was (probably) a descendant of the old royal family of Emesa in central Syria, and included in his ancestry many of the same royal families of several eastern lands, from Thrace to Media, as his wife. This marriage was thus very obviously a political arrangement, aimed at widening the basis of Elagabalus' support beyond the very narrow group of Syrian and royal families, and his purported connection to the Severus family. A distant relative, C. Septimius Severus, cousin of the emperor Septimius, had governed Lykia-Pamphylia in the 150s,[115] though this is scarcely relevant. In Perge a statue of a lady as priestess of Artemis has been linked by style to the Severan family;[116] again this is only a very tenuous connection between the family and the city.

In a way the uncertainty as to whether Hadrian actually visited Pamphylia on his grand tours typifies the whole relationship of the cities of Pamphylia with the empire. At Perge Plancia Magna paid for the construction of the triumphal arch carrying statues of the three emperors Nerva, Trajan, and Hadrian, and four imperial women, Plotina (Trajan's wife), Sabina (Hadrian's wife), and Sabina's mother and grandmother.[117] The preponderance of women in a monument designed for Hadrian, and paid for by a rich, well-connected, and politically active woman is interesting, to say the least. Hadrian had in his train at this

---

[111] *SEG* XXXVIII, 1332; C. Brixhe and R. Hodot *D'Asie Mineure du Nord au Sud*, Nancy 1988, no. 39.

[112] All the contemporary records are either silent with regard to Pamphylia or ambiguous: cf. Schäfer, *Phaselis*, 153–154; neither A. R. Birley, *Hadrian, the Restless Emperor*, London 1997, 261, nor E. Speller, *Following Hadrian*, London 2002, can do more than suggest that Hadrian visited the area; it is not evidence of his visit that local people put up arches and statues to him.

[113] *Scriptores Historiae Augustae*, Verus 6–9; A. Birley, *Marcus Aurelius*, London 1966, 168.

[114] P. Weiss, 'Auxe Perge; Beobachtungen zu einem bemerkenserten städtischen Document des späten 3 Jahrhundert n. Chr.', *Chiron* 21, 1991, 313–38; R. Merkelbach, 'Kaiser Tacitus erhebt Perge zur Metropolis Pamphyliens und erlauft einen Agon', *Ep. Anat.* 29, 1997, 69–74.

[115] Settipani, *Continuité*, 456 and 467.

[116] *Inscriptions Latines d'Algérie*, 1.1283.

[117] A. Schmidt-Colinot, 'Eine Severische Preisten aus Syrien in Perge', *Ist. Mitt.* 41, 1991, 39–445.

point a local poet, Paion of Side;[118] at Phaselis another arch was put up and at least four statues presented by different sponsors.[119]

None of this, the emperor's friends, his poet, or the various buildings honouring him, is proof of the emperor's actual presence in any of the cities of Pamphylia. These monuments were erected partly in anticipation of his visit, partly as an inducement to him to arrive, partly as an acknowledgement of his proximity – or they may just have been examples of the hubris of the local rich – the arch of Plancia Magna at Perge, with its imperial women, may have something of that about it. And four statues of Hadrian at Phaselis seems extravagant. It is, one would suspect, more a sign of local internal political and social competition than anything to do directly with the emperor as a person or a visitor.

For these people were, of course, only partly honouring the emperor. Their main purpose was to have their own cities take note of their generosity. It was above all a local reputation they sought; the emperor's possible visit was merely the occasion for their display of local benevolence and generosity; if he had not been travelling then they would have spent their money on a different monument, perhaps something more useful than a statue or an arch. Triumphal arches are spectacular, but a bath building or an aqueduct, or even a temple, or the repair of an old and worn-out facility, might be more welcome to the citizens. That is, the empire was a distant and barely relevant factor in local life, even if an emperor seemed likely to pay a visit; for the inhabitants local life and reputation were more important.

The local elites made certain that their work was noticed by setting up inscriptions recording their attentiveness and generosity. In the manner of one hand washing the other, a particularly notable deed – such as helping feed the population in a time of dearth – would be marked by a collective commemoration. The net result would be a display of elite boasting which would surround the population at every turn. The best local surviving example of this ensemble is at Termessos, where several hundred of these inscriptions have been located in the city centre;[120] at Phaselis there are also numerous records;[121] at Sillyon the dossier of inscriptions associated with Menodora and her family pointedly recalled their spending of a million *denarii* to benefit the city and its citizens.[122]

---

[118] *I. Perge*, 101–109.

[119] L. Robert, 'Deux poètes grecs à l'époque impériale', *Stele: Mélanges Kontolion*, Athens 1980, 1–20;.

[120] Schäfer, *Phaselis* 153–154.

[121] O. van Niff, 'Inscriptions and Civic Memory in the Roman East', in A. Cooling (ed.), *The Afterlife of Inscriptions*, London 2000, 21–36.

[122] D. J. Blackburn, 'The Inscriptions', in Schäfer, *Phaselis*, 138–163.

The display is always keyed to an act which will benefit the community, and even the self-commemoration of victory or victories in the games is done in the name of honouring the victor's own city.[123] In the same spirit as providing food at a time of famine is the foundation of alimentary schemes at Attaleia, by one of the Calpurnii of that city, and at Sillyon, by Menodora.[124]

The case of Menodora has been noted more than once already; it may be helpful to go into more detail.[125] She was the daughter of a man called Megakles, and had married her uncle, Apollonios. The family traced its ancestry back for three generations before Megakles, and was clearly very wealthy. Menodora survived her husband and the hopes of the survival of the family lay with her son, another Megakles; there was also a daughter, probably called Theodora. Menodora was very active politically in the city, holding priesthoods (of 'all the gods' and Demeter), *damiourgos* of the city, honoured as *gymnasiarchos* 'for the giving of oil', no doubt the prize at the competitions, and *dekaprotos*; women were not normally entitled to hold these offices, but they were liturgies and the wealthy were expected to take up the formal burden; wealthy women did not escape.

After her husband's death, Menodora's father adopted her son as his own son, making the young Megakles his direct heir. Menodora's activities were therefore based on her control of the family's wealth as her son's guardian. But Megakles died young, leaving Menodora the heiress of the whole family's wealth. The inscriptions recounting her generosity to the city, paid for no doubt by the lady herself, recalled, amongst other gifts, one of a statue of the boy. The genealogy of the family has been worked out as in Chart VI.

The inscriptions cannot be dated much more precisely than 'the middle of the second century AD', which would refer to the aftermath of the death of Megakles (III); Menodora was born,therefore, early in that century, and, allowing a quarter-century for each generation, the first Megakles would have been adult at the beginning of the first century AD. This therefore is a family which was very prominent in the affairs of Sillyon for at least a century and a half, so prominent that Menodora, despite her sex, was able to hold numerous local offices normally held by men. All due to her wealth, of course, but we must also assume a strong force of personality there as well.

[123] Van Bremen, 'Family from Sillyon'.
[124] O. van Niff, 'Local Heroes: Athletics, Festivals and Elite Self-fashioning in the Roman East', in S. Goldhill (ed.), *Being Greek under Rome: Cultural Identity, the Second Sophistic and the Development of Empire*, Cambridge 2001.
[125] C. P. Jones, 'Eastern Alimenta and an inscription of Attaleia', *JHS* 109, 1991, 189–191; van Bremen, 'Family of Sillyon'.

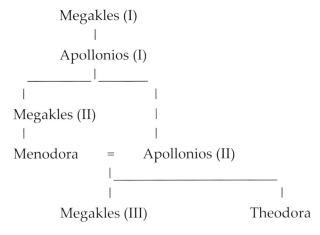

Chart VI. The Family of Menodora

Menodora is only one of several women who are prominent in affairs in Pamphylia in the second century AD. Plancia Magna at Perge has been noted already, but there is another example, not a lady politically active so far as we can tell, nor living in a city, but whose life suggests one reason for the importance of such women – the same reason, essentially which led to the prominence of both Plancia Magna and Menodora. A series of inscriptions on a small tower at the olive-oil producing village of Lyrboton (just north of modern Varsak) concerns, as with Menodora, an inheritance. The central person in the case was Kille, whose marital career must have been the engine for the accumulation of the property bequeathed by her son. The family genealogy works out as follows (Chart VII), based on the inscription and on a group of inscribed sarcophagi from the village.[126]

The generation of Demetrios and Apollonios flourished in and before the time of the Emperor Domitian, whose name was removed from one of the inscriptions. Kille therefore probably lived in the reign of Antoninus Pius and Marcus Aurelius. The story is another unhappy ending, however, for the inscriptions record the extinction of the family. Kille had been the guardian for Timotheos, whose decisions on the inheritance are recorded in the inscription. His own children presumably being dead, he left everything to Harmax, his

[126] The inscriptions were first published by H. A. Ormerod and E. S. G. Robinson, 'Notes and Inscriptions from Pamphylia', *ABSA* 17, 1910–1911, 216–249; they have been studied afresh by S. Sahin, 'Studien zu den Inschriften von Perge II de Gesändte Apollonios und seine Familie', *Ep. Anat.* 25, 1995, 1–24.

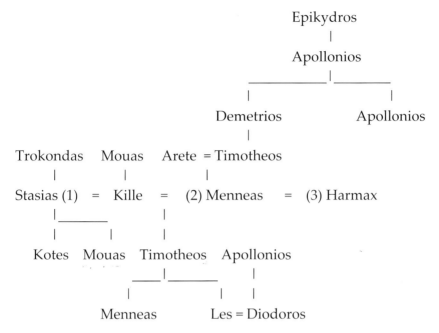

Chart VII The Family and Marriages of Kille of Lyrboton kome

mother's third husband, who was to hold it for his lifetime, and it was then to go to Apollo, whose temple presumably was in the village.

From the century of the women we have another geographer's swift survey of the region, in Ptolemy's *Geography*. It is only a list, essentially, like that of the sailor Ps.-Skylax five centuries before, and the two lists are very similar. Ptolemy notes all the usual cities, beginning at Olbia and going along the coast to Side; Korakesion and the Melas River are put in Rough Kilikia, and Perge, Sillyon and Aspendos are listed separately, because they were inland. Sillyon is spelled 'Sileion', which suggests that the pronunciation of the name was changing – it would be Syllaion a century later.[127]

The local oligarchs' generosity to their cities – as they claimed it to be – depended on their continuing to be rich. J. Nollé has argued that Side at least showed signs of prosperity in the second half of the third century,[128] but in that period there are repeated indications that elsewhere this source of civic upkeep was failing. The games and festivals faded away gradually during

[127] Ptolemy V.1–7.
[128] J. Nollé, 'Die Blutezeit der Stadt Side in der 2 Hälfte des 3 Jahrhunderts n. Chr.', Pamphylische Studien 10, *Chiron* 17, 1987, 254–265, repeated in shorter form with the same title in *AST* IV 1986, 269–272.

the century; the slow spread of Christianity will also have reduced both their popularity and their necessity, but the weakening of the wealth of the local rich was another, and perhaps more important, factor; the decline in the practice of epigraphic commemoration also hides from us their possibly similar decline. The commemoration of the emperors very largely stopped altogether with the end of the Severi. Building projects ceased, and existing buildings sometimes failed, the elaborate aqueduct at Aspendos did.

From outside there came raids by the Goths, who at one point in the 250s or 260s, laid formal siege to Side.[129] The attack was unsuccessful, but the presence of the invaders must surely have damaged the countryside, at least in the short term; no doubt it was this attack which necessitated the third century repairs to the city's aqueduct. The Isaurians beyond the Taurus were in insurrection for some decades, though their main target seems to have been Kilikia. In 276 the city of Cremna in Pisidia, to the north of Perge, was the centre of a major conflict, when it was besieged by the imperial Roman army – this being the occasion for the visit of the Emperor Tacitus to Perge. This insurrection was surely damaging to a wide area all around.[130] The siege was successful, but it was followed by a spread of banditry through the mountain areas.[131]

One of the most curious aspects of the third century is the evidence the cities provide for both competition with their neighbours and for a spirit of reconciliation with them. These are both visible in the coins produced in the cities. The economic problems affecting the empire, including inflation, lead to an increased production of coinage, and also to a competition for imperial favours, which could bring imperial subsidies. When achieved, these favours were advertised on the coins. Perge and Side competitively boasted of their appointments as *neocoroi*, which may be seen as a new version of the old rivalry, even hostility, between Side and Aspendos. By now Perge was the most important of the cities of the plain – its only competitor was Side. It does not seem that the largest of the cities, Attaleia, entered this competition; or perhaps it was the fact that Perge had by far the largest *chora* of all the Pamphylian cities which enhanced its strength and importance.

At the same time there is evidence of continued cooperation between the cities. The coins which commemorated the games at nine- or ten-year intervals,

---

[129] Dexippus, *FGrH* 100 F29; C. Foss, 'Bryonianus Lollianus of Side', *ZPE* 26, 1977, 161–171, dates the siege to the reign of Gallienus (252–268); J. Nollé, in *I. Perge* 79, opts for 269.

[130] S. Mitchell, *Cremna in Pisidia*, London and Swansea 1995, 211.

[131] S. Mitchell, 'The Siege of Cremna', in D. French and C. S. Lightfoot (eds), *The Eastern Frontier of the Roman Empire*, BAR S553, Oxford 1989, 311–328; C. Wolff, *Les Brigands en Orient*, Rome 2003, ch. 5.

issued by Perge and Aspendos, might indicate their cooperation in regional games (and is evidence of the continuing good relations between them). And there is a curious group of coins which proclaimed *homonoia* – concord (the Latin word would be *concordia*), unity, agreement between the cities. These coins linked the pairs of cities who made the agreements, and who then issued coins to celebrate and publicize it. They come from the middle of the third century, the reigns of Gordian III, Valerian, and Gallienus (i.e., 238–268), but mainly between 253 and 268. Side was the most active in this, as befitted an active trading city with old contacts, linking itself with Alexandria-by-Egypt, Delphi, Myra in Lykia, and Sagalassos in Pisidia, and, within Pamphylia, with Perge, Attaleia, and Aspendos. Concord with Aspendos and Perge is somewhat of a surprise, but it was clearly reciprocated, at least for the moment, and similar coins came from those cities. Perge was the only other city to make more than one or two such agreements: besides Side, it reached out to Delphi (it may be that the initiative was Delphi's), and Ephesos, which was another Artemis city.[132]

It is perhaps suitable to end this chapter with an event which was unique in Pamphylia's history, which is recorded uncommonly well, which draws together several of the many threads of this chapter, and which in several ways marked the end of the early imperial 'Roman' period. In AD 276 the Emperor Tacitus made his headquarters at Perge, during the final stages of the campaign to reduce rebellious Cremna to obedience. His sojourn provoked extravagant comments by Perge that it had become the capital of the world, and an elaborate declaration of its prominence in Pamphylia. Perhaps this sentiment persuaded the emperor to give grants of similar honours to the other cities. All Pamphylia clearly participated in the celebrations.

A chant of acclamations was devised at Perge and recorded in an inscription in which the city's honours were recited: 'metropolis' was a title conferred by Tacitus himself, but earlier the Emperor Caracalla had given the city the title of 'friend and ally', and Perge compared itself with Ephesos, one of its 'concord' cities. The chant went on with alternating shouts of 'Long Live Perge' ('*auxe Perge*') and praises of the city, which included the statement (or claim) that it was 'the greatest city of Pamphylia'. The city clearly had a wonderful time while the emperor was there.[133]

---

[132] Head, HN 701–705; P. R. Franke and M. K. Nollé, *Die Homonoia-Münzen Kleinasiens und der thrakischen Randgebiet*, Saarbrucken 1997.

[133] I. Kaygusuz, 'Perge, unter Kaiser Mittelpunkt der Welt', *Ep. Anat.* 4, 1984, 1–4; P. Weiss, 'Auxe Perge' (note 109).

But this was an end, not part of the onwards process. This is the only certain visit of any emperor to Pamphylia in the history of the empire, and Tacitus is the last emperor whose head appears on coins minted in any of the Pamphylian cities. Indeed the rest of the cities had already ceased minting, and Perge's mint still operated only because of the momentary imperial needs. By this time, also, new building had ceased, and even repairs were abandoned (as with Aspendos' aqueduct). None of the old oligarchic families, not even the Plancii, seem to have survived. Those elements – local coining, local families, civic building by the rich – which were all the essential parts of the culture of the first centuries of the Roman Empire, and of the preceding Hellenistic, ceased. The people of the following centuries inherited much of that culture, but the emphasis changed. Above all the religious impulse was to be directed into Christianity, and the local autonomy, which had been an essential element, was to be greatly reduced as the grip of the central government tightened. The extravagance of Perge's reaction to the presence of the emperor in the city was a final celebration of the old culture, an ending.

9

The Effects of Christianity

The Roman Empire recovered from the travails of the third century AD, but at the cost of an increased weight of government. The autonomy of cities was heavily restricted, the power of local provincial governors greatly increased, and the effects of this are to be seen in the cities. The patronage formerly exercised by the local rich now appears in the names of the governors in many cases, or of people who had been born in the cities and had made good in a career in central government. In other words, the former city council men had moved into the imperial bureaucracy; but this in many ways severed the direct links of the cities and the rich men.

The period of 'Late Antiquity', the fourth to early seventh centuries, exhibits many different signs of local prosperity until near the end. The re-establishment of internal order, and fending off of external attacks, the general reduction in internal warfare, all permitted the resumption of normal economic life. In the mid-fourth century the *Expositio Totius Mundi et Gentium*, a compilation of paragraphs giving thumbnail sketches of regions around the Mediterranean, characterized Pamphylia as a 'very lovely land, self-sufficient, and an exporter of oil; it has two splendid cities, Perge and Side',[1] and it is these two cities in which the best evidence for this period remains.

The basic economy of all the cities was, as ever in the ancient world, agriculture. The export of olive oil had been something noted at Aspendos in the Hellenistic and Roman Imperial periods, and this clearly continued in and after the fourth century. Side was the exception among the original cities in that it was a more accomplished trading city than the others, and its harbour was extensively altered in the fifth century.[2] Phaselis was similarly a city very oriented to trade, but the others did not neglect such activity: Attaleia and Magydos were ports, and Aspendos and Perge were accessible by river. In fact, it seems likely that the

---

[1] *Expositio Totius Mundi et Gentium*, ed., J. Rougé, Paris 1966, 181.
[2] P. Knoblauch, *Die Hafenlagen und die Anschliessenden Seemauer von Side*, Ankara 1977; compare his illustrations 85 and 86.

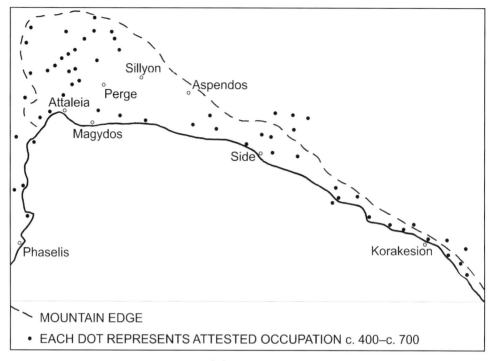

Map 15. Pamphylia: Late Antique settlements

river ports suffered from the deposition of silt and sand along the coast, which
blocked their rivers, while the bridge over the Eurymedon south of Aspendos,
now a Seljuk construction but built on solid and obvious Roman piers, will
have restricted access to river boats only; in this period near the mouth of the
river, at modern Bogazak, below the bridge, a settlement developed, which may
well have been an outport for Aspendos. Also near the mouth of the Kestros,
Perge's river, by the early sixth century there was the port of Emporion – the
name itself is a sign of mercantile activity – and this was clearly Perge's outport.
There also developed an anchorage at Kynosarion, which was due south of, and
probably in the *chora* of, Sillyon. Sillyon's river, in particular, has clearly been
diverted from its original mouth to flow east for ten kilometres before reaching
the sea, and was probably useless for navigation at all times. But Kynosarion was
apparently no more than an open beach, the sort of landing place the sailors of
the time used as their nightly resting place.[3]

The need for such ports testifies to the continuing flow of commerce. And
for once we have the helpful survey of rural settlements, the *Tabula Imperii*

---

[3] For these places, cf. *TIB* 2.486 (Bogazak), 529 (Emporion), 676 (Kynosarion).

Byzantini, to put beside the cities which are necessarily the first objects of study. This survey has identified many settlements that show evidence of occupation in and after Late Antiquity. Their first period, the fourth to seventh centuries, shows villages and villas spread throughout Pamphylia, but the distribution of those located is uneven. Perge and Side, as would be expected, have numerous rural settlements in their *chorai,* but Aspendos has only a few; Sillyon has none, except for Kynosarion, presumed to be in the city's territory; Phaselis, if it controlled the Çandır valley, still had several places in its mountainous and difficult territory. Attaleia, with only a small territory, had only one that can be identified (Map 15).

This distribution confirms the archaeological findings at the cities, and the evidence from the written sources. Perge and Side were the two pre-eminent cities of Pamphylia in Late Antiquity. This situation had been developing all through the earlier Roman Imperial period, of course, and the acclamations for the brief visit of the Emperor Tacitus emphasised it for Perge. This contrasts with the Hellenistic period, when Aspendos was the most prominent and important city, and with the post-AD 650 period when Attaleia was the most important, indeed almost the only, city.

Side, on the other hand, had retained its importance, in a local sense, all through from its origin, when it was the only urban place in Pamphylia. It rivalled Aspendos in the Hellenistic, and Perge in the Roman and Late Antique periods, and it bade fair to rival Attaleia for a time after AD 650. The basis for this was obviously its trade, its considerable territory, as shown by its *chora,* and its position at the mouth of the Melas River route to the interior. In addition it had more varied types of land – shore, river valley, plain, hills, forests – than most of the others, whose territories were essentially the plain, or, at Phaselis, the hills. It is obviously relevant that Perge and Side lay on the most useful routes leading to the Anatolian interior; Phaselis, Sillyon, and Aspendos had no such relatively easy access; Attaleia, different as ever, had its port and its size and its fortifications as its main assets; it also had access, like Perge, to the Anatolian interior; these were to bring it to prominence later.

The sources for this period are somewhat different from those available for earlier periods. The ending of local mints removes the numismatic evidence, except for that provided by some local hoards; archeologically there is *TIB*'s competent survey for the rural areas, though this is not reinforced by much excavation; the written sources are as fragmentary and oblique as ever, but they now also include a certain amount of information from Christian documents.

The major changes to conditions of life were, therefore, first of all the general, if slow, adoption of Christianity, with its new *ethos* and its requirement for new and different buildings; and the closer attention to local affairs by the agents of the central and provincial governments. In this latter case it was the imperial successors of the Emperor Tacitus, notably Diocletian, who began the process.

Perhaps as a consequence of the rebellion by Cremna, the Pisidian section of the province of 'Lykia and Pamphylia' was detached, leaving Lydia and Pamphylia still linked. This probably took place in Diocletian's reign (284–305), certainly by 308–311 when Pisidia is regarded as under the governor of the diocese of Asia.[4] This was part of a long, slow process by which the provinces were subdivided into smaller areas, while super-provinces, the dioceses, were erected over them; all of which provided the central government with a much closer control over local affairs. By the end of the fourth century, Lykia and Pamphylia had also been separated, so that they were then two provinces; as a result Pamphylia was, for the first time, governed as a single unit.[5] This was still the situation at the end of the fourth century, as is shown in the *Notitia Dignitatum*, which appears to reflect the position about 395, the date of the death of the Emperor Theodosios I.[6]

Looking at these changes from the viewpoint of Pamphylia, while inevitable in the context of my subject, may give a misleading impression of the overall purpose of the changes. This was not a matter of providing Pamphylia with a particular provincial government; it was perhaps more a matter of Pamphylia being left after the other areas had been removed from the former much larger province. Pisidia was removed, to be added to Lykaonia, which later took in Isauria also, in order to provide a unified government for the troublesome mountain areas – the rebellion of Cremna in 276 and its suppression left a poisonous legacy of brigandage which lasted for many years.[7] With Pisidia gone, there was no reason not to separate Lykia and Pamphylia, since it seems that smaller provinces such as these were the imperial government's preference by the fourth century; the two areas had in fact little in common, and their only link was the provincial governor. Once again, however, these measures were being taken, which affected Pamphylia, but not with Pamphylia's well-being particularly in mind.

The Late Antique governors of the province are little known. Only a dozen are known by name and only half these can be assigned a precise date for their incumbency; in the last century and a half, before the Arab attacks changed everything, only one governor is known by name. Their effective anonymity is

---

[4] A. H. M. Jones, *The Later Roman Empire 284–602*, Oxford 1964, 43.

[5] A. H. M. Jones, 'The Date and Value of the Verona List', *JRS* 44, 1954, 21–29.

[6] Jones, *Later Roman Empire*, 1417–1460: Pamphylia is on 1457.

[7] S. Mitchell, *Cremna in Pisidia*, London and Swansea 1995, ch. 6, and is 'Native Rebellion in the Pisidian Taurus', in K. Hopwood (ed.), *Organized Crime in Antiquity*, London 1995.

not deceptive: their work was increasingly controlled from Constantinople, and anyway, Pamphylia retained its overall unimportance in the imperial scheme of things. Another reason for the governors' general anonymity is the new custom of men using only single names – Christian names – which deprives us of the means of detecting their family connections.[8] This brings us to the other great social change, the general adoption of Christianity.

As with all too much of the social history of Pamphylia, the process of Christianisation in the area is all-but invisible. Paul of Tarsos passed through Perge on one of his journeys, and through Attaleia on his return, but we have no evidence that his passage had any result locally.[9] No doubt the number of Christians grew slowly during the first two centuries AD. Two local men, Nestor of Kibyra and Tribimis of Perge, were martyred in the brief persecution under the Emperor Decius (250–251), and their memory was certainly kept alive both locally and in Constantinople for several centuries,[10] but what they did to earn, or provoke, such a dubious honour is not known. During Diocletian's reign the shrine of Artemis at Perge was damaged or destroyed by a couple of Christians,[11] an action which provided the local believers with two more martyrs to remember, and an enlivening, but unbelievable, story describing their deaths. These developments and deaths imply that at least a part of Perge's population was by that time Christian, and militantly so, and that the devotees of Artemis were incapable of stopping them – unless it was no more than a small scale guerilla action. Presumably the temple and the goddess's image were repaired, for the worship of the old gods was still the official religion for another thirty years after the attack. Some time later, Lykia-Pamphylia was the source of at least one petition for the restoration of paganism,[12] and the pagan Emperor Julian was commemorated at Side as a god.[13] It all proved to be too late, and Constantine's final victory over Licinius in 324 put the Christians everywhere in control. As with all totalitarian revolutionaries, once in power they denied to their opponents the toleration which they had generally been allowed beforehand.

---

[8] A list of governors is provided in *TIB* 1, appendix A.

[9] Acts 13.13.14.

[10] C. Brixhe and R. Hodot, *L'Asie Mineure de Nord au Sud*, Nancy 1988, no. 14, a shrine of Tribimis.

[11] 'Meniologium Graecum Basilinum, Aug 1', in P. G. Migne. *Patrologia cursus completa ...,* vol. 117, 568. The two perpetrators were Alexander and Leontius; the story of their deaths was that the beasts in the arena would not kill them, so they were decapitated; this was clearly regarded as exemplary; cf. McKay 'Major Sanctuaries', 2075.

[12] *OGIS* 564; Jones, *Later Roman Empire*, 72–73; J. H. Smith, *Constantine the Great*, New York 1971, 98–99.

[13] *I. Side* 50.

The visible results of this at the several cities are the remains of churches built during the following three centuries. Attaleia shows the remains of at least four. The largest, the Church of the Panaghia, was converted into a mosque later (the Kesik Minare), which has meant that much of it survives, though the building is now in ruins. It is of an unusual plan, evidently based on the Roman *basilica*, though with pillars supporting a central dome, so that the centre of the building is the focus, not one end. It has a certain resemblance in plan to the Church of Hagia Sophia in Constantinople, which has suggested a date for its construction in the early part of the sixth century. It used much recycled stonework in its building, including a variety of inscriptions, and was decorated with carved marble and floor mosaics and wall frescos.[14]

One other church, of St. Demetrios, is wholly ruined, and two other churches are known of in the city.[15] This is the only city in Pamphylia to have been continually inhabited since its foundation; recycling of cut stone (and even the importation of cut stones from other sites) was normal, and the change of religion to Islam in the thirteenth century ensured that as churches went out of use they were allowed to collapse, their stones were removed, or they were converted into mosques.

Perge, relatively well explored, therefore provides a better indication of the scale of church building in Late Antiquity. This was the city in which no temples existed in the imperial period, for it was always overshadowed by the temple of Artemis (Plates 5, 6). The temple was closed down at some point, probably in the fourth century. If my supposition that the temple prevented the establishment of other cults in the city is correct, then this would go all the more so for Christianity, yet a church was built in the city's southward extension, by the South Gate, in the fourth century[16] (Map 7 'G'). Inside the city, in a commanding position just to the west of the colonnaded main street, and central to the whole city, a much greater church was built probably in the same period (Map 7, 'G1'). It was a large building, 32 metres wide and 45 long, with five aisles, plus an atrium and a narthex.[17] Still using the basic

---

[14] M. Balance, 'Cumanin Camii at Antalya: A Byzantine Church'. *Proceedings of the British School at Rome* 23, 1955, 99–114; G. Grassi, 'Precisazioni sulla Panaghia di Antalya', *Milion* 1, 1988, 81–104, and id., 'Scultura architettonica e *spolia* marmoree della Panaghia in Antalya', *Milion* 2, 1990; the inscriptions are noted by N. Gokalp, 'Epigraphische Mitteilungen aus Antalya IV: Inschriften aus Attaleia', *Ep. Anat.* 31, 1999, 72–76..

[15] H. Rott, *Kleinasiatische Denkmäler*, Leipzig 1908, 32–44.

[16] *Ibid.*, 47–50.

[17] *Ibid.*, 50–57; preliminary excavation reports on this church are in IX *Kazı*, 1987, 187–188, and X *Kazı*, 1989, 212–213.

basilican plan, it has all the appearance of a triumphant Christian cathedral planted in the place where the Lady of Perge would never have allowed it; it was actually built on the highest part of the lower city. In the cathedral a relief of Artemis was incorporated, apparently standing in for one of the Virgin Mary.[18]

Perge had no less than six churches, the two just noted, two (and a chapel) on the acropolis (Map 7, 'G2', G3'), and a sixth on the southern hill, where the former temple may have been. Not all these are well dated, and the chapel on the acropolis was certainly of Byzantine date (that is, eighth century or later). Those below the acropolis were built before the Arab attacks, which began about 650, and which compelled the evacuation of the lower city; but another, at the main street crossing was perhaps of post-650 date (Map 7, beside 'S'). It was all a substantial building investment, almost comparable with that which had been made in the earlier Roman period.

In addition there were other works carried out in the city, particularly repairs and renovations of existing buildings. Apart from the churches, the only new buildings which have been detected are a fountain near the theatre, and the curious 'tetraconch' building inserted at a slightly disturbing angle into a large *palaestra* (Map 7, 'G4') The city walls were repaired and the buildings put up outside the southern gate were now enclosed in an extension of the walls (Plate 9, Map 16). The Roman *agora* to the east of the gate had been built over part of the old Hellenistic walls, and the new extension of the walls was constructed of recycled stones. Various shops in several parts of the city were repaired or altered, and the *nymphaeum* below the acropolis was renovated and improved. By this time, of course, apart from the churches, the city had the full set of buildings needed for the continuing life of an ancient city, and new buildings were not needed. What was done shows that the city fabric was carefully maintained and that any gaps in provision were supplied. The city lived and prospered.[19]

Besides building churches in several parts of the city and nearby, Perge could also claim its own saint. This was a lady of the city who became revered as St Matrona of Perge, though her sanctity was earned at Constantinople, not in her home city. It is possibly significant that the cathedral was dedicated to the Virgin, and that the city's own saint was a lady.[20] Surely this can be seen as an

---

[18] A. Pekman, *Perge Tarihi/History of Perge*, Ankara 1973, 98, referring to S. Onurkan, 'Perge Artemis Kaburtmaları ve Artemis Pergaia', *Belleten* 33, 1969, 319; Rott, *Kleinasiatische*, 48–56.

[19] These works are detailed, with references, in Foss, 'Cities', 16–18.

[20] J. Featherstone and C. Mango, 'Life of St Matrona of Perge', in A. M. Talbot, *Holy Women of Byzantium; Ten Saints' Lives in English Translation*, Washington DC 1996, 13–64.

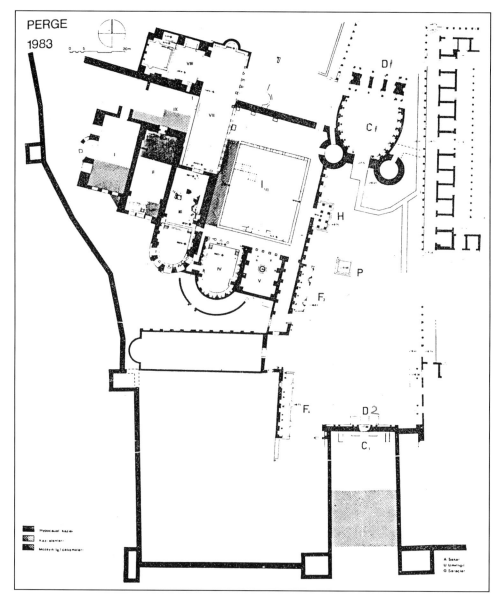

Map 16. Perge: south gate

ingrained, ancestral continuation of the influence of the defunct, dethroned Lady of Perge.

Side was Perge's great rival, insisting on the same or better privileges during the Roman period. This rivalry extended into the Christian period, when the two cities' bishops were eventually recognized as equals, and Pamphylia was divided between them; the bishop of Side's territory was that of the old *polis*, from the old boundary with Aspendos eastwards, plus the hills and coastlands to the south and east; Perge's bishop had authority over the cities of the plain, including Sillyon and Aspendos. Side also had its martyrs, who had also attacked the city's Artemis temple. Their condemnation, like those in Perge, was foiled by the unwillingness of the animals to kill them, and they were then decapitated, very like those at Perge. One wonders which story was copied from which. But Side went one better in having nine martyrs, to Perge's two.[21]

Side had suffered a violent, if unsuccessful, siege by the Goths in the 260s, and was in the front line of the Isaurian emergency between 350 and the end of the century. The city was never captured, but it will have received damage particularly in its rural areas. The aqueduct needed extensive repairs at the end of the third century, accomplished by a local equestrian called Bryonianus Lollianus, his wife, and his son.[22] The walls were strengthened and remodelled, towers were added, and gateways were narrowed; the old notion that the Hellenistic walls were abandoned in the fourth or fifth century has been discarded.[23] The North Gate was extended by taking an extra-mural *nymphaeum* as the basis for a new wall, rather as at Perge, by which the old Hellenistic gate, with its now decorated, semi-circular entranceway, was made into an inner gateway: the new outer gate was flanked by square towers, and had a more determined and deterrent look to it. Other work was done at the South Gate, also aimed at strengthening it.[24] Within the city, as at Perge, most building work was in the form of repairs, and almost every building shows evidence of repair or even rebuilding during Late Antiquity. Some new buildings, however, including more than one fountain, were put up, as were, possibly, a new suite of baths.

Bryonianus Lollianus is something of a puzzle. He lists his career as *primipilarius*, *procurator*, and *ducenarius*, which earlier would have meant a military career followed by a transfer to the civil branch, rising therefore from private soldier to the aristocracy; he married a lady of a senatorial family. But if, as seems likely, he was active towards the end of the third century, his offices may well actually have been all civilian, for *primipilarius* became an honorary civil rank as the legionary army faded away. For his generous help to his city he

---

[21] J. Nollé in *I. Side*, 186–194.

[22] C. Foss, 'Bryonianus Lollianus of Side', *ZPE* 26, 1977, 161–171.

[23] C. Foss, 'Attius Philippus and the Walls of Side', *ZPE* 26, 1977, 172–180.

[24] J.-M. Carrie, 'Bryonianus Lollianus de Side ou les Avatars de l'ordre équestre', *ZPE* 35, 1979, 213–224, backs up Foss's dating with further detailed argument.

was honoured as *ktistes*, and his wife as Pegasis, a nymph who provided water – he had repaired the aqueduct.[25]

The main new buildings, of course, were the churches. It would seem that, despite the martyrs, Christianity only slowly prevailed in the city. The Emperor Julian was honoured with a statue – the inscription calls him a god[26] – and the Christian emperors Valentinian II, Theodosius I and his sons, were commemorated with a statue erected 'according to the traditional ritual' – pagan, that is – by a pagan praetorian prefect whom they later executed.[27] The local aristocracy was evidently largely pagan throughout the fourth century, and Julian's statue and inscription were not removed later. There is a church dated to the early fifth century in the city, built on the basilican plan. It appears to be the earliest church in Side; no doubt the dominant pagans were tolerant, to their subsequent discomfiture, but were able to maintain control of the city's planning system.[28]

Other churches in the city are dated, rather vaguely, to the fifth and sixth centuries, by which time the full weight of the imperial government was insisting on Christianity, and pagan worship was suppressed. These include an elaborate complex of buildings inside the East Gate, consisting of a large church, thought to be the city's cathedral, a bishop's palace, associated buildings, and a chapel (Map 9, '28'). (It is perhaps not surprising to learn that the church is rather bigger than the main church at Perge.) In the sixth century, probably, the site of the twin temples of Apollo and Athene at the harbour, which by then were in ruins, was taken over and a large basilican church built there: Christ now acted as the sailors' landmark in place of Apollo and Artemis (Map 9, '20', Plate 22). A temple near the harbour, probably to Men, was also reused, but as what is not known.[29]

The pattern seen at Perge is, though its citizens and bishops may not have liked the thought, more or less repeated at Side; the main difference might be the slower acceptance of Christianity at the latter city, but even that is not certain, for Artemis at Perge was a powerful force for resistance, well rooted in the local city and in the local aristocracy. The initial martyrdoms were not repeated in later years, and the fourth century, as elsewhere in the empire, was

---

[25] Foss, 'Cities', 31–33; A. M. Mansel, *Die Ruinen von Side*, Berlin 1963, 27–39.

[26] *I. Side* 50.

[27] *I. Side* 52.

[28] S. Eyice, 'L'Église cruciforme Byzantine de Side en Pamphylie', *Anatolia* 3, 1958, 35–42.

[29] Foss, 'Cities', 31–43; S. Eyice, 'L'Église Byzantine de Side', *Anatolia* 2, 1957, 36–42, and 'Un baptistière byzantine à Side en Pamphylie', *Actes des Congrès Internationales d'Archéologique Chrétienne*, Paris 1957, 577–582; Rott, *Kleinasiatische*, 61–65.

a period in which the rival religions jostled each other, with Christianity slowly winning the competition. Otherwise civic life continued, as the renovations in both cities attest. Commercial activity remained strong, and Side's harbour was kept usable by removing windblown sand and silt,[30] while Perge's outpost at Emporion was important enough to be given a building to act as a house for the poor by the Emperor Justinian in the sixth century.[31]

Phaselis exhibits the same continuity, if perhaps on a smaller scale – but it was also a smaller city. It too retained its generally prosperous condition. The municipal amenities – baths, walls, the theatre, the *agorai*, the harbours – were repaired and maintained. Churches were the only new buildings erected, one in the old rectangular *agora*, using up half its area, and another on the acropolis.[32]

A *basilica* and church (of St Andreas) is known at Magydos,[33] and Aspendos and Sillyon provide small fragments of evidence of continued occupation and general prosperity. The lack of information is in large part due to a lack of investigation of all these cities, but churches have been noted in all. Aspendos rebuilt its Roman *basilica*, and two bath buildings on the lower land south of the acropolis have been dated to the period of Late Antiquity; one of them is enormous (Map 5, 'Y'), and both show substantial remains even now; the failure of the aqueduct, and so of the water supply to the upper city, was perhaps the basic reason for these new baths, which were closer to the river, from which, presumably, they drew their water. The city renamed itself 'Primupolis' at some point, possibly after a local martyr called Primus.[34] At Sillyon, there is a church, though small, which reused an earlier building, and a hall attached to it. The construction may be dated only roughly to the fifth or sixth centuries. The city had a bishop by that time, and these may be his cathedral and palace, though it is rather small for such a designation.[35] At Korakesion a small Byzantine church still exists, built into a tower of the city wall, and a second one is on the top of the hill; both are probably of later build.[36]

The purposes of civic building thus changed, and some of the old constructions tended to fall out of use: theatres were not abandoned, being useful for many civil functions, but the games festivals were discontinued; the baths were maintained,

---

[30] P. Knoblauch, *Die Hafenenlagen und die Anschliessenden Seemauer von Side*, Ankara 1977.

[31] Procopius, *De Aedificiis*, 5.9.38.

[32] C. Foss, 'The Lycian Coast in the Byzantine Age', *DOP*, 48, 1999, 1–52.

[33] M. Adak and M. Atvur, 'Epigraphische Mitteilungen aus Antalya II: Die Pamphylische Hafenstadt Magydos', *Ep. Anat.*, 31, 1999, 57.

[34] Foss, 'Cities', 19–24.

[35] Nethercott and Ruggieri, 50–153; see also the comment by Foss, 'Cities', 19–20, and his note 83.

[36] Bean, *TSS*, 80–82.

and new ones built, and the aqueducts which fed them were maintained where possible; fountains were installed and repaired. The fourth century saw a major change in civic priorities, one of which was the gradual adoption of Christianity, and this had an obvious effect on other activities. Those which had a pagan religious basis, as with the games, were discontinued, those without such a basis, such as the baths, could continue. They were replaced or supplemented by other activities with all the appearance of the old civic obligations of the pagan period applied in a new way, just as new churches replaced, sometimes physically, the older temples. Charity funds were channelled to the Church, and the Church's holdings of land greatly expanded. For both of these the main source of funds was always the local oligarchy. The great increase in wealth and power of the Church made the bishops part of the local power structure, in the same way as the former pagan and imperial priesthoods had been. Once this became clear, the oligarchs rapidly colonised the episcopate,[37] just as the increased importance of the imperial bureaucracy proved similarly attractive.

All the cities, and even Olbia, are recorded as bishoprics in the fourth and fifth centuries. A series of councils were held, whose episcopal attendees were recorded, and this gives a helpful record of the continuing life of the cities at the time, since it may be assumed that the existence of a bishopric meant the presence of a relatively substantial congregation; however, confirmatory evidence is needed by the time we reach the later Byzantine period. Aspendos appears once as 'Primupolis', but then reverted to its original name. Several bishoprics in Side's area were in places which had been villages earlier, and do not otherwise give indications of civic life. Olbia, where there was also a bishop, appears in one list as a *demos*, a people, not actually as a city. The implication is that this ancient city was no longer functioning as such; it also appears only in Hierokles' list, not in attendance at the several councils; perhaps we can assume it was absorbed by its close neighbour Attaleia – there had surely been a blight on Olbia since Attaleia's foundation, but the absorption had taken centuries to become final. The bishops of the cities inherited the *chorai* of their cities as their bishoprics. In the cases of Perge and Side these were, of course, large, and so promoted the bishops' own status; by the fifth century the predominance of these two cities led to their recognition as metropolitan sees; Perge enfolded the old cities of the plain in its area, plus Attaleia and Magydos; Side had to be content with only Korakesion of the Pamphylians, plus village bishops.[38]

---

[37] Jones, *Later Roman Empire*, 920–929, on the social origins of the clergy.

[38] See the lists in Appendix 4 of Jones, *Later Roman Empire*, and those conveniently tabulated by W. M. Ramsey, 'Antiquities of Southern Phrygia and the Border Lands', *AJA* 4, 1888, 6–21.

The attention of the emperors was, as always, habitually directed to other concerns than Pamphylia. A visit to Side by Helena, the mother of Constantine I, in 327, was only a momentary event.[39] Rather more violent events in the region appear to have affected Side more than any other city. The Isaurians' raids in the 350s brought troops into the area. In 354 an Isaurian attack was blocked by 'the legions' which were stationed in the city.[40] Then in the time of the Emperor Valens (364–378) the Isaurians are said, contradictorily, to have sacked cities in Lykia and Pamphylia, and yet were unable to tackle walls, and so they ravaged the countryside.[41]

These raids did not begin until the 350s, it seems, for Ammianus comments that in 354 the area 'was long unmolested', but he also notes that there were 'strong garrisons' in the cities.[42] Precisely what this means is not clear, since he says no more about it, but it is certain that these local troops could defend the city but were not sufficient to prevent the attacks, and it took imperial expeditionary forces to beard the raiders in their dens. This suggests that the 'strong garrisons' were actually the militia forces of the various cities, probably poorly armed and nearly untrained. One of the imperial expeditions was mounted by the *vicarius* of Asia, Musonius, in which he was defeated and killed;[43] another was sent about 400 by the Goth Gainas;[44] soon after another one was necessary, in which the commander succeeded at last in reaching deep into the mountains, so stopping the raids for a time.[45]

Pamphylia was rarely in the imperial limelight. Under normal conditions, and for long periods, the outside world's intrusion into Pamphylia was concerned with administration and taxation and little else. The military operations in the second half of the fourth century are very unusual. But then there was also the never-distant problem of corrupt officials, and this would be particularly unpleasant when the culture of the administrators turned larcenous. For Pamphylia we have a little story of about AD 400 where the extortions of a governor called Hierax were compared to the ravages of the Isaurian raiders; Hierax was caught, and divested of more wealth than his ill-gotten gains amounted to, though it is

---

[39] *I. Side* 47, 48; L. Robert, 'L'Impératrice Anatrophé à Side', *Revue de Philologie* 41, 1967, 82–84.

[40] Ammianus Marcellinus 14.2.8 and 10.

[41] Ammianus Marcellinus 4.20.

[42] Ammianus Marcellinus 14.2.8 and 10; the 'legions' at Side are a puzzle, as is the number of men in a legion at this time; perhaps Ammianus simply means legionaries, or possibly merely soldiers; it seems unlikely that two (or more) legions were stationed at Side at this time. On legionary size, see P. Southern and K. R. Dixon, *The Late Roman Army*, London 1996, 31–33.

[43] Ammianus Marcellinus 27.9.6.

[44] Zosimus, *Historia Nova* 5.15.

[45] Zosimus, *Historia Nova* 5.25.

unlikely that any was returned to their original owners.[46] Just how common this behaviour was is unknown, and the point of the story is that Hierax was caught. How far his behaviour was typical, and whether his exposure was unusual, is a mystery. It was probably a periodical matter, a problem which revived when the supervisory functions of the higher bureaucracy were directed elsewhere. To become rich, was, after all, one of the purposes of joining the imperial bureaucracy, and there were few administrative restraints on their activities.

The fifth century saw the loss of the western empire, but imperial events, crises at Constantinople, the barbarian invasions, and the problems of the west were all distant events having little direct effect in Pamphylia. The Isaurian raids were awkward and threatening, but were suppressed during the later fourth century, and anyway had mainly been directed into Kilikia.[47]

In 542, however, the plague arrived in Egypt, and was rapidly exported north across the Mediterranean. It will have reached Pamphylia, probably at Side, which had old connections with Alexandria, or perhaps Attaleia. We have no precise information on its effects in Pamphylia, but it cannot be doubted that the land was fully involved in the great demographic crisis which followed. Contemporary estimates suggest a very heavy death toll, of the order of between a fifth and a half of the urban population. The disease, thought to be bubonic plague, affected cities most of all because of the dirt and crowding, and the cities of Pamphylia will have suffered with the rest. This was a disease which struck repeatedly, on average every fifteen years or so, never allowing the depleted population to recover. There can be no doubt that the Pamphylian cities' population declined seriously in the century after the plague's arrival.[48]

This did not necessarily mean that the cities physically reduced in size. Side has been taken as a particular example of shrinkage, where an inscription recording the repair of the city wall at the instigation of Attius Philippus was noted in the new, later, wall which cuts the city in half (Map 9, '29', Plate 23). This was held to imply the reduction of the city to less than half its Roman size in the fourth and fifth centuries. But it is now recognised that the inscription

[46] Eutropius, frag. 71 (R. C. Blockley, *The Fragmentary Classicising Historians of the Later Roman Empire*, Liverpool 1989, 114–117.

[47] S. Mitchell, 'Native Rebellion in the Pisidian Taurus', in K. Hopwood (ed.), *Organised Crime in Antiquity*, London 1999, 155–176; M. Zimmermann, 'Probus, Carus und die Räuber in Gebiet des Pisidien Termessos', *ZPE* 110, 1996, 265–277.

[48] Procopius, *Persian Wars* 2.21–23, (on the outbreak at Constantinople in 542); *Chronicle of Ps.-Dionysios of Tell Mahre* III, 74–98, who quotes John of Ephesos as reporting an official casualty total of 290,000 in the city, when counting stopped; cf. S. Mitchell, *A History of the Later Roman Empire, AD 284–641*, Oxford 2006, 372–375.

is a re-used stone, incorporated later in the new wall, and therefore that the city probably maintained its larger size into the late period.[49] If Side did so, then the other cities presumably survived just as well: the existence of churches in all the cities demonstrates their continuation, and the identification of six churches at Perge implies continued prosperity and no diminution in the city's size. But size is not directly related to population, and the damage the plague caused, which is unambiguous in general terms, surely meant that the number of people in the cities was drastically reduced. The size of the city would not necessarily have to be reduced because there were fewer people, though, since the reduction in population was maintained by the repeated outbreaks of plague, we must assume that the cities became steadily more depopulated, with empty houses, underused facilities, and repairs not made. By the time the troubles of the seventh century arrived, the cities which had existed in the fourth century still existed, dilapidated, and, as it turned out, vulnerable.

---

[49] C. Foss, 'Attius Philippus and the Walls of Side', *ZPE* 26, 1977, 172–180.

10

The End of Greek Pamphylia

Standing at the year AD 600, the history of Greek Pamphylia was one which a Pamphylian could have contemplated with some complacency and a deal of civic satisfaction. The various cities were, of course, ailing, but they had survived the various troubles of empires and kings with little difficulty – only Phaselis and Korakesion, for example, had ever been captured in war and most of the rest that never even been attacked. The population, so far as we can see now, all spoke Greek – so that the Hittites and Luwians, Pisidians, and the Italian immigrants, imported slaves, other immigrants, had been fully assimilated. The population, after some resistance, but with few serious conflicts, was now Christian, with a bishop in every city, though there may have been a pleasant glow of the memory of past paganism. Like the immigrants, Christianity had been assimilated to the local society, its social revolutionary purpose had been successfully blunted, and there was a certain continuity between the gods of the past and the present religion, as with the prominence of the Virgin in Artemis' city of Perge, and the re-use of the harbourside temples of Side for a Christian church.

If any did so reflect, the years following AD 600 provided a rude awakening. From that time onwards Greek Pamphylia was on the defensive, and ultimately it was defeated and destroyed. But that destruction took a very long time. It may be said to have begun with the Persian War which began in 602; by 615 Syria and Palestine had been systematically conquered by the enemy, and next year Egypt as well – and in that year a Persian army invaded Asia Minor.

This invasion was aimed at Constantinople, and actually reached Chalkedon on the Bosporos. It will have by-passed Pamphylia in the same way as every other invader: the country was scarcely a priority target in such a war. The theory that it was these invasions which contributed most to the urban collapse in Asia Minor[1] – the Arabs had received the exclusive blame beforehand – cannot apply

[1] C. Foss, 'The Persians in Asia Minor and the end of Antiquity', *English Historical Review* 90, 1975, 721–743.

in Pamphylia. So far as can be seen, the Persians never did reach the area, though having captured Syria they took Cyprus and Rhodes. The Arab assaults which began in the second half of that century, however, were much more sustained and extensive, and they came by sea, as well as by land, and to such an attack Pamphylia was very vulnerable. The damage caused by the Persians may have begun the process of urban collapse in central Asia Minor – though the plague had weakened the cities beforehand – but the Arabs' actions certainly prevented any recovery, and for Pamphylia the Arabs were the real enemy. The Persian presence in Asia Minor was in fact relatively brief. Several raids took place over the years between 610 and 626, mainly directed into Kappadokia or against Constantinople, but then from 626 the Emperor Heraklios successfully invaded Persia in reply, so deflecting any further raids.[2]

For some years after the Arab conquest of Syria and Egypt in 634–635, the Pamphylian cities again remained unaffected, but once the Arab governor of Syria, Muawiya ibn Abu Sufyan, organised the Phoenicians of Syria into a fleet, the Pamphylians became a target. The fate of the cities is not documented in any detail, however, and making assumptions about the extent of destruction or survival is difficult and dangerous. The Arab fleets sailed along the south coast of Asia Minor from their Syrian and Egyptian bases, aiming primarily for the Aegean and Constantinople, and any city along the way would clearly be in danger. Lowland Kilikia became an evacuated and devastated no-man's-land, and the Taurus passes were fortified; Pamphylia was once more protected to some degree by its geography, though it had now come much closer to danger than before.[3]

The first Arab naval attacks were directed at Cyprus, and then at the island of Arados, which seems to have held out when the rest of Syria had been conquered.[4] After a brief truce, negotiated by the Emperor Constans II, a new Arab naval campaign followed in 655, which resulted in a great battle off Phoenix (modern Finike) in Lykia; this was called Dhu al-Sawari – 'battle of the masts' – by the Arabs, from the large number of ships involved. It seems to have been a confused melee, with little form to it. The sources suggest that it

---

[2] Theophanes, *Chronicle* 304–306.

[3] H. Ahrweiler, 'L'Asie Mineure et les invasions arabes (VIIe–IXe Siècles', *Revue Historique* 227, 1962, 1–22, notes that 'les côtes de Pamphylie, de la Lycie et d'Ionie ont été les plus exposées', but this is only passive; the actual Arab raids need to be documented.

[4] Sebeos 147; Theophanes 343–344; Dionysios, *West Syrian Chronicles* 173–178; L. I. Conrad, 'The Conquest of Arwad: a Source-Critical Study in the Historiography of the Early Medieval Near East', in A. Cameron and L. I. Conrad (eds), *The Byzantine and Early Islamic Near East, 1. Problems in the Source Material*, Princeton 1992, 317–350.

was an Arab victory, and the emperor was forced to flee, but it has been pointed out that, if so, it had few results.[5] Partly this was because the casualties on both sides were very large, in men and ships, and partly because the Arab Caliphate collapsed into a civil war in 656. This lasted for five years, but it is noticeable that no other naval campaigns were mounted for several more years even after the civil war ended. The battle showed much inexperience on both sides: this was the first Arab seaborne expedition, and the Byzantine naval arm had been neglected for generations.

In all this, as is all too usual, Pamphylia is not mentioned, and it is not possible to assess what damage, if any, the region suffered. If it is correct, as has been suggested by A.N. Stratos, that the Arab fleet stopped at Phoenix to cut wood – though the notion, in the midst of a campaign which was supposed to attack Constantinople, is a trifle bizarre – then it seems probable that both Lykia and Pamphylia will have suffered, since the Arab fleet would clearly have had time to disperse and loot. On the other hand, a later Arab naval offensive, probably in 672, which seized and colonised the island of Rhodes, was much more dangerous.[6]

The seizure of Rhodes allowed the Arab fleet to sail west from Syria, rest and reprovision at the island, and then use its harbour as a base for raiding throughout the Aegean: Crete, Smyrna, Kos, and Lykia are all mentioned as suffering.[7] One must expect that all the Asian coasts from Kilikia to Constantinople were also well ravaged on a regular basis, and this would clearly include the Pamphylian cities. But only one of those cities is mentioned in these years, and it is rather surprising to see that it is Sillyon (written as 'Syllaion'), where in 677, according to Theophanes, an Arab fleet on its way back to Syria, was wrecked by a storm.[8]

This notice is curious for two reasons. First, Sillyon is the furthest from the coast of any of the cities of Pamphylia, and is the least likely of the cities to be used to locate a shipwreck. It may be that the section of the coast where the wreck took place was part of Sillyon's territory, and I have argued earlier that the three cities of the plain probably each had a share of the coastland; Kynosarion

---

[5] Theophanes 345–346; Sebeos 170–171; Dionysios 179–180; A. N. Stratos, 'The Naval Engagement at Phoenix', *Charanis Studies*, New Brunswck, 1980, 229–247; V. Christides, 'The Naval Engagement of Dhat as-Sarari, AH 34/AD 655–656, a Classical Example of Naval Warfare Incompetence', *Byzantina* 13.3, 1985, 133–1345, who instances some sources Stratos missed.

[6] Theophanes 354–346; Brooks, 'Arabs', 187; K. Y. Blankinship, *The End of the Jihad State: the Reign of Hisham al-Malik and the Collapse of the Ummayads*, New York 1994, 25–26.

[7] Theophanes 354–355; Brooks, 'Arabs', 187–189.

[8] Theophanes 354.

seems to have been Sillyon's port in Late Antiquity. Yet Theophanes is locating the wreck of large fleet of ships, which surely spread over a longer length of coast than Sillyon controlled.

The second reason for this curious naming is that it may be a sign that Sillyon, even as early as the 670s, had emerged as much more important than the other cities of Pamphylia. The very fact that it is located farther from the coast than other inland cities gave it a certain advantage in the conditions of Arab maritime raids. The first targets of the raiders would presumably be the coastal cities – Phaselis, Olbia, Attaleia, Magydos, Side – so that the three cities of the plain are likely to be attacked later, and of the three Perge and Aspendos were more vulnerable than Sillyon, being less well fortified and closer to the coast. And if these other cities had been badly damaged by raids before 677, then it seems possible that Sillyon had become the refuge for the survivors. This is not a particularly strong argument, being based only on the occurrence of a single name, but other indications (which will be returned to later in this chapter) carry the same implication – that Sillyon had become a much more important city at this period than ever it had been earlier.

The cities, with their walls and substantial populations, might well hold out against the raiders, who were normally not equipped to conduct lengthy sieges, but the surrounding rural areas could not. The *TIB* map of the region shows that most of the places occupied in the preceding centuries were abandoned from the eighth century onwards. In Perge's territory only two places survived; in Side's only one; elsewhere only a single coastal place north of Phaselis. The four ports, however, all show signs of continuing life, though how vigorous it was at Magydos is unknown.[9] The rural settlements had been wiped out; survivors will have fled to their cities (Map 17).

The destruction of the rural population meant that the cities could be fed only with difficulty, and all of them, with the exception of Attaleia, shrank physically. This was in part the result of the raids, but also of the reduction of population over the previous century because of the recurring plague. The Pergeans abandoned the lower city, with its walls and great buildings, and retired – those of them who had survived – to the acropolis. The pottery excavated in the great baths beside the South Gate shows continuous use of the establishment into the seventh century; from the eighth century onwards the pottery became rare, implying only occasional occupation.[10] A small church was built at the

---

[9] *TIB* vols 1 and 2, *passim*.
[10] N. Atik, *Die Keramik aus den Südthermen von Perge*, Tubingen 1995.

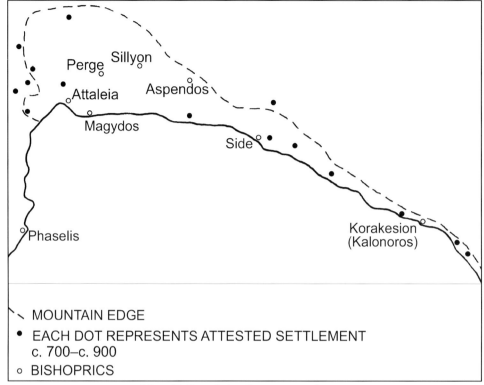

Map 17. Pamphylia: Byzantine settlements

crossing of the main city streets: it lay directly in front of the path to the acropolis and may have been thought to provide some protection for the surviving city on the hill, and across the canal along the main street, which thus no longer flowed. The acropolis had two churches, and it is in this period that a rock-cut chapel and the chamber for a group of monks were made.[11]

Aspendos retained its bishop for some time, but there is little or no sign that the city remained inhabited; its hill is not as defensible as either Perge's or Sillyon's, though later generations found the theatre worth converting into either a royal residence or a caravanserai.[12] Phaselis, like Perge, abandoned its well-built areas, and retreated to the acropolis and the low peninsula of land connecting it to the mainland, where a group of buildings, including the church set into the old market, and the main paved street had to be held if the harbours were to continue to be useful. The mainland extensions of the city, the *Nordsiedlung* and

[11] Foss, 'Cities', 18–19.

[12] J. Freely, *The Eastern Mediterranean Coast of Turkey*, Istanbul 1998, 81–82, says 'it was a royal residence for the Seljuk Alaettin Kay Kubad I, c.1220'; the sign at the site claims it was a caravanserai; both are possible, of course.

the *Weststadt*, were both abandoned. The city was now essentially a naval base, and there was little of the old city, either in its institutions or its inhabitants, still recognizable.[13] Without the possibility of seaborne trade, which scarcely existed for the time being, Phaselis had lost its reason for existence.

Side's kilometre-long Hellenistic city walls proved to be too extensive to be defended with the reduced population and resources of the city. They were abandoned and a new wall, a third of the length of the old, was built across the city at the point where the peninsula joined the mainland (Map 9, Plates 23, 24). The buildings between these walls were usable only if the raiders did not come; no doubt they were burnt and looted at the first opportunity; much of the town shows signs of being burnt, but the date and occasion are not known. These buildings represented important aspects of the city's public life, for they included the large *agora*, one of the largest baths, the cathedral, the bishop's palace, the baptistery, and the complex of buildings associated with them, also the *nymphaeum* which was the terminus of the aqueduct, as well as the great Hellenistic-Roman walls, which still stand to this day. Further, the new walls used the *scena* of the theatre as part of their length, which left that building unusable, and its access to the *agora* was blocked; the inner wall of the *palaistra* was also used as part of the new wall and that building was thus also abandoned; the triumphal arch of Vespasian now became the main gate of the reduced city, but was itself also partially blocked, to reduce the size of the ingress, and thus the danger of penetration (Plate 21). At that point the wall wound round some important water storage cisterns to include them in the city.

A whole set of changes to the reduced city was now necessary: a new marketplace was needed, a new administration, and new churches. Two of the last are known, but are very small. One was built inside the nave of the former church in the abandoned area outside the new wall; the other was similarly placed within the large basilican church beside the harbour[14] (Plate 22). This last had already replaced the former temples of Apollo and Athena; now the great reduction in size is eloquent of the drastic reduction in the size of the city's population. The small church between the walls was clearly vulnerable in the event of a raid. It is reminiscent of the similarly placed church at Perge, at the street intersection; no doubt both cities put a good deal of faith in God's protection. At Side, at Perge, at Phaselis, at Aspendos, life had been reduced to a more basic level, the leisurely luxury of the rich of the high Roman Empire was abandoned, as was the elaborate city government. The general impression

---

[13] C. Foss, 'The Lycian Coast in the Byzantine Age', *DOP* 48, 1994, 1–52.
[14] Foss, 'Cities', 43–45.

at Side, as at Phaselis, is that the city now existed largely to defend the harbour, which indeed had also been reduced in size; much of it was silted up, but a new mole was built to provide a smaller harbour.[15]

By the end of the seventh century Pamphylia had become part of the naval command of the Kibyrrheotai. The Arab harassment of Anatolia compelled the Byzantine government to reorganise the military and naval defences of the whole empire, so that it was divided into *themai*, each with a commander, a staff, and an army. The Kibyrrheot command had originally been part of a much larger *thema*, the Karabisianoi, which covered the whole south-west of Asia Minor – Pamphylia, Lykia, and Karia – which were the very areas of the mainland most subject to raiding from Syria and Rhodes, especially during the Arabs' occupation of the latter between 672 and 680. The greater *thema* included some of the islands of the Aegean, and was at first a naval command with its headquarters at the island of Samos. It may be that the pressure exerted by the Arab control of Rhodes proved too much, but the Karabisianoi *thema*, which certainly existed by 645 or thereabouts, became divided into three separate *themai* later.[16]

Pamphylia became the Kibyrrheot *thema*, with Attaleia as its centre and main base, and the commander of the *thema* became the local governor. When it was set up as an independent command is unclear, but the *thema* certainly existed as a separate and specifically naval command by 697, when its fleet was sent to attempt the recovery of Carthage.[17] Rhodes had been evacuated by the Arabs in 680, on the accession of a new caliph, Muawiya's son Yazid I.[18] A second Arab civil war began in 683 and lasted ten years; this involved making a ten-year truce with the Roman Empire.[19] This was the international setting for an attempt by the government of the Emperor Leontios (695– 698) to recover control of the province of Africa, lost in 695. The expedition succeeded briefly, but when its commander returned for reinforcements he was displaced in a plot, and the commander of the fleet detachment of the Kibyrrheots which had been left in Pamphylian waters, Apsimar, was proclaimed emperor in opposition to Leontios, who himself was a recent usurper. Leontios was removed, and Apsimar became Emperor Tiberios III (698– 705).[20]

---

[15] P. Knoblauch, *Die Hafenenlagen und die Anschliessenden Seemauer von Side*, Ankara 1977.
[16] This is a great historical problem in Byzantine studies; cf. J. Haldon, *Warfare, State and Society in the Byzantine World, 565–1204,* London 1999, 74–85 and 109–115, for a concise summary; also. A. J. Toynbee, *Constantine Porphyrogenitus and his World*, Oxford 1973, 258–261.
[17] Theophanes 370.
[18] Blankinship, *End of the Jihad State*, 26.
[19] *Ibid.*, 27.
[20] Theophanes 370; Nikephoros the Patriach, *History*, 40.

Once again the fleeting appearance of a place name gives a clue to the situation. Apsimar, the new usurper, had commanded the Kourkotai, which was the naval force stationed at Korykos, the anchorage used centuries before by Antiochus III and later fortified by Attalos II. It was a useful advanced base, protecting the main *thema* base at Attaleia, and assisting communications with both Constantinople and Africa. Korykos may also have been preferred to Phaselis, which is a better harbour and was certainly in use at the time, since a fleet stationed at Korykos would protect Phaselis as well, and would be closer to Cape Gelidonya if the enemy fleet sailed directly across the Bay of Antalya to make landfall there and head on westwards.

Why this *thema* was named for Kibyra, the small *polis* west of Side on the eastern Pamphylian coast, is not known. (It cannot have been named for the main Kibyra, which was outside its boundaries altogether.) The Emperor Constantine VII Porphyrogenitus claimed that it was coined as an insult, which may be so.[21] Perhaps it originated with a rival commander; or Kibyra may simply have been its eastern boundary – perhaps the *thema* was described as 'the command as far as Kibyra', which was one of the fleet's bases, no doubt like Korykos. Side was surely another, as would be Korakesion. Kibyra stood in the same relationship to Side as Korykos did to Attaleia, as a picquet placed in advance to give warning of attacks. It is a sheltered bay and harbour partly protected by a low-lying island. Side was refortified in the seventh century, enclosing an area which could defend only part of the city, but which was designed above all to defend the harbour, which was in turn improved.[22] In the same way Phaselis' harbour was defended and the quays maintained, with new buildings added, partly made of statue bases, in the eighth century.[23]

The one city which did not fall on such hard times was Attaleia. This was the headquarters of the *thema* and of the fleet, and the city was later also noteworthy for its merchants, who were able to combine the roles of merchant and military intelligence officer, and to travel fairly freely in Syria, according to the Arab historian Ibn Hawkal.[24] The city also had a slave market where Muslim prisoners were held for ransom or for sale. Together with Side's new fortifications, which might have reduced the city's defensible area by over half but which also imply a certain continuing vigour, and which were seventh century in date, this shows a certain continuing vitality in Pamphylia in the vulnerable coastal cities, though

[21] Constantine Porphyrogenitus, *De Thematibus*, 38.
[22] Notes 13 and 14.
[23] Foss, 'Lycian Coast'.
[24] Ibn Hawkal, quoted by A. A. Vasiliev, *Byzance et les Arabes*, vol 2, part 2, 413–414 and 419.

the inland cities suffered badly. The cessation of raids for much of the period between 680 and 700 will have helped at least to stabilize the situation, as would the presence of the fleet, which was manned locally, a practice which will surely have invigorated local energies.

Korykos as the headquarters of a substantial fleet is as unconvincing as Kibyra, and this may suggest that it was no more than a temporary anchorage; the fleet, after all, is only recorded as being there because that was where it was at one stage in the imperial usurpation by its commander. Attaleia's harbour is rather enclosed, and could well be difficult for a fleet to get out of in an emergency; a foul wind might block a fleet in that corner of the bay while an enemy fleet sailed past out at sea. Korykos was obviously a better base from which to control traffic across the mouth of the Pamphylian Sea, but it seems unlikely to have been much more than a station for a few ships. Pamphylia was clearly being defended by sea. Attaleia and Side were active port- and harbour-cities, though both were much reduced.

In the second half of the seventh century, therefore, Pamphylia became a frontier land, its cities shrunken and defensive, its countryside subject to frequent ravaging, its governor a military man. The Arab Caliphate dominated the coastline as far west as Rough Kilikia, and for a time its ships were able to raid at will all along the south coast of Asia Minor and into the Aegean. Perhaps from 655 and certainly by 697, the Roman Empire, through the Kibyrrheot fleet, patrolled the coast as far east as (at least) Kibyra Minor, using Attaleia, Side, Kibyra, Phaselis, and Korykos as naval and presumably military and administrative bases.[25]

The cities of Pamphylia had therefore presumably suffered early and devastating attacks, as is implied by the record of their shrinkage, and the region had changed its strategic function, from a sleepy and contented backwater to an active, perhaps fearful, frontier in a never-ending war. Yet it will not do to write off these ancient cities too quickly. It is worth recalling that we have no records at all of any ravaging of Pamphylia until the ninth century, and, while it is not reasonable to assume that this reflects reality, it is the case that any periods during which ravaging took place were relatively brief – in 655, perhaps, and in the 670s. The area may also have been the target of pirate raids, by single ships or small groups, but these would not be serious enough to destroy cities, nor even villages. That is to say, whatever damage the cities and villages

---

[25] The officers associated with the Kibyrrheot *thema* are collected and listed by A. G. C. Savvides, 'The Secular Prosopography of the Byzantine Maritime Theme of the Carabisiai/Cibyrrheots', *Byzantinoslavica* 59, 1998, 24–45.

sustained in the wars, such damage did not amount to total destruction and the elimination of all human life. Damage, yes; massacre, very likely; removal of people into slavery or death, certainly. But the cities survived these initial attacks, in however shrunken a form.[26]

Some estimates can be made of the populations of the reduced cities. The approximate areas still in use – that is, within the newly defended areas – were about twenty hectares at Side and about eleven hectares at Phaselis, reduced from fifty and twenty-six hectares respectively, that is, by about sixty per cent in both cases. Using the formula of 200 inhabitants per hectare employed earlier – though this is perhaps optimistic – this would imply an urban population of 4000 at Side and 2200 at Phaselis. These are certainly serious reductions, and should be regarded as maxima. They do not mean the complete extinction of city life, though such populations will have been hard put to do much more than survive and defend themselves. Defence, in fact, would have been difficult, for a population of only 4000 implies a potential maximum military force of less than a thousand men, not nearly enough to be able to form a serious defence against an Arab fleet of a hundred or more ships. Further, such a population was scarcely large enough to be able to support much in the way of games and pastimes. Life had become grey and grim and hard work; no doubt the churches became ever more important as substitutes for entertainment.

Attaleia was certainly still a functioning city, in the sense that it is recorded occasionally in the sparse records of the period in ways which show that it was more than just a naval base. It housed the local bishop; it was the government centre for the Kibyrrheot *thema*; it was a naval base; it was a trading centre, with a slave market with connections to Syria. It is the only Pamphylian city which does not seem to have shrunk physically, and the old walls were maintained on the line laid out in the second century BC, making it by far the biggest urban centre in Byzantine Pamphylia.[27] In 685, as part of the truce terms concluded by the Emperor Justinian II with the Caliph Marwan I, the city received a reinforcement of 12,000 Mardaite refugees, who had conducted a serious rebellion against the Muslim Caliphate in the Lebanese Mountains for several years.[28] This might suggest that the city had been substantially depopulated in the previous

---

[26] For a general summary, cf. W. Brandeis, *Die Städte Kleinasiens in 7 und 8 Jahrhundert*, Berlin 1985.

[27] These walls are recorded as being repaired and maintained into the nineteenth century; H. Rott, *Kleinasiatische Denkmäler*, Leipzig 1908, 48–56; B. Pace, 'Adalia', *Annuario* 3, 1916–1921, 3–21.

[28] Theophanes 363; P. Charanis, 'The Transfer of Population as a Policy in the Byzantine Period', Comparative Studies of Society and History 3, 1960/1961, 140–154.

generations, but it clearly still existed and was in a defensible state. It is surely not a coincidence that this figure, 12,000, is the same as that calculated to have been the likely urban population of the original city; the refugees were, that is, intended to do two things: fill up the urban space, and also repopulate the nearby countryside; they also constituted a major military reinforcement.

But the settlement of these 12,000 refugees in and about the city means that there had been room for them at that time, in a city whose territory was always small, though in the new situation it seems highly unlikely that the old city territories retained any meaning, except in ecclesiastical terms. The previous century of warfare had clearly had a damaging effect on the population of the city, though perhaps less so on the fabric of the city. As a government centre it would be the obvious destination for refugees from round about, and this will have helped maintain the population of the place to some degree. The other cities, not being deliberately supported by the central government or reinforced by the arrival of refugees and the emplacement of local government functions, clearly scarcely survived.

From then on, Attaleia does not appear again in the notably exiguous sources for nearly two centuries. In 860 it was captured by an Arab fleet, but held only briefly;[29] this was an episode of the continuing intermittent warfare. In the 850s the Byzantine fleet twice attacked Damietta in Egypt, and more than once the Arab fleet menaced Attaleia, and even on one occasion Constantinople.[30] The Mardaites remained a separate community with its own chief, a *Catepan*, whose authority was separate from and independent of that of the Kibyrrheot commander. The naval commander was also the governor of the *thema* – a situation which inevitably produced friction with the *catepan*,[31] and which in the early tenth century developed into a serious dispute which could only be settled by the Emperor Leo VI in 910.

This emperor strengthened the fortifications of the city, above all by doubling the walls,[32] and Ibn Hawkal described it as a strong fortress which was one of the empire's most important trading posts.[33] In the eleventh century it was made an archbishopric, and in the twelfth it was further refortified.[34] All in all this

---

[29] *Cambridge Medieval History* IV.1.713.

[30] A.A. Vasiliev, *Byzance et les Arabes* (note 2).

[31] Constantine Porphyrogenitus, *De Administrando Imperio*, 228–231; Toynbee, *Constantine Porphyrogenitus*, 249.

[32] Bean, *TSS*, 22; H. Grégoire, *Receuil des Inscriptions Chrétiennes d'Asie Mineure*, Paris 1922, nos 302–304.

[33] See note 23.

[34] Bean, *TSS*, 22; see also Foss, 'Cities'.

is essentially as continuous a history of the city as is possible given the poor sources, and one which contrasts powerfully with the decline and shrinkage of the other cities. It was the only Pamphylian city to maintain its original size, and the failure of the rest left it as the pre-eminent city of the whole south coast; the promotion of its bishop in the eleventh century was a belated recognition of his city's importance.[35]

The city's geographical and maritime position made it a trading centre, as Ibn Hawkal noted. It was also a shipbuilding centre, using wood from the mountains. The fleet of *dromons* based at the city needed repair, and new ships had to be built. There was also a type of transport ship in the period called *pamphyloi*, presumably named for a local type of vessel. In 911 a fleet was sent from the Kibyrrheot command to take part in the attempted reconquest of Crete, consisting of fifteen *dromons* and sixteen *pamphyloi*, manned by a total of about 6,000 rowers and 1,000 soldiers; the Mardaites contributed about 5,000 men.[36] A navigational treatise of about the same date, ascribed to the Mardaites' 'wisdom', confirms the active participation of their new home city in naval warfare; a second treatise is ascribed to the commander (*protospatharios*) of the Kibyrrheot fleet. Both of these documents are, of course, designed for use by naval commanders, but one cannot doubt that the city was an active sea-trading centre as well, with a wealth of seafaring knowledge in its mixed population.[37]

Only one of the inland cities of Pamphylia had any history in this period: Sillyon now came into its own at long last. This is the city of Pamphylia of which the least is known. It had no great games, no important harbour, no great temple, but in these new and dangerous conditions its real importance was revealed, for it was relatively distant from the threatening sea, and was eminently defensible even with a reduced population. This was a revival of the reason for which the site had been chosen for habitation originally. The sheer natural cliff walls of the city gave it a strength none of the other cities, not even Attaleia, could match. This had been seen once already, if briefly, when it defied Alexander, but never since, for its strength had not been needed or tested. Now it was. So where all the other cities of Pamphylia succumbed at one time or another to Arab attacks, even if, like Attaleia, only temporarily, Sillyon gained a reputation for invincibility;

---

[35] Constantine Porphyrogenitus, *De Caeremoniis*, 651–660; H. Ahrweiler, *Byzance et la Mer*, Paris 1955, 410–415.

[36] A summary history is in I. Erdem, 'Bir Ortacag Kenti Antalya: Gec Antik Donemden Selçuklularin Sonona Genel Bir Yaklasim (I)', *Adalya* 5, 2002/2002, 163–171.

[37] S. Dagron, 'Das Firmament soll christlich werden. Zu zwei Seefahrtskalendera des 10 Jahrhunderts', in S. Prinzing and S. Simon, *Fest und Alburg in Byzanz*, Munich 1990.

the hagiography of St Andrew Salos (Andrew the Fool) was able to take this city's strength as proverbial: 'Sylaion will be called and never be seized or captured'.[38] The date of this prediction is not certain,[39] but its sentiment implies that the city, in contrast to the other Pamphylian cities, had resisted attack successfully, just as had Thessalonika, before its capture in 904, and Constantinople. In another part of the same hagiography Sillyon was named as one of the possible successors to Constantinople as imperial capital, once Constantinople had sunk into the sea, as the author prophesied.[40] This extraordinary prediction only makes sense if Sillyon, like Constantinople, was a conspicuous resister. The ninth century might be an appropriate date for the document.

Another hagiography, of St Stephen the Younger, referring either to be early ninth or the mid-eighth century, suggests that Sillyon would be a suitable place as a refuge for iconodules – those in favour of retaining and venerating icons – and this in turn suggests it would be a place where a man could be safe from both persecution and the Arabs.[41] Both threats were thus ever present to the author: a matter emphasised by a battle in 790 when the governor of the Kibyrrheot *thema* was captured by Arab raiders in the bay in front of Attaleia;[42] he was taken off to Baghdad and there executed when he refused to apostasize.

A new governor of the city was appointed in 821/822, a man called Echimos, who took the Christian name of John. He came from the 'South' and was a Syriac-speaker, and so probably originally a Moslem from Syria converted to Christianity; his original name of 'Echimos' seems to be a hellenization of 'Hakim'.[43] By this time some new construction had been undertaken in the city. No doubt the population had been seriously reduced by the evil times, and the size of the circuit, even with the relative smallness of the city, was too great for making an effective defence. Part of the circuit was walled off on the south-east to form an acropolis or castle about 200 metres square; the lower land below this area was also walled off as a barbican. Within the city a large three-storey building, called the palace, was constructed, much of whose walls

[38] L. Ryden, 'The Andreas Salos Apocalypse', *DOP* 28, 1974, 199–261.

[39] The date is disputed: L. Ryden, 'The Date of the Life of Andreas Salos', *DOP* 32, 1978, 129–155 argues for a composition in the 950s; C. Mango, 'The Life of St Andrew the Fool Reconsidered', *Rivista de Studi Bizantini e Slavi*, 2, 1982, 297–313, argues for the late seventh century; neither is wholly convincing.

[40] Ryden, 'Apocalypse', 216.

[41] G. Huxley, 'On the Vita of St Stephen the Younger', *Greek, Roman, and Byzantine Studies,* 18, 1977, 97–108.

[42] *Cambridge Medieval History* IV.1.706.

[43] F. Halkin, 'Saint Antoine le Jeune et Patronas le Vainqueur des Arabes en 863 (d'après une texte inédit)', *Analecta Bollandiana* 2, 1944, 187–225.

remain[44] (Plate 12). All this makes Sillyon the most determinedly defended of any of the inland cities; if the enclosed area was fully inhabited, the population would be only a few hundreds, but it has the appearance more of a citadel of refuge, so some of the population may well have lived outside, in the older city. The rural areas round about were also inhabited to some extent, as the stories connected with John/Echimos note.

John/Echimos remained as governor of the city for several years, during which he defeated the pretensions of a momentarily successful rebel, Thomas the Slav, and repelled an attack on the city by an Arab fleet. John, warned of the fleet's approach by the watchman, put into effect what was clearly a pre-arranged plan of defence. The whole population manned the walls, the women dressed in men's clothing. The Arab fleet disembarked a force of sixty cavalry and an uncertain number of infantry, and marched to the city. John interviewed their commander from the wall, conversing in Syriac, his native tongue. John emphasized the city's poverty, and threatened the Arabs with the wrath of God; but it was a bribe but which actually persuaded the Arab general to go away.[45]

The whole episode sees everyone playing the part in a well-understood process. The Arab force did not wish to settle in to a siege; the commander and the troops merely wanted loot, and bribes were a good and easy substitute. But it is clear that the forces available to John were very few – why else pretend that the women were soldiers? – and it was the practice to have a watchman searching the sea approaches (the coast was several kilometres from the city) on the assumption that a raiding force might appear at any moment. (At the highest point of the site, to the north, there is a cylindrical tower, still standing about ten feet high, and built of the re-used stone typical of the Byzantine construction methods.) It is unlikely that, while the two commanders were elegantly conversing, the ordinary Arab soldiers refrained from looting and destroying in the countryside. This case may stand as an example of all the other raids, which includes those which had already eliminated Perge and Aspendos, and which were in process of killing off Side and Phaselis, both of which were abandoned by the end of the ninth century.

In 825 John resigned to become a monk, and, taking the name Anthony, went to sit at the foot of the column of a stylite called Eustathius who lived near Sillyon, taking yet another new name, Anthony. (Actually he deserted his post, and only his evident holy sincerity prevented the *thema* commander from executing him on the spot.) John/Echimos/Anthony had already exhibited

---

[44] Foss, 'Cities', 20–21.
[45] Halkin, 'Saint Antoine le Jeune'; Foss, 'Cities', relates the story, 21–22.

signs of the partiality for the cenobitic life, and later moved to Bithynia, where he finally died in about 865. These items, like the references to Sillyon's fame and invicibility, suggest strongly that the city had emerged as a major centre of loyalty and resistance. Note that the stylite lived outside the city, and he cannot have been the only person to do so.

Sillyon also had its church just outside its walls, as had Perge and Side, and perhaps Phaselis, but this was on top of the hill, and less likely to be accessible to raiders. There is a chapel on the hill also; otherwise the only evidence in the buildings of construction at this period other than the castle is the round tower and repairs to other buildings.[46]

By the time of John's governorship at Sillyon, Aspendos had been long abandoned, and Perge, if not wholly abandoned, had sunk into insignificance. The former metropolitan bishopric had combined with Sillyon, for no bishop of Perge is recorded from 787 until the tenth century, and even before that Perge and Sillyon were regularly combined under one man. Since Sillyon was the surviving city of the two, it was at Sillyon that the bishop will have resided.[47] Perge had in effect ceded the local civic supremacy, which it had held during Late Antiquity, to Attaleia. In the face of the assaults of militant Islam the Church had taken refuge in the strongest defended place. Attaleia suffered capture in 860, while Sillyon maintained itself against the attack of 824.[48] Sillyon was a notable religious centre by this time, a place with a stylite, Eustathios, formerly of Jerusalem (John/Echimos/Anthony's inspirer), and which had communities of monks and nuns which are noted in the description of a John's defence of the city; but then there was hardly anywhere else in the area for them to go, and this perhaps fits with the note of the Arab fleet being wrecked near 'Sylaion' in 677.[49]

Sillyon is noted as having a harbour in this time.[50] This is unlikely to have been still at Kynosarion, which was an exposed anchorage and can scarcely be called a harbour. It may therefore have been the outport of either Perge or Aspendos (that is, Emporion or Bogazak), now disused by those defunct cities. At a guess it would be at Perge's Emporion, which was nearer to Sillyon than Bogazak, and Perge and Sillyon were linked ecclesiastically.

This prominence of Sillyon is clearly the result both of its resistance to the Arab raids and of the ruin of the other cities, while it was also more remote

[46] Chapel and church: V. Ruggieri and J. F. Nethercott, 'The Metropolitan City of Syllaion and its Churches', *Jahrbuch der Österreichen Byzantinistik*, 36, 1986, 154–155; tower: Lanckoronski, 69–71.

[47] See the chart in Ruggieri and Nethercott, 'Metropolitan City of Syllaion', 143–145.

[48] *Ibid.*, 140–142.

[49] Theophanes 354.

[50] Nikephoros the Patriarch 37.

from the sea, being, that is, more distant from the enemy. On the other hand, Attaleia does seem to have stood out even more than before as the main city of the region from the time of the foundation of the Kibyrrheot fleet and *thema*. Attaleia's position on the coast gave it the prominence due to its governmental and mercantile roles and to its size, but it was also, because of these factors, a more tempting target, and its coastal position made it more vulnerable; Sillyon's reputation was based on the fact that the city was never captured – at least until the time of the composition of the hagiography. Being the most distant city from the coast was partial protection, and its small size may well have made it an unattractive target, but the most effective element was its formidable cliffs and walls. The ideological atmosphere of the Byzantine Empire, of its self-image as a besieged Christian state suffering heretical and enemy and pagan attacks, would certainly imply divine protection for Sillyon – hence perhaps the stylite, the monasteries, the nunneries, and the churches in front of the various cities.

The city was also early involved in the iconoclast problem, and it was a bishop of Perge/Sillyon, Constantine, who was acclaimed patriarch of Constantinople at the decisive iconoclast council of Hereia in 754; in addition, two of the Emperor Constantine V's main advisers at that council were bishops Basil of Pisidia, formerly of Perge, and Sisinnios, his successor there.[51] It would seem that Pamphylia was a centre of iconoclastic opinion at the time, and in the middle of the eighth century both Sisinnios and Constantine were based at Sillyon. It would do no harm for the patriarch to be known to have been bishop of the 'invincible' Sillyon.

And yet, fifty years later, in 807, the city was recommended to iconodules as a suitable refuge. This has led to the suggestion that the city and its region had been lost to the Arabs for a time; this does not necessarily follow from the recommendation, and seems fairly unlikely, given its later reputation for invincibility.[52] Not long after, an iconoclast monk, Antonius, was appointed bishop of the joint sees, and was then promoted to patriarch in 821 by the Emperor Michael II. The sympathies of the city and its bishop and its monasteries clearly wavered, but in the final crunch, they continued to defend the city.

The urban condition of Pamphylia by the end of the eighth century was thus parlous, but not wholly desperate. Phaselis was reduced to its acropolis; its harbour had been maintained and repaired, but it cannot be seen as much more

---

[51] J. Herrin, *The Formation of Christendom*, Oxford 1987, 368–370; for Constantine: Theophanes 428.

[52] Huxley, 'St Stephen the Younger'.

than a naval base; by the ninth century it was virtually uninhabited, and at that time stones from the site were being taken to Attaleia to be used as building material.[53] Perge was reduced to its acropolis as soon as Arab attacks began, and its bishop had to move to Sillyon for refuge; effective abandonment of the city, including the acropolis, is very likely by the end of the eighth century. The absence of Aspendos in any record would suggest the same condition there.

Side had now shrunk to its inner core; occupation continued there into the ninth century, when a coin hoard containing coins of the Emperor Basil I (867–886) was deposited within the city limits, but that seems to have been the end, and the city is reckoned to have been deserted by about AD 900.[54] Around that date the bishop of Side, Eustathios, wrote a letter in which he suggested abandoning the site and moving the see elsewhere. He gave no reason, which would suggest that his addressee knew the condition of the place already: depopulation is the obvious assumption.[55] At some point the whole city was burnt, and the archaeologists found traces in many parts of the site.[56] The date of this is not known, nor even if it was a single conflagration or a series, an accident or the deliberate act of enemies. There is no doubt that the place was vulnerable to attack, and its reduced population would obviously find it difficult to maintain the harbour, always subject to silting. The failure of the aqueduct – which would be one of the first targets of any attack – drastically reduced the water supply. Not far inland, at Manaua, a minor port on the Melas River, a castle was built on a hill, using recycled stone (and so probably of this period). This site provided much better local protection, both in allowing warning of an attack, and by the existence of the fortified castle.[57] The site of Side may not have been wholly abandoned, but as a functioning city it had clearly ceased to exist when Bishop Eustathios decided he had to leave.

Korakesion, never an important city, is also never referred to in these centuries, yet it may well have continued to be inhabited; its great rock is, after all, eminently defensible. Its name changed, which is a sign that it continued to be inhabited: by the eleventh century it was being called Kalonoros – 'beautiful

[53] *TAM* II.3.1191 and 1210, inscriptions from Phaselis built into the walls of Attaleia; cf. Blackburn in Schäfer, *Phaselis*, 37.

[54] Bean, *TSS*, 59; Brandes, *Die Städte Kleinasiens*, 103; Foss, 'Cities', hesitates over the city's abandonment, at one point using coin evidence to suggest continued occupation, but in the end seeming to plump for an ending.

[55] J. Compronass, 'Zwei Schriften des Arethas von Kaisareia', *Studi Bizantini e Neoellenici* 4, 1936, 89–135.

[56] A. M. Mansel, 'Side', *RE* Supp 10, 1965, 888.

[57] J. Nollé, 'Pamphylische Studien: Manaua', *Chiron* 21, 1991, 242–244.

mountain'[58] – which may imply that it was being praised for its constancy and Christian faithfulness, just as Sillyon gained a reputation for invincibility.

The Arab raiders damaged the countryside even more than the urban areas, which could make at least some attempt at resistance behind their walls and on their hills. The rural inhabitants might be able to take refuge in the cities, but they could not protect their crops and flocks and homes; the repetition of the raids depleted rural resources, just as the repetition of the plague had reduced the population, and both also reduced urban resources without hope of easy recovery. For an area depending for much of its income on the production of olive oil, raiders who cut down the olive trees inflicted permanent damage. The village of Lyrboton in Perge's territory, which had been populous enough to support three churches in the Late Antique period, continued to be occupied on a small scale, but the traces are few.[59] This will have been the fate of many of the villages and small towns as well. Pamphylia's protection was the Kibyrrheot fleet by sea and the walls of Attaleia and Sillyon by land. But by 900 only those two places were left as functioning urban centres – perhaps Kalonoros/ Korakesion as well, though only the rock was defensible – and the countryside must have been largely abandoned. Side, Aspendos, Perge, Phaselis, Magydos, had all effectively died; it is not even known if Kibyra, the name-town of the fleet and *thema*, survived.[60]

The extraordinary capacity of the Byzantine Empire to stage recoveries after disasters produced a revival of imperial power from about AD 900, in particular after the recovery of Crete in 961 (which had been under Muslim control since 827), and the establishment of full control over Cyprus in 965, both of which events indicate that naval dominance had been achieved over the Arab raiders, whose political base had fragmented from about 900.[61] Even in the 850s the empire had been able to send naval raids as far as Egypt, and during the first half of the tenth century Arab raids into Anatolia through the Taurus passes were progressively blunted and then stopped. All this did not necessarily provide full security for Pamphylia, but it did lessen the Arab menace; the maritime threat

[58] Bean, *TSS*, 77.

[59] N. Çevik, 'An Olive Oil Production Centre in Pamphylia: Lyrboton Kome', *Lycia* III, 1996/1997, 79–104; cf. also J. Keil, 'Die Lyrboton Kome in Pamphylien', *Jahreshefte des Österreiches Archäologischen Instituts an Wien*, 23, 1926, 89–106.

[60] *TIB* 2.629–630.

[61] Control of Cyprus by a naval power clearly had important implications for the security of Pamphylia. The island had been occupied by neither Greeks nor Arabs between 688 and 965, though the agreement on this was broken by both sides at times: R. J. H. Jenkins, 'Cyprus between Byzantium and Islam, AD 688–965', in G. F. Mylonas and D. Raymond (eds), *Studies presented to David M. Robinson*, St Louis MO 1953, vol. 2, 1006–1024.

was now more from piracy than from a full-scale assault, and a walled city had little to fear from a pirate raid. The frontier territory could begin to recover.[62] But in the event it was given only a short time, no more than a century or thereabouts, to do so.

The eleventh century invasions of Anatolia by the Seljuk Turks created a new setback. By that time Attaleia was a wealthy town again and Pamphylia was exporting cereals north to the Anatolian interior.[63] The countryside had clearly benefited from the restored security, and had been resettled to some extent, though the old deserted cities did not revive, so far as can be seen, and Sillyon had lost its *raison d'etre* with the decline of the Arab threat. The Turkish invasions of the interior spilled over into Pamphylia from inland soon after the great Byzantine defeat at Manzikert in 1071, which opened up the whole of the interior to their attacks. By the time the First Crusaders passed through Asia Minor in 1097, much of Pamphylia, like most of the peninsula, was under Turkish rule.[64]

The Crusaders' defeat of the Turks permitted the recovery of much of western Asia Minor by the Emperor Alexios I Comnenos, and this included Pamphylia. This recovery was precarious, and Attaleia was no longer a safe place for the next century, for the recovery of the city did not mean the recovery of control over the countryside. In 1147, the Second Crusaders discovered that it was very difficult even for the large French army under King Louis VII to march south from the Maiandros valley into Pamphylia, and once there they found that Attaleia had lost control of its fields, and was importing its food by sea;[65] the road had in fact been cut intermittently for the previous thirty years;[66] in 1182 the city was put under siege by the Sultan of Konya.[67] Control of the city did remain with the empire for the whole of the twelfth century, however, even if it was precarious for much of the time, and the city continued to be an important naval base, with enough shipping to provide transport for King Louis and his staff, but not for the whole army, in 1147. At that time the governor in the emperor's name was an Italian, Landulf, though his loyalty to the emperor

---

[62] For the decline of the Caliphate, and the slow cessation of the raids, cf. P. K. Hitti, *History of the Arabs*, seventh ed., London 1961, ch. 31.

[63] J. Darouzes, *Epistoliers Byzantins du Xe siècle*, Paris 1960, 198–199; S. Vryonis, *The Decline of Medieval Hellenism in Asia Minor and the Process of Islamization from the Eleventh through the Fifteenth Century*, Berkeley and Los Angeles, 1971, 14.

[64] This follows from the fact that it was retaken by the Byzantines as a result of the First Crusade.

[65] William of Tyre 16.26; Odo of Deuil, ed. Waquet, Paris 1949, 73–76.

[66] Anna Comnena, *Alexiad* 14.1, for example.

[67] Niketas Choniates 340.

was minimal.[68] Emperor John II had sufficient control in the south in the early 1140s to contemplate setting up Pamphylia and its neighbouring areas as a semi-independent appanage for his son, though in the event the deaths of two of his sons meant he did not do so,[69] and the presence of the French crusaders attracted Turkish attacks close to the city in 1148.

The Turkish problem was thus more difficult and far more threatening than the Arab raids had been. The Byzantine disaster at Manzikert in 1071 permitted the invasion of central Anatolia by Turkish nomads, who took over the inland areas, and who were unwilling to acknowledge anyone, Turk or Greek, as their ruler. They were a permanent presence, not raiders who returned home. They cut the urban centres off from their sources of food supply, and had a habit of converting arable land to pasture. The towns rapidly withered throughout inland Anatolia, partly because they lost control of their countryside, partly because of the damage resulting from the fighting and the passage of all the various armies, and partly because they were repeatedly assaulted or captured by both sides. Byzantine recovery thus now required an initial military conquest, followed by a constant military presence designed to repel further Turkish incursions, and the physical expulsion of the wandering Turkish nomads. Only when this had been done could urban and then rural resettlement take place. And only briefly did any part of the empire enjoy sufficient stability for this resettlement to happen.[70]

On the Turkish side, it took some time for a competent political authority to emerge which could exercise control over the invading nomads, who were generally unwilling to obey anyone. For a long time, a series of weak emirates controlled small parts of Anatolia, though they wholly failed to control the wandering Turkmen. These nomads reached Pamphylia during the twelfth century and behind them came the fragile authority of the emirs. Attaleia's lands were severely damaged by the mid-twelfth century, as the French crusaders discovered, and the city had to import its food by sea – but the city itself was not vulnerable to the nomads, who did not have the resources and manpower to mount serious sieges. As Byzantine power receded in the interior Pamphylia was cut off from contact with Constantinople by land, though the sea lanes remained open. The cities had to fend for themselves, which they perhaps could

---

[68] Odo of Deuil 71–76.

[69] M. Angold, *The Byzantine Empire 1025–1204*, Harlow 1984, 156.

[70] For the Greek side of the story cf. Vryonis, *Decline*; for the Turkish viewpoint, cf. C. Cahen, *The Formation of Turkey: the Seljukid Sultanate of Rum, Eleventh to Fourteenth Centuries*, trans P. M. Holt, Harlow 2001.

have managed to do if their enemies were only the Turkmen. But the Turkmen could call in help from the emirs, and from the Seljuk Sultan in Konya, who emerged as the greatest of the Turkish rulers in Anatolia. In 1207 the Sultan Kilij Arslan mounted another serious attack on Attaleia. Despite help from the Franks of Cyprus, the city fell, after its lands had been, once more, badly ravaged. It suffered a three-day sack, and was annexed by the sultan; he had to retake the city in 1215 after a rebellion.[71] Kalonoros/Korakesion, whose survival was also no doubt due to its coastal situation as well as its fortified rock, followed a few years later, taken by Kilij Arslan's son Ala-ed-din Kay Qubadh I (who is also said to have resided at the theatre at Aspendos). He besieged the place for two months before its Greek ruler caved in on generous personal terms. The sultan liked his new conquest and made it a centre of his power, carrying out extensive building works. It became called Alaiye (now Alanya) after him.[72]

These cities were scarcely cities at all by the time they fell. Attaleia's population was incapable of defending the city, even with considerable outside help; the Greek lord of Kalonoros preferred to retire with his wealth to an estate in the interior, leaving his daughter in the harem of the city's conqueror. Metropolitans of the Greek Church continued at Attaleia for a century or so after the final conquest, but by 1400 even that vestige of autonomy had faded away.[73] It cannot have helped the local Christians to survive when Attaleia became the target for attacks by sea by Christian rulers; Peter I of Cyprus seized the city in 1361 and it was held until 1373; it was attacked a century later by a Venetian expedition, which failed to take it.[74] This was a curious reversal of the previous Arab threat: the sea was the source of enemies whoever ruled in Pamphylia.

There is no indication that any of the other cities was inhabited by the end of the tenth century. The excavations at Side have turned up three coin hoards, one of the mid-eleventh century, and two, probably parts of the same hoard of Western European coins of the mid-twelfth century; these last may be a relic of the Second Crusade, part of whose men tried to reach their destination along the coast. But these hoards do not suggest that the place was still inhabited.[75] There was still a metropolitan bishop of Side, for instance, but he was non-resident.

[71] Cahen, *Formation of Turkey*, 48; I. Erdem, 'Bir Ortacag Kenti Antalya: Gec Antik Donem'den Selçuklularin Sonona Genel Bir Yaklasim (II)', *Adalya* 6, 2001/2002, 291–303.
[72] K. Bilici, 'Alanya'nin Fethi Meseleri Bit Tebit', *Adalya* 4, 1999–2000, 282–292; Vryonis, *Decline* 230.
[73] Vryonis, *Decline*, 314 and 315.
[74] These minor episodes left a few relics behind: F. W. Hasluck, 'Frankish Remains in Adalia', *ABSA* 15, 1908/9, 270–273.
[75] S. Yetkin, 'The Turkish Monuments in Sillyon (Yankoy Hisari)', in *Mansel'e Armagon/Mélanges Mansel*, vol 2, Ankara 1974, 861–872, but see the comment of Foss, 'Cities', note 92.

Sillyon's long and successful resistance to Arab attack was not repeated when the Turks arrived. When the city finally fell is not known, but its bishop reverted to Perge as his title (and was also non-resident), and the Turks seized the Church's property. The site of Sillyon has some small and ill-built mosques, built from the rubble of the ancient city; no doubt they were the work of the nomads, to be used when they were in the area;[76] they are not real signs of inhabitation. Yet even these are a sign of the reputation of the place, for it is even less convenient for nomad occupation than for arable farmers. The same signs of use have not been located at other abandoned cities – apart from the coin hoards at Side. Rather more impressive mosques were built at Alaiye and Attaleia, where they were often converted from churches.

And yet these city sites still existed. Their buildings did not fall down at once; they could still be lived in if the conquerors chose – as some of them certainly did at Attaleia and Korakesion/Alaiye. Indeed, even now, after ten centuries and more of neglect, there are walls and even whole buildings still standing. But the new conquerors did not wish for a city life. The final conquests were accomplished by the sultans and their armies, but the occupiers of the land, before and after those conquests, were the nomads.

For the next several centuries nomad bands used Pamphylia as their home. Their life-style ignored the cities, though they were not wholly inimical to arable agriculture. It is fortunate that their life was studied in the mid twentieth century, before it finally disappeared.[77] There were some groups who migrated between Pamphylia, their base in winter, and the summer pastures in the interior of Anatolia around the great lakes; there were also groups, described as 'semi-nomads', whose migrations were over shorter distances, between their winter villages on lower land and their summer pastures in the nearby hills. In such a life some villages were more or less permanent, but with a fluctuating population; some groups lived largely in tents. All were pastoralists above all. In such a situation Pamphylia ceased to be a settled land, except for fields of catch-crops, and gardens around at Attaleia (now Antalya, or Adalia).[78]

The clearest sign that the old cities had vanished, even as places of residence

[76] X. de Planhol, *De la Plaine Pamphylienne aux lacs Pisidiens, Nomadisme et vie Paysanne*, Paris, 1958.

[77] Evliya Celebi repeatedly notes the huts of Turkmen: H. Crane, 'Evliya Celebi's Journey through the Pamphylian Plain in 1671–1672', *Muqarnas* 10, 1993, 157–168; he also noted the well-fortified Attaleia, and found no urban settlement between Attaleia and Manaua.

[78] Planhol, *Plaine Pamphylienne*, fig. 10. He shows Aspendos and Perge being stages on the road, but it was not the old cities which were involved; Seljuk occupation of the countryside around Alanya is implied by the instances of pavilions: S. Redford, 'Seljuk Pavilions and Enclosures in and around Alanya', *AST* 14(1), 1996.

for a significant population, came when the Seljuk government organised the trade route through Pamphylia. This is marked by a series of well-built caravanserais spaced a day's journey apart along the route, which is somewhat different from the earlier Roman road. Several of these hostels survive, spread along the modern Turkish routes 400 and 650.[79] Only Alanya and Antalya (Korakesion and Attaleia) of all the old cities are included;[80] all the rest of the old Greek cities are ignored. This route which still existed in the early 1800s, followed step by step by European travellers such as Leake.[81]

From the Arab invasions to the Turkish conquest, that is, from about AD 650 to about 1200, we can see a fairly constant, if not quite regular, decline in the cities of Pamphylia. There was a rapid decline in the second half of the seventh century, under the impact of Arab raids upon the under-inhabited cities, reducing them to minimal occupation, and in some cases (Perge, Aspendos, Phaselis) to abandonment within another century. This was modified by a brief recovery in the tenth and eleventh centuries at those places where urban life still survived. There was a decline not just in the size and population of the old cities, but a change in the composition of their people as well. By the time Attaleia came under assault from the Sultan of Konya early in the thirteenth century, it was partly populated by Turks and by western Europeans from France and Italy as well as by Greeks and Mardaites; when Korakesion fell its population was replaced by Turks, as Attaleia's was after the sack. The rural population became in large part nomad Turks. In all this the area mirrors the history of the rest of Anatolia rather more closely than earlier. Greeks survived in small numbers in Attaleia until the 1920s, when much of the Greek population was finally removed, but as a Greek country, Pamphylia was mortally wounded in the seventh and eighth centuries and died in the twelfth.

---

[79] The surviving caravanserais are surveyed in *Antalya I, Selçuklu Esesleri Seminarin*, Antalya 1986; the old Roman bridge over the Eurymedon was repaired, according to the inscription recovered at the site, by the Sultan Kaykusrau in 1239/1240: Z. K. Bilici, 'Koprupazar (Belkis) Koprusu Kitabesi Uzerine', *Adalya* 5, 2001/2002, 73–182.

[80] Alanya survived as a fort: S. Lloyd and D S. Rice, *Alanya (Ala'iyye)*, London 1958; M. O. Arik, 'Alanya – Inner Citadel Excavations (1985–1991)', *Anatolia*, 1992, 119–127. See also R. Mason, 'The Medici-Lazara Map of Alanya', *Anat. St.* 39, 1989, 85–105.

[81] W. M. Leake, *Journal of a Tour in Asia Minor*, London 1825, 125–133. He took six days along muddy and difficult roads with little cultivation until the neighbourhood of Antalya; the caravanserais are being converted into more economic uses, which is only suitable, at Alara Han and Serabta Han; Kirkhoz Han is still empty. Each is of different construction; all are planted in geographically well-chosen places.

Conclusion

A Land of the Greek Periphery

Pamphylia was a country of Greek-type cities for almost two thousand years, longer than England has so far been English; and four times as long as Europeans have been in America. At any time during that period, except perhaps during its last century, this would have seemed a natural and permanent state of affairs. Yet from about AD 1200 Greeks in Pamphylia were in an urban minority, of little or no account, no more than a remnant. And once that is understood, then it can be remembered that before 800 BC or thereabouts, it was not a Greek land at all. In the largest historical perspective, the Greek presence in Pamphylia was only temporary.

The Greeks in Pamphylia were always flanked by non-Greeks – Lykians, Pisidians, Isaurians, Etenneis, Kilikians. In many cases these adopted Greek forms, even the Greek language, but remained firmly non-Greek in their choice of *ethnos*; they may have been hellenised, but they were never Hellenes. In terms of social geography, the Pamphylian Greeks were an island, surrounded by the sea and by the lands of non-Greeks, just as in physical geographical terms they lived in a land which was hemmed in and blocked off by the sea to the south and the mountains to the east, north, and west. And, of course, the population of Pamphylia may have spoken Greek and lived in cities like Greeks elsewhere, with Greek constitutions, but their mixed origins, as Luwians, Italians, as well as Greeks, was always clear, in their religion, their names, and in the very name of their country.

'Greek' Pamphylia was, that is to say, on the periphery of the Greek world. The Greek settlers combined with the indigenous inhabitants and formed themselves into a society of cities, which were generally fairly small, and all of them adopted the dominant Hellenic culture. This facility for absorbing Greek culture was also one for assimilating non-Greeks, so that the Italians who arrived in the first centuries BC and AD were absorbed within a century. The acceptance of Christianity did not change this – it was another process of absorption – but it removed the distinctive religion of the Lady of Perge, the last remnant of the Luwians.

This facility for integrating foreign elements sets the area apart from other parts of the Greek world, where racial exclusiveness was the general rule. It was clearly part of the local political and social culture in Pamphylia, for the apparent lack of social conflict and political violence also suggests a culture of local toleration. Politically this is perhaps also reflected in the submissiveness with which the several conquerors were greeted – Persians, Hellenistic kings, Romans.

The barrier set by the monotheistic religions, however, did not permit the absorption of the next group of immigrants. The pattern was set by the Arab raids, which were resisted to the point of destruction, so that only Attaleia and Sillyon held out. But the Arabs did not stay or settle, merely raided destructively. The Muslim Turks did arrive with the intention of settling, but in a most drastic way. They were alien, in speech, in religion, and in economy, and could not be absorbed. Once that became clear, the isolation of Pamphylia doomed it to slow and detailed conquest, for the first time, and the Greek society there to destruction.

It was this isolation, however, which had also been the salvation of Greek Pamphylia for the previous two millennia. In the great clashes of kingdoms and empires, Pamphylia was always unimportant. Separated from the rest of the Greek world by the sea and the mountains, and with no particular wealth of its own, and with no major route passing through it, the area was of only marginal interest to the great conquerors. Kroisos, the Akhaimenids, Athens, Alexander, the Hellenistic kings, Rome, the Arabs, all paid attention to the place only briefly and in passing. Alexander's passage was in this sense typical: a swift march, an incomplete conquest, and a rapid departure. Kroisos, Ptolemy I, Antiochos III, P. Servilius Vatia, Cn. Pompeius, did much the same, passing through in order to go somewhere else more important, or richer, or more interesting. The Akhaimenid Great Kings and the Roman emperors largely ignored it, except to take tax monies out of it. The Arabs merely raided it, making no attempt to conquer. Only the Turks, looking for lands to graze, made a serious, and successful, effort to take it over.

The cities themselves had varied origins: Side was wholly indigenous, Phaselis wholly immigrant, as were perhaps Olbia and Magydos. Attaleia was founded by an outsider king. The three cities of the plain, Perge, Sillyon, Aspendos, were of mixed indigenous Luwian and (by this time) indigenous Greek origin, and they parcelled out their mutual plain between them peaceably. These three were close together geographically, which might have been expected to promote quarrels. Instead, over a period of several hundred years, they repeatedly formed political alliances with each other to defend themselves against threats and attacks. Of all the cities, only indigenous Side and colonist Phaselis were belligerent.

The evidence for the friendship of these cities of the plain is certainly tenuous, but their origins in apparent mutual agreement in the seventh century BC, their concerted reaction to Alexander in the 330s, their joint coinage and alliance in the face of the Seleukid threat at the end of the third century BC, their joint approach to the Romans in 169 BC, and in the end their joint participation in the metropolitan bishopric of Perge/Sillyon, all lay out a pattern of political behaviour which can only be characterised as repeated mutual help in the face of outside pressure. From this mutuality Side and Phaselis were generally excluded, emphasising once again the difference between these two and the three cities of the plain.

Each new threat provoked a different reaction, designed to meet the specific threat which had developed. The problem of turmoil in Anatolia and the threatening presence of Greeks at sea led to the foundation of the cities. The passage of Alexander produced submission, though Sillyon had to fight since it was occupied by a Persian force; both Side and Phaselis, different again, tried to use Alexander's power for their own ends. The Ptolemaic approach led, probably, to submission, but that of Antiochos III and Akhaios produced a mutual alliance, which spread to Phaselis and Termessos – Side standing aloof as before. The intrusion of Attalid interest perhaps came up against the same unity, for the new city of Attaleia was planted in a place which was less than ideal, as though shunted to one side. The Roman arrival produced submission again. All this was assisted by the out-of-the-way nature of Pamphylia's geographical situation.

What had happened was that the original cooperation in city-founding left a mutual determination that the best way to meet a threat was to act together. But within that shelter the relationships of the three cities changed. In the Akhaimenid period and into the Hellenistic, Aspendos was the most important, and richest, of the three; by the Roman period this description lay with Perge, thanks to its rich temple, its facilities for trade, its large *chora*; in the end it was Sillyon which lasted longest.

The emergence of Sillyon in the face of the Arab raids was another manifestation of this mutual relationship, for it occurred at the same time as that city became a refuge for the Pergean bishops. Indeed the mutual peaceableness of this whole set of cities is remarkable: the only belligerent members were Side, with its quarrels with Aspendos and Perge and its hostility to the Etenneis, and Phaselis, which tended to fight its neighbours, but never, so far as we know, other Pamphylians.

All this puts Pamphylia as a Greek land on the very edge of the Greek world, not just geographically, but socially and politically as well. It lay outside the mainstream, and this was to its collective benefit. It was rarely fought over, until the end; it was usually relatively prosperous, but it was always on the periphery, never at the centre of events.

In the end, though, all this was not enough. The new world of Christianity and Islam had no room for political quiescence and mutual toleration. The wars of Byzantium against the Arabs and the Turks were marked by the failure of the usual pattern of integration of incomers. This may be put down to the rigidities introduced into Pamphylian social attitudes by the adoption of monotheistic Christianity – together, of course, with the similarly intolerant and monotheistic ways of Islam. And in the end, for the first time in their two millennia-long presence in Pamphylia, the Pamphylians were faced by a situation which had occurred to all other Mediterranean peoples as far back as the Greek Archaic age: the intrusion into their land of organised bands of peoples determined to take their lands from them. It was an ironic development given the long history of local peace and integration and absorption. Christianity compelled the Pamphylian cities to change their age-old attitudes, and so effectively destroyed them by refusing a sensible compromise with their new enemies. The cities were killed by their Christianity.

The peripheral situation of Pamphylia was therefore maintained through till the end. The Byzantine government could do little to assist in the final agony, and was even prepared to contemplate separating off the area as a semi-autonomous principality, just as had the Hittites three millennia before. At no point was Pamphylia valued for itself, except presumably by its inhabitants. But the cities fought for their lives, and as they died, even as Attaleia was being fought over by Turks and Franks, just possibly a Pamphylian Greek could reflect that for many centuries these cities had provided a secure and comfortable life for their people, usually tolerant and usually peaceful. They were certainly peripheral to Greece, Rome, and Greek culture, but they had long been successful as cities and communities; and when under dire threat, they had fought for what they believed in, even to the death.

Appendix 1: A Ruler in Pamphylia in Plato

Plato, in the *Republic* (10.615) has a story in which an Ardiaios is said 'a thousand years before', to have been 'tyrant of a city in Pamphylia'. This does not appear to be a real person. The reference comes in a story about the punishment of evil-doers, so that 'Pamphylia' is not to be seen as a reference to an actual place, but as a synonym for 'somewhere'. There is an earlier reference to 'Er, son of Ananaias, a Pamphylian' (10.614), which is even more obviously an invention. There never was an Aridaios, and so far as we known there is no record of any man being a tyrant of any city in Pamphylia, or for that matter any city in Pamphylia in the fourteenth century BC. The reference should go the way of Plato's invention of Atlantis, into the fiction records.

Appendix 2: City Statistics

The following numbers are all approximations since the territories of the cities are all of uncertain size, and so their populations are also. They are listed here largely to give some notion of comparative sizes. They must not be taken as 'correct'. The basis is 200 persons per hectare in urban areas, and one person per hectare in rural.

A. Urban Areas

City	Approx Useful Territory (Sq. Km)	Acropolis/Original Site (Ha)	Expanded Site (Ha)	Theatre Capacity	Population of Urban Centre
Aspendos	370	23	35	20,000	7,000
Attaleia	80	4	60	–	12,000
Korakesion	?	24/36	30/42	–	4,000*
Magydos	40	–		–	–
Olbia	?	–		–	–
Perge	600	15	45+4	14,000	9,000/9,800
Phaselis	240	6	26	10,000	5,200
Side	480	22	50	22,000	10,000
Sillyon	210	28	28	–	5,600

+ – this is the minimum; absence of information on chora or city size
* – figure reduced to take account of difficult topography

B. Populations (at 200 persons per urban ha. and 200 per rural sq. km.)

City	City area (ha.)	City Population	Chora (sq km.)	Chora Population	Total Population
Aspendos	35	7,000	370	37,000	44,000
Attaleia	60	12,000	80	8,000	20,000
Korakesion	30/42	4,000	–	–	–
Magydos	–	–	40	4,000	4,000+
Perge	49	9,800	600	60,000	70,000
Phaselis	26	5,200	240	24,000	29,000
Side	50	10,000	480	48,000	58,000
Sillyon	28	5,600	210	21,000	26,600

+ – this is the minimum; absence of information on chora or city size
* – figure reduced to take account of difficult topography

Bibliography

1. Sources

The written sources are detailed in their places; here I assemble the other ancient materials.

A. Archaeological

H. Abbasoğlu and W. Martini, 'Perge Acropolis'ndi 1996 Yilinda Yapılar Çalısmalar', XIX *Kazı* II, 1997, 102.

M. Adak and O. Atvur, 'Epigraphische Mitteilungen aus Antalya II: die Pamphylische Hafenstadt Magydos', Ep. *Anat.* 31, 1999, 53–68.

M. O. Arik, 'Alanya – Inner Citadel Excavations (1985–1991)', *Anatolica* 18, 1992, 119–127.

N. Atik, *Die Keramik aus den südthermen von Perge*, Tubingen 1995.

M. H. Ballance, 'Cumanin Camii at Antalya: a Byzantine Church', *Proceedings of the British School at Rome*, NS 10, 1955, 99–114.

M. Ballance, 'The Roman Basilica at Aspendos 1956 and 1992', *AST* XI, 1993, 453–457.

E. Y. Bostanci, 'Researches on the Mediterranean coast of Anatolia: a new Palaeolithic Site at Belbina near Antalya', *Anatolia*, 11, 1967, 203–217.

C. Brixhe, 'Une tablette de juge d'origine probablement Pamphylienne', *BCH* 90, 1966, 653–663.

H. Cuppers, 'Getriedemagazin am forum in Aspendos', *BJ* 161, 1961, 25–35.

F. W. Hasluck, 'Frankish Remains at Adalia', *ABSA* 15, 1908/9, 270–273.

H. Hormann, 'Das Nymphäum zu Aspendos', *Jahrbuch des Deutsches Archäologisches Institut* 44, 1929, 263–274.

J. Inan, 'Der Demetrios und Apolloniosbogen in Perge', *Ist. Mitt.* 39, 1989, 237–244.

J. Inan and W. Martini in 17, 18, and 19 *Kazı* (on Perge).

I. Kayan, A. Minzoni-Deroche, I. Yalçinkaya, 'Prospection Préhistorique dans la Region d'Antalya, Notice Préliminaire', in B. Remy (ed.), *Varia Anatolica I: Anatolia Antiqua/Eski Anadolu*, Istanbul and Paris 1988, 9–12.

P. Kessener, 'The 1998 Campaign of the Aspendos Aqueduct Research Project', XVII *AST*, 1999, 263–269.

P. Kessener and S. Piras, 'The Pressure Line of the Aspendos Aqueduct', *Adalya* 2, 1998, 159–187.

P. Kessener and S. Piras, 'The 1998 Campaign of the Aspendos Aqueduct Research Project', XVII *AST*, 1999, 263–269.

P. Knoblauch, *Die Hafenanlagen und die Anschliessenden Seemauern von Side*, Ankara 1977.

M. Küpper, 'Sillyon, Research Work, 1995', XIV *AST*, II, 1996, 451–462.

M. Küpper, 'Landliche Siedlungsplätze in Sillyon', *Lykia* II, 1995, 62–74.

M. Küpper, 'Landliche Siedlungstrukturen in Pamphylien am Beispiel Sillyon', *Adalya* II, 1995, 97–115.

M. Küpper, 'Sillyon, Bericht uber die Arbeiten 1996', XVI *AST* II 1998, 475–496.

H. Lauter, 'Die Hellenistische Agora von Aspendos', *BJ* 170, 1970, 77–101.

H. Lauter, 'Das Hellenistische Südtor von Perge', *BJ* 172, 1972, 1–11.

A. M. Mansel, 'Fouilles de Side et de Perge', *Anadolu* 2, 1955, 58–62.

A. M. Mansel, 'Ein Basaltkessel aus Side', *Anadolu* 3, 1958, 1–13.

A. M. Mansel, *Die Agora von Side*, Ankara 1956.

A. M. Mansel, *Die Ruinen von Side*, Berlin 1963.

A. M. Mansel, 'Bemerkungen über die Landmauer von Side (Pamphylien)', in *Mélanges Offerts à K. Michalowski*, Warsaw 1966, 541–551.

A. M. Mansel, 'Die Nymphaeen von Perge', *Ist. Mitt.* 25, 1975, 367–32.

A. M. Mansel, *Side 1947–1966, Yillari Kazıları ve Arastirmalarinin Sonucları*, Ankara 1978.

W. Martini, 'Die Akropolis von Perge, Survey und Sondagen, 1994–1996', *AMS* 34, 1999, 155–161.

J. Mellaart, 'Preclassical Remains in Southern Turkey', *Anat. St.* 5, 1955, 176–178.

H. Metzger, 'Tête en terre cuite du Musée d'Adalia', *REA* 54, 1952, 13–17.

S. Mitchell, *Archaeological Reports, Asia Minor, ABSA* 1979–1999.

G. Moretti, 'Oggetti antichi esistenti in Adalia, *Annuario* 3, 1916–1921, 23–27.

E. Ozgur, 'Aspendos Orenyeri 1991 Yili Kazı Onarim ve Cevre Duzenleme Çalismalari', *Muze Kurtarima Kazıları Seminari III, 1992*, Ankara 1993, 251–255.

R. Paribeni and P. Romanelli, *Monumenti Antichi* 23, 1914.

W. M. Ramsey, 'Antiquities of Southern Phrygia and the Border Lands', *AJA* 4, 1888, 6–21.

S. Redford, 'Seljuk Pavilions and Enclosures in and around Alanya', *AST* 14(1), 1996,

F. E. Winter, 'Notes on Military Architecture in the Termessos Region', *AJA* 70, 1966, 53–58.

S. Yetkin, 'The Turkish Monuments in Sillyon (Yankoy Hisari)', in *Mansel'e Armagon/Mélanges Mansel*, vol 2, Ankara 1974, 861–872.

B. Epigraphic

R. D. Barnett, 'A Phoenician Inscription from Eastern Cilicia', *Iraq* 10, 1948.

G. E. Bean, 'Notes and Inscriptions from Lycia', *JHS* 68, 1948, 46–56.

G. E. Bean, 'Epitaphs from Aspendos', *Jahrbuch für Klein-Asiatische Forschung* 2, 1952/1953, 201–266.

G. E. Bean, 'Inscriptions in the Antalya Museum', *Belleten* 22, 1958, 21–70.

C. E. Bean and T. B. Mitford, *Journeys in Rough Cilicia in 1962 and 1963*, Vienna 1965.

G. E. Bean and T. B. Mitford, *Journeys in Rough Cilicia 1964–1968*, Vienna 1970.

E. Bosch and S. Atlan, 'Epigrafya: Antalya Kitabeleri', *Belleten* 11, 1946.

R. van Bremen, 'A Family from Sillyon', *ZPE* 104, 1996, 43–56.

C. Brixhe, 'Documents inédits de Pamphylie', *Anadolu* 11, 1967, 203–217.

C. Brixhe, 'Un nouveau document épichorique de Side', *Kadmos* 8, 1967, 143–151.

C. Brixhe, 'L'Alphabet épichorique de Side', *Kadmos* 8, 1969, 54–84.

C. Brixhe, *Le Dialecte grec de Pamphylie*, Paris 1976.

C. Brixhe, 'Corpus des Inscriptions Dialectales de Pamphylie, Supplement IV', *Kadmos* 35, 1996, 72–88.

C. Brixhe and R. Hodot, *D'Asie Mineure du Nord au Sud*, Nancy 1988, no. 39.

C. Brixhe and G. Neumann, 'Die Griechische-Sidetische bilingue von Seleukeia', *Kadmos* 27, 1988, 35–43.

H. Cambel and J. D. Hawkins, *Corpus of Hieroglyphic Luwian Inscriptions*, vol 2, 2000.

N. Gokalp, 'Epigraphische Mitteilungen aus Antalya IV: Inschriften aus Attaleia', *Ep. Anat.* 31, 1999, 72–75.

H. Grégoire, *Receuil des inscriptions grecques Chrétiennes d'Asie Mineure,* Paris 1922.

F. W. Hasluck, 'A French Inscription at Adalia', *ABSA* 16, 1909/10, 24–26.

D. Hereward, 'Inscriptions from Pamphylia and Isauria', *JHS* 78, 1958, 57–67.

J. Inan, 'Bemerkungen zu Lykischen und Pamphylischen Inschriften', *Ep. Anat.* 17, 1991, 113–138.

B. Iplikçioğlu, 'Bati Pamphylia ve dogu Lykia'da Epigrafya Arastirmalari 2002,' *AST* XXI, 2003, 75–78.

F. Isik, 'Pamfilya ve Anadolu Gercegi', *Adalya* 1, 1996, 23–24.

C. P. Jones, 'The Plancii of Perge and Diana Planciana', *Harvard Studies in Classical Philology* 80, 1976, 231–238.

C. P. Jones, 'Eastern Alimenta and an inscription of Attaleia', *JHS* 109, 1991, 189–191.

C. P. Jones, 'A Decree from Perge in Pamphylia', *Ep. Anat.,* 25, 1995, 29–33.

C. P. Jones, '"Joint Sacrifice" at Iasus and Side', *JHS* 118, 1998, 183–186.

C. P. Jones, 'Old and New in the Inscriptions of Perge: I. The Foundation of M. Feridius', *Ep. Anat.* 31, 1999, 8–13.

C. P. Jones and C. Habicht, 'A Hellenistic Inscription from Arsinoe in Cilicia', *Phoenix* 43, 1989, 317–346).

I. Kaygusuz, *Belleten* 40, 1980, 249–256.

I. Kaygusuz, 'Eine Neue Ehrung für Quintus Voconius Saxa Fidus in Perge', *Ep. Anat.,* 2, 1983, 37–39.

I. Kaygusuz, 'Perge, unter Kaiser Tacitus Mittelpunkt der Welt', *Ep. Anat.* 4, 1984, 1–4.

H.-J. Kellner, 'Zwei neue Flottendiplome: Zur Grenze von Pamphylien und Kilikien', *Chiron* 7, 1977, 315–322.

T. Korkut and R. Rekoğlu, 'Grabinschrift aus Pamphylien und Lykien', *ZPE* 143, 2003, 105–116.

R. Merkelbach, 'Kaiser Tacitus erhebt Perge zur Metropolis Pamphyliens und erlaubt einen Agon', *Ep. Anat.* 29, 1997, 69–74.

R. Merkelbach and S. Sahin, 'Die Publizierten Inschriften von Perge', *Ep. Anat.* 11, 1988, 97–169.

S. Mitchell, 'The Plancii in Asia Minor', *JRS* 64, 1974, 27–39.

S. Mitchell, 'The Siege of Cremna', in D. French and C. S. Lightfoot (eds), *The Eastern Frontier of the Roman Empire*, BAR S553, Oxford 1989, 311–328.

S. Mitchell, 'Termessos, king Amyntas, and the War with the Sandaliotai, a New Inscription from Pisidia', in D. French (ed.), *Studies in the History and Topography of Lycia and Pisidia in Memoriam A. S. Hall*, Ankara 1994, 95–105.

P. G. Mosca and J. Russell, 'A Phoenician Inscription from Cebel Ires Dagı in Rough Cilicia, Ep. Anat. 9, 1987, 1–28.

G. Neuman, 'Zur Entzifferung der Sidetischen Inschriften', *Kadmos* 7, 1968, 75–85.

O. van Niff, 'Inscriptions and Civic Memory in the Roman East', in A. Cooling (ed.), *The Afterlife of Inscriptions*, London 2000, 21–36.

O. van Niff, 'Local Heroes: Athletics, Festivals and Elite Self-fashioning in the Roman East', in S. Goldhill (ed.), *Being Greek under Rome: Cultural Identity, the Second Sophistic and the Development of Empire*, Cambridge 2001.

J. Nollé, 'Die Eintracht der Mehlsieber und Brotformer in Side', *Ep. Anat.*, 1, 1983, 131–140.

J. Nollé, 'Die 'Charaktere' im 3 Epidemienbuch des Hippokrates und Mnemon von Side', *Ep. Anat.*, 2, 1983, 85–98.

J. Nollé, 'Pamphylische Studien', *Chiron* 15, 1985, 199–212.

J. Nollé, 'Pamphylische Studien 6–10', *Chiron* 17, 1989, 235–273.

J. Nollé, 'Pamphylische Studien 11–12', *Chiron* 21, 1991, 331–344.

J. Nollé, 'Die feindlichen Schwestern – Betrachtungen zur Rivalität der pamphylischen Städte', in G. Robesch and G. Rehrenbak, *Die Epigraphische und Altertumskundliche erforschung kleinasiens*, Vienna 1993, 297–317.

J. Nollé, S. Sahin, Ch. Vorster, 'Katalog der Inschriften im Museum von Alanya', *Ep. Anat.* 19, 1985, 125–146.

H. A. Ormerod and D. W. Robinson, 'Notes and Inscriptions from Pamphylia', *ABSA*, 17, 1910–1911, 215–249.

B. Pace, 'La Zona costiera da Adalia a Side', *Annuario* 3, 1916–1921, 29–53.

G. Radet and P. Paris, 'Inscriptions d'Attaleia, de Perge, d'Aspendos', *BCH* 10, 1886.

G. Radet and P. Paris, 'Inscriptions de Syllion en Pamphylie', *BCH* 13, 1886, 486–497.

J. and L. Robert, 'Bulletin Épigraphique', *Revue des Etudes Grecques* 61, 1948, 198–203.

L. Robert, 'Hellenica', *Revue Philologique* 13, 1939, 154–155.

L. Robert, *Le Sanctuaire de Sinuri près de Mylasa*: I. *Les Inscriptions grecques*, Paris 1945, 35–57.

L. Robert, 'Deux Textes inutilisés sur Perge et sur Side', *Hellenica* 5, Paris 1948, 64–76.

L. Robert, 'Inscriptions Grecques de Side en Pamphylie', *Revue de Philologie* 32, 1958, 15–53.

L. Robert, 'Decret héllénistique de Termessos', *Docs*, 53–58.

L. Robert, 'Un pierre à Phaselis et une inscription de Cilicie', *Docs*, 42–44.

L. Robert, 'L'Impératrice Anatrophé à Side', *Revue de Philologie* 41, 1967, 82–84.

J. Russell, 'A Roman Military Diploma from Eastern Pamphylia', *AJA* 95, 1991, 469–488.

S. Sahin, 'Ti. Iulius Frugi, Proconsul von Lycia-Pamphylia unter Mark Aurel und Verus', *Ep. Anat.*, 3,1984.

S. Sahin, 'Bemerkungen zu lykischen und pamphylischen Inschriften', *Ep. Anat.* 17, 1991, 133–134.

S. Sahin, 'Perge Kentinin Kuruculari ve Plancia Magna', *Adalya* 1, 1996, 45–52.

S. Sahin, 'Studien zu den Inschriften von Perge III: Marcus Plancius Rutilius Varus und C. Iulius Plancius Varus Cornutus', *Ep. Anat.*, 27, 1996, 115–125.

S. Sahin, 'Epigraphische Mitteilungen aus Antalya I: Inschriften aus Pamphylien und Lykien', *Ep. Anat.* 31, 1999, 40–45.

S. Sahin, 'Epigraphische Mitteilungen aus Antalya V: Olbia und einige andere Küste norte bei Kemer in Westpamphylien', *Ep. Anat.* 33, 2001, 145–167.

M. Segre, 'Decreto de Aspendos', *Aegyptos* 14, 1934, 253–268.

P. de Souza, 'Romans and Pirates in a late Hellenistic Oracle from Pamphylia', *Classical Quarterly* 47, 1997, 477–481.

J.-Y. Strasser, 'Inscriptions agonistiques de Side', *Ep. Anat.* 35, 2003, 3–76.

R. S. Stroud, 'An Argive Decree from Nemea concerning Aspendos', *Hesperia* 53, 1984, 193–216.

R. Stuppich, 'Das Grabmal eines Konsularen in Attaleia', *Ist. Mitt.* 41, 1991, 417–422.

P. Weiss, 'Ein agonistisches Bema und die isopythischen Spiele von Side', *Chiron* 11, 1981, 315–346.

P. Weiss, 'Auxe Perge; Beobachtungen zu einem bemerkenswerten städtischen Document des späten 3 Jahrhundert n. Chr.', *Chiron* 21, 1991, 313–38.

P. Weiss, 'Ein neuer Prokonsul von Lycia-Pamphylia auf einem militardiplom (165/166 n. Chr.)', *Ep. Anat.* 31, 1999, 77–82.

A. M. Woodward, 'Inscriptions from Western Pisidia', *ABSA* 17, 1910–1911, 205–214.

A. M. Woodward and H. A. Ormerod, 'A Journey in South-Western Asia Minor', *ABSA* 16, 1909–1910, 76–136.

M. Worrle, 'Leben und Sterben wie ein Furst: Überlegungen zu den Inschriften einer neuen Dynastengrabes in Lykien', *Chiron* 18, 1988, 77–83.

F. C. Woudhuizen, 'Origins of the Sidetic Script', *Talanta* 16/17. 1984/1985.

C. Numismatic

S. Atlan, 'Eine in Side geprägte Lykische Münze', *Anatolia* 3, 1958, 89–95.

S. Atlan, 'Die Münzen des Stadt Side mit Sidetischen Inschriften', *Kadmos* 7, 1968, 67–80.

N. Baydun, 'Die Münzen von Attaleia in Pamphylia', *JNG*, 26 1975, 33–75 and 1976, 37–78.

C. Boehringer, *Zur Chronologie Mittelhellenistischer Münzserien 220–160 v. Chr.,* Berlin 1972.

C. Brixhe, 'Tetradrachmes de Side à monogramme épichorique', *Kadmos* 16, 1977, 168–174

S. Bulut, 'Erken Donem Likye Sikkelerinde Triskeles Motifi', *Adalya* VII, 2004, 15–68.

H. Chantaine, 'Schatzfund von Antalya', *JNG* 28, 1976, 89–106.

H.J. Colin, *Die Münzen von Perge in Pamphylia aus hellenistischer Zeit,* Koln 1996.

C. Foss, 'A Hoard of the Third Century AD from Pamphylia', *Coin Hoards* V, 1980, 37–40.

P.R. Franke and M. K. Nollé, *Die Homonoia-münzen kleinasiens und der thrakischen Randgebiete,* Saarbrucken 1997.

H. Graebler, 'Die Losurne in der Agonistik' *Zeitschrift für Numismatik* 39, 1929, 271–312.

C. Hiepp-Tamer, *Die Münzpragung de Lykischen Stadt Phaselis in Griechischen Zeit,* Saarbrucken 1993.

G. F. Hill, 'Greek Coins acquired by the British Museum in 1919', *Num. Chron.*, 20, 1920, 97–116.

G. F. Hill, 'Some Coins of Southern Asia Minor', in W. C. Calder and J. Keel (eds), *Anatolian Studies presented to W. H. Buckler,* Manchester 1939, 207–224.

F. Imhoof-Blumer, 'Münzen von Selge und Aspendos', *Zeitschrift für Numismatik* 5, 1878, 133–142.

C. M. Kraay, 'Notes on the Mint of Side in the Fifth Century BC', *Num. Chron.* 1969, 15–20.

C. M. Kraay, 'Hoards, Small Change, and the Origin of Coinage', *JHS* 84, 1964, 76–91.

H. de Longprière, *Rev. Num.* 1869, 50–52.

O. Mørkholm, 'The Era of the Pamphylian Alexanders', *ANSMN* 23, 1978, 69–75.

O. Mørkholm, *Early Hellenistic Coinage,* Cambridge 1991.

J. C. Mossop, 'An Autonomous Coin of Magydos in Pamphylia', *Num. Chron.* 10, 1970, 319–320.

M. J. Price, *The Coinage in the Name of Alexander the Great and Philip Arrhidaeus*, London 1991.

G. Le Rider, 'Les Tetradrachmes Pamphyliens de la fin du IIIe siècle et du debut de IIe siècle avant nôtre ére', *Rev. Num.*, 2e série, 14, 1972, 253–259.

L. Robert, 'Monnaies et Divinités d'Aspendos', *Hellenica* XI –XII, Paris 1960, 177–188.

H. Seyrig, 'Monnaies Héllénistiques', *Rev. Num.*, 2e serie 5, 1963, 7–64.

M. Thompson, 'The Cavalla Hoard', *ANSMN* 26, 1981, 33–49.

H. A. Troxell, *The Coinage of the Lycian League*, New York 1982.

2. Modern works

A. General accounts

H. Ahrweiler, 'L'Asie Mineure et les invasions arabes (VIIe–IXe Siècles', *Revue Historique* 227, 1962, 1–22.

H. Ahrweiler, *Byzance et la mer*, Paris 1966.

Antalya 1: Selçuklu Eserleri Semineri, Antalya 1986.

G. G. Aperghis, *The Seleukid Royal Economy*, Cambridge 2004.

R. E. Allen, *The Attalid Kingdom, a Constitutional History*, Oxford 1983.

M. Angold, *The Byzantine Empire 1025–1204*, Harlow 1984.

E. Babelon, *Les Perses Achémenides*, Paris 1893.

E. Badian, 'Nearchus the Cretan,' *YCS* 24, 1975, 147–170.

R. S. Bagnall, *The Administration of the Ptolemaic Possessions outside Egypt*, Leiden 1976.

D. W. Baronowski, 'The Status of the Greek Cities of Asia Minor after 190 BC', *Hermes* 119, 1991, 450–463.

G. F. Bass, 'Cape Gelidonya: a Bronze Age shipwreck', *TAPA* 57/58, 1967.

C. Baurain, *Les Grecs et la Mediterranée Orientale des siècles obscurs à la fin de l'époque archaique*, Paris 1997.

E. Bikerman, 'Notes sur Poybe, I: Le Statut des villes d'Asie Mineure après la paix d'Apamée', *Revue des Études Grecques*, 50, 1937, 217–239.

P. Bilde *et al.* (eds), *Centre and Periphery in the Hellenistic World*, Aarhus 1997.

A. Birley, *Marcus Aurelius*, London 1966.

A. Birley, *Hadrian, the Restless Emperor*, London 1997.

K. Y. Blankinship, *The End of the Jihad State: the Reign of Hisham al-Malik and the Collapse of the Ummayads*, New York 1994.

J. Boardman, *The Greeks Overseas*, London 1973.

A. B. Bosworth, *Conquest and Empire, the Reign of Alexander the Great*, Cambridge 1988.

W. Brandes, *Die Stadt Kleinasiens in 7 und 8 Jahrhundert*, Berlin 1985.

K. Broderson, 'The 'Urban Myth' of Euboean Kyme', *Ancient History Bulletin*, 15, 2001, 25–26.

E. W. Brooks, 'The Arabs in Asia Minor (641–750), from Arabic Sources', *JHS* 18, 1898, 182–204.

E. W. Brooks, 'The Campaign of 716–718 from Arabic Sources', *JHS* 19, 1899, 1–33.

E. W. Brooks, 'Byzantines and Arabs in the time of the Early Abbasids,' *English Historical Review* 15, 1900, 728–747 and 17, 1901, 84–92.

T. R. S. Broughton, 'Some Non-Colonial Coloni of Augustus', *TAPA*, 46, 1935, 18–24.

T. R. S. Broughton, *The Magistrates of the Roman Republic*, New York, 1951–1960.

P. A. Brunt, 'C. Fabricius Tuscus and an Augustan Dilectus', *ZPE* 13, 1974, 161–185.

T. Bryce, *The Lycians*, vol. 1, Copenhagen 1986.

T. Bryce, *The Kingdom of the Hittites*, Oxford 1998.

A. R. Burn, *The Lyric Age of Greece*, rev.ed., London 1978.

C. Cahen, *The Formation of Turkey: the Seljukid Sultanate of Rum, Eleventh to Fourteenth Centuries*, trans P. M. Holt, Harlow 2001.

Cambridge Ancient History.

Cambridge Medieval History, vol. IV.

P. H. J. Houwink ten Cate, *The Luwian Population Groups of Lycia and Cilicia Aspera during the Hellenistic Period*, Leiden 1965.

P. Charanis, 'The Transfer of Population as a Policy in the Byzantine Empire', *Comparative Studies in Society and History* 3, 1960–1961, 140–154.

V. Christides, 'The Naval Engagement of Dhat as-Sarari AH 34/AD 655–656. A Classical Example of Naval Warfare Incompetence', *Byzantina* 13.2, 1985, 1331–1345.

C. R. Cockerell, *Travels in Europe and the Levant, 1810–1817*, London 1903.

G. M. Cohen, *The Hellenistic Settlements in Europe, the Islands and Asia Minor*, Berkeley and Los Angeles, 1995.

J. N. Coldstream, 'Status symbols in Cyprus in the eleventh century BC', in E. Peltenburg (ed.), *Early Society in Cyprus*, Edinburgh 1989, 325–335.

S. Colvin, 'Names in Hellenistic and Roman Lycia', in S. Colvin (ed.), *The Greco-Roman East*, *YCS* 31, 2004, 44–84.

L. I. Conrad, 'The Conquest of Arwad: a Source-Critical Study in the Historiography of the Early Medieval Near East', in A. Cameron and L. I. Conrad (eds), *The Byzantine and Early Islamic Near East, 1. Problems in the Source Material*, Princeton 1992, 317–350.

J. M. Cook, *The Persian Empire*, London 1983.

M. Crawford, *Roman Statutes*, London 1996.

A. H. Fahmy, *Muslim Sea-Power in the Eastern Mediterranean in the 7th to 10th Centuries*, New Delhi 1966.

R. Fleischer, *Artemis von Ephesos und Verwändte Kultstatuen aus Anatolien und Syrien*, Leiden 1972.

C. Foss, 'The Persians in Asia Minor and the end of Antiquity', *English Historical Review* 90, 1975, 721–743.

C. Foss, 'The Lycian Coast in the Byzantine Age', *DOP* 48, 1994, 1–52.

P. Freeman, 'The Province of Cilicia and its Origins', in P. Freeman and D. Kennedy (eds), *The Defence of the Roman and Byzantine East*, BAR S297, vol. 1, 1986, 252–275.

D. H. French, 'Sites and Inscriptions from Phrygia, Pisidia and Pamphylia', *Ep. Anat.* 17, 1991, 51–58.

J. Garstang and O. R. Gurney, *A Geography of the Hittite Empire*, London 1959.

J. D. Grainger, 'The Campaign of Cn. Manlius Vulso in Asia Minor', *Anat. St.* 54, 1995, 23–42.

J. D. Grainger, *The Roman War of Antiochos the Great*, Leiden 2002.

P. Green, *Alexander of Macedon*, 2nd ed., Harmondsworth 1974.

Jack P. Greene, *Peripheries and Center, Constitutional Development in the Extended Polities of the British Empire and the United States, 1607–1788*, New York, 1986.

E. S. Gruen, *The Hellenistic World and the Coming of Rome*, Berkeley and Los Angeles 1984.

O. R. Gurney, 'The Annals of Hattusilis III', *Anat. St.* 47, 1997, 127–139.

R. Haensch, *Capita provinciarum, Statthaltersitze und Provincialverwaltung in der Römischen Kaiserzeit*, Mainz 1997.

J. Haldon, *Warfare, State and Society in the Byzantine World, 565–1204*, London 1999.

M. H. Hansen and T. H. Nielsen (eds), *An Inventory of Archaic and Classical Poleis*, Oxford 2004.

M. Hassall, M. Crawford, and J. Reynolds, 'Rome and the Eastern Provinces at the end of the Second Century BC', *JRS* 64, 1974, 195–220.

J. Herrin, *The Formation of Christendom*, Oxford 1987.

P. K. Hitti, *History of the Arabs*, 7th ed., London 1961.

S. Hornblower, *Mausolus*, Oxford 1982.

C. Huart, *Ancient Persia and Iranian Civilisation*, London 1927.

G. Huxley, 'On the Vita of St Stephen the Younger', *Greek, Roman, and Byzantine Studies,* 18, 1977, 97–108.

J. Inan and E. Rosenbaum, *Roman and Early Byzantine Portrait Sculpture in Asia Minor*, Oxford 1966.

S. Jameson, 'The Lycian League; Some Problems of its Administration', *ANRW* II.2.

M. Jasink, 'Kizzuwatna and Tarhuntassa, their historical evolution and interactions with Hatti', in *La Cilicie, Espaces et Pouvoirs Locales*, Istanbul 2001, 47–56.

R. J. H. Jenkins, 'Cyprus between Byzantium and Islam, AD 688–965', in G. F. Mylonas and D. Raymond (eds), *Studies presented to David M. Robinson*, St Louis MO 1953, vol 2, 1006–1024.

A. H. M. Jones, *The Later Roman Empire 284–602*, Oxford 1964.

A. H. M. Jones, 'The Date and Value of the Verona List', *JRS* 44, 1954, 21–29.

R. M. Kallet-Marx, *Hegemony to Empire, the Development of the Roman Imperium in the East from 148 to 62 BC*, Berkeley and Los Angeles 1995.

K. H. Karpat, *Ottoman Population 1830–1914, Demographic and Social Characteristics*, Madison WS 1985.

W. F. Keppie, 'Legions in the East from Augustus to Trajan', in P. Freeman and D. Kennedy, *The Defence of the Roman and Byzantine East*, BAR S287, Oxford 1986.

E. Lanciers, 'Die Vergottlichung und die Ehe des Ptolemaios IV und der Arsinoe III', *Archiv für Papyrusforschung*, 34, 1988, 27–32.

M. Launey, *Recherches sur les Armées Héllénistiques*, Paris 1948, rev. ed., 1987.

W. M. Leake, *Journal of a Tour in Asia Minor*, London 1825.

B. N. Levick, *Roman Colonies in Southern Asia Minor*, Oxford 1967.

J. Ma, *Antiochos III and the Cities of Western Asia Minor*, Oxford 1999.

D. Magie, *Roman Rule in Asia Minor,* Princeton, NJ, 1950.

F. G. Maier, 'Priest Kings in Cyprus', in E. Peltenburg (ed.), *Early Society in Cyprus*, Edinburgh 1989, 376–391.

C. Mango, 'The Life of St Andrew the Fool Reconsidered', *Rivista di Studi Bizantini e Slavi*, 2, 1982, 297–313.

B. C. McGing, *The Foreign Policy of Mithradates Eupator King of Pontus*, Leiden 1986.

R. Meiggs, *The Athenian Empire*, Oxford 1973.

M. Miller, *The Sicilian Colony Dates*, Albany NY 1970.

S. Mitchell, 'Roman Residents and Roman Property in Southern Asia Minor', *Proceedings of the Xth International Congress of Classical Archaeology, Ankara/Izmir 1973*, Ankara 1978, 311–318.

S. Mitchell, *Anatolia*, Oxford 1989.

S. Mitchell, 'Amyntas in Pisidien – der lëtzte könig de Galater', *AMS* 12, 1994, 97–103.

S. Mitchell, *Cremna in Pisidia*, London and Swansea 1995.

S. Mitchell, 'The Administration of Roman Asia from 133 BC to AD 250', in W. Eck (ed.), *Lokale Autonomie und römische Ordnungsmacht in den kaiserzeitlichen Provinzen vom 1 bis 3 Jahrhundert*, Munich 1999.

S. Mitchell, 'Native Rebellion in the Pisidian Taurus', in K. Hopwood (ed.), *Organised Crime in Antiquity*, London 1999, 155–176.

A. T. Olmstead, *History of the Persian Empire*, Chicago 1948.

H. A. Ormerod, *Piracy in the Ancient World*, Liverpool 1926.

R. Osborne, *Greece in the Making, 1200–479 BC*, London 1996.

D. Pohl, 'Kaiserzeitliche Tempel in Kleinasien under besondere Beruchsichtigung der hellenisticher Vorläufer', *AMS* 43, 2002, 217–219.

M. P. Popham, 'Precolonisation: early Greek contact with the East', in G. R. Tsetskhladze and F. de Angelis, *The Archaeology of Greek Colonisation, Essays dedicated to Sir John Boardman*, Oxford 2002, 11–34.

W. M. Ramsay, 'Antiquities of Southern Phrygia and the Borderlands', *AJA*, 4, 1888, 6–21.

B. Rémy, *L'Évolution Administrative de l'Anatolie aux trois premiers siècles de Nôtre Ére*, Lyon 1986.

D. Ridgeway, *The First Western Greeks*, Cambridge 1992.

L. Robert, *Noms Indigènes dans l'Asie Mineure Greco-Romaine*, Paris 1963.

L. Robert, 'Hellenica XXI: Trihemiolies Athéniennes', *Opera Minora Selecta*, 3, 1377–1383.

L. Robert, 'Deux poètes grecs à l'époque impériale', *Stele: Mélanges Kontolion*, Athens 1980, 1–20.

E. Rosenbaum, G. Huber, S. Onurkan, *A Survey of Coastal Cilicia*, Ankara 1967.

H. Rott, *Kleinasiatische Denkmäler*, Leipzig 1908.

L. Ryder, 'The Andrea Salos Apocalypse', *DOP* 28, 1974.

G. Salmeri, 'Hellenism on the periphery: the case of Cilicia and an etymology of Soloikismos', in Colvin (ed.), *The Greco-Roman East*, *YCS* 31, 2004, 181–206.

O. Salomies, 'Roman Nomina in the Greek East', *Arctos* 35, 2001, 139–174.

M. K. Sanders, *The Sea Peoples, Warriors of the Ancient Mediterranean 1250–1150 BC*, rev. ed., London 1985.

M. H. Sayer, 'Strassenbau in Kilikien unter den Flaviern nach einem neugefundenen Meilenstein', *Ep. Anat.* 20, 1992, 58–61.

C. Settipani, *Continuité Gentilice et Continuite Familiale dans les familles Senatoriales Romaines à l'époque impériale*, Oxford 2000.

R. A. Sherk, *Rome and the Greek East to the Death of Augustus*, Cambridge 1984.

J. H. Smith, *Constantine the Great*, New York 1971.

P. de Souza, *Piracy in the Greco-Roman World*, Cambridge 1999.

E. Speller, *Following Hadrian, a second century journey through the Roman Empire*, London 2002.

M. P. Spiedel, 'Citizen Cohorts in the Roman Imperial Army: new Data on the Cohorts Apula, Campana and III Campestris', *TAPA* 106, 1976, 339–341.

M. P. Spiedel, 'The Roman Army in Asia Minor: Recent Epigraphical Discoveries and Research', in S. Mitchell (ed.), *Armies and Frontiers in Roman and Byzantine Anatolia*, BAR, S156, Oxford 1983.

D. Stockton, 'The Peace of Kallias', *Historia* 8, 1955, 61–79.

A. N. Stratos, 'The Naval Engagement at Phoenix', *Studies in Seventh Century Byzantine Political History*, 1983.

R. Syme, 'Observations on the Province of Cilicia', in W. C. Calder and J. Keel (eds), *Anatolian Studies presented to W. H. Buckler*, Manchester 1939, 299–332.

R. Syme, *Anatolica*, Oxford 1995.

M. Tameanko, *Monumental Coins, Buildings and Structures on Ancient Coinage*, Iola WI, 1999.

M. Thompson, 'The Cavalli Hoard', *ANSMN* 26, 1981, 33–49.

A. J. Toynbee, *A Study of History*, XI, *Historical Atlas and Gazetteer*, London 1959.

A. J. Toynbee, *Constantine Porphyrogenitus and his World*, Oxford 1973.

J. Vanschoonwinkel, 'Mopsos: legendes et réalité', *Hethitica* 10, 1990, 185–211.

A. A. Vasiliev, *Byzance et les Arabes*, Brussels 1950 and 1968.

S. Vryonis, *The Decline of Medieval Hellenism in Asia Minor and the Process of Islamisation from the Eleventh through the Fifteenth Century*, Berkeley and Los Angeles, 1971.

J. Weisehofer, *Ancient Persia*, London 1996.

C. Wolff, *Les Brigands en Orient*, Rome 2003.

J. Yakar, *The Later Prehistory of Anatolia, the Late Chalcolithic and Early Bronze Ages*, BAR S268, Oxford 1985.

J. Yakar, *Ethnoarchaeology of Anatolia: Rural Socio-Economy in the Bronze and Iron Ages*, Tel Aviv 2000.

M. Zimmermann, 'Probus, Carus und die Räuber in Gebiet des Pisidischen Termessos', *ZPE* 110, 1996, 265–277.

B. Works concerning all Pamphylia

S. Alparslan, 'The Evaluation of the Motifs and Styles of the Architectural Sculpture of the Byzantine Age in Antalya and Lycia', *Adalya* VI, 2003, 251–258.

R. D. Barnett, 'Mopsos', *JHS* 73, 1953, 140–143.

G. E. Bean, *Turkey's Southern Shore*, London 1975.

F. Beaufort, *Karamania*, London 1817.

E. Blumenthal, *Die Altgriechische Siedlungscolonisation aus Mittelmeerraum unter besonderer Berucksichtigung der Südküste Kleinasiens*, Tubingen 1963.

H. Brandt, 'Gesellschaft und Wirtschaft Pamphyliens und Pisidiens in Altertum', *AMS* 7, 1992.

G. Camodeca, 'Un Nuovo Proconsole del Tempo di Caracalla – I Gavii Tranquilli di Calatia, *Ostraka* 3, 1999, 467–471.

M. Christol and T. Drew-Bear, 'D. Fonteius Fronto, Proconsul de Lycie-Pamphylie', Greek, *Roman and Byzantine Studies* 32, 1991, 397–413.

H. Crane, 'Evliya Celebi's Journey through the Pamphylian Plain in 1671–72', *Muqarnas* 10, 1993, 157–168.

M. and B. Dincol, J. Yakar, and A. Taffia, 'The Borders of the Appanage Kingdom of Tarhuntassa – A Geographical and Archaeological Assessment', *Anatolica* 26, 2000, 1–19.

T. M. P. Duggan, 'A Short Account of Recorded Calamities (Earthquakes and Plagues) in Antalya Province and Adjacent and Related areas over the past 2,300 years – an incomplete List, Comments and Observatons', *Adalya* 7, 2001, 123–162.

A. Erzen, 'Das Besiedlungsproblem Pamphyliens im Altertum', *Archäologischer Anzeiger* 1973, 388–401.

C. Foss, 'The Cities of Pamphylia in the Byzantine Age', in *Cities, Fortresses and Villages of Byzantine Asia Minor,* Aldershot 1997.

A. E. Gordon, *Q. Veranius, Consul 49 AD*, Berkeley CA, 1952;

V. Grace, 'Imports from Pamphylia', *Études Déliennes, BCH Supplement* 1, 1973, 197–198.

F. Halkin, 'Saint Antoine le Jeune et Patronas le Vainqueur des Arabes en 863 (d'après une texte inédit)', *Analecta Bollandiana* 2, 1944, 187–225.

A. S. Hall, 'An Unidentified Governor of Lycia-Pamphylia under Vespasian', *Ep. Anat.,* 4, 1985, 27–35.

S. Jameson, *Lycia and Pamphylia under the Roman Empire from Augustus to Diocletian*, Oxford D. Phil., 1965.

R. Kanel, 'Eine Beschriftete Römische Porträtbuste aus Pamphylian', *Ep. Anat.*, 13, 1989, 123–124.

Count K. Lanckoronski, *Städte Pamphyliens und Pisidiens*, Vienna 1890.

T. S. McKay, 'The Major Sanctuaries of Pamphylia and Cilicia', *ANRW* II, 8.3, 2045–2130.

H. A. Ormerod, 'The Campaign of Servilius Vatia against the Pirates', *JRS* 12, 1922, 35–56.

H. Otten, *Die Bronzetafel aus Boghaskoy: ein Staatsvertrag Tuthalijas IV*, Wiesbaden 1988.

I. Piso, 'Die Laufbahn eines Ritters aus Pamphylien', *Chiron* 8, 1978, 515–527.

X. de Planhol, *De la plaine pamphylienne aux lacs pisidiens*, Paris 1958.

L. Ryden, 'The Andreas Salos Apocalypse', *DOP* 28, 1974, 199–261.

L. Ryden, 'The Date of the Life of Andreas Salos', *DOP* 32, 1978, 129–155.

A. G. C. Savvides, 'The Secular Prosopography of the Byzantine Maritime Theme of the Carbisians/Cibyrraeots', *Byzantinoslavica* 59, 1998, 24–45.

V. Sevin, 'Kroisos ve Pamphylia', *Belleten* 40, 1976, 185–193,

A. N. Sherwin-White, 'Rome, Pamphylia and Lycia, 133–70 BC', *JRS* 66, 1976, 1–14.

T. A. B. Spratt and E. Forbes, *Travels in Lycia*, London 1947.

F. Stark, *The Lycian Shore*, London 1956.

F. Stark, *Alexander's Path*, London 1958.

R. Syme, 'Galatia and Pamphylia under Augustus: the governorships of Piso, Quirinus and Silvanus', *Klio* 27, 1934, 122–148.

R. Syme, 'Pamphylia from Augustus to Vespasian', *Klio* 30, 1937, 227–231.

C. Works concerning individual Cities

H. Abbasoğlu, 'The founding of Perge and its development in the Hellenistic and Roman periods', in D. Parrish (ed.), *Urbanism in Western Asia Minor, Journal of Roman Archaeology Supplement* 45, Portsmouth RI 2001, 173–188.

D. J. Blackburn, 'A Brief History of the City, based on the Ancient Sources', in J. Shäfer (ed.), *Phaselis*, Tubingen, 1981.

K. Bilici, 'Alanya'nin Fethi Meselesi: Bir Tesbit', *Adalya* 4, 1999–2000, 287–292.

Z. K. Bilici, 'Koprupazar (Belkis) Koprusu Kitabesi Uzerine', *Adalya* 5, 2001/2, 173–182.

H. Brandt, 'Kulte in Aspendos', *Ist. Mitt.* 38, 1988, 237–250.

J.–M. Carrie, 'Bryonianus Lollianus de Side ou les Avatars de l'Ordre Équestre', *ZPE* 35, 1979, 213–224.

N. Çevik, 'The Localisation of Olbia on the Gulf of Pamphylia', *Lykia* 1, 1994, 90–95.

N. Çevik, 'Antalya-Hurma, Koyu'nde Bir Ciftlik Yerlesimi', *Lykia* 2, 1995, 39–61.

N. Çevik, 'An Olive Oil Production Center in Pamphylia: Lyrboton Kome', *Lykia* III, 1996/1997, 79–104.

H. J. Drexhage, 'Die Kontackte zwischen Side, Alexandria und Ägypten in der Römische Kaiserzeit (1–3 n. Chr.), *AMS* 3, 1991, 75–90.

W. Eck, 'L. Marcius Celer M. Calpurnius Longus, Proconsul von Achaia und Suffektkonsul unter Hadrian', *ZPE* 86, 1991, 97–106.

I. Erdem, 'Bir Ortacag Kenti Antalya: Gec Antik Donem'den Selçuklularin Sonuna Genel Bir Yaklasim (1)' *Adalya* V, 2001/2, 163–177 and (II), *Adalya* VI, 2002/3.

S. Eyice, 'L'Église cruciforme Byzantine de Side', *Anatolia* 2, 1957, 36–42.

S. Eyice, 'Un baptistière byzantine à Side en Pamphylie', *Actes des Congrès Internationales d'Archéologique Chrétienne*, Paris 1957, 577–582.

J. Faucounau, 'Remarques sur l'Alphabet des inscriptions "Barbares" de Side', *Belleten* 44, 1980.

J. Featherstone and C. Mango, 'Life of St Matrona of Perge', in A. M. Talbot, *Holy Women of Byzantium; Ten Saints' Lives in English Translation*, Washington DC 1996, 13–64.

C. Foss, 'Attius Philippus and the Walls of Side', *ZPE* 26, 1977, 172–180.

C. Foss, 'Bryonianus Lollianus of Side', *ZPE* 26, 1977, 161–171.

H. Geyikoglu, 'Antalya'nin Ilk Turk Mulki Amiri ve Kumandani Mubarizettin Ertokusun Faaliyetleri ve Eserleri', *Adalya* 5, 2001–2002, 187–201.

J. Inan, *Eine Antike Stadt in Taurusgebirge, Lyrbe? – Seleukeia?*, Istanbul 1993.

J. Keil, 'Die Lyrboton Kome in Pamphylien', *Jahreshefte des Österreiches Archäologischen Instituts an Wien*, 23, 1926, 89–106.

R. Mason, 'The Medici-Lazara Map of Alanya', *Anat. St.* 39, 1989, 85–105.

J. Nollé, 'Zum Landbau von Side', *Ep. Anat.*, 1, 1983, 119–129

J. Nollé, 'Die Blutezeit der Stadt Side in der 2 hälfte des 3 Jhdts n. Chr.', *AST* 4, 1986, 269–272.

J. Nollé, 'Side, zur Geschichte einer kleinasiatische Stadt in der römischen kaiserzeit im spiegel ihrer Münzen', *Antike Welt* 21, 1990, 244–265.

S. Onurkan, 'Artemis Pergaia', *Ist. Mitt.* 19/20, 1969/1970, 289–298.

S. Onurkan, 'Perge Artemis Kaburtmalari ve Artemis Pergaia', *Belleten* 33, 1969.

B. Pace, 'Adalia', *Annuario* 3, 1916–1921, 3–21.

B. Pace, 'Diana Pergaia', in W. H. Buckler and W. M. Calder (eds), *Anatolian Studies presented to Sir W. M. Ramsay*, Manchester 1923, 297–314.

A. Peknan, *Perge Tarihi/History of Perge*, Ankara 1972.

J. Raeymaekers, 'The Grain Hoarders of Aspendos: Philostratus on the Intervention of Apollonius of Tyana', in L. Moore (ed.), *Politics, Administration and Society in the Hellenistic and Roman Worlds, Studia Hellenistica* 36, Leuven 2000.

L. Robert, 'La Sanctuaire d'Artémis Pergaia et la voilement des femmes', *Hellenica* V, Paris 1948, 64–69.

V. Ruggieri and J. F. Nethercott, 'The Metropolitan city of Syllaion and its Churches', *Jahrbuch fur Osterreichen Byzantinistik*, 36, 1986, 133–156.

J. Schafer (ed.), *Phaselis*, Tubingen 1987.

A. Schmidt-Colinet, 'Eine Severische Preisten aus Syrien in Perge', *Ist. Mitt.* 41, 1991, 439–445.

Index

The cities which are the main subject of this book are distinguished in bold type.

Asitawadas 8–9

Aspendos xii, xv, 1, 8, 12, 15, 52, 63, 65,
67, 166, 226; abandoned 220, 222, 223;
and Akhaios 111; and Alexander 70,
71–73, 74–76, 77, 114; and Arab raids
209–10, 230; and Argive alliance 80–82;
and Athens 54, 56, 65; autonomy
154, 168; bishopric 202; buildings of
59–60, 88–91, 97, 103–108, 174–5,
188, 201; *chora* of 33, 34–36, 37, 38,
193; coins of 56–59, 66–67, 87, 110,
112–24, 154, 176–7, 180, 181, 198; and
emperors 182; founding 9, 23–24, 27,
39, 62; games at 59, 176, 176–7, 188–9;
government institutions 87; importance
of 75–76, 193, 231; Italian families in
166–9; and Pamphylian alliance 112–25;
and Perge 179; and Persia 49, 51, 52,
54–55, 64; population of 32–33; port
44, 46, 49, 191; prosperity 88, 97, 171–
2, 201; and Ptolemaic kingdom 80, 81,
84, 85, 86; Roman citizenship 168–9;
and Rome 137, 144, 149, 154; and Side
74–75, 81, 112, 137, 155, 170, 188–90;
site of 23, 27–29, 30, 34–35, 88; size
and expansion of 31, 33, 40, 88, 135;
trade of 66, 191–2

Assyrian empire 24–25

Athene, goddess 57, 87, 98, 101, 105, 180,
200

Athens 10, 31, 41, 59, 142; and Pamphylia
49–51, 53–55, 56, 136; and Phaselis 53,
63, 65, 113, 120, 134

Attaleia xii, 3, 15, 22, 154, 204; alimentary
scheme 185; and Arab raids 209, 216,
218; autonomy 155; bishopric 216–7,
226; buildings of 131, 175, 196, 216;
chora of 36–37, 129–31, 188, 193;
coins of 132, 140, 155, 179–80; *colonia*
181; colonists in 161, 162–5; and
emperors 181–2; founding of 39, 40,
129–33, 134, 136, 231; importance
of 193; Italian families in 162–5, 169;
military and naval headquarters 212–3,
216–7, 221; and pirates 152, 155, 158;

population of 33, 131, 215–6; port
133–4, 195, 214; and Rome 137, 138,
139–40, 145, 149, 150; and Side 189;
site of 38, 129; size of 131; trade 171–2,
191, 213; and Turkish attacks 224–5,
227, 228; *see also* Antalya

Attalid kingdom 129, 149, 150

Attalos I, Pergamene king 110

Attalos II, Pergamene king 129, 133, 134,
136, 158, 213

Attalos III, Pergamene king 129, 136–7,
138, 158

Attius Philippos 204–5

Augustus, emperor xi, 153, 154, 177

Babylon 77

Babylonian kingdom 25, 42–45

Basil, bishop 221

Basil I, emperor 222

Bithynia-Pontus, Roman province 156, 165

Bosporos 53, 206

Black Sea 54, 66

Bogazak 192, 220

Bryonianus Lollianus 199–200

Byzantiuon 141

Caecilia Tertulla 162

Caecilius Metellus Nepos, Q. 147

Cakirlar 130

Caligula, emperor 181

Calpurnius, M. 162

Calpurnius Longus L., governor 162–3

Calpurnius Longus, L. Marcius Celer,
consul, governor 163–4, 171

Calpurnius Rufus M., governor 162–3

Candir, river 22, 33, 36–37, 70, 130, 178

Capria, Lake 2

Caracalla, emperor 181, 189

Catal Huyuk 2

Cebel Ires Dagi, Kilikia 18

Celebi, Evliy 75

Chalkedon, Bithynia 206

Chalkis, Euboia 17

Charisenos, slave, of Aspendos 168

Chelidonian Cape 51, 53–54, 142 – *see also*

Plates

1

1. The Borders of Pamphylia.

A picture taken looking south from the mouth of the caves at Karain. The line of the mountains stretches into the distance, and continues south as far as Cape Gelidonya. To the left is the uppermost of the 'shelves' of limestone, this one at 500 metres above sea level. In the Ice Age, when the cave was inhabited, this would have been barren, and in the time of the melting of the ice, it would have been regularly flooded. The cave is 150 metres above the shelf, giving the inhabitants a good view and a safe refuge.

2

3

4

2. The Plain.

A view looking north from the acropolis of Perge. The plain is more or less flat, but with hills intervening, which are usually wooded. In the distance are the Taurus Mountains, ever present and looming everywhere in Pamphylia. This is part of Perge's *chora*, now very fertile, and devoted increasingly to cultivating fruits and vegetables under glass. This is a recent development, and when Perge was founded much of this area would have been under wood.

3. Perge.

A view looking south from the acropolis of Perge. The main street of the city has been excavated, from the nymphaeum just below the hill to the South Gate. The towers of the city wall can be seen to the right in the middle distance but the overgrowth hides much of the other excavations. On the horizon are the two hills, Koca Belen to the right and Iyilik Belen to the left; the great temple was on one of them, probably Iyilik Belen.

4. Perge, the Main Street.

Looking north towards the acropolis. The water channel is marked by the stones along the middle of the street, which was colonnaded in the Roman period. In fact the visible remains are all of the Roman period, though the layout of the city at this point was mainly Hellenistic. To either side were the rectilinear streets of that earlier period. The acropolis dominates the city.

5   6

7

8

5. Perge, Artemis.

This is a carving high on a reconstructed column in the main street, showing a Greek, or Hellenised version of the local goddess. Neighbouring columns show a leaping stag – she was Mistress of the Animals in the Greek pantheon – and a man sacrificing at an altar (no. 6).

6. Perge, a Man Sacrificing.

This is another carving on another reconstructed column. The man is sacrificing, and is facing towards the goddess on the next column (no. 5).

7. The Main Street at Perge

The excavations at Perge have concentrated on clearing the line of the main street, flanked in the Roman period by a colonnaded pavement. Much of the street surface survives, though the columns have been re-erected. A covered water channel runs along the centre of the street, with open pools at intervals. The street is now the habitat of many local people selling their products, giving a pleasing air of continuity to the place.

8. Perge, the Stadium.

Perge's stadium is south of the city, outside the walls, as were all the local stadia. It lies on flat land, and the seating was supported on barrel vaults, in which were shops; the visible remains are all of Roman date. Beyond can be seen several of the towers which line the city walls, with the South Gate to the right. Beyond again is the acropolis, where was the first city; the view gives a good impression of the acropolis as a fortified refuge, with its vertical cliffs all around.

9

10

11

9. Perge, The Acropolis.

A view along the edge of the acropolis, near the south-west corner. The difficulty of access to this, and similar sites at other cities, is very clear, and there was only one point at which access could be said to be possible. But also note the large cistern, which has been exposed by the collapse of part of the cliff. No doubt the excavation of the cistern has helped to weaken the cliff at that point, but it is also the case that bits of the acropolis have regularly fallen off. Cisterns are a hazard to anyone walking the acropolis now, and many of them are close to the cliff edge, no doubt because that was where the water ran to when it rained.

10. Perge, South Gate.

The Late Antique gate, in front of the older semi-circular Hellenistic Gate. The earlier gate was converted into a more ceremonial entrance to the city in Plancia Magna's time, when it was lined with the portraits of those identified as 'founders' of the city. The contrast between the gates is stark, for this newer gate is clearly designed for defence, blank and sheer, with a very narrow opening.

11. Sillyon.

A street of steps. The steps and the footings of the buildings are carved out of the rock, with the upper parts of the walls, largely now missing, constructed of looser stones. This has meant that the houses lasted a long time, and any rebuilding was done on the old foundations. The edge of the cliff, and its progressive collapse is also visible.

12

13

14

12. Sillyon – the Cliff.

A view of the edge of the city at the point where the theatre was built. The few remains of the theatre can be seen to the left; an Odeon which was next to it has now wholly disappeared. The way the cliff breaks and collapses can be seen clearly. Much of the visible collapse has taken place in the past few years. In 2003 a lot more of the theatre survived, though with wide cracks in it; this view was taken in 2006.

13. Sillyon – the City.

A view towards the city from the south. The easiest modern access is along the path which slopes up from right to left across the hillside, and this was also the path of the ancient ramp. Defensive towers can be seen in front of the city – they seem to have been free-standing. To the right, on either side of the tree, there are the Byzantine buildings of the last but one phase of the city; the last phase is represented by the small mosques.

14. Phaselis – the Acropolis.

The acropolis seen from the *Weststadt*. The bay formed the South Harbour. The hill is now densely covered with trees and undergrowth, but its peninsular situation is clear. Behind the camera, the sandy peninsula terminates at the steep hills of the Lykian Mountains; access inland was very difficult.

15

16

17

15. Phaselis – the hinterland.

A view from the car park (which is close to the northern end of the centre of the city, looking north-west over the marsh towards the mountains. In the distance are those mountains, steep and formidable. To the right is the cliff edge of the *Nordsiedlung*, the third part of the city; the *Weststadt* is behind the tree to the left.

16. Antalya – the Hadrian Gate.

The gate was rebuilt as a gesture to Hadrian, a rather more useful gesture than a mere arch. The walls to either side of the gate survive to their full height, but show repeated repairs and rebuildings. Behind (or through) the gate can be seen the lane which is one of those indicating the survival in the modern city of the grid layout of the original Hellenistic foundation.

17. Antalya – Hidirlik Tower.

A tomb for a very rich and important member of the Calpurnius family. No name is inscribed on the building, but twelve fasces are carved beside the door on the east side (to the right facing away), which indicates that the occupant was a consul. In later years, not surprisingly, the building was incorporated in the defences of the city, and the wall around the top, made of small irregular stonework, was added.

18

19

20

18. Aspendos – the Aqueduct.

A view north from Aspendos. The piers of the aqueduct are in the right foreground, with the modern village next to it. Beyond are, first, the plain which was part of Aspendos' *chora*, then a line of hills which marked the limestone outcrop which formed the boundary between Aspendos and Sillyon. The flat-topped hill in the left centre is Sillyon; it is a separate hill from those to either side of it, and several kilometres further off. The Taurus and Lykian Mountains can just be made out in the haze on the horizon. The aqueduct tapped a source in the Taurus.

19. Aspendos – the Chora.

Another view from the Aspendos hill, this time looking north-east, past the piers of the aqueduct and over the nearby *chora* towards the hills and mountains. The *chora* was, as can be seen, somewhat constricted at this point. The hills are, and probably always were, forested.

20. Aspendos – the Stadium.

The cliff edge is less obvious at Aspendos than at Perge or Sillyon, but it is visible on the left in this view looking from above the theatre northwards. The stadium has not been overwhelmed by falling rock, despite its closeness under the cliff. Two of the tombs which lined the street beyond the stadium can just be made out. Note again the closeness of the hills and mountains. The plain is flat, required draining to make it usable, and the river is to the right, lined with trees.

21

22

23

21. Side.

The street which leads south from the North gate of the city has recently been cleared for much of its length. Note the water channel leading along it. The ecclesiastical complex is at the far end.

22. Side – the Arch.

The arch originally put up to honour Vespasian became one of the central points of the city, with the *agora* to the left, the theatre inside the city behind the fountain on the left, a bath (behind the camera), and a helpful fountain close by. The aqueduct passed on the right, supplying the bath (now the museum), the fountain, and a set of cisterns (behind the wall on the right). When the city shrank in the seventh/eighth century the arch became the main entrance to the city, and was partly blocked to render access difficult. It is now once more the main entrance to the city.

23. Side – Two Churches.

A large church was built behind the remains of the temples of Apollo and Athene at the harbour entrance. The temples are behind the camera, and the large church's remains are the wall on the right and the far wall with the doorway; this shows no more than a quarter of the building. After the decline of the city set in, a smaller church was built (the building to the left), within the ruins of the older one. It is a vivid indication of the shrinkage of the city in its last century.

24

24. Side – the Later Wall.

With decline of the city a new wall was built. It cut off the Hellenistic extension and the great ecclesiastical centre, and incorporated the theatre into its line. Here, in a view looking north, the later wall, with its formidable tower, is visible, with the theatre beyond. To the right of the tree remains of the *agora*, also abandoned, are visible as a heap of stones. The structure on the left is part of the 'official *agora*', which may actually be a gymnasium. Much of the essential public life of the ancient city was thus abandoned in the struggle to survive.